abjection incorporated

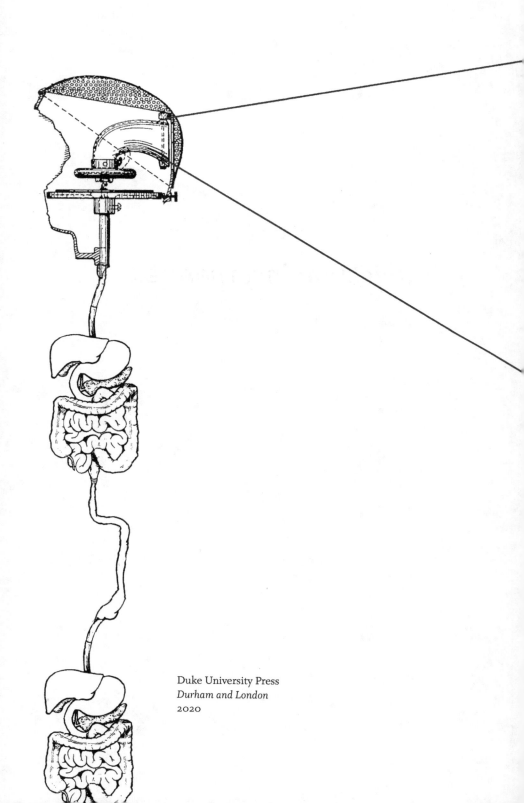

Duke University Press
Durham and London
2020

abjection

incorporated

mediating

the politics

of pleasure

& violence

edited by

maggie hennefeld

& nicholas sammond

© 2020 Duke University Press
All rights reserved

Designed by Aimee Harrison
Typeset in Whitman by Westchester Publishing Ser
vices

Library of Congress Cataloging-in-Publication Data
is available at the Library of Congress
ISBN 9781478001898 (hardcover: alk paper)
ISBN 9781478003021 (pbk: alk. paper)
ISBN 9781478003410 (ebook)

Cover art adapted from Christoph Adolf Giebeler-
Wanke, "United States Patent: 1325013 A—
Phonetic Doll," December 16, 1919.

Color versions of artworks featured in this volume,
and additional images, may be found at http://
scalar .usc.edu/works/abjection-incorporated-
insert/index.

contents

acknowledgments

We would like to thank our contributors, who patiently supported the development of this project and who thoughtfully revised their essays when the 2016 presidential election and numerous #MeToo revelations moved us to rework our concept of abjection. We are immensely grateful to Elizabeth Ault, our inspiring and brilliant editor, and to Courtney Berger, Ken Wissoker, Kate Herman, and the rest of the team at Duke University Press for shepherding the volume through production. Vanessa Cambier, Alicia Fletcher, and Sarah Crawley provided crucial editorial assistance. Nicholas Sammond would like to thank Mike Zryd, Cannon Schmidt, and Chris Dingwall for reading iterations of his essay, and Agata Szmygin for her wry smiles and unwavering support. Maggie Hennefeld would like to thank Nicholas Baer for his extensive, insightful feedback and moral support, as well as Cesare Casarino, Alison Griffiths, Laura Horak, Kathleen Karlyn, Linda Mizejewski, Kyle Stevens, her comedy students, her family, the volume contributors and Nic, and everyone who attended our scms panel at nine o'clock on Sunday morning for their generosity and intellectual engagement with this project, and Alex Tolleson for his always joyful, intelligent, and loving support.

Color versions of artworks featured in this volume and additional images may be found at http://scalar.usc.edu/works/abjection-incorporated-insert/index.

Not It, or,
The Abject Objection

maggie hennefeld
& nicholas sammond

The abject is the violence of mourning for an "object" that has always already been lost. —Julia Kristeva, *Powers of Horror*

In the final analysis, oppressors must be reduced to sovereignty in its individual form: on the contrary, the oppressed are formed out of the amorphous and immense mass of the wretched population.
—Georges Bataille, "Abjection and Miserable Forms"

This volume springs from the existential fault lines that now characterize contemporary politics and culture, like weeds growing out of a crumbling sidewalk. Anonymous internet trolls spew hate speech, neoliberal policies accelerate rampant inequality, climate change threatens irreversible catastrophe, as does authoritarianism worldwide, and traditional journalistic organs are frequently compared to varieties of putrid garbage. Abjection both drives and defines this moment. Yet, strangely, in the midst of this mad race to claim a rapidly diminishing higher ground, there accrues political value in emphasizing one's own social persecution and economic dehumanization. While some of us are always already abjected—marginalized because of our race, gender, sexuality, class, ability, nationality—other self-styled minorities, such as men's rights groups and white supremacists, have attempted to co-opt the rallying cries of the truly oppressed, claiming the status of the outcast. Every genuine liberation protest is now echoed by its scandalous inversion, exemplified by perverse chants such as "Blue Lives Matter," "Affirmative Action for White Applicants," or "Men's Rights Are Human Rights." If social authenticity is a currency that derives from a wounded identity, abjection is its lingua franca. In other words, many people normally associated with the dominant culture are increasingly claiming an abject status in order to adopt, ironize, and undermine the markers of marginalization by which damaging social and power hierarchies have traditionally been administered and enforced.

Though abjection is utterly ubiquitous in twenty-first-century politics, its theorization is too often itself abjected in critical humanities scholarship: it gets pigeonholed as either one more facet of the bad object of psychoanalysis, or as an outmoded offshoot of Enlightenment philosophies of class conflict (i.e., old materialisms). Indeed, the two most influential twentieth-century theorists of abjection, whose works map tidily onto those debased fields, are undoubtedly Julia Kristeva and Georges Bataille. Kristeva has generatively defined the abject in *Powers of Horror* (1982) as "that which is cast out." This abominable matter further comes to symbolize all the reviled forms of difference by which meaning and identity are delineated in language and culture. Kristeva writes: "There looms, within abjection, one of those violent, dark revolts of being, directed against a threat that seems to emanate from an exorbitant outside or inside, ejected beyond the scope of the possible, the tolerable, the thinkable. It lies there, quite close, but it cannot be assimilated."[1]

In Kristeva's psychoanalytic approach to abjection and selfhood, the child, as it learns to identify as a sovereign subject, regards the products of its own body (and the bodies of others)—blood, snot, piss, shit, mucus, sperm, rotting flesh—as vile, disgusting, and in need of suppression, rejection, and regulation. The latency of such infantile abhorrence, as Bataille notes, has an irresistible political influence. For example, when the invocation of "Mexican rapists," "nasty women," and a news anchor accused of "bleeding from her wherever" can aid in restoring the ultimate sovereign white male subject, a robust, critical, and sustained engagement with the abject is absolutely necessary.[2] Sadly, Donald Trump's campaign, then his presidency, have given us daily (if not hourly) reminders of the toxicity of this dynamic between infantile narcissism and regressive nationalist politics.

Kristeva's semiotic-psychoanalytic account of the abject—that unbearable excess that the ego will always scramble to reject—primarily concerns issues of subject formation, particularly the negotiation of boundaries between the child and its mother, or the corporeal regulation of the sovereign subject. In contrast, Georges Bataille emphasizes not the psychic training of the ego but the politics of the social. "Abjection and Miserable Forms" (1934), written during Hitler's rise to autocratic power in 1930s Europe, focuses on the oppression of the wretched masses by sovereign rulers. For Bataille, it simply does not matter if the individual ego has the will to cast out certain gross or reviled matter, because "general abjection," he argues, is "wreaked by impotence under given social conditions." In other words, abjection is imposed on the social body by a sovereign imperative, regardless of one's developmental bodily discipline. He adds that "filth, snot, and vermin are enough to render an infant vile; his personal nature is not responsible for it, only the negligence and helplessness of those raising it." Though written nearly fifty years before *Powers of Horror*, "Abjection and Miserable Forms" still offers crucial context for the structural theories of abjection and individual subjectivity that Kristeva would later articulate.

Abjection Incorporated explores the tensions between (and beyond) these critical paradigms, presenting perspectives on a historical moment in which a meaningful distinction between the self-disciplining subject who reviles gross bodies and the sovereign imperative that excludes wretched social masses is in constant threat of collapse. In this neofeudal moment epitomized by Donald Trump and a growing host of other tin-pot autocrats, individual self-governance and political sovereignty are understood by many as one and the same (consider how the president's inflammatory tweets can carry greater political significance than his official executive statements). To this point, Trump's ascent to sovereignty (or at least to the office of the American presidency) has unleashed a firestorm of competing performances of abjection. For many, Trump and his followers embody the abject underbelly of a democratic body politic, the "deplorables."[3] In contrast, for Trump's supporters, "draining the swamp" means cleansing government of soft-hearted progressives and moderate Democrats and Republicans—"cucks" and "basic bitches" in the language of the "alt-right"—rather than addressing endemic corruption. To paraphrase Judith Butler, Trump's presidency delivers "the perfect ideological contradiction," in that Trump has channeled rising populist anger over class inequality and the ongoing immiseration of the working poor under global neoliberalism and pinned it onto differences in culture, geography, and racial or ethnic identity.[4] Perversely, the permanent struggle for equity and social justice has a nemesis in the violent bigotry that abjects a slew of cultural Others: women, people of color, immigrants, gays, trans folk . . . the usual scapegoats of misogynistic white bigotry and structural racism. The Trump presidency, then, is a timely and painful illustration of how abjection has become central to the negotiation of social identity—both in one's difference from the Other and in one's estrangement from the self.

A key problem posed by this volume, and an existential issue in this political moment, is how to distinguish between who gets to be a sovereign ego and who has to be abjected for that ego to feel (temporarily) secure in its own sense of self. Who is being sacrificed on behalf of the nostalgic, ethno-nationalist wager to "Make America Great Again"? Amid mass displacements, deportations, perpetual war, environmental degradation, an emboldened police state, and the declining prospects of well-paying jobs for a shrinking middle class, the threat of abjection—of falling into a miserable place—remains a pervasive reality. Yet, at the same time, appearing to be socially abject, although strongly undesirable in daily life, can generate widespread sympathy and even institutional redress—payback for what Wendy Brown has called "wounded attachments."[5] Being abject (or performing self-abjection) often carries significant political capital. Like the charlatan crying "fake news," however, the wolf garbs itself in sheep's clothing, seeking sympathy not as a perpetrator but as a victim—of an allegedly oppressive majority of minorities. Though cynically nihilistic, these tactics have the effect of minimizing actual crimes and obfuscations, also making it extremely difficult (or at least mentally exhausting) to articulate the difference between the compulsory social abjection of minoritized others and right-wing opportunistic appropriations of rhetorics of marginalization.

The essays in this volume strive to elucidate that vital distinction between involuntary abjection by dominant social forces, and performances of (self)-abjection that proliferate with the withering of the neoliberal state. For feminist/queer and critical race theorists (such as Judith Butler, Mel Y. Chen, or Darieck Scott), the individualizing drive toward abjecting unwanted elements from the body politic intrinsically forms the basis of normative, white, patriarchal, and heterosexual iterations of the (unmarked) self, which underpin the sovereign subject. The exclusion of the abject shores up the defensive circumscription of the ego in its potential spectrum of social and corporeal identifications. In Bataille's terms, "The imperative forces do not exercise their coercive action directly on the oppressed: they content themselves with excluding them by prohibiting any contact" with the Other (say, by building a wall).[6] Although contact with the wretched masses is forbidden to the sovereign subject, those masses, paradoxically, can never be eliminated. In fact, this "wretched population" must remain present as an object of disgust and fascination, and as an abject lesson that drives the individual oppressor's maintenance of sovereignty and self-rule.

This volume plumbs that fragile and contested zone of permeability between the wretched and the ruler. What are the murky affects, partial objects, and ambivalent attachments, we ask, that mediate between the sovereign ego and its teeming outside (or repressed inside)? In differing ways and to varying degrees, the essays in this volume offer case studies for delineating between cynical, voluntary self-abjection, and involuntary social abjection. Abjection—properly understood, deployed, and critiqued—offers a contested but necessary instrument to resist the wholesale dismantling of civically inclusive spaces, of democratic social practices and political institutions, and of economic processes that might foster equity—or, at the very least, less grossly unequal distributions of wealth, power, and resources. In other words, the abject and abjection have become pivotal terms in the accumulation, contestation, and deployment of power in twenty-first-century life.

Horrible Laughter at the Limits of Abjection

It would be funny if it wasn't so sad.
—Bernie Sanders (in reference to Jeff Sessions's
appointment as the US Attorney General)

Why does the spectacle of abjection so often provoke grim, morbid laughter rather than demeaning ridicule or cynical mockery? We often describe genres of comedy that linger between referential horror and obscene farce as "dark," "black," "cringeworthy," "gallows humor," or sometimes "anticomedy" (jokes with bad taste and no apparent point). While these modes at their best resist "punching down" and making laughing stocks of already marginalized subjects, their social politics are also more complex than merely "punching up" by lambasting those with undue power, influence, or normative legitimacy. Abject humor, then, engages the liminality of affect and the ambiguity of social relations by confronting the grinding operations of power with a perverse mixture of joy and dread. Abjection, as a state of being or as a rubric for critical reading, may lend itself to horror as well as to comedy, but its ultimate stakes are bigger than either. The abject objection derives from and contributes to an extremity of affect, a dislocation of the self, in which screams and laughter become indistinguishable, the sound of what Kristeva (following Jacques Lacan) calls *jouissance*. For her, "*Jouissance* alone causes the abject to exist as such. One does not know it, one does not desire it, one joys in it. Violently and painfully. A passion."[7]

A good example that helps tease out the multiple valences of abjection is the popular film *Get Out* (dir. Jordan Peele, 2017), a horror/satire allegory about the history of slavery and race relations in America. The film projects its social critique through an absurd lens that further sharpens its urgent political message. Peele depicts a racial dystopia in which black bodies are enslaved not through forced labor or mass criminalization, but through fantastic neurosurgical body swapping. As one white character puts it, "Black is in fashion," so the late-capitalist mode of antiblack slavery turns on possessing the Other's body in the most literal form imaginable: by placing one's failing consciousness into it. Black bodies are auctioned off to elderly, disabled, or cosmetically abjected white consumers, while black consciousness is banished to the "sunken place": a free fall into an inner space from which one watches one's own body continue to act as through a distant screen.

The abject objection lurks in the often reproduced tearful, silent gaze of the protagonist, Chris (Daniel Kaluuya), a look of mute terror and grief, as he realizes the utter banality of the horror he faces: that what happens in *Get Out* isn't fantastic. It's merely the logical extension of a long-standing tradition of physical, then cultural, appropriation—one that has always been rooted in the total, debased alterity of the black Other. The next logical step, argues Peele, rather than simply co-opting the art, culture, and lifeways of black people, is that white consumers occupy their bodies. The film is a parody of an abject white liberal fantasy of becoming black: to be inside a black body but to somehow remain white. The black body imprisons the black soul, and the white consciousness that inhabits it assumes the mantle of warden and beneficiary.

As with abjection itself, Chris's look when he is compelled toward the "sunken place" appears neither comic nor horrific. His eyes glisten with tears, and in them we can see a reflection of something, perhaps ourselves. His face presents itself to the camera, to the audience, for the experience of the *jouissance* about which Kristeva writes—not merely joy nor horror nor any singular, nameable emotion, but a raw experience of the terrible possibility of (not) being. Yet while Kristeva in her own racial formation would only imagine the audience for *Get Out* as white, Bataille might well see, in his notion of social abjection, the bottomless dread of that unrelenting structure of white supremacy and racial violence by other means. That horror has fueled African American comedy for generations, and it runs through the work of Richard Pryor, Paul Mooney, Dave Chappelle, and Wanda Sykes, a humor in which laughter is always tinged with grief, horror, anger, and exhausted sadness at the implacability of that formation.[8]

The tension between laughter and terror that Peele mines presents two key facets of abjection, but they are not the only ones. The abject, in eliciting the nameless affect through which the sovereign subject emerges—as Thomas Lamarre reminds us in this volume—is not so much a stable heuristic as something illuminated in its situational specificity—legible only through its objects and practices. The film's "off-color" or "dark" sense of humor refuses the spectator a comfortable position, a stable vantage point for disavowing the evident parallels between the film's voyeurism of racialized bodies and its allegory of the "sunken place." Laughter at screenings of *Get Out* is a scandal—a necessary but impossible mode of affective experience, provoked by horrifically comical situations just exaggerated enough to distort the trauma of their referential violence.

In this instance, then, abjection allows one to understand the already ambiguous category called "comedy" (is it a mode or a genre?) in its capacity to do far more work than simply elicit laughter. (This derives from the Aristotelian presumption that laughter is always less than other, serious affects, and that laughter can only signify humor.) While laughter is often mistaken for a mere displacement of abjection, comedy itself is frequently devalued within the cultural hierarchies that ascribe authenticity or social relevance to a given genre or aesthetic mode. This is the case because comedy—no matter how graphically violent, offensively crude, or vividly grotesque—has the power to present even the most disturbing content as entirely unserious. From the bawdy, sacrilegious play of the medieval carnival, to the brutal comic beatings celebrated by the Italian *commedia dell'arte*, to the spectacles of bodily explosion (decapitation, dismemberment, diarrhea) prevalent in children's cartoons, there is nothing exceptional about finding ecstatic delight in the abject genres of laughter. Now, however, "as both an aesthetic mode and a form of life," Lauren Berlant and Sianne Ngai write, comedy's "action just as likely produces anxiety: risking transgression, flirting with displeasure, or just confusing things in a way that intensifies and impedes the pleasure."[9] In other words, comedy is not reducible to an escapist flight from the traumas of brutal reality, as in theories of the carnivalesque (Bakhtin), gallows humor (Freud), or benign violation (McGraw and Warren). When all culture increasingly appears to be in a state of permanent carnival, there is nothing particularly exceptional or liberating about subverting the exclusion of reviled matter. As comedy expands to encompass the anxious and the horrible, it signals the abjecting of a tidy poetics of being, of anything ever again being "just a joke."

To dwell a bit longer on the collective trauma/avatar named Donald Trump, part of what has made his presidency so horribly compelling (though for many unsurprising) is his utter lack of conventional orthodoxy: his self-caricaturing persona, his gleeful replacement of standard Republican dog-whistle race baiting with indifferently inadvertent acts of overt racism, and the ease with which liberal laughter defers outrage or action in the face of his daily defilement of American political decorum: who would possibly take this buffoon seriously? When Congressman Keith Ellison first suggested, on ABC News in July 2015, that Trump might be the Republican nominee (let alone the next POTUS), his ominous prophecy provoked not cautious dread but incredulous laughter from his fellow panelists.[10] (Kristeva reminds us, "Laughter is a way of displacing abjection.") Yet, even while Trump's casual statements elicit pure outrage and disgust—condoning white supremacy, denying climate change, and authorizing mass deportations of immigrants and refugees—laughter still adheres to him (and to the burgeoning cast of characters once close to him and now purged, from Sean Spicer to, as of this writing, Kirstjen Nielsen). As John Oliver put it in January 2017, "A Klan-backed misogynist Internet troll is going to be delivering the next State of the Union address. . . . That is not normal. That is fucked up."[11] Defensive laughter against Trump (provoked by late-night commentators such as Samantha Bee or Trevor Noah) thus oscillates between dismissive mockery and sheer outraged howling. As Walter Benjamin has written (also in the context of rising fascism and looming war), dreadful laughter can provide an inoculation against "mass psychosis."[12] In this vein, late-night political satire, at its best, provokes modes of laughter more potent than simple outrage and mere disgust; at its worst, it incites the weary chuckling of a smug yet rapidly failing liberalism. Beyond relief or deflection, it helps frame the tangled and ever mobile line between the laughable and the horrible—yet always at the risk of anesthetizing a viewer exhausted by the onslaught of countless political outrages.

The essays in this volume go well beyond the distancing laughter of deferred abjection by lingering in zones of contamination—between repudiation and redemption—wherein attempts at abject defacement recoil back onto the sovereign subject.[13] While some laughter thrives on disavowing its own fascination with the abject, other affects refuse that narrow exclusionary logic—not simply displacing abjection, but confronting it head-on. Many essays in this volume take up the tipping point where the abject becomes funny, playful, solicitous, and irresistible; others examine how the violence of repulsion is further shaped by unlikely absurdities, unexpected horrors. Above all, the essays in this volume treat the comic as important and significant, but as only one facet of the abject.

Yet a moment's reflection on the abject in comedy may not only help to trace its ubiquity in the current cultural landscape, but also to offer a way into abjection in other modes, other affects. Concisely put, even laughter has its Other. Comedy, as it has been conventionally defined, involves the reversal of expectations by playing on misperceptions between appearance and reality. Something about the image of a paradigmatic ideal assaulted by its own carnal, degrading physicality—such as a pompous and dapper gentleman falling into a mud puddle—provokes irresistible laughter. As Alenka Zupančič puts it (invoking Lacan's famous argument that the madman who believes he is a king is no crazier than the king who also believes he is a king), "What is really funny and makes us laugh most . . . is not simply that the baron falls into the puddle but, much more, that he *rises* from it and goes about his business as if nothing had happened."[14] He acts as if his very baron-ness requires that he ignore the mud on his all too human body. Beyond the dangers of failing to recognize the potential for physical violence inherent in absurd nonsense, thus blinding ourselves to its real political perils, the social dynamics of how incongruous bodies become funny are extremely complex.

Classical theories of comedy generally view laughter as a means of regulating social relations of power. In Henri Bergson's well-known definition of the comic, laughter functions as a "social corrective" by cruelly or callously deriding those whose behavior appears out of step with the pace of modern life—because their bodies strike laughing observers as overly mechanical, rigid, or thing-like. In contrast, in recuperative theories of laughter (such as the carnivalesque), dejected, vile, and grotesque bodies revolt against their own exclusion and therefore become the basis of contagious laughter and collective refusal.[15] Yet, scholarship on grotesque comedy similarly strips the body of its abject instability by locating exceptional difference in a transparently subversive (and necessarily temporary) power. The carnality of comical abjection resides between these two familiar paradigms: between a disciplinary trap and a subversive escape. It represents a volatile effect, unleashed from the impossibility of consigning excessive comicality to either total discipline or momentary subversion. Bodies (both real and social) signify, and abjection's business is to get rid of that which muddies the sign, to differentiate between signal and noise. Comedy revels in the noise (uncanny spectacle, graphic corporeality, violent imagery), emphasizing its messy entanglement with the signal (i.e., with plain language)—their constant raveling and unraveling.

Recent scholarship on comedy and difference has focused on theorizing the ambiguities of comical affect, particularly the ambivalences of comedic pleasure in relation to the liberating performance of self-abjection. In Ngai's critique of affective labor and neoliberal capitalism, for example, she asserts "the zany" as a significant aesthetic category of post-Fordist production.[16] In zaniness she finds the quirky exuberance and eccentric warmth that often drive the production of affective labor in allegedly "dematerialized," flexible, and networked economies of value. In this vein, studies of gender and humor (M. Alison Kibler, Rebecca Krefting, Linda Mizejewski),[17] race and satire (Bambi Haggins, Jacqueline Najuma Stewart, Glenda Carpio, Mel Watkins),[18] and ethnicity and laughter (Gayatri Devi, David Gillota, Robert Stam)[19] have proliferated in response to the recent explosion of comedies about corporeal identity and socioeconomic marginalization. Feminist comedians have been emboldened to celebrate their own difference through graphic slapstick (Ilana Glazer, Bridget Everett, Leslie Jones), biting self-referential stand-up (Margaret Cho, Tig Notaro, Maria Bamford), and defiant confessional literature (Lindy West, Roxane Gay, Gabourey Sidibe). Yet, at the same time, these women are predatorily harassed with *ad hominem* scorn and online death threats. Again, debates about whether grotesque bodily display is liberating or shaming are no longer adequate in a climate of permanent carnival and rampant transgressive discourse.

Feminist scholarship on affect and emotion has repeatedly refused to consider laughter with the same degree of nuanced complexity offered to other ambiguous expressions of emotion. Instead, many of these works, such as Sara Ahmed's *Cultural Politics of Emotion* and *The Promise of Happiness*, consider only the negative feelings: pain, hate, fear, disgust, shame—with "love" as the ultimate horizon of collective affirmation. Ahmed glosses over laughter, she explains, because communal laughter has a coercive element that may force bodies into false and constrained senses of affective intimacy: "When we are laughing, we are facing each other; our bodies are mirroring each other. I might hear the joke, and when I register what has been said, I might find that I do not find it funny, or even that I find it offensive. When I hear the joke, it becomes a crisis . . . if I stop laughing, I withdraw from bodily intimacy."[20] Since "affect" refers not to an individual state of experience but to a shared economy of intimate circulation, for Ahmed laughter and humor stem from unequal structures of feeling. Like Ngai's notion of the neoliberal mandate to happiness (or what Berlant has theorized as "cruel optimism"), laughter compels a bodily response and is imagined to be coercive on this register.[21]

Even the joys of whimsical laughter are not beyond these gift economies of affect as reciprocity and obligatory participation. As Ahmed argues in "Feminist Killjoys," "To revitalize the critique of happiness is to be willing to be proximate to unhappiness. . . . There can even be joy in killing joy. And kill joy, we must and we do."[22] This raises a paradox of joy and its relation to violence: Does "killing joy" necessarily exclude the affects of joy, particularly laughter? To invoke Bataille in "The Practice of Joy before Death," "There are explosives everywhere which perhaps will soon blind me. I laugh when I think that my eyes persist in demanding objects that do not destroy them."[23] Bataille's fatalistic joy is a far cry from the manipulative forms of capitalist happiness that Ahmed and Berlant (and others) have critiqued. Abject laughter—not the laughter that displaces abjection, but that embraces contamination—is part of the wager of this volume. Laughter, we argue, has the power to shatter the coercive constraints of prescribed happiness by launching the feeling subject toward the threshold of abjection. There, comedy gives way to a range of raw, ineffable experiences, in which the precarity of our sovereignty punctuates its value.

Abject comedy plays on the failure of laughter to prop up the faltering boundaries of the ego, or to erect a safe distance between the laughing subject and the comic object. Laughing in relation to the abject is not a mechanism of disavowal (as in callous or cynical laughter), but an experience of radical openness to the simultaneous necessity and permeability of all boundaries and borders. (There is no such thing as a truly closed border, since even sovereign borders must also leave themselves open to the privileged bodies and the multifarious forms of capital and traffic that have license to cross them.) Abjection often returns—resisting displacement—in forms that may be violent and gruesome, and just as often, surprisingly funny. Part of Bataille's project to dismantle the abject formations of authoritarian politics involved significant experimentation with the intermingling of seemingly incompatible feelings, such as joy, anguish, pleasure, violence, poetic sacrifice, outrage, and disgust.[24]

This volume builds on that crucial project, confronting the abjection of difference by channeling its uncertainties of affect and instabilities of experience. The title of this volume, *Abjection Incorporated*, goes beyond the intentional agency of a single sovereign subject, taking up the immanence of collective refusal—when a deliberate displacement by abjection is embraced and absorbed—incorporated—at the very moment of exclusion and repudiation. At the same time, "incorporation" is a pun on the freewheeling cultural capital that now accrues from performances of social marginalization. On both fronts, it is crucial to rethink the relationship between pleasure and violence, acceptance and rejection, that awaken the ongoing task of critique: to resist the compulsive and unthinking disavowal contained within every act of abjection—and to confront the uncontained messiness lurking at all levels of culture, society, and politics.

Abject-Oriented Materialisms

There is no theory of abjection without the trace of an agentive, embodied subject. Our commitment in this volume to rethinking the abject stems, in part, from our discomfort with the diminishing place of the subject in certain discourses in the critical humanities. The displacement or elimination of the subject in variants of affect theory, new materialisms, actor-network theory, and object-oriented ontology (ooo), while important for theorizing life in an increasingly networked society, also effectively declares the subject largely irrelevant just at that moment when the possibility of laying claim to a sovereign subject status, and through it some degree of effective political agency, has been (grudgingly) extended to those generally described as its Other(s). At the risk of stating the obvious, this would include people of color, the poor (working or otherwise), women, queers, the differently abled—those who have been abjected in the name of securing the ongoing efficacy of an unmarked, transcendental subject. With the death of the subject and recession of the human, Jane Bennett argues in *Vibrant Matter*, "All bodies become more than mere objects, as the thing-powers of resistance and protean agency are brought into sharper relief."[25] Bennett (like Gilles Deleuze, Brian Massumi, or Tony Sampson, for instance) draws on the metaphor of the network to explain this inextricable linking of all forms of bodies and matter. The abject has at best a tenuous place within this critical paradigm, because the counter-politics of abjection require the oppressive weight of actual and residual boundaries—divisions between self and other, between sovereign individuals and unruly masses—and would be obscured, if not eliminated, by the epistemic erasure of those boundaries. In other words, the abject exists in necessary opposition to the productive fantasy of the individual or social body as an agential or sovereign being: it erupts from the impossible fantasies and repressed violence underpinning that sovereign subject. The strands and nodes of the network, we argue, are spattered with blood, pus, and a simmering stew of corporeal excreta—or at the very least need to be viewed as such. In this vein, the abject has much to offer variants of new materialisms. It provides methodological traction for recognizing the productive ability of matter to connect us, yet in ways that avoid resurrecting the old specters of the desiring subject, the decisional sovereign, or agency grounded in an outmoded and unreflexive humanism. One need only look at the fierce ongoing debates today in the United States about who "matters" to appreciate the continued importance of the abjectly material, agentive subject—and the political urgency of its possibilities and effects.

The abject objections articulated in this volume provide a vital means of troubling both the sovereign subject and its problematic diminution in theories of networked society. The authors in this volume claim no unified stance on the relative value of the reported death of the subject, yet we argue that our turn toward abjection in this instance offers a middle way: a chance to engage productively with Deleuzian immanence and *assemblage* (what Erin Manning, returning to Deleuze's original, has termed *agencement*) without wholly discarding the subject, or the imperfect, uneven, and contingent agency produced in, around, and through it. New materialist scholars, such as Bennett, Massumi, Jussi Parikka, Nigel Thrift, or Sampson, have offered nuanced revisions to the trap of the overdetermined subject when it is located in networked social and new media environments. In theoretically distinct ways, they emphasize sociotechnical instances in which classic humanist subject-object relations do not obtain, or within which agency is better understood as a momentary accretion of immanence, rather than resident in discrete bodies (as in *Get Out's* satirical dystopia). They position themselves between heuristics of distributed affect and constitutive violence. Varying in approach, each has described monadic formations in which a relatively ephemeral subject acquires agency at and through impermanent affective nodes. This model of the subject differs from the humanist notion of a stable and ongoing predicate entity that exists independently of its momentary networked iterations.

Our description of new materialism(s), of course, oversimplifies a varied field of inquiry, the boundaries of which are often in dispute. More fluid versions of new materialism, for instance, are aligned with poststandpoint or intersectional feminisms, and they recognize the importance of questioning the primacy of the sovereign subject over other forms of collectivity and distributed cognition and affect. At the same time, however, such approaches note the inescapable systems of power and domination that are nonetheless maintained within the "posthuman" landscape. The withering of the nation-state, for instance, and with it the traditional foundation for the sovereign subject, goes hand in hand with the globalization of capital flows and the concentration of power in fewer and fewer hands. Similarly, the matrix of affiliation and affect asserted by social networks such as Facebook or Twitter is predicated on economies of attention that harness the decentered subject in apparently involuntary, unremunerated, and (paradoxically) self-commodifying labor. As we have learned in the aftermath of the 2016 election, the status hierarchies developed, maintained, and contested through such social media—who earns more "likes" for their posts—are quite visible. Yet less visible is their value for data mining through devices as seemingly innocuous as a quiz that asks "which Smurf are you?," the likes of which were mobilized by the Trump campaign to produce fine-grained voting maps and to target its message in precise (and politically effective) ways.[26] Here the economy of "liking" and of recirculating (as in "retweeting")—converting the violence of appropriation into transient tokens of affection—serves as an effective (albeit flawed) hedge, an ephemeral act of subjectivation that takes the place of sovereign subjectivity.

One response to the ongoing operation of increasingly decentralized power is what Karen Barad has termed "agential realism," the analysis of contingent and situational agency and subjectivity.[27] Arguing for a fluid subjectivity that is inherently local and situational, Barad articulates "a theory which insists on the importance of constructed boundaries and also the necessity of interrogating and refiguring them." For Barad, "boundaries are not our enemies," because

> they are necessary for making meanings, but this does not make them innocent. Boundaries have real material consequences—cuts are agentially positioned and accountability is mandatory. The shifting of boundaries often helps bring to the surface questions of power which the powerful often try to submerge. Agential realism insists that mutually exclusive, shifting, multiple positionings are necessary if the complexity of our intra-actions are to be appreciated.[28]

As with Mel Y. Chen's concept of *animacies*—a continuum of agencies from the seemingly inert to the human that is deeply imbricated in regimes of race, gender, sexuality, and class—this is a new materialism that decenters the subject without displacing it entirely. It is that ambivalent (or multivalent) subject and the ephemeral agency it gains at the boundary between subject and object (and ego and abject), the comic and the violent, between matter and being, that the essays in this volume explore. Our notion of agency is always partial, momentary, and sometimes only clearly intentional after the fact. It is an agency produced both by the constitutive violence of subjective and corporeal difference, and by the impossibility of ever erasing or normalizing the oppressive power of structural hierarchy.

In this vein, Barad and others (such as Chen) offer alternatives to overly reductive humanisms and to narrow new materialisms. They critique what they describe as excessively celebratory accounts of subject-object disruption, which they argue ultimately fail to articulate actual relations of power adequately, and many of which are enacted by privileged subjects. Such accounts may reveal interesting and significant assemblages of actants, but at the cost of abjecting others, of effacing power and its real and often local, individual, and human effects. Conversely, previous work by theorists of the abject in popular culture, such as Tina Chanter, Barbara Creed, or Carol Clover, too often risk stepping into a cul de sac of critical exegesis by imagining that merely gesturing toward and delineating processes of social abjection renders them somehow less effective. The implicit expectation in such works is that exposure to the harsh light of critical analysis will reveal the mechanisms by which privilege asserts itself through abjection. This has certainly been a conceit of comedy studies: to valorize the exposure of bodies marked as grotesque, abject, excessive, or corporeally debased (cf. Haggins, Kohen, Mellencamp, Rowe).[29] Such ideological critiques, though crucial, inevitably reach a political impasse in their attempts to subvert the effects of abjection, producing a model of sovereignty that clothes the normative sovereign subject with the markers of exceptional identity, attaching a hyphen as a compromise.[30]

This is exactly the argument that Jane Bennett poses in *Vibrant Matter*, a touchstone of new materialism for many. Attempting to move past what she sees as a stultifying negative dialectics, and working to articulate a model of agency distributed across a range of actants (some of which are human), Bennett critiques the vulgar Marxist notion of *demystification*—a belief in the evaporation of false consciousness in the face of dialectical thinking. Claiming that what "demystification uncovers is always something human, for example, the hidden quest for domination on the part of some humans over others, a human desire to deflect responsibility for harms done, or an unjust distribution of (human) power," Bennett claims forcefully that "demystification tends to screen from view the vitality of matter and to reduce *political* agency to *human* agency." "Those are the tendencies," she avers, "I resist."[31] In Bennett's vital materialism, agency extends also to nonhuman actors, wherein participation requires ceding notions of individual effectiveness or responsibility in favor of distributed affectivity.

This conceptual/theoretical move has the virtue of calling out or unseating sovereign subjects deeply imbricated in privilege, and of aptly modeling the monadological distribution of power and affect-as-power in and through networked social life.[32] Yet it does so at the considerable cost of naturalizing the distribution of power through its accumulation in the hands of increasingly fewer sovereign subjects—and this, to put it in Bennett's terms, many of the authors in this volume *resist*. To be a node in vibrant matter is to be part of a relatively undifferentiated mass, which for a theorist of abjection (such as

Bataille and Kristeva) is to be the necessary Other to those who still lay claim to the increasingly rare and valuable privilege of sovereign individuality.

Such attempts to decenter the human-ness of all forms of matter (both inert and corporeal) have the troubling potential to erase the violence bound up in the exercise of power.[33] Privilege owes a great deal to hierarchies of sovereign subjectivity that predate and still underpin much of networked society. Which is to say, it's a straight line from Gamergate to the alt-right presidency of Donald Trump, in which a billionaire could appeal to young white men (and 53 percent of white women) whose sudden experience of precarity, their fear of sharing or losing the seat of sovereignty, has translated into virulent rage and a fierce need to violently abject feminists, queers, immigrants, and people of color as Other.

The abject has always concerned the fragility of boundaries between pleasure and disgust. "Spasms and vomiting protect me," Kristeva claims. "I use them throughout my life, in my repugnance—the intermittent retching that will distance me from, and allow me to avoid, objects and extreme situations that I experience as menacing and dangerous: defilement, sewage, sordidness, the ignominy of compromise, in-between states, betrayal. Fascination and rejection at the same time, abjection is the jolt that leads me into the abject but also separates me from it."[34]

Yet what are we, as parts of a social body, to do with our disgust? To give an intermediated example, actress of color Leslie Jones was singled out on Twitter in the summer of 2016 by sexist white supremacist fans of the original *Ghostbusters* (1984). When Jones fought back in the same forum, many on the internet were shocked and appalled by her retweets of the racist and misogynistic abuse that had been leveled at her.[35] The only woman of color in a celebrity cast of female comedians, Jones was targeted by a coordinated campaign of vicious online harassment—abhorrent but sadly unexceptional compared with the hateful attacks that female public figures of color often encounter. Samantha Bee has succinctly described the gender politics of online participation: "Being a woman on the internet means receiving frequent bouquets of chivalrous offers to tear you in half . . . especially if you have the nerve to run for president, talk about politics on TV, or criticize literally any video game."[36] In addition to demonstrating the habitual racist vitriol endemic to many spaces of networked discourse, Jones's example also reinforces the point that hierarchies of subjectivity have their roots in an old materialism that is still very much alive.[37]

The refusal to see an African American as fully American (or as fully human) is an old form of bigotry; the circulation of that bigotry across multiple platforms—from 4chan (and 8chan) trolls harassing stars of color to neo-Nazi marches protesting the removal of Confederate statues—represents a remediation of an all-too-familiar legacy of structural racism and institutional enslavement. To say that black lives matter, then, is to invoke a fraught material history in which African American slaves were fungible commodities in a system predicated on their circulation as *objects*, and on the denial of their status as subjects. Nicholas Mirzoeff invokes Jane Bennett's notion of vital matter to make this point when he demonstrates how race can become especially symptomatic in the new materialist account:

> The denial of agency to matter central to Bennett's agenda (and with which I am sympathetic in itself) is equated via a quote from Bruno Latour to the moment "when the Founding Fathers denied slaves and women the right to vote." Quite apart from the false equation of slavery and the right to vote, what happened to understanding the chattel part of chattel slavery, so central to *Dred Scott*? An enslaved person was an "article of property," an object, non-human and commodified. Whether we agree with this classification or not, we must accept its immense and continuing significance. Race, in Bennett's account, is a problem only for what she calls political ecology, not the theorizing of materialism.[38]

Like Mirzoeff, who argues that the idea of vibrant matter effectively whitewashes the capitalist history of chattel slavery, many of the authors in this volume share a concern about the violent erasures that occur when matter displaces issues of subjectivity, (non)sovereignty, and human desire.

In many essays in this volume, such as those by Eugenie Brinkema, James Cahill, and Meredith Bak, abjection represents something more graphic and unsettling than vibrant: something between embodied vibrant matter speaking back and the return of the repressed. As Mirzoeff puts it, "My anxiety with the material, nonhuman and universalist turns in academic discourse is, then, how quickly we seem to forget all the work that has been done to establish how and why so many people have been designated as non-human and bought and sold as material objects."[39] The bodies and persons who have been abjected, enslaved, trafficked, and dehumanized argue for self-critical, subject-oriented materialist approaches to counter the erasure of their exceptional difference and violent expropriation.[40] While such ideological critique inevitably runs the risk of reaching a political impasse in its attempt to subvert the effects of abjection, new materialist approaches often underplay the importance of the production and regulation of subject-object relations to dynamics of power in intermediated existence. The harassment of Leslie

Jones is a case in point: the rise and fall of trending topics on Twitter perform the seemingly organic distribution and flow of affect, but for some the effect of the flow is anything but abstract—as when someone like Jones struggles to be a subject in that flow while suffering as the repeated object of its violence.

Or, to put it in Butler's terms, the bodies that matter—those abjected to secure the sovereignty of the dominant minority—form an abject objection to their erasure by new materialisms. More than a backlash against their abjection, this is the result of a principled objection. When Jones was castigated for retweeting the most offensive of the slanders against her to underline their offensiveness, she revealed the violence by which intermediated subjects are *repeatedly* stripped of their agency and sovereignty. Darieck Scott, in his discussion of gay African American men in literature and in social life, asks, "Is this question [of the role of abjection and domination in racialization] ultimately best focused on identifying those elements of that experience, that history, which tend toward the overcoming and surpassing of domination and defeat?" That is, if one is still actively abjected, does a heroic recounting of moments of resistance to that abjection really get at the ways in which being abject, and not overcoming, transcending, or denying it, may be a form of resistance? Discussing abjection as lived by American gay black men, he continues, "What can the historical, inherited experience of . . . enslavement and what it might have taught, conscious and unconscious, provide for us by way of useful lessons or templates?"[41] This is an urgent claim for future scholarship in fields that intersect with and complement the critical study of race and oppression. The point is not simply, following Mirzoeff, to delimit the materiality, the mattering, of race and its erasure in new materialisms and elsewhere (though that is important). It is also to explore in rigorous detail the *productivity* of those moments of abjection. As Scott puts it, "Within human abjection as represented and lived in the experience of being-black, of blackness—we may find that the zone of self or personhood extends into realms where we would not ordinarily perceive its presence; and that suffering seems, at some level or at some far-flung contact point, to merge into something like ability, like power (and certainly, like pleasure) without losing or denying what it is to suffer."[42] When one is the thing abjected, rejected in defense of the security of others (of their need to be other than Other), that abjection is not without the possibility of a perverse form of agency. Living such contradictions—simultaneously as an admittedly contingent subject and as a castoff to ensure the (greater) subjectivity of one's "betters"—cannot be corrected through simple demystification. Nor can abjection be subverted easily by disrupting the boundary between subject and world—by becoming disruptively *present as subject*. Rather, only by walking that border, tracing its variations between agent, self, and other—between boundary, interior, and exterior—may one call into question, even for a moment, the transitory and ephemeral subjectivation of the nodal, networked, and indeterminate self of the new materialist age. Expanding on and moving past Kristeva, Chen describes this as "a clashing embodiment of dignity as well as of shame." The abjected agent, she argues, is rich in affect, imbricating "high stature and base animality, the blendings embody an intensity, a fraught collision between humanity and 'zeroness.'"[43] For Chen, abjection does not simply organize subjectivity; it also creates the potential for an affinity with the abjected, with the animal materials that have just been cast off at the ground zero of subject production.

Some might object that to explore abjection, particularly in psychoanalytic terms, is not new—not in the paradigm-shifting way in which new materialisms are new. Yet, by definition, novelty has never been the point for the return of the repressed. Novelty as a value is a hallmark of late capitalism and, in the case of human (academic) commodities, of the neoliberal (approaching neofeudal) imperative to embrace rather than deny one's commodity status, to update, upgrade, and adopt early and often. In the networked age, we offer ourselves up as willing objects, rejecting subjective agency in favor of being the "LinkedIn," "searchable," and ultimately fungible agents of a cloud-based sovereignty. The point of the abject stems from its urgency: it is useless except inasmuch as it helps to produce those subjects that are supposedly no longer relevant.

The Road to Abject Incorporation Is Paved with Negative Critique

Critiques of the abject in art, media, and popular culture often describe the act of abjection as punitive and isolating—the maintenance of social norms through the agency of the ego. Each essay in this volume is dedicated to moving beyond that valuable but narrow conception to consider the ways in which the abject may be summoned and deployed as an *objection*—a means of preemptively producing exceptional difference to undermine the stability of normative discourse. Taking in a variety of topics in visual and material culture, from talking dolls to postwar graphic media to stand-up comedians, the contributors to this volume share a common interest in moving the abject and abjection beyond the narrow confines of the psychoanalytic (and especially the even narrower defile of the mother-child dyad), the punitive, and the exclusionary. Building on the foundational theories of abjection outlined by Kristeva and Bataille, they rethink these unconscious-oriented approaches by examining an intermedial and interdisciplinary range of texts. Above all, they pursue the productive disruption that may follow the dissolution of boundaries between the real and the feigned, the subject and its objects, the sublime and the profane, out of which abjection forms the space for an objection. They do not attempt to recuperate the comic from the violent, nor to cordon off violence from the laughable, but to explore their common (and generative) threat to the self, and to the social body.

Because these tensions between the state and its sovereign subjects figure so centrally to our account of the abject objection, it seems appropriate to open this book with Sylvère Lotringer's "The Politics of Abjection," an excursus on George Bataille's 1934 essay "Abjection and Miserable Forms." For Bataille (and for Lotringer), abjection is not simply constitutive of culture through the individual, but also derives from and contributes to larger operations of sovereign subjectivation and social immiseration. For any oppressive ruling class to understand itself as justly sovereign, it must find its abject Other among the masses of the oppressed, and thereby demarcate the filth and decay from which it is inherently different (yet to which it is necessarily related), through means that are seemingly benign but manifestly cruel. This act of imperative exclusion is neither inherently comic nor directly violent. Rather, it becomes a graphic inscription of the relations of power on the social landscape. "Abjection results not from a dialectical operation," Lotringer explains, merely "feeling abject when 'abjectified' in someone else's eyes, or reclaiming abjection as an identifying feature." Instead, he argues, it happens "precisely when the dialectics break down." This broken dialectic, then, becomes the condition of possibility for the abjected masses to object to sovereign rule and to assert the autonomy of their social existence.

Abject Performances:
Subjectivity, Identity, Individuality

The first section of the volume, "Abject Performances: Subjectivity, Identity, Individuality," redraws the line between social performances of abjection and the living bodies that produce and animate them. Each of the three essays in this section, by Michelle Cho, Rebecca Wanzo, and Maggie Hennefeld, explores a different aspect of performativity, locating its abject politics within economic, geographic, and intersectionally identitarian contexts. The constitution of the body politic through comedy is frequently gendered, too often by abjecting women (especially women of color), and thereby limiting or regulating their powers of comedic protest or resistance.

Michelle Cho considers one national inflection of these conjunctions between abject comedy and female corporeality in "Popular Abjection and Gendered Embodiment in South Korean Film Comedy." Cho poses a notion of "the beautiful abject," which she understands as "a new form of popular abjection" in which "gender transgression, made pleasurable as abject spectacle, signals both the endurance and the instability of patriarchal gender norms." Drawing on the feminist and queer theories of Judith Butler, Lauren Berlant, Kathleen Rowe, and Jane Park, Cho reads the ubiquity of female grotesque types (or gendered abject comedy) in South Korean media as a symptom of the crisis of masculinity in the nation's militaristic patriarchal society. Looking at both domestic and international receptions of South Korean romantic comedies, such as *My Sassy Girl* (2001) and *200 Pounds Beauty* (2006), Cho argues that "spectacles of abject excess disavow the actual violence of gendered abjection, as a fundamental condition of mainstream, late-capitalist Asian modernity." She thus extends the notion of abject comedy as constitutive of the social body politic to explore the gendered and racial mediation of international flows of commodity capital and cultural images.

In "Precarious-Girl Comedy: Issa Rae, Lena Dunham, and Abjection Aesthetics," Rebecca Wanzo looks at two recent comedies, Issa Rae's *The Misadventures of Awkward Black Girl* (2011–13) and Lena Dunham's *Girls* (2012–17), both for their obvious differences (race) and for what they have in common: a predicate condition of abjection that situates the millennial woman in a state of being always already precarious. In these and several other recent gendered sitcoms, Wanzo notes, abjection is deployed to signal the protagonist's precarity. (Contrast this, for instance, with *Friends* (1994–2004), in which a cast of underemployed and unemployed [white and stereotypically beautiful] characters live in relative luxury.) Yet for Wanzo, abjection is more than simply a sign of precarity; it is the very condition that drives the comedy of these series, even as it dooms their protagonists. "Inhabiting a world in which mobility is frozen—economically, politically, romantically," Wanzo warns us, "these women's bodies become sites of the modern mire of economic and intimate abjection."

Maggie Hennefeld's chapter, "Abject Feminism, Grotesque Comedy, and Apocalyptic Laughter on *Inside Amy Schumer*," returns to the bodily violence popular in feminist satirical comedy. Hennefeld theorizes an "abject feminism" as a political response to the social contradictions between individual self-making and collectivist advocacy in contemporary popular feminisms. Given the inadequacy of recent arguments based in intersectionality to resolve this driving contradiction between identity and collectivity, Hennefeld claims, images of apocalyptic or world-shattering violence (spontaneous decapitation, cannibalistic self-petrification, and ritual mass suicide) provide impossible but necessary rejoinders to the impasses of feminist politics. Theorizing the gendered stakes of the distinction between abject comedy and carnivalesque unruliness, Hennefeld argues that abject feminist laughter provides a space "for acting out the contradictory meanings and ideals of gender identity and its shape-shifting relationship to feminist politics in the twenty-first century."

Abject Bodies: Humans, Animals, Objects

The essays in "Abject Bodies: Humans, Animals, Objects," by Yiman Wang, Rijuta Mehta, Meredith Bak, and James Leo Cahill, and the art of Mark Mulroney, focus on the dynamic between (non)human subject formation and the disciplinary paradigms that circumscribe it. Abjected bodies often serve as allegorical figures during tumultuous moments of national struggle. A case in point is found in Yiman Wang's analysis of the brief resurgence of slapstick comedy during the 1950s in the People's Republic of China (1949–66). In her chapter, "The Animal and the Animalistic: China's Late 1950s Socialist Satirical Comedy," Wang looks at two rarely discussed zoo-themed comedies, *An Unfinished Comedy* (dir. Lv Ban, 1957) and *A Nightmare in the Zoo* (dir. Shi Lan, 1956), a fictional film featuring a Chinese comic duo in the style of Laurel and Hardy. The latter film was condemned for physiologically repulsing its audiences with performances of animalistic slapstick and for producing dehumanizing satires of state officials. As Wang argues, the subsequent denigration and prohibition of such modes of comedy played a crucial role in "enabl[ing] the very formation of the socialist body politic." Methodologically, Wang draws on an innovative range of theories of animality, comedic physiognomy, and political governance (from Bataille and Derrida to Cai Chusheng and Pang Zhaolin) to shed light on this forgotten archive of Chinese socialist film satire from 1956–57. She thereby teases out a "a strand of vexed *inter(dis)course* between the animal, the animalistic, and the socialist new human in the late 1950s cultural-political landscape," arguing that the comedies unleashed "animalist specter(s)" that "continue to unsettle and haunt socialist projections of ideological purism."

Rijuta Mehta puts a sharp point on the role of abjection in political dis-course, illustrating its crucial urgency to theories and aesthetics of state violence. In "Anticolonial Folly and the Reversals of Repatriation," Mehta locates an abjection based in the process of nation formation, the inscrip-tion of social relations on the ground and on the bodies of those who suf-fered under the "follies of repatriation" in Pakistan, India, and Bangladesh in the middle of the twentieth century. Comparing representations of women and men during partition in the short stories of Saadat Hasan Manto and in photographs contemporary with those stories, Mehta suggests that the "new sovereign state produced an abject script not only for Manto's comic irony, by naming it 'unclean,' 'filthy,' 'taboo,' and 'disgusting' under obscenity law, but also for native subjects, especially the women photographed in repatriation portraits between 1947 and 1956." The "abject scripts" that Mehta considers are specific to the violent, painful, and unresolved tensions and experiences of state partition. Similarly, the comic irony that she locates in Manto's work is tinged with the pathos of those violent and graphic productions of nation-hood. Like other essays in this volume, Mehta's readings of partition litera-ture and photography forge productive and unexpected connections between theories of the abject and ironically absurd eruptions of state violence—such as the possibility of cosmic laughter at unbearable images of sexual assault and state brutality in postpartition South Asia.

Yet that which abjects is not always of the living; instead, it may refer to the basis of life in death, to the stillness by which we try to understand ani-mation. Meredith Bak's chapter, "Between Technology and Toy: The Talking Doll as Abject Artifact," reverse engineers the uncanny creepiness of one of the all-time most popular children's toys: the talking doll. The abject violence lurking in this allegedly innocent plaything derives from the toy's oscillation between humanoid companion and cold, mechanical apparatus—it is a vio-lence to the very idea of flesh. "Talking dolls encourage traditional nurturing doll play," Bak claims, "but also often require the child to perform strange, violent, or invasive actions to trigger speech." Bak historicizes the talking doll's abject status through an analysis of patent records from the late nine-teenth century to the present. Focusing on the technological devices used to record the doll's cooing, gurgling "mama" and "papa" sound effects, she excavates a media archaeology of the doll's morphing voice box technologies, from bellows and valves, to phonograph records and cylinders, to magnetic tapes and digital clouds. She argues that the talking dolls invite children to "engag[e] an ongoing power dynamic to nurture and provide care, but also to abuse and destroy. These conflicting impulses exemplify the 'vortex of summons and repulsion' characteristic of the abject." By analyzing talking doll patents, Bak demonstrates that even primal abjection has its own intellectual and commercial genealogy, hence archival history. Rather than throw the baby out with the bathwater, Bak builds on foundational psychoanalytic readings of talking dolls (as uncanny object and transitional plaything), while opening them to alternative notions of time and historiography than those of the archaic unconscious.

James Cahill's contribution also moves beyond the body—whether fat, animalized, or absurd—via the big toe, "the most human part," according to Bataille. "Absolute Dismemberment: The Burlesque Natural History of Georges Bataille" theorizes the abject dialectics between animality and the human by finally giving the big toe its due as the very "threshold between human and animal life," to assert an anti-anthropocentric critique of the limits of humanism. First, however, Cahill accepts an unresolved dare (or even surrealist prank) laid down by the French intellectual Raymond Queneau: to imagine a dialectical, natural history based on the surrealist writings of Bataille. Cahill does so, he says, "in part for the pleasure of trying it, but also for the economy with which it draws together important strands of Bataille's thinking about animality, aesthetics, abjection, and comic laughter, demonstrating their mutual entanglements in his thought, as well as their untimely productivity in [this] era of accelerated and often frightful metamorphoses, extinctions, exhaustion, and death on a planetary scale." Looking at texts that predate Bataille's 1934 essay on abjection, Cahill's critical antics pose further challenges to the compartmentalization of humanities disciplines today—such as anthropology and natural history—making evocatively perverse use of G. W. F. Hegel's notion of "picture thinking," as the materialist filter for universal truth.

The volume then takes a break from the formal essay for a trip into an autobiography of abjection. Reporting from the trenches of vernacular objection in present-day cultural production, visual artist Mark Mulroney offers an interlude in which he graphically recounts his personal exploits in an abject education system. Sparing no detail, Mulroney depicts (in both word and image) a bio-graphical narrative of his profound confusion at (poorly) mediated sex education, a disciplining made worse by its being delivered in a Catholic school. There, he was instructed in the meanings of his body and the bodies around him while the crucified Christ gazed down on him from the front of the room. Of that Christ, Mulroney observes, "Sure he was dead, but he was also *very sexy*." (Consider yourself trigger-warned.) Mulroney's art translates the eroticism of the martyrs into vernacular form—or, rather, updates the vernacular to account for the production of new martyrs.[44]

Abject Aesthetics: Structure, Form, System

The final section views abjection in aesthetic terms. The essays in part 3—by Nicholas Sammond, Eugenie Brinkema, Thomas Lamarre, and Rob King—approach the abject as a vital critical category for understanding the fraught relationship between pleasure and violence—in all its forms and surface guises. First drafted before the 2016 elections, these essays excavate the abjected objections long simmering just beneath the surface of American political life and cultural values. They help us understand how abjection has long been incorporated in and by the national body politic.

In "A Matter of Fluids: EC Comics and Vernacular Abjection," Nicholas Sammond explores the circulation of immanent and persistent wartime traumas—both the nightmarish residues of World War II and the unthinkable and unremitting possibility of nuclear war—in Cold War–era pulp comics, especially in *Mad* magazine. Sammond discusses how romance, horror, and satire comics and magazines mobilized the abject in their images (especially those of corrupted flesh, blood, spit, and sweat), as well as through destabilized graphic designs. He argues that in their insistent repetition they formed objections to an increasingly pervasive domestic authoritarianism that marked the early days of the Cold War. Sammond notes that vernacular media such as comics translated the extreme abjection of an already heavily constrained postwar femininity into blatantly misogynistic social commentaries—even though media makers imagined that misogyny as an incisive critique of normative performances of gender and social repression during the Cold War. "Life in the vernacular," Sammond claims, "plowed the furrows of the banal, offering in the mundane and repetitive themes of love, sex, and death a riotous rebellion against a postwar project that could only imagine . . . a deathless fantasy of love in the service of the future."

In "Spit * Light * Spunk: Larry Clark, an Aesthetic of Frankness," Eugenie Brinkema demands that we see abjection as form, refusing to assimilate the abject's graphic excess into the symbolic order to which (in some accounts) it stands as Other. Closely reading the cinematic and photographic work of Larry Clark through the lens of radical formalism, Brinkema insists on moving beyond "the canon of *signs* of abjection," which mistakes that which is abjected for the act of abjection. Instead, she argues for a critical practice that relinquishes "the easy ascription of abjection to things presented to the eye and mind, thrown in the path of the subject as a nameable, precise sensual content—the definite article of *that* sticky load, *this* maimed corpus." For Brinkema, rather than incorporation, the more productive move is to argue for "abjection's notion of downcasting, lowering, casting off to describe a formal language of uncluttered openness, sincerity, simplification, clarification, a brutalizing of visual language through a paring down to a radical program of exclusion."

The abject, in this formulation, presages an eruption, whether into laughter or violence (or laughter as violence), wherein the expulsive force of abjection is often preceded by a dis-ease, a sense of irritation. Thomas Lamarre looks at manga comics for teenage girls, such as *The Wolf Girl and the Black Prince* (Hatta Ayuko, 2011–), surveying their meticulously administered worlds for how they inflect and refract abjection. "A Series of Ugly Feelings: Fabulation and Abjection in Shojo Manga" mounts a detailed critique of Kristeva's "weight of meaninglessness" through what Sianne Ngai calls the "ugly feelings" that haunt popular Japanese shōjo manga, comics marketed primarily to female adolescents. "Ngai stresses how difficult it is to determine whether ugly feelings are resistant or acquiescent in political terms," Lamarre argues, "precisely because they are not object oriented." He analyzes the "objectless feeling of irritation" that arises in encountering manga, both through its depiction of interspecies role-playing scenarios, and in the diffusion of the story across different serial media. Focusing on manga's formal heterogeneity, Lamarre argues provocatively that the irritation that serialization inspires "generates a feedback effect that allows for the conveyance of abjection, as information for the series," and in this case is "the noise whose amplified feedback makes the *Wolf Girl* series into a self-organizing multimedia franchise system."

Last but not least, Rob King disentangles two terms that might at face value be taken as synonymous: the abject and the absurd. "Powers of Comedy, or, the Abject Dialectics of *Louie*" examines the tension between absurdist flight and abject self-degradation in the short films and television shows of the comedian Louis C. K. King focuses on C. K.'s self-authored, autobiographical FX sitcom, *Louie* (2010–15), from its initial reception through the recent revelations about C. K.'s offscreen behavior and his attempted apologies for that behavior. Beginning with C. K.'s short films from the 1990s, such as *Ice Cream* (1993) and *Hello There* (1995), King locates the absurd in *Louie* as the dialectical other to the stand-up comedian's routine self-exposure (grotesque irony noted) through abjection. Rather than viewing the abject as underpinning a comedian's own truth-telling authenticity (a familiar account adopted by John Limon, Rebecca Krefting, David Gillota, and others), King argues that C. K.'s use of the absurd reorganizes the horror of abjection into a new modality in American comedy: abject-absurd dialectics. Drawing primarily on Deleuze's argument for opposing trajectories of sense and nonsense in *The Logic of Sense* (1969), King argues that, "in *Louie*, absurdist fantasy . . . is an interiorized response to an externalized abjection that seeks to sublate it in thought, to find refuge in an absurdist imaginary that galvanizes the self against the sickening lure of abject states of affair or filthy objects." By invoking the absurd as spectral other to the abject, C. K. avoids the redemptive reading of abject comedy, wherein simple naming of the abject gestures toward regulating the body politic and restoring a conservative and rational order.

The Aftermath of Abjection

Abjection as a heuristic, as a mode of incorporation, as an objection, goes beyond either laughter or horror and cuts to the radical imbrication of these seemingly opposed affects. Methodologically, abject objection is not simply about demystifying the misogyny in horror films, nor just about articulating the affect that motivates the self-loathing comedian. Indeed, limiting studies in abjection to comedy repeats the error of a previous generation of scholars who confined them to horror. This is not merely a generic or modal claim; it is an argument about the timely utility of the concept of abjection and the abject across a range of disciplinary boundaries. Each essay in *Abjection Incorporated* points to a multivalent understanding of abjection as a social, political, and aesthetic operation designed to separate those who *are* or *should be* from those who *are not* or *should never be,* and more recently to provide perverse cover for those who feel their own sovereign subjectivity suddenly threatened by the mere acknowledgment of the Other. As the chapters in this volume vividly detail, the *idea* of abjection—the sovereign reinforcement of the self or the social body through the charged, violent, and perversely pleasurable denial of the other—far from fading, has increasing currency today. The effects of this abjection are very real, though they often unfold in images and events that seem altogether unreal. Laugh, cry, gawk, quake, shudder, or freeze in terror—these encroaching imperatives of abjection can and should continue to produce renewed energies for collective refusal and resistance: for saying "no" instead of always insisting "not I." The abject objection demands more of us than quietude, acquiescence, and incorporation. It is a challenge, asking us who the hell we think we are.

Notes

Epigraphs: Julia Kristeva, *Powers of Horror: An Essay on Abjection*, trans. Leon S. Roudiez (New York: Columbia University Press, 1982), 1; Georges Bataille, "Abjection and Miserable Forms," in *More and Less*, ed. Sylvère Lotringer, trans. Yvonne Shafir (1934; Cambridge, MA: MIT Press, 1993), 9.

    Color versions of artworks featured in this volume, and additional images, may be found at http://scalar.usc.edu/works/abjection-incorporated-insert /index.

1 Kristeva, *Powers of Horror*, 1.

2 Hunter Walker, "Donald Trump Just Released an Epic Statement Raging against Mexican Immigrants and 'Disease,'" *Business Insider*, July 6, 2015, http://www.businessinsider.com/donald-trumps-epic-statement-on-mexico -2015-7; Michal Addady, "Outrage Persists over Donald Trump's 'Blood' Remark about Megyn Kelly," *Fortune*, August 9, 2015, http://fortune.com/2015 /08/09/trump-blood-megyn-kelly/.

3 Angie Drobnic Holan, "In Context: Hillary Clinton and the 'Basket of De-plorables,'" *Politifact*, September 11, 2016, http://www.politifact.com/truth-o -meter/article/2016/sep/11/context-hillary-clinton-basket-deplorables/.

4 Judith Butler, "Talking Politics," November 17, 2016, in *Talking Politics*, pro-duced by David Runciman and Catherine Carr, podcast, 54:03, https://www .acast.com/talkingpolitics/judithbutler.

5 Wendy Brown, "Wounded Attachments," in *States of Injury: Power and Freedom in Late Modernity* (Princeton, NJ: Princeton University Press, 1995), 52–76.

6 Bataille, "Abjection and Miserable Forms," 9.

7 Kristeva, *Powers of Horror*, 9.

8 See, for instance, Bambi Haggins, *Laughing Mad: The Black Comic Persona in Post-Soul America* (New Brunswick, NJ: Rutgers University Press, 2007); or Glenda Carpio, *Laughing Fit to Kill: Black Humor in Fictions of Slavery* (New York: Oxford University Press, 2008).

9 Lauren Berlant and Sianne Ngai, "Comedy Has Issues," *Critical Inquiry* 43 (Winter 2017): 233.

10 "Keith on ABC 'This Week'—7/26/15," Keith Ellison for Congress, video, 0:32, May 4, 2016, https://www.youtube.com/watch?v=FHkPadFK340.

11 Benjamin Lee, "John Oliver on Trump: 'A Klan-Backed Misogynist Internet Troll' Is President," *Guardian* (London), November 14, 2016, https://www .theguardian.com/tv-and-radio/2016/nov/14/john-oliver-trump-wins-election -last-week-tonight.

12 Walter Benjamin, "The Work of Art in the Age of Its Technological Repro-ducibility (Second Version)," in *The Work of Art in the Age of Its Technological Reproducibility and Other Writings on Media*, ed. Michael W. Jennings, Brigid Doherty, and Thomas Y. Levin (Cambridge, MA: Harvard University Press, 2008), 38.

13 Bataille, "Abjection and Miserable Forms," 9.

14 Alenka Zupančič, *The Odd One In: On Comedy* (Cambridge, MA: MIT Press, 2008), 30.

15 Mikhail Bakhtin, *Rabelais and His World*, trans. Hélène Iswolsky (Bloomington: Indiana University Press, 1984).

16 Sianne Ngai, *Our Aesthetic Categories: Zany, Cute, Interesting* (Cambridge, MA: Harvard University Press, 2012), 10.

17 M. Alison Kibler, *Rank Ladies: Gender and Cultural Hierarchy in American Vaudeville* (Chapel Hill: University of North Carolina Press, 1999); Rebecca Krefting, *All Joking Aside: American Humor and Its Discontents* (Baltimore, MD: Johns Hopkins University Press, 2014); Linda Mizejewski, *Pretty/Funny: Women Comedians and Body Politics* (Austin: University of Texas Press, 2015).

18 Haggins, *Laughing Mad*; Jacqueline Najuma Stewart, "'Negroes Laughing at Themselves?': Black Spectatorship and the Performance of Urban Modernity," in *Migrating to the Movies: Cinema and Black Urban Modernity* (Berkeley: University of California Press, 2005), 93–114; Carpio, *Laughing Fit to Kill*; Mel Watkins, *On the Real Side: Laughing, Lying, and Signifying—The Underground Tradition of African-American Humor that Transformed American Culture, from Slavery to Richard Pryor* (New York: Simon and Schuster, 1994).

19 Gayatri Devi and Najat Rahman, *Humor in Middle Eastern Cinema* (Detroit, MI: Wayne State University Press, 2014); David Gillota, *Ethnic Humor in Multiethnic America* (New Brunswick, NJ: Rutgers University Press, 2013); Robert Stam, *Subversive Pleasures: Bakhtin, Cultural Criticism, and Film* (Baltimore, MD: Johns Hopkins University Press, 1989).

20 Sara Ahmed, *The Promise of Happiness* (Durham, NC: Duke University Press, 2011), 87; Ahmed, *The Cultural Politics of Emotion* (Edinburgh: Edinburgh University Press, 2004).

21 Lauren Berlant, *Cruel Optimism* (Durham, NC: Duke University Press, 2011).

22 Ahmed, *Promise of Happiness*, 87.

23 Georges Bataille, "The Practice of Joy before Death," in *Visions of Excess: Selected Writings, 1927–1939*, ed. and trans. Allan Stoekl (Minneapolis: University of Minnesota Press, 1985), 239.

24 Bataille, "Practice of Joy Before Death," 239.

25 Jane Bennett, *Vibrant Matter: A Political Ecology of Things* (Durham, NC: Duke University Press, 2010), 13.

26 McKenzie Funk, "Cambridge Analytica and the Secret Agenda of a Facebook Quiz," *New York Times*, November 19, 2016, http://www.nytimes.com/2016/11/20/opinion/the-secret-agenda-of-a-facebook-quiz.html?_r=0.

27 Karen Barad, "Meeting the Universe Halfway: Realism and Social Constructivism without the Contradiction," in *Feminism, Science, and the Philosophy of Science*, ed. L. H. Nelson and J. Nelson (London: Kluwer, 1996), 187. Unfortunately, in some selective interpretations of Barad's nuanced approach to decentered subjectivity, agential realism becomes merely a variant of ooo, one that imagines the disruption of subject-object relations as automatically

creating space for new and more radical social formations. See, for instance, Carol A. Taylor, "Close Encounters of a Critical Kind: A Diffractive Musing In/Between New Material Feminism and Object-Oriented Ontology," *Cultural Studies* 16, no. 2 (2016): 201. See also Richard Grusin, ed., *The Nonhuman Turn* (Minneapolis: University of Minnesota Press, 2015).

28 Barad, "Meeting the Universe," 187.

29 Haggins, *Laughing Mad*; Yael Kohen, *We Killed: The Rise of Women in American Comedy* (New York: Sarah Crichton Books, 2012); Patricia Mellencamp, *High Anxiety: Catastrophe, Scandal, Age, and Comedy* (Bloomington: Indiana University Press, 1992); Kathleen Rowe, *The Unruly Woman: Gender and the Genres of Laughter* (Austin: University of Texas Press, 1995).

30 Bakhtin, *Rabelais and His World*.

31 Bennett, *Vibrant Matter*, xv.

32 Bennett sees in this move, borrowed very much from Bruno Latour (among others, such as Michel Foucault and Diana Coole), the opportunity to chart complex phenomena with more nuance (ecological crises, biomedical interventions at other than the gross somatic level, or global agricultural production), and in certain instances to begin to intervene in unexpected ways, through avenues other than the human.

33 For example, laughter marks a vestige of Bennett's central delineation between human agency and vital matter. She elaborates this encroachment through Franz Kafka's spool-of-thread character, Odradek, "who/that can run and laugh"; Kafka describes Odradek's laughter as having "no lungs behind it" and "sound[ing] rather like the rustling of falling leaves." Bennett, *Vibrant Matter*, 7–8. See also Grusin, *Nonhuman Turn*.

34 Julia Kristeva, *Hatred and Forgiveness* (New York: Columbia University Press, 2010), 185.

35 Ijeoma Oluo, "Leslie Jones' Twitter Abuse Is a Deliberate Campaign of Hate," *Guardian* (London), July 19, 2016, https://www.theguardian.com /commentisfree/2016/jul/19/leslie-jones-twitter-abuse-deliberate-campaign -hate.

36 Matt Willstein, "Samantha Bee Warns Trump after Victory: 'Nasty Women' Not Going Away," *Daily Beast*, November 9, 2016, http://www.thedailybeast .com/articles/2016/11/09/samantha-bee-warns-trump-after-victory-nasty -women-not-going-away.html.

37 And this very point was repeated when NBC chose Jones to cover the Rio Olympics, where she celebrated herself and her fellow athletes as Americans, and whereupon she was met with even more contemptible online hatred.

38 Nick Mirzoeff, "It's Not the Anthropocene, It's the White Supremacy Scene, Or, The Geological Color Line," in *After Extinction*, ed. Richard Grusin (Minneapolis: University of Minnesota Press, 2018), 4–5.

39 Mirzoeff, "It's Not the Anthropocene," 4

40 Recent stories posted from Dubai, India, New York, and Britain suggest that chattel slavery is far from a thing of the past and is sometimes carried out

with the same level of sophistication and organization once practiced by Euro-American slavers. See, for instance, Jamie Grierson, "UK Family Found Guilty of Enslaving Homeless and Disabled People," *Guardian* (London), August 11, 2017, https://www.theguardian.com/uk-news/2017/aug/11/uk -family-found-guilty-of-enslaving-homeless-and-disabled-people.

41 Darieck Scott, *Extravagant Abjection: Blackness, Power, and Sexuality in the African American Literary Imagination* (New York: NYU Press, 2010), 6.

42 Scott, *Extravagant Abjection*, 15.

43 Mel Y. Chen, *Animacies: Biopolitics, Racial Mattering, and Queer Affect* (Durham, NC: Duke University Press, 2012), 40.

44 Color versions of images in Mulroney's chapter may be found at http://scalar .usc.edu/works/abjection-incorporated-insert/index.

chapter one

The Politics of Abjection

sylvère lotringer

Georges Bataille introduced the notion of "abjection" in the late 1920s in the journal *Documents* as a way of countering the "sublimating" tendencies at work among the French cultural avant-garde. The surrealists resorted to higher spiritual values to protect themselves from what they considered to be a sordid reality. To foil this all-too-bourgeois transposition, Bataille deliberately brought up shocking, repulsive, "and even abject" elements. This "anti-aesthetic" stance was eventually adopted—and adapted—by Nord-American artistic circles bent on, as Julia Kristeva wrote, "disturbing identity, system, order."[1]

Most of what circulated about the abject at the time in English-speaking countries derived from Kristeva's essay *Powers of Horror: An Essay on Abjection*, and the notion eventually gained currency in the United States with *Abject Art: Repulsion and Desire in American Art*, a 1992–93 exhibition at the Whitney Museum.[2] For a while, it seemed, obscenity and abjection swept over the American continent, ostensibly challenging "dominant culture"—patriarchy, homophobia, religious fundamentalism.

The wonder is that, despite this scatological fever, so few people would have paid attention to Bataille's original concept. His seminal essay, "Abjection and Miserable Forms," was not translated at the time, despite heated theoretical discussions about the nature and special consistency of uncontrolled substances, like piss and shit, which had found their way into various art venues, often for purposes diametrically opposed to those that Bataille had in mind.

Bataille wrote his short essay on abjection at a time when Europe was on the brink of disaster. French society was increasingly polarized, and the dehumanization of labor (assembly lines) was feeding into violent social struggles. A social revolution seemed imminent, but it didn't come from the Left, as was expected. In January 1933, Hitler was elected chancellor of the Third Reich, and nothing seemed able to stop the irresistible rise of fascism in Germany. In October 1933, just back from Vienna, in a famous public lecture, Louis-Ferdinand Céline denounced "the kind of unanimous amorous, almost irresistible impatience for death" that was throwing entire people toward extreme, aggressive, ecstatic nationalism. And Hitler wasn't the last word, he cautioned: "We will see far more epileptic yet than he, here maybe."[3] This was an accurate prophecy, and a self-prophecy to boot. Three years later Céline succumbed to the same violence, resorting to an age-old remedy—antisemitism.

In "The Notion of Expenditure," published in January 1933, Bataille turned to Marcel Mauss's notion of the potlatch to identify the roots of social antagonism; and then, reshuffling his concepts in light of Freud and German phenomenology, he quickly wrote in November of the same year another prescient essay, "The Psychological Structure of Fascism," published in *La Critique sociale*, an anti-Stalinist Marxist journal to which philosopher Simone Weil also contributed. In it he showed that the godlike master was heterogeneous to the rest of society. Unlike the French Left, which dismissed the threat of fascism in France as propaganda or demagoguery, Bataille took it seriously. He acknowledged the "destructive force" of the fascist movement, the contagious character of its myths, the religious outlook of a political revolution capable of mobilizing "the immense resources of affective life"[4] toward a convulsive and catastrophic end: a pure expenditure celebrating the positive value of destruction and loss. It was the first time that Bataille was totally in sync with what was happening to the world at large. The triumph of fascism in Germany had opened up the prospect of fascism in France. A few months later, the unlikely alliance of Communists, goons, and police managed to crush a royalist-fascist putsch against the Chamber of Representatives on the Place de la Concorde on February 6, 1934. For the first time in France, the fascist threat had become a domestic reality.

Wasting no time, Bataille resolved to write a book on "Fascism in France." He never completed it—the threat didn't materialize—and it was only published posthumously with the innocuous title *Essays in Sociology*.[5] In this context, and with this intention, Bataille wrote his short chapter on "Abjection and Miserable Forms," elaborating on a few remarks that he had made earlier in "The Psychological Structure of Fascism." Until then Bataille had used "abjection" as a disruptive strategy; now he set out to turn it into a full-fledged concept.

Bataille analyzed fascism as a topical reanimation of royal power. Like the old sovereign, the fascist master is *something other* than the rest of the population. So is the slave at the other extreme, but in a different way. The slave's heterogeneous nature "is akin to the filth in which his material situation condemns him to live, that of the master is formed by an act excluding all filth: an act pure in direction, but sadistic in form."[6] The master's imperative act of exclusion precipitates the slave into a debased condition, but this condition only becomes properly "abject" when the slave proves unable to fend off the contamination by filth. In terms of sadomasochism, Bataille postulated that the two agencies could remain exclusive of each other: "The sadistic attitude can be manifested by an imperative person to the exclusion of any corresponding masochistic attitude. In this case, the exclusion of the filthy forms that serve as the object of the cruel act is not accompanied by the positioning of these forms as value."[7] In the psychotic universe of fascism, each position kept looping on itself at a distance from the other.

Both masters and slaves were heterogeneous to the rest of society, but their respective heterogeneity remained heterogeneous to each other. The two simply did not communicate. The master's sadism can exert its cruelty at the expense of the slaves without ever touching them or acknowledging their humanity. Breaking apart Freud's concept of *sadomasochism* into two co-independent agencies, Bataille brought out in advance the psychopathic character of fascist violence and the dehumanization it induces in its victims.[8] He was also right to recognize in the "brilliant purity" of fascist sadism elements that are usually attached to "a great number of religious attitudes."[9]

Bataille's concept of the abject could certainly have been used to bring out sadistic elements present in the American fundamentalist Right's attack on sexual minorities, but the kind of abject experience that he elaborated, which involves humiliation, dehumanization, and confinement in one's own debasement, could hardly have been reappropriated by their opponents as a dialectical model for liberation strategies. It starkly pointed instead to the extermination camps.

Walter Benjamin considered "The Psychological Structure of Fascism" politically dangerous. It wasn't an analysis of fascism, he said; it was in fact working *on behalf of* fascism. Bataille's fascination, he implied, was all too apparent. But wasn't fascination what fascism intended to elicit in the masses? How could one understand anything about fascism without acknowledging this disturbing effect? Hitler's rise to power in Germany suddenly propelled Bataille out of the confining surrealist orbit and into the most controversial question of the period.

Bataille considered Hitler's ascension "one of the most sinister events of our time." Yet wasn't it something of the kind that he had wished to happen, the coming to the fore of cruel masters capable of "maintaining drastically the principle of expenditure"?[10] Bataille wasn't a fascist, but he howled with them out of his own hatred for the bourgeoisie.[11] In "The Notion of Expenditure," he deplored "the attenuation of the masters' brutality,"[12] openly expressing his contempt for the sordid materialism, the selfishness, the abysmal hypocrisy of the bourgeois petty masters. Modern upper classes, he wrote, now are prey to some kind of "passive indifference." They "no longer have the force to recognize the results of their own destructive acts," and even less the sadism and cruelty associated with power.[13] Bataille may not have meant this as a direct invitation for strongmen to take over from cowardly bosses, as was just happening in Germany, yet his contempt for the bourgeoisie and his exaltation of irrational violence were undoubtedly resonating with the event. The ultimate goal of real industrial masters, he asserted, was not profit or accumulation, but the will to turn workers into pure "refuse." Instead of extracting surplus value from the wretched population working in factories, the strong masters enjoyed a surplus value of cruelty.

Bataille was being more Marxist than Marx. Marx had always refused to interpret workers' misery as a natural cause or a deliberate theft—he just considered it the inevitable outcome of capitalist production. The raison d'être of capitalism wasn't to reduce workers to hunger: the creation of poverty was inherent to its own development. Upping the ante on Marx's theory of absolute pauperization, Bataille on the contrary saw in this act of separation, only "antisocial in appearance," between noble and ignoble men the will to segregate workers into "a category of dejection and abjection." Pushing Marx into the hands of Nietzsche, Bataille asserted that the force of the nobles could no more refrain from crushing the weak and powerless than capitalism could make them such. But this was a perverse reading of Nietzsche, whose aristocrats derive their values from mindless cruelty and triumphant self-affirmation—expenditure—not from calculated oppression. The cynical character that Bataille attributed to the master class was already turned toward this power now coming to the fore: fascism. The rich create for the dregs of the earth, Bataille wrote, "a category which opens the way to slavery."[14] Although conceived on the Greek model, *slavery still was a thing to come.*

Hatred for the bourgeoisie didn't automatically lead to fascism. Actually it could lead both ways. Bataille denounced the "revolutionary idealism" of the surrealists as a poetical deviation that could only be satisfied by a military fascism; instead they rallied communism. Like them, Bataille was a fascist by default. Expecting nothing else from the revolution than revolution itself, he remained this strange political hybrid—an ultra-leftist mystic; a fanatic without a cause. Simone Weil was an ultra-leftist mystic as well, but she fought for justice. The two could never see eye to eye in *La Critique sociale.*

In "Abjection and Miserable Forms," Bataille distinguished two forms of miserable existence, itself torn apart and divided by the reciprocal hate and repulsion of its parts: the union of miserable "reserved for subversion" and the other, "the dregs of the people," welded to their misery, were left without any "possibility of affirmation whatsoever." The abject condition that Bataille considered "positive"—organized workers—could counter the masters' aversion by an "antisocial" act of insubordination. But it could just as well elicit a perverse desire, a twisted eroticism, masochistic in nature, a will to humiliation and sainthood, as happens in the "mental agonistic orgy"[15] often encouraged by Christianity at the expense of real struggles.

Wretched men rejected into "negative" abjection, on the other hand, were "without inclination towards it and may even share the horror of abjection, but in a state of daze and tiredness."[16] This is how Simone Weil described the workers whose condition she volunteered to share, miserable reduced to "the dull mental state and hopelessness that accompanies total exhaustion," at best "a kind of mechanical happiness, rather degrading" whenever the pace of the assembly line increased.[17] Industrial work, she realized, excludes any feeling of solidarity, and even any idea of resistance. Passive abjection merely confirms one's condition.

Bataille also gave two distinct values to the masters' imperative gesture: the positive act, which "rejects humans in a negative attitude, a powerlessness"; and the negative act, which "simply excludes abject positive things."[18] Denying abjection exposes oneself to the masters' repression, and accepting abjection internalizes it. Abjection only assumes its true dimension and reaches its absolute form when it turns into a separate destiny. It is not just the objective condition into which someone is forced but the infinitely repeated consciousness of one's own ignominy reflected in the glorious transcendence of the masters.

Bataille's definition of abjection was unprecedented. Detaching the concept from any specific substance, social situation, cultural determination, or racial or biological distinction, he defined it by its own performativity. People become abject not just because they're treated like things, but because they become things to themselves. Only then, when they're being invaded and exposed to the vertiginous experience of existing apart from the human race, does abjection set in. For people, abjection results "from the material impossibility of avoiding any contact with abject things: it is but the abjection of things passed on to those who are exposed to them."[19] Abjection results not from a dialectical operation—feeling abject when "abjectified" in someone else's eyes, or reclaiming abjection as an identifying feature—but precisely when the dialectics break down. When it ceases to be experienced as an act of exclusion and becomes an autonomous condition, then, and only then, does true abjection set in.

Notes

1 Julia Kristeva, *Powers of Horror: An Essay on Abjection* (New York: Columbia University Press, 1982), 4.

2 Kristeva, *Powers of Horror*.

3 Louis-Ferdinand Céline, "Homage to Zola," speech delivered at Médan, October 1, 1933, trans. Alexander Jacob. http://lf-celine.blogspot.com/2016/06/louis-ferdinand-celine-homage-to-zola.html. The text was first published by Robert Denoël in 1936 in *Apologie de Mort à credit*.

4 Georges Bataille, "The Psychological Structure of Fascism," in *Visions of Excess: Selected Writings 1927–1939*, ed. Allan Stoekl, trans. Allan Stoekl with Carl R. Lovitt and Donald M. Leslie Jr. (Manchester: Manchester University Press, 1985), 159.

5 Georges Bataille, *Oeuvres completes*, vol. 2 (Paris: Gallimard, 1970).

6 Bataille, "The Psychological Structure of Fascism," 146.

7 Bataille, "The Psychological Structure of Fascism."

8 Gilles Deleuze followed suit in his *Coldness and Cruelty* (New York: Zone Books, 1991).

9 Bataille, "The Psychological Structure of Fascism," 146.

10 Georges Bataille, "The Notion of Expenditure," in *Visions of Excess*, 125.

11 Bataille advocated taking over fascist weapons, not to fight fascism, but to turn them against the bourgeoisie.

12 Bataille, "The Notion of Expenditure," 126.

13 Bataille, "Psychological Structure of Fascism," 126.

14 Bataille, "The Notion of Expenditure," 125.

15 Bataille, "The Notion of Expenditure," 127.

16 Georges Bataille, "Notes, V: Abjection," in *Oeuvres completes*, vol. 2 (Paris: Gallimard, 1970), 437.

17 Simone Weil, *Formative Writings, 1929–1941*, ed. and trans. Dorothy Tuck McFarland and Wilhelmina Van Ness (Amherst: University of Massachusetts Press, 1987), 167.
18 Bataille, "Notes, V: Abjection," 437.
19 Bataille, "Notes, V: Abjection," 437.

abject

performances

subjectivity,

identity,

individuality

part I

chapter two

Popular Abjection & Gendered Embodiment in South Korean Film Comedy

michelle cho

If a person opposes norms of binary gender not just by having a critical point of view about them, but by incorporating norms critically, and that stylized opposition is legible, then it seems that violence emerges precisely as the demand to undo that legibility, to question its possibility, to render it unreal and impossible in the face of its appearance to the contrary.
—Judith Butler, *Undoing Gender*

The most popular Korean television show of 2014 was a time-travel romantic comedy serial called *My Love from the Star* (*Pyŏresŏ On Kŭdae*; Seoul Broadcasting System [SBS], December 18, 2013–February 27, 2014).[1] A bonafide viral phenomenon, the show was streamed more than 2.5 billion times in China and dominated viewership across the broader Asian region, with much attention focused on the show's celebrity cast.

Starring as a gorgeous but neurotically self-absorbed starlet with a penchant for public mishaps, actress Jeon Ji-Hyun (aka Gianna Jun) reprised a role that she made famous in the 2001 rom-com hit *My Sassy Girl* (*Yŏpkijŏgin Kŭnyŏ*; dir. Kwak Jae-Young), a battle-of-the-sexes gender- and genre-bender with nods to gross-out physical comedy (figure 2.1).[2] Based on a popular

figure 2.1 Jeon Ji-Hyun (Gianna Jun) as a neurotic, self-absorbed starlet in *My Love from the Star,* posting an embarrassing selfie on social media.

internet novel, *My Sassy Girl* presents the story of a mild-mannered college student named Gŏn-u, who meets and falls in love with a crude and bullying young woman he encounters by chance and who subjects him to various trials. *My Sassy Girl* is hailed as one of the South Korean film industry's first pan-Asian hits, and it features a title character who drinks, pukes, and punches her way to her beloved's heart.[3] The term translated as "sassy"—*yŏpki*—bears connotations of the bizarre, grotesque, perverse, and disgusting, and the film indeed bases its humor on forms of abject corporeality.

A renowned "natural" beauty in an industry well known for endorsing cosmetic surgery, Jeon single-handedly invented the comic figure of the abject beauty—a classically beautiful woman rendered abject by the contrast between her appearance and her behavior. Beyond generating a comic trope, Jeon's breakout performance as the sassy girl also gave form to a nascent ideology that promotes pragmatically conventional gender presentation as all-purpose indemnity for gender-transgressive behavior, allowing the *appearance* of stable gender norms to cover for a rapidly transforming division of labor (particularly as increasing numbers of women enter all sectors of the workforce and traditionally male-dominated institutions). Following the film's success, a *yŏpki* craze swept the Asian region, as the ideal of Jeon's sassy girl became a trendy form of twenty-first-century feminine agency. Moreover, the sassy girl's pairing of masculine behavior with feminine presentation anticipated the ways in which the South Korean plastic surgery industry would profit from the exchange value of normative beauty ideals in a global economy of entrepreneurial self-investment.[4] The sassy girl trope—the conventionally feminine body performing comedic gender transgression—soon proliferated in a rash of copycat romantic comedies like *Oh! Happy Day* (dir. Yun Hak-Yeol, 2003) and *The Two Faces of My Girlfriend* (dir. Lee Suk-hoon, 2007). Echoes of *My Sassy Girl* continue into the present, from the aforementioned *My Love From the Star* to *My New Sassy Girl* (dir. Jo Geun-sik, 2016), a Chinese-Korean coproduced sequel, and a television serial version of *My Sassy Girl* (dir. Oh Jin-seok, SBS, May 29–July 18, 2017).

In this chapter, I consider the popularity of the abject beauty, both with domestic audiences and across the Asian region. I argue that this figure presents a new form of popular abjection whereby gender transgression, made pleasurable as abject spectacle, signals both the endurance and the instability of patriarchal gender norms. The dual signification of abjection, through which mainstream comedies shore up gender norms while offering the spectacle of their transgression, suggests that entertaining spectacles of abject excess disavow the actual violence of gendered abjection, as a fundamental condition of mainstream, late-capitalist Asian modernity. In other words, the popular abject functions to distract from the violence of gender norms in South Korea's fiercely patriarchal and militarized culture and society. Thus, popular comedies' stigmatization of nonnormatively gendered bodies suggests a regulatory function whose light presentation via the rom-com genre belies its severity.

The popular abject thus opens up a critique of the rom-com's violent subtext, revealing the continuity in the gender politics of popular genre cinemas and art cinemas. Since the turn of the millennium, the reputation of East Asian cinemas in international festival circuits and cult-film spectatorship, influenced by a marketing discourse of "extremity," has often centered on racialized and gendered embodiment.[5] Fans and detractors alike highlight the excessive corporeality of "Asia Extreme's" visceral images of bodily trauma and sexual transgression. The affectivity of "extreme" cinemas has also been theorized vis-à-vis European national and regional cinemas, including the "New French Extreme" and the corporeal experiments of European auteurs like Michael Haneke and Lars Von Trier.[6] What has yet to be discussed, however, is the relationship between extreme cinema's affective uses of gendered embodiment and those of body humor in mainstream physical comedies. In the former, violence is often taken to index the real, even in works by Asian cult auteurs like Miike Takashi, in which cartoonish gore often serves campy or absurdist ends. Auteurist New Korean cinemas by Kim Ki-duk, Kim Jee-Woon, and Park Chan-wook present violence as a desublimated form of social critique or as a touchstone of their genre aesthetics. Extreme violence in their oeuvres aims to serve as catharsis or ameliorating shock, despite, as critics have suggested, often veering into exploitation.[7] In many of the most notorious cases, for example, in Kim Ki-duk's 2000 film *The Isle*, the affective intensity of violent spectacle relies in particular on gendered, corporeal violation, through tropes of rape, prostitution, or self-mutilation.[8] Across art, auteur, and popular genres, the body is subjected to injury, as slapstick remains the most prevalent form of comedy in Korean film and television, raising the question of the extent to which gendered violence underwrites the aesthetic and artistic value of extreme cinemas.

Against an approach that cathects the body as a site of authenticity or im-mediation, I emphasize the ways in which gendered embodiment in the films I address foregrounds the body's performativity, sociality, and discursive production. I assess abjection's cultural politics across a millennial trajectory of physical comedy in South Korea to contextualize its particularly gendered form in popular cinema of the late 1990s to the early 2000s: the transposition of comic abject performance from pathetic masculinity to unruly femininity that indicates the latter's compensatory relationship to the former.[9] I thus consider the *normativity* of abject corporeality in mainstream comedies, to show how films encourage spectator identification with the abject, which shores up hetero-patriarchal social relations in the oppressively gendered domain of South Korean commercial screen media. The question remains, however, of whether the abject can be fully appropriated for normative ends.

While the spectacle of abjection is a steady feature of mainstream television and film comedy, the *popular abjection* that I theorize here emerges specifically in comedies of the late 1990s through the early 2000s, the period of Korean film production to which critics and scholars date the resurgence or renaissance of Korean national cinemas after three decades of Cold War censorship and industry stagnation. This period also immediately follows the Asian financial crisis, in which the South Korean economy narrowly avoided bankruptcy via an International Monetary Fund (IMF) bailout and accompanying reform agenda. The economic collapse and seemingly regressive subordination to the West, particularly to South Korea's Cold War steward, the United States, was experienced as a striking blow to notions of liberal democratic self-determination and a crisis of sovereignty for a nation that had endured colonization, partition, foreign occupation, military dictatorship, and democratization in the span of three generations. Millennial genre cinemas

michelle cho

in South Korea localized popular regional trends, like the Hong Kong martial arts action comedy and Japanese yakuza films, in the development of gangster comedy. Having historical precedent in the B-grade action flicks of the seventies and eighties, inspired by the popular slapstick of stars like Jackie Chan, some of the most commercially successful films of the late 1990s and early 2000s were gangster comedies with screwball tendencies, particularly in their turn to gender farce.[10]

The gendered comic figure that emerged in the genre of gangster comedy—the gangster stooge—embodied a laughable, pathetic masculinity amid the crisis of national sovereignty and economic development triggered by the debt crisis and subsequent IMF intervention. In this context, I propose *My Sassy Girl* as an extension of the gender-reversal gangster film, the culmination of a trajectory of physical comedy that grounds the humor of inverted gender roles in a strictly binary approach to gender, to displace anxiety over the actual fluidity of gender positions in this period.[11] The aesthetics of abject embodiment, in other words, the visual forms given to abject bodies and the ways in which they signify, displace pathetic masculinity through its transformation into unruly femininity in *My Sassy Girl*. This observation helps to then contextualize the success of the film *200 Pounds Beauty* (*Minyŏnŭn Koeruwŏ*; dir. Kim Young-hwa, 2006)—the next most popular Korean romantic comedy of the early 2000s—a simultaneous critique and endorsement of extreme body modification through plastic surgery.[12]

While *200 Pounds Beauty* moves away from the forms of physical violence found in *My Sassy Girl* that are associated with the gangster as a generic figure of outmoded, inflexible ignorance, it similarly demonstrates the ways in which the malleability of gender presentation shores up normative ideals that are violently inscribed on the body. This manner of correlating identification and abjection through protagonists who embody abject femininity has unpredictable consequences: the classical body authorizes the enjoyment of gender transgression as comedy; however, the disavowal that makes the sassy girl's gender inversion acceptable also subjects the boundaries of normative gender roles and embodiment to ridicule, inadvertently revealing conventional femininity as an outgrowth of transgender performance and the embrace of artifice. Additionally, the films characterize *normal* heterosexual relationships as sadomasochistic, as heterosexuality is shown to entail the violent imposition of gender norms. Thus, violence and cruelty as mechanisms of desire are no longer perverse, but rather, necessary to a process of social reproduction of gender conventions. I argue that these films offer gendered embodiment as the provisional guarantee of a binary gendered division of labor in late-stage East Asian capitalism. Popular abjection also underscores, however, the continual failure of gender's reparative function, instead foregrounding the rift between presentation and identification, gender essentialism and constructivism, to present pragmatic gender bending as a dominant though disavowed contemporary ethos.

From Sad Sacks to Sassy Girls

Laughing is a way of placing or displacing abjection.
—Julia Kristeva, *Powers of Horror*

Since its emergence in the early 2000s, English-language scholarship on Korean cinema has centered on gendered genres and their symptomatic expression in popular cinema. From the management of contradictory passions in the women's weepies of midcentury "Golden Age" melodrama to "New Korean Cinema's" project of remasculinization, cinema has been a frequent stage for the disciplining of gender, in a manner that arguably corresponds to the aggressive gendering of nationalism in South Korea (aka ROK or Republic of Korea) throughout the postwar period.[13] Moreover, as different media become associated with gendering frameworks, with cinema deemed a "masculine" form and television adopting the quotidian rhythms and domestic concerns of soap opera's serial repetition, the embedded gendered connotations of genre and medium overdetermine the treatment of shifting gender roles at the narrative level. These tensions are evident in popular comedy film from the early 2000s.

Jinhee Choi places the subgenre of gangster comedy, with notable works including *No. 3* (dir. Song Seung-han, 1997), *My Wife Is a Gangster* (dir. Jo Jin-kyu, 2001), and the *Marrying the Mafia* series (dir. Jeong Heung-sun, 2002–6), within the late 1990s and early 2000s boom in gangster films, which Choi attributes to their successful niche marketing by new production companies of the period.[14] Choi and Jinsoo An also situate the gangster antihero in the genealogy of colonial resistance, as an alternative agent whose abject status owes to the injustices of colonial occupation, which requires a stripping away of institutionally conferred power to highlight instead the efficacy of naturalized masculine right. Particularly in Im Kwon Taek's *The General's Son* series (1990–92), the association of Korean gangsters with colonial resistance has legitimated the gangster code, producing an investment in physically violent masculinity and the trope of righteous criminality over other sanctioned

michelle cho

forms of authority. In gangster melodramas of the early 2000s, like *Friend* (dir. Kwak Kyung-taek, 2001) and *A Dirty Carnival* (dir. Yu Ha, 2006), the gangster's pathos stems from his social marginality, wherein he is prevented from achieving middle-class respectability and upward mobility by the gravitational pull of class prejudices and archaic codes of conduct. Corrupted by an underground cash economy that accompanies state-orchestrated, high-growth development, the urban gangster of postauthoritarian gangster noir becomes a melancholic figure who must be contained by the developing nation through his transformation into myth.[15] Thus, I argue that gangster comedy demystifies the heroic, militant, or melancholy gangster figure and replaces him with a crude, uneducated, infantile bully, an abject form of masculinity then parodied through gender inversion.[16]

In the paradigmatic case of *My Wife Is a Gangster* (Korean title: *Mafia Wife*), a naïve, rule-bound bachelor weds a female mafia boss in a marriage of convenience orchestrated by her gang because their *hyŏngnim* (the honorific term for "older brother" that is the customary form of address to a male superior within the gang fraternity) needs to get pregnant and produce an heir. As a crime boss, the "mafia wife" leads her organization with calculated efficiency. Yet, her incompetence in the domestic sphere pushes her into the arena of campy female drag, as she painstakingly learns how to be a woman from her buffoonish underlings' misogynist translation of femininity.

By placing a representative of abject femininity into the role of gang patriarch, *My Wife Is a Gangster* parodies paternalism as the perverse symptom of a woman at the mercy of her biological clock. With class divisions amplifying in South Korea's new postindustrial, globalizing economy, popular figures of ideal male subjectivity in the early 2000s elevate the "soft" masculinity of the wealthy metrosexual over the physicality of the brawny, brainless gangster.[17] The film's portrayal of brute masculinity in a female body satirizes the paranoia over deposed masculine authority, while nonetheless preserving the comedic abjection of gender swapping. In my reading, this ambivalent, abject spectacle culminates in the unsettling physical comedy of the sassy girl's *yŏpki*, or perverse embodiment.

My Sassy Girl establishes the perversity of the title character by emphasizing her crude, masculine behavioral tics of binge drinking and bullying in the name of moral education—a misdirected attempt to call out strangers' misbehavior in the service of the public good. Told from Gŏn-u's perspective, the sassy girl—who is given no name but simply referred to as "that girl"—soon reveals her manic behavior to be a symptom of melancholia.

figure 2.2
A portrait of Gŏn-u
dressed as a girl,
in a flashback
sequence detailing
Gŏn-u's gender
troubles.

She tries to both remake Gŏn-u into her tragically deceased ex-boyfriend and repel him with her extreme behavior, out of guilt over betraying the memory of her former lover, whom Gŏn-u now threatens to replace. While "the girl's" aggression never fully neutralizes her physical attractiveness for Gŏn-u, he is repelled by her use of alcohol as a multipurpose excuse for unladylike behavior such as vomiting, passing out in public, and, especially, using violence as a mode of persuasion. The film presents Gŏn-u's horrified reaction shots to underscore "the girl's" perversity, yet Gŏn-u's corresponding perversion is also an excessive gender confusion, which the film's opening sequence explains as a result of his having been raised "as a girl" for the first several years of his life, because his parents had hoped for a daughter (figure 2.2). Reversing the traditional preference for male offspring in South Korea, the film offers parallel gender inversions for its central romantic pair, which it then sets about resolving through the restoration of proper patriarchal heteronormativity.

Although *My Sassy Girl* unswervingly follows the prescribed rom-com formula (the meet-cute, obstacle, separation, and reunion), it also foregrounds its reflexive stance on narrative conventions. The film abounds with intertextual references, from canonical Korean literary texts to popular action and martial arts cinema, to the metafictional framing of the internet novel from which the film is adapted (the film is produced by ShinCine, which is the company that appears in the last section of the film as the studio to which Gŏn-u pitches his autobiographical script, based on the actual internet novel that is *My Sassy Girl's* source material). This collage of references enhances the realism of the contemporary Seoul setting, despite the film's contrived three-act narrative structure, genre clichés such as fate and parental interference, and the tonal shift from comedy to melodrama, which is a dominant feature

michelle cho

of Korean mainstream narrative cinemas. Balancing the estranging effects of formalism and the affective appeal of popular generic modes, *My Sassy Girl* maintains a commitment to binary oppositions throughout its narrative: masculine-feminine, abject-ideal, comedy-melodrama.

The Tears of the Unruly

Both *My Sassy Girl* and *200 Pounds Beauty* present familiar, transnationally legible genre conventions, particularly the figure of the "unruly woman," as theorized in the context of gendered comedy by Kathleen Rowe, but with crucial differences that undercut Rowe's assertion of the unruly woman's resistant function.[18] Rowe's characterization of the unruly woman follows a Bakhtinian lineage in the ludic sensibility of the carnivalesque. The unruly woman is thus associated with gender inversion or masculinity, jokes, androgyny, dirt, liminality, looseness, and bodily excess. The unruliness of *My Sassy Girl*'s eponymous heroine stems not just from her perverse or *yŏpki* behavior and the violence of her actions as the "woman on top." These behaviors are presented ambivalently, as enjoyable parodies of patriarchy that soon tip into signs of the girl's pathological and abject status. The most iconoclastic effect of the girl's gender inversion is that her aggression is so out of step with her idealized feminine appearance as to be surprising each time it erupts onscreen.

Hanna, the protagonist of *200 Pounds Beauty*, maintains consistently feminine personality traits and romantic desires and lacks the gleeful irreverence of the comedic, unruly woman celebrated by Rowe. Instead, her unruliness stems solely from her uncontrollable body. Actress and model Kim Ah-Jung, who plays Hanna, dons a latex fat suit, to later regain her familiar physical form after the character's transformation through plastic surgery. A source of slapstick laughs, the rubbery mass that is her "fat" body overwhelms every space that seeks to contain it, particularly in an early scene in which Hanna's attempt to bow in the narrow confines of a fortune teller's lair sets off a string of mishaps that culminates in the destruction of the huckster's Buddha icon. Later, as she dances to a pop song on a small underground stage platform, the wooden floorboards collapse under her weight. Elastic and uncontainable, Hanna's body radiates mayhem. Although Hanna's transformation via plastic surgery reins in the grotesquerie associated with the fat body, it unleashes another type of excess, a disruptive beauty that literally stops traffic. Hanna finds this social transformation in visibility both empowering and embarrassing. Thus, Hanna's extremes, which exclude her from the category of normal

figure 2.3 Hanna (Kim Ah-Jung) prepares to go under the knife.

female bodies, are the basis for the film's claim that "beautiful women suffer," which is the literal translation of the film's Korean title.[19]

200 Pounds Beauty, aka *Beautiful Women Suffer*, tells the story of a woman who finds self-actualization by calibrating her outer appearance to her inner beauty. Hanna is a spunky, sweet, and sympathetic rom-com heroine with a beautiful voice, who resorts to extreme body modification only after realizing that the cruelty of South Korean gender norms and extreme fat phobia prevent her from having a life, that is, the ability to move about public space without eliciting disgust and ridicule, much less pursue a singing career in the extremely image-centered popular music industry. At the beginning of the film, Hanna is a phone sex operator and ghost singer for a pop diva named Ammy, whose manager is Hanna's mentor and secret crush. After overhearing Ammy and the manager joke about her naïveté and easy exploitation, Hanna falls into depression and attempts suicide. Her failed attempt leads her to the decision that plastic surgery is her last chance at a livable existence (figure 2.3).

Blackmailing a phone sex client who also happens to be a plastic surgeon, Hanna is reborn after much blood, sweat, tears, and silicone as Jenny, a rising new pop star. Hanna/Jenny realizes however, that the transformation from duckling to swan has plunged her into further depths of self-hatred, after she is forced to cut off ties with her disabled father, her best friend, and worst of all, her former, pure-hearted self.

The film resolves Hanna's transformation *not* by returning her to her previous form, but by repairing the rift between old and new self through public confession. As the jealous Ammy stands poised to send photos of fat Hanna to the press to ruin Hanna/Jenny's fledgling career, Hanna panics at her

michelle cho

figure 2.4 Hanna/Jenny (Kim Ah-Jung) panics at her concert, tearfully confessing her deception to the audience, with images of her pre–plastic surgery self projected behind her.

first stadium concert and outs herself to the audience, weepily apologizing for deceiving them (figure 2.4). Unexpectedly, the audience responds with sympathy to her public performance of tormented self-alienation, allowing Hanna to regain her "true" self, now fully realized by the correspondence between her beautiful spirit and her beautiful body. This "true" self is achieved through copious tears and public atonement, as the film enacts a now ubiquitous formula for Korean romantic comedy: the bimodal form of tragicomedy, where slapstick comedy shifts abruptly into melodrama.[20]

While both films mobilize the genre conventions of physical comedy through slapstick, gender inversion, body humor, and, as Linda Mizejewski writes, "the ability of disruptive behavior to be interpreted as laudable individualism," they also both rely on the embodied dimensions of melodramatic affect to suture their representations of gender transgression to familiar and comforting narratives. *My Sassy Girl* ends in heterosexual coupling, and *200 Pounds Beauty* affirms neoliberal self-fashioning as liberal self-determination. Moreover, the films melodramatically recuperate abject femininity as a collective act, either as an expression of specifically national sentiment or as a means by which pop culture performance forges community bonds.

Both films situate the popular abject in the domain of contemporary celebrity or entertainment culture, an arena that is carnivalesque in its inversion of truth and semblance, such that the best performance is also the most authentic. One of *My Sassy Girl*'s running jokes is that the girl is a budding screenwriter who writes scripts that would never be greenlighted and, in one scene, that actually elicit violent bodily rejection, when an attempt to pitch one of the girl's works to a film production company ends with the producer racing to a toilet, overcome with nausea. The girl's scripts are all derivative and cliché genre films, from a thinly disguised version of *The Terminator* to a *wuxia* period film to a perverse rendition of "Rain Shower," a classic Korean tale of first love. Yet they express her version of her "true" self by rewriting sentimental, nostalgic narratives into horror or action genres, with inverted gender roles as alternatives to conventional gendered characterization. For example, the girl's "Rain Shower" script turns the tragic story of a teenage girl dying of consumption, who asks to be buried in the clothes that she wore when she met her first love during a summer rain shower, into a horror film, where the dying girl decrees that her love interest be buried alive with her, so that they can be together for eternity. The effect of the carnivalesque is revisited in amplified form in *My Love from the Star*, in which the reflexivity produced by the character played by Jeon Ji-Hyun is also redoubled in her role as a Korean wave star, whose star image is always being threatened by her "real" self—her emotional vulnerability, her unladylike antics, and her ignoble narcissism.

In *200 Pounds Beauty* the sphere of pop entertainment/celebrity is carnivalesque, not just because it offers the possibility of upturning the relationship between artifice and authenticity, but also because it is literally underwritten by the grotesque. Hanna's unruly fat self as the "voice" for Ammy, and then the beautiful Hanna/Jenny as the grotesque creature of extreme body modification, underscores the notion that normative femininity is always an index of the feminine grotesque. The popular abject thus signifies and reproduces disgust over the fleshly material that is plasticized by scalpels, fat suction and redistribution, implantation of inorganic material like silicone, and the injection of toxins for the sake of aestheticized paralysis. *200 Pounds Beauty*'s notion that a non-shame-inducing body can emerge only via a passage through the condition of grotesquerie makes abjection indeed the mainstream condition and concretizes the celebrity form as the undoing of the boundary between the acceptable and the abject body.

Ultimately, *200 Pounds Beauty* supports the strict observance of feminine beauty ideals through the plasticized beauty's self-policing—the process of taking the violence of social norms as an occasion to remake oneself through plastic surgery's disciplinary technology. Embodiment as empowerment is achieved by jettisoning a naïve insistence on naturalism; this knowing disenchantment with "nature" is coded as feminine agency in the patriarchal order. The politics of self-making rely on reflexive awareness of gender performativity, while maintaining an assertively binarized gender system. Similarly, the *yŏpki* girl rehabilitates the dispossessed, emasculated gangster by redirecting humor away from him, in the direction of the hysterical feminine, but in a way that constantly points to masculinity's dependence on feminine submission. Only the revelation of the girl's pathological mourning gives Gŏn-u the opportunity to recode his femininity as the reasoned, responsible, and mature form of the masculine (if the sassy girl is the infantile, undisciplined masculine form).

Misogyny and Militant Beauty

Beauty is my weapon / I'm a beautiful girl
—lyrics from "Beautiful Girl," 200 *Pounds Beauty* soundtrack

If both *My Sassy Girl* and 200 *Pounds Beauty* denaturalize gender, reveling in its performative construction, they can also be read through a transgender lens, particularly in the normative social influence imputed to the feminine. *My Sassy Girl's* protagonist is behaviorally masculine though visually feminine; Hanna/Jenny sings about her beauty as weaponry, even if narratively the humor in 200 *Pounds Beauty* relies on the character's seeming innocence of the manipulability of appearance and sexual attractiveness as a means of feminine empowerment. The militance of beauty in both of these cases takes the form of grounding gender identity in the prescriptive dimension of femininity as masculinity's guarantor.

   My Sassy Girl offers a curious turning point in the power dynamic between Gŏn-u and the *yŏpki* girl, in a sequence involving a military deserter who must be persuaded to return to the fold of normative masculinity, healed of his misogynist and misanthropic rage at being abandoned by his girlfriend while captive in his mandatory military service.[21] What ensues is a curious shift in the film's point of view, which has thus far framed the *yŏpki* girl's perverse masculinity through absurdity and body humor. What occurs here is the transition from a straightforward male POV, that of Gŏn-u, the narrator, to a focus on the girl's feminine interiority, as she delivers an impassioned monologue about love and loss that reduces the conscript to tears. This shift to the girl's perspective downplays the metatextual framing device that the film is the adaptation of the internet novel that Gŏn-u writes about their relationship. From this point onward, the film reforms the *yŏpki* girl via a trope of self-reflection, as she progressively verbalizes her inner thoughts and motivations, and thus "works through" her interminable mourning for her deceased ex-boyfriend. At this pivotal moment, the *yŏpki* girl successfully instructs the soldier in how to achieve manhood by embracing the magnanimity of true love, which can only be achieved by letting go, that is, by mourning his ex-girlfriend. Attributing his antisocial act of desertion to immaturity, the girl exhorts the soldier to grow up, to develop the unconditional care for another that would allow him to part with his ex-girlfriend without recrimination. In counseling the soldier, the *yŏpki* girl also happens to be verbalizing her own passage from melancholia to mourning, suddenly becoming a voice of reason, successfully disciplining the soldier into reassuming his commitment to national service.

This scene's transgender dimension is highlighted in what enables the *yŏpki* girl to have this heart-to-heart conversation with the deserter, to counsel him in a role that would customarily be served by a wise male superior. Moreover, in contrast to Gŏn-u, who cowardly begs the soldier to keep the girl and let him go, the *yŏpki* girl saves them both by bravely facing down the soldier's violent, reactionary masculinity, even though he takes the couple hostage at gunpoint. The militant beauty here is the *yŏpki* girl, who will ultimately be shown to have served a pedagogical function, not only in this instance, but in Gŏn-u's life as well. The girl's character here instructs in the no-nonsense, hard-hitting, truth-telling fashion, but she can only convey these lessons because she simultaneously embodies the object of desire—the girl who got away and drove the army deserter into heartbroken irrationality in the first place. The wound at the heart of gendered nationalism can only be repaired by women, who must perform dependency as a safeguard for militarized masculinity.

In this scene's gendered comedy, whereby a character simultaneously neuters and shores up militarized masculinity through her feminine embodiment, gender binaries function in multiple ways. If, in gangster comedies, masculine right is rendered farcical by the gangster's demotion to subaltern or rube, the gender-reversal comedy displaces this abjection, feminizing this form of behavior as male hysteria. Although Kristeva contrasts hysteria and abjection, writing that hysteria "brings about, ignores, or seduces the symbolic but does not produce it," while "the subject of abjection is eminently productive of culture," I suggest that the gendering function of hysteria as a feminine neurosis renders its transposition across bodies, in these works, symbolically productive.[22] Gender binaries are openly derided, the source of humor and the generic code, to be built up again and protected by the power attributed to femininity as the underwriter of masculine integrity. This is further lampooned in *200 Pounds Beauty*, through the exaggerated power of feminine embodiment as a form of physical dominance over men, a weapon in an ongoing war of the sexes. Humor issues from mass disavowal of the actual violence of gender norms and the prevalence of gender inequity, maintained through the popular mythologies of ideal gendered embodiment distributed through popular cinema, among other mass-mediated forms.

Militant beauty thus signals the very real effects of gender oppression, both in the trauma of military conditioning for male conscripts, many of whom are traumatized by their experiences of hazing and corporal punishment in the hierarchized disciplinary apparatus of the military, and in the everyday misogyny that gives rise to the weaponization of feminine beauty. While the latter is a source of comic hyperbole in *200 Pounds Beauty*, the notion of beauty as *defensive* highlights the normalized hostility women face in everyday life. As Hanna and the *yŏpki* girl's self-actualization narratives attest, femininity entails a kind of public availability, a publicity that issues from the gender binary. Because both Hanna and the *yŏpki* girl are ideally gendered bodies, they can safely internalize the violence of gender norms as a reparative gesture, to overcome their split identifications through the performance of public confession.

Conclusion: Mass Disavowal and the Abject Ideal

I conclude here by highlighting popular abjection's production of an ideal of inclusive exclusion in these transnationally appealing South Korean comedies. Bodies produce affect in comedic and then sentimental modes. Making gender transgression funny disavows the actual violence of gendered constraints. Then, the reversal of comedy into melodrama registers—through a chain of displacements—the broader implications of the mass abjection produced by dissolving gender frameworks of legibility. Comedy blows the cover off naturalized gender, while melodramatic tears repair gender's lost objects. Both *My Sassy Girl* and *200 Pounds Beauty* suggest that abjection is a state of exclusion that is common to all who are subjected to normative gender frameworks, but this abjection is a precondition to self-making projects, as it is a state to be overcome via self-cultivation, whether through the pursuit of beauty or through therapeutic self-narration. We must reckon with what's at stake in the compulsive repetition of this abject ideal, by which one produces oneself through one's expulsion, recognition, and radical reconstruction.

While the Gangnam area of Seoul is more popularly known internationally as the setting of the comedic music video and pop single "Gangnam Style" (Psy, 2012), for the South Korean public, it has recently become a flashpoint for public debates over gender inequality. On May 17, 2016, a twenty-three-year-old woman was murdered in a public restroom by a thirty-four-year-old male whom she did not know. The perpetrator claims that he was motivated by hatred toward women because they belittled or ignored him, yet, since he has a history of mental illness, police investigators in the case do not consider this a hate crime. While women across the country argue otherwise, men's rights groups have taken to social media and public rallies to decry the claim of misogyny in discussions of the case, arguing that men are being unduly harmed by identification with the perpetrator. A makeshift memorial at the Gangnam subway station has drawn thousands to express their grief and to question the state of gender relations in a country that the World Economic Forum ranks 115 out of 145 countries for gender equality.[23]

Accounts of the nation's stunning pace of development and the millennial success of its culture industries as a dominant source of pop culture content in East and Southeast Asia disavow this inequality and the persistence of conservative, patriarchal gender norms in South Korea. I press the need to contextualize the representations of gendered abjection in popular works in a historical view of mainstream attitudes toward gender relations. Scholars have detailed the production of militarized masculinity as a central ideological tenet of South Korean nationalism since the nation's inception after World War II, throughout the Cold War, in the ongoing tensions with North Korea, and as a key node in a US-led military-industrial complex across the Pacific.[24] The production of the masculine national subject and the corresponding feminine abject is further embedded in the history of colonization by Japan, from 1905 to 1945, and industrial modernization under successive military dictatorships from 1961 to 1987.

The popular abjection that I discuss here emerges shortly after the transition to democratic governance in the 1990s and bears the traces of this postwar, postcolonial trajectory, founded on the remediation of colonized, abject masculinity. In the early 2000s, in response to new media forms and the rapid integration of digital networks, an obsession with self-reflexive entertainment emerged along with a broad national project of globalization across industries and economic sectors. The current availability of Korean popular culture on digital platforms around the world is a direct outcome of this state-sponsored national branding project. Through this national-global initiative, Korean popular media has become associated with plasticity—metaphorically, in the penchant for pastiche and syncretic adaptation, and more literally, in the ubiquity of plastic surgery among Korean entertainers. Korean media have thus mainstreamed the abject and grotesque body through popular media forms, across film, television, and pop music, which are also key cultural exports.

michelle cho

Since the postwar period, South Korean comedians, or "gagmen," in film and television have traditionally played the role of the fool who serves as the alibi for the persistence of physical and social hierarchies. Gagmen and gagwomen generally perform slapstick routines on variety shows or situation comedies, and their bodies are presented as foils to the beautiful, classical bodies of film and TV melodrama actors. By presenting the gagwoman in the classical body of the melodramatically emotive movie star or pop singer, *My Sassy Girl* and *200 Pounds Beauty* present an abject ideal that confounds signification, while making legible new models of gendered subjectivity, particularly in the chiasmic relation between pathetic masculinity and unruly femininity. Both films offer the subversion of gender roles for entertainment, along with the concomitant pleasure of restoring gender and genre norms. Yet, spectator identification with the abject body, through Hanna's public confession or the *yŏpki* girl's interminable mourning, offers abjection as a condition that makes traditional gender roles worth preserving *only* because they can be denaturalized over and over again. The collective mourning for the loss of these social conventions thus offers a means of belonging in a sentimental public.[25] As the genre conventions of the South Korean romantic comedy specifically entail an abrupt transition from comedy to melodrama, from the abjection of the female condition to the abjection of affectively constituted cultural citizenship, this bipolarity may express something about a transnational, millennial zeitgeist: if you're not laughing, you're crying, or first as farce, then as tragedy. A performance of unruliness that disciplines in *My Sassy Girl* and a performance of docility (made potent and unruly through self-transformation via surgical construction) in *200 Pounds Beauty* offer a fantasy field for intemperate desires, particularly those of a nonbinary gender identification that can simultaneously preserve the security and legibility of gendered forms of social being.

Notes

I would like to thank Maggie Hennefeld and Nic Sammond for their encouragement and editorial brilliance. I'm also grateful for generous feedback on previous versions of this essay from Sunyoung Park, Moonim Baek, Bishnupriya Gosh, Bhaskar Sarkar, and Kim Icreverzi, as well as research support from Yonsei University's Future-Leading Research Initiative. Epigraphs: Judith Butler, *Undoing Gender* (New York: Routledge, 2004), 35; Julia Kristeva, *Powers of Horror: An Essay on Abjection*, trans. Leon S. Roudiez (New York: Columbia University Press, 1982), 8.

1   In March 2014, the *Washington Post* reported that delegates at the meeting of China's National People's Congress, a highly symbolic annual parliamentary meeting at which the Chinese Communist Party's social, economic, and military initiatives are unveiled, spent an entire morning session speculating about why South Korean television dramas eclipsed the popularity of Chinese-produced content in the region. William Wan, "Chinese Officials Debate Why China Can't Make a Soap Opera as Good as South Korea's," *Washington Post*, March 7, 2014, http://www.washingtonpost.com/world/asia _pacific/chinese-officials-debate-why-china-cant-make-a-soap-opera-as-good -as-south-koreas/2014/03/07/94b86678-a5f3-11e3-84d4-e59b1709222c_story .html.

2   *Gross-out* refers to a subgenre of American comedy often directed at younger audiences ("gross-out teen comedy") that foregrounds crude sexual, scatological, or grotesque body humor. *American Pie* (dir. Paul Weitz, 1999) and *There's Something about Mary* (dir. Bobby Farrelly and Peter Farrelly, 1998), two examples that define the transformations of the genre, from its inception in the 1970s, share with *My Sassy Girl* the turn-of-the-millennium production context. See Lesley Speed, "Loose Cannons: White Masculinity and the Vulgar Teen Comedy Film," *Journal of Popular Culture* 43, no. 4 (2010): 820–41.

3   Jane Chi Hyun Park, "Remaking the Korean Romcom: A Case Study of *Yeopgijeogin geunyeo* and *My Sassy Girl*," in *Complicated Currents: Media Flows, Soft Power and East Asia*, ed. Daniel Black, Stephen Epstein, and Alison Tokita (Melbourne: Monash University ePress, 2010), 13.1–13.12. http://books .publishing.monash.edu/apps/bookworm/view/Complicated+Currents/122 /xhtml/chapter13.html.

4   The early 2000s gave rise to the terms *momzzang*—"best body"—and *ulzzang*—"best face"—in fan discourse and social media. Jeon Ji-Hyun often appeared on best body/face celebrity rankings. Joanna Elfving-Hwang analyzes the preservation of key tenets of Confucian family values in the Korean extreme makeover show *Let Me In*. In her reading of the show's authorization of body modification as a form of filial piety, Elfving-Hwang outlines the important qualifiers with which to read cosmetic body enhancement and surgical modification in accordance with local cultural norms. Plastic surgery thus has far more complex and embedded connotations than mere vanity or the pursuit of "Westernized" beauty ideals. Joanna Elving-Hwang, "Cosmetic Surgery and Embodying the Moral Self in South Korean Popular Makeover Culture," *Asia-Pacific Journal* 11, no. 24 (2013): 1–11.

5   Chi-Yun Shin analyzes the marketing phenomenon of "Asia Extreme" in "Art of Branding: Tartan 'Asia Extreme' Films," *Jump Cut* 50 (2008), https://www .ejumpcut.org/archive/jc50.2008/TartanDist/text.html.

6   Critiques of the aesthetics of the extreme in art-house cinemas claim that the hyperviolent aesthetics of discomfort operate as justification for cinematic exploitation. In a now infamous screed against the "New French Extremism," published in *Art Forum* in 2004, James Quandt writes against what

he perceives as "an international vogue for 'porno chic,' widely apparent in art-house films from Austria to Korea." "Flesh and Blood: Sex and Violence in Recent French Cinema," reprinted in *The New Extremism in Cinema: From France to Europe*, ed. Tanya Horeck and Tina Kendall (Edinburgh: Edinburgh University Press, 2011), 24–25.

7   In Manohla Dargis's March 25, 2005, *New York Times* review of Park Chan-wook's cult hit *Oldboy*, she writes, "The most interesting thing about 'Oldboy' is that . . . it is a B movie tricked out as an A movie. Once, a film like this, predicated on extreme violence and staying within the prison house of genre rather than transcending it, would have been shot on cardboard sets with two-bit talent. It would have had its premiere in Times Square."

8   One of the most polarizing Korean films to screen internationally, *The Isle* presents scenes of self-mutilation, including one in which a prostitute stuffs fishhooks into her vagina, that had viewers passing out or vomiting at its Venice Film Festival premiere.

9   Following the authors of the volume *New Millennium South Korea: Neoliberal Capitalism and Transnational Movements*, ed. Jesook Song (New York: Routledge, 2010), I use *millennial* as both a period category and a sociocultural formation by which the timing of the Asian financial crisis shortly after democratic reforms and the liberalization of public and commercial culture in the 1990s accelerates the development of neoliberal consensus/common sense, which comes to define social relations and practices of self-making in the twenty-first century.

10   The majority of successful comedies of the late 1990s and early 2000s would fit the "gangster slapstick" label. Notable examples include *My Boss, My Hero* (dir. Yoon Je-kyun, 2001), *Hi! Dharma!* (dir. Park Cheol-kwan, 2001), and *Kick the Moon* (dir. Kim Sang-jin, 2001).

11   Both Jinhee Choi and Jane Chi Hyun Park write about *My Sassy Girl* in the context of genre considerations of the popular Korean rom-com. Choi also includes an extensive genealogy of various South Korean gangster films in her book *The South Korean Film Renaissance: Local Hitmakers, Global Provocateurs* (Middletown, CT: Wesleyan University Press, 2010). While both scholars mention gender role reversal as a comic device with reference to the popular comedy *My Wife Is a Gangster* (*Chopok Manura*; dir. Jo Jin-kyu, 2001), they see *My Sassy Girl* as a fundamentally different genre of film comedy.

12   Jane Park explains that the film hit the number one spot in Hong Kong and Singapore and "catapulted Kim Ah-Jung, the actress who plays Hanna, to *hallyu* fame, eclipsing Jeon Ji-hyun's popularity from *My Sassy Girl* five years earlier." See "Tragicomic Transformations: Gender, Humor, and the Plastic Body in Two Korean Comedies," in *A Companion to Film Comedy*, ed. Andrew Horton and Joanna E. Rapf (Malden, MA: Wiley-Blackwell, 2012), 437.

13   Cf. Kyung Hyun Kim, *The Remasculinization of Korean Cinema* (Durham, NC: Duke University Press, 2004); Nancy Abelmann and Kathleen McHugh,

eds., *South Korean Golden Age Melodrama: Gender, Genre, and National Cinema* (Detroit, MI: Wayne State University Press, 2005); and Kelly Jeong, *Crisis of Gender and the Nation in Korean Literature and Cinema: Modernity Arrives Again* (New York: Lexington Books, 2011). For a critique of gendered nationalism, see Seungsook Moon, *Militarized Modernity and Gendered Citizenship in South Korea* (Durham, NC: Duke University Press, 2005). For discussions of the ROK-US military alliance and its reliance on economies of sexual labor, see Katherine S. Moon, *Sex among Allies: Military Prostitution in US-Korea Relations* (New York: Columbia University Press, 1997); and Jin-kyung Lee, *Service Economies: Militarism, Sex Work, and Migrant Labor in South Korea* (Minneapolis: University of Minnesota Press, 2010).

14 Choi, *South Korean Film Renaissance*, 60, 64.

15 Chi-Yun Shin directly links the abject figure of the dispossessed gangster to the IMF crisis and the concomitant crisis of masculinity produced by widespread economic instability, mass layoffs, and the discourse of national humiliation in the context of an emphatically masculinized nationalism produced by the formative influence of the military's political hegemony since the founding of the Republic of Korea in 1948. See Chi-Yun Shin, "Two of a Kind: Gender and Friendship in *Friend* and *Take Care of My Cat*," in *New Korean Cinema*, ed. Chi-Yun Shin and Julian Stringer (Edinburgh: University of Edinburgh Press, 2005), 123.

16 According to Choi, "Korean gangster cinema presents the same core conflicts as male coming-of-age stories . . . individual vs. society, desire vs. duty, rebellion vs. conformity, and longing vs. contentment—and in both, the male protagonists neither make successful transitions from adolescence to adulthood nor come to terms with their own identities" (*South Korean Film Renaissance*, 70). By arguing for *My Sassy Girl*'s place in this genealogy, I want to consider what is signified when women rebel, and whether girls' coming-of-age stories share these core concerns.

17 "Soft masculinity" is Sun Jung's term for the masculine mode popularized in K-dramas and pop idols. See her *Korean Masculinities and Transcultural Consumption: Yonsama, Rain, Oldboy, K-pop Idols* (Hong Kong: HKU Press, 2011).

18 Kathleen Rowe, *The Unruly Woman: Gender and the Genres of Laughter* (Austin: University of Texas Press, 1995).

19 Jane Chi Hyun Park translates this film's title as "It's Tough Being Beautiful," which perhaps captures something of the sentiment that being burdened by excessive admiration because one is so attractive is an enviable state. Given the film's overall turn to melodramatic confession, however, I prefer the literal translation for the purposes of this chapter (Park, "Tragicomic Transformations," 436).

20 Park, "Tragicomic Transformations," 436.

21 Given the ongoing conflict with North Korea, as no peace treaty was signed after the armistice agreement of 1953, meaning the North and South Korean

states are still technically at war, all male citizens of the ROK between the ages of eighteen and thirty-five are conscripted into military service for a period of twenty-one to twenty-four months. Most young Korean men dread their military service, fueling claims of gender discrimination, since women are not required to serve an equivalent term.

22 Kristeva, *Powers of Horror*, 45.

23 World Economic Forum, *The Global Gender Gap Report 2015*, http://reports .weforum.org/global-gender-gap-report-2015/.

24 See Chungmoo Choi and Elaine Kim, eds., *Dangerous Women: Gender and Korean Nationalism* (New York: Routledge, 1997); and Moon, *Militarized Modernity*.

25 I adapt this concept from Lauren Berlant, *The Female Complaint: The Unfinished Business of Sentimentality in American Culture* (Durham, NC: Duke University Press, 2008).

chapter three

Precarious-Girl Comedy: Issa Rae, Lena Dunham, & Abjection Aesthetics

rebecca wanzo

Comedy has long trafficked in shame and abjection to produce laughter. Shame may emphasize the superiority of the audience to the humiliated, trigger a feeling of recognition, or do both. The relationship between alienation and identification may be most transparent with the comedy of people who are "other" in some way, as the shamed subject can function as representative of an alienated group and produce the hybrid affect of discomfited pleasure. Issa Rae, creator and star of the comedy web series *The Mis-Adventures of Awkward Black Girl* (2011–13), organized her show around the nexus of identification and alienated shame by depicting a young African American woman struggling with what many people might find incongruous—being both black and awkward. Her character J's inability to inhabit a black "cool pose," an identity most associated with men but one that clearly resonates in the everyday performance culture of African American women as well, was embraced by "black geeks" as a revolutionary media representation.[1]

A year after *Awkward Black Girl*'s premiere, another program was hailed as innovative and representative of a particular alienated demographic. In 2012, the actress, writer, and producer Lena Dunham and her new series were ubiquitous in the popular press. Dunham created and starred in the HBO dramedy *Girls* (2012–17), which follows recent college graduate Hannah and her girlfriends in Brooklyn as they navigate lives that seem profession-ally directionless and romantically and sexually wretched. Many critics im-mediately hailed the series as "brilliant," "perfect," "authentic," "original," and a "breakthrough."[2] *New York Magazine* television critic Emily Nussbaum claimed that *Girls* "was a bold defense (and searing critique) of the so-called Millennial Generation by a person still in her twenties . . . the show [felt] 'for us, by us.'"[3]

Nussbaum's language—"for us, by us"—was similar to the claims of many black women fans of *Awkward Black Girl*, although they were not referring to the same "us." In fact, feminists of color often attacked *Girls* for its racial homogeneity.[4] But the shows actually have a great deal in common, and they are representative of a millennial female subject who has begun appearing in twenty-first-century comedy. Like *Girls*, Issa Rae's *The Mis-Adventures of Awk-ward Black Girl* depicts a woman who comes from a fairly comfortable class position; struggles to find a satisfying job after college; has romantic encoun-ters that challenge her sense of self-worth; and is socially awkward, inept, and abject in most situations. And these shows are not anomalies. Women who seem to be experiencing arrested development—economically and often psychologically—are the protagonists in several television and web series that emerged at the same time, such as *Broad City* (web series, 2009–11; Comedy Central, 2014–), *2 Broke Girls* (2011–17), and *How to Live with Your Parents (For the Rest of Your Life)* (2013). These sitcoms are indicative of network executives' belief that there is a market in depicting a perpetual girlhood pro-duced not only by the greater economic insecurity that middle-class women have been facing post–Great Recession, but by a variety of social factors that generate feelings of immobilization and isolation. Abjection is often a princi-pal sign of these characters' precarity—they inhabit spaces where they often recoil from others and others recoil from them, and their constant associa-tion with the gross (things like dirt, vomit, and feces) are habitually signs of what emotional and economic insecurity has wrought.

The nexus of abjection and precarity characterizes what I term precarious-girl comedies in the new millennium. Lauren Berlant argues that a new cinema of precarity in European melodrama records the "loneliness of col-lective singularity," which can nevertheless produce a new kind of solidarity in neoliberal times.[5] The precarious-girl comedy makes endless alienation a source of humor and evolves from comedic traditions that use abjection and what Kathleen Rowe calls the "unruly woman" to disavow the possibility of solidarity with people of similar historical identities and social locations, embracing the otherness found in abjection as a desired end and expression of an authentic self.[6] These shows are also somewhat haunted by their television predecessors—the women's melodrama that is organized by an (often thwarted) desire for the happy ending and, in the case of *Awkward Black Girl*, racial uplift cinema and television.[7] Both highly racialized genres are operationalized by attachments to the lost possibility of a "good life," but in the precarious-girl comedy, the protagonist embraces the idea that she repels others as a sign of her individuation. If she cannot escape the conditions that make her alienate others, then perhaps she can escape her feelings about her immobility by treating acceptance of her abjection as a form of psychological growth and development.

Race may make a critical difference in how middle-class millennial abjection is represented as a path toward freedom. While the protagonists of both *Girls* and *Awkward Black Girl* ultimately depict acceptance of the abject self as a more evolved self, Western black subjects nonetheless have a different relationship to abjection. As Darieck Scott has argued, "Blackness is constructed by a history of abjection and is a form of abjection."[8] For middle-class white subjects, abjection has not historically been a defining characteristic of white identity; thus, the embrace of abjection for Hannah means coming to terms with a new, uglier place to inhabit. But since black subjects are always already abject in the Western imagination, reframing the affective response to that history and taking away some of that history's power to wound has been the work of many black cultural producers, including Issa Rae. While *Girls* is a study in the classic psychoanalytic account of abjection, often depicting Hannah Horvath as a dehumanized object full of disappointed drives, *Awkward Black Girl* humorously blends the historical weight of black abjection with other kinds of abjection, so that the abjection J uses to define herself is not one determined by the history of white supremacy. The term *awkward* becomes a synonym for abjection and yet also a modification of it, lessening its power to wound. There may be freedom in a middle-class white "girl" associating herself with sexual abjection, dirt, and feces, given traditional representations of pure white womanhood; but, perhaps unsurprisingly, a black "girl" may resist or play with Western constructions of the concept.

As numerous feminist media scholars have noted, the somewhat narrow treatment of feminism on television has often been of a liberal feminist mold, in which women "move forward" professionally or contest traditional domestic roles.[9] Yet "moving forward" is somewhat antithetical to the abjection aesthetics modeled in these series. These programs hinge on immobility as a mode of being. Depicting female subjects who will never entirely escape abjection, they also highlight the differences race and class may make to embracing not only this twenty-first-century form of comedy, but also modes of self-fashioning in neoliberal times.

You're Not Gonna Make It After All: From Prefeminism to Abjection in Women's Sitcoms

Neither *Girls* as a dramedy nor *Awkward Black Girl* as a web series have all the characteristics of traditional sitcoms, but the programs nevertheless replicate many of the most important characteristics of the situation comedy format. They are also indebted to previous representations of urban single women in sitcoms that explore women's issues. Television shows such as *Ally McBeal* and later programs featuring "enlightened sexism," in Susan Douglas's terms, characterized the "postfeminist" television culture of the 1990s and early twenty-first century. Douglas argues that such shows focused on successful women who eschewed feminism as unnecessary in their embrace of hyperfeminine, sexualized identities, or they depicted troubled "fantasies of empowerment" that undercut women.[10] *Girls* and *Awkward Black Girl* are part of this postfeminist moment, but its protagonists also epitomize a new economic and interpersonal insecurity of the American middle class. While clearly shaped by what we might term "feminist representational progress on television"—diversified protagonists, transformations in and removal from the domestic sphere, workplace comedy, and complex and varied representations of sexuality—the programs also reflect somewhat of a regression. "Girl" as opposed to "woman" has reemerged as a way to talk about women in their twenties, featuring women who seem ill-equipped for adult life.

Millennial women (born in the 1980s and 1990s) in the United States have been increasingly represented as stuck in the mire of a "post" without futurity. Several popular articles have described the "end of men," given the decreased mobility of men in a downsized economy, but discourse about American women's precarity reflects progress and failure simultaneously.[11] The discourse about precarious white masculinity revolves around the effects of various social revolutions and globalization on men's supremacy, and precarity for men of color (even middle-class men) involves state violence in addition to the threats posed by the economic recession. In contrast, the various strands of women's precarity involve the successes and unfulfilled promises of feminism and other civil rights projects. Poor subjects (often people of color) who have always been living precarious lives find that their suffering only increases in periods of greater economic stratification.[12] And, as the economic downturn also challenges men, heteronormativity becomes even less of an assured path for economic and personal security for women than it was in previous generations.[13] Those who have imagined that they should benefit from the gains of feminism and the civil rights movement may find that they are failing to succeed because of their limited options. This is not to say that success is elusive to all women; but how should we understand those who have less and now expect less, who have internalized many of the claims of second-wave feminism (but may not admit it), who have embraced identities that are not tied to traditional models for women in love and work but feel disappointed by their limited options? Moreover, what kind of narrative tropes, aesthetic practices, or genres and generic conventions might emerge in relation to this moment of precarity?

Lauren Berlant argues that we have "a whole new precarious public sphere, defined by debates about how to rework insecurity in the ongoing present and defined as well by an emerging aesthetic."[14] In fact, multiple aesthetics have emerged, and in the woman-centered sitcom, abjection has been an important affective mode, disrupting the genre's narrative tendency to support a domestic status quo or move women toward marriage and greater professional fulfillment. Abjection has been fairly central to the US tradition of comedy—particularly stand-up. Drawing from Julia Kristeva, John Limon argues that the essence of comedy is "abasement" and "a psychic worrying of those aspects of oneself that one cannot be rid of." Describing stand-up comedians who made a career of constructing personae who are always stuck, making humor out of some identity or personality traits that they cannot discard, he suggests that abjection became not just a role they play but the *only* character they play.[15] The stand-up comedian's monologue is a genre of the present; a glimpse of future happiness would take us out of the moment of comedy, away from the comedian who continually inhabits a place of shame. But the odd temporality of the sitcom depends on both stagnation and movement toward the episodic happy ending that the format demands.[16] In precarious-girl comedies, the abjection aesthetic requires that they remain stuck, even as the format of the comedy requires that they move forward. Thus this form of comedy offers one solution to the question above, suggesting that when women have ambitions, politics, and desires for which they have no outlet, they can make a virtue of accepting their immobility when they cannot craft the world around them. Inhabiting a world in which mobility is frozen—economically, politically, romantically—these women's bodies become sites of the modern mire of economic and intimate abjection. And their bonding, too, is characterized by isolation, even in a social group. They are all uniquely Other, interpellating viewers who recognize these subjects.

rebecca wanzo

As these comedies demonstrate, gender and race make a difference in how precarity-induced abjection is articulated. White male versions of arrested affective and professional development—evident in white bromance film comedies such as *Knocked Up* (2007) and *I Love You, Man* (2009), as well as in television shows like *Two and a Half Men* (2003–15)—are recuperated as demonstrating the need for joie de vivre in adulthood on the path to greater responsibility. The female versions that have been appearing on television, however, depict women who often remain somewhat stuck; their personal and professional failures rarely lead them down the path to happiness.[17]

In many representations of women in comedy or dramedy series, the characters may be awkward but really good at their jobs; moments of incompetence or failure are often configured as something they will overcome; or they might have been examples of unruly women, exerting power through their excess or inappropriate behavior. In contrast, in both *Girls* and *Awkward Black Girl*, we see that the characters will move forward professionally, but we still have serious doubts about their ability to be successful. Romantic progress is probable, but it is not the cure to an abjection that is not just a stage or phase but a mode of being. The difference between the precarious-girl comedy and other postfeminist comedy representations is that the latter still revolve around women's success, even with fewer romantic or professional expectations, while the precarious girl only demonstrates progress by embracing abjection without ambivalence.

Repugnant Subjectivity: Hannah Horvath and the Freedom to Repel

In the cold opening of the *Girls* pilot, Hannah Horvath's parents cut her off financially. This scene immediately establishes two much-discussed characteristics of millennials: post-college-graduate dependence on parental support and increased narcissism.[18] Toward the end of the episode, Hannah goes to her parents' hotel room to try to change their minds about not supporting her financially. Knocking on the door and announcing her presence with an infantile "papa," she wakes them up and tells them to read her book right away: "I don't want to freak you out, . . . but I think I may be the voice of my generation." The reaction shot shows her parents' amusement at her hyperbole, aligning the audience with their affect. Even she can see herself through their response and clarifies, "Or at least . . . a voice of *a* generation." The program constantly calls attention to how her self-importance alienates her from others—not just her friends and family but the viewers as well.

Being a frustrated writer is just one of her sources of disappointment. In the pilot we learn she has a "sort of" boyfriend who makes her feel devalued and uncomfortable and that she is prone to dramatic exaggerations and lies to compensate for her unhappiness. What Hannah wishes to expel is this thing that makes her insecure, unworthy, and unable to move about successfully in the world. She seems to be experiencing what Kristeva, in her discussion of abjection, would describe as the "weight of meaninglessness" in this precarious moment. But she cannot face that reality because acknowledging her limited opportunities would result in an annihilation of her sense of self.[19] For Hannah, graduation and limited opportunities function as an inaugural loss of all her hopes and fantasies. And on some level, she recognizes that she is or has become a creature of thwarted desires.

This is, obviously, a hard space in which to dwell. Hannah's compensation is *jouissance*—a complex concept in psychoanalysis, but most easily understood in Kristeva as a kind of painful pleasure shaped by the crisis and dissolution of the subject. The phallocentric focus of jouissance becomes an aspect of women's creation for French feminist theorists like Hélène Cixous and Kristeva, but for Kristeva it is linked to the abject. Hannah's outlet for finding a self occurs once her original sense of self (or fantasy about herself) is shattered. Since she cannot quite grasp the things that make her miserable—lack of success, a feeling that she alienates others but that she cannot change the aspects of her self that alienate—she crafts agency in the experience of abjection. The alienation then becomes sublime as a mode of compensation.[20] This is why, according to Kristeva, "so many victims of the abject are its fascinated victims."[21] Claiming difference, alienation, isolation, and specialness is part of how Hannah shores up her identity—particularly as a writer. *Girls* imagines modes of women's creation in the face of a precarity that disrupts subjectivity and agency.

Hannah is often accused of being narcissistic, a precondition of which is abjection, as the idealized image of the self is the lost object of the abject self. Thus part of the comedy aesthetic of abjection is constantly calling attention to the lost love object, the ideal self. Hannah's way of gaining composure is to embrace abjection as her *new* ideal self. As a writer whose brilliance should, she believes, take priority over others' needs, Hannah's idealized self repels. She feels that her parents should sublimate their concerns about their financial planning to support her. When the editor of her e-book dies, Hannah pesters his widow about the status of her manuscript at the funeral. Narcissism, Freud tells us, might be a characteristic of all human beings, and it is essential to the project of self-preservation.[22] Thus we can understand why

rebecca wanzo

an inflated sense of importance can be a useful defense mechanism in precarious economic times.

Abjection is also central to Hannah's identity as a writer—a slight modification of the narrative that "one must suffer to write." Kristeva recognizes a relationship between writing and abjection; writing is an exercise in expelling that ungraspable, nasty thing from the self, as well as a way of dwelling and externalizing abjection by being able to define what the thing is in a way that is impossible when it remains only in the mind. Abjection can thus become what Hannah is and what she creates. Lena Dunham is not Hannah, but her character's abjection is well within the tradition of the "psychic worrying of the self" common to the US stand-up tradition, which has transferred well to television, as viewers repeatedly return to watch performers (mostly men) like Louis C. K. and Larry David represent the shaming they describe in their routines, anxious as they watch the character's inevitable missteps. The representation of shame eliminates the distance that partially provides pleasure in the always retrospective stand-up, as the performer has survived to provide commentary, whereas these representations drag us into a heightened anxiety as we anticipate excruciating encounters.

In one episode, Hannah tells her friends about how her employer has been patting her on the ass and touching other female employees inappropriately. Her friend Jessa suggests that Hannah is actually flattered and should have sex with him so that she can write about the experience. Hannah decides to approach her boss in his office about it: "Be honest with me, Rich. . . . I know you want to fuck me. . . . At first it was repulsive to me, but now I'm game, so I think we should just do this, before I change my mind." He is shocked, despite his own inappropriate behavior, as his pats are of the still-sexist-if-not-sexual paternalistic sort, and he tells her that her speech is "an inappropriate way to talk to your employer." Hannah replies, "Rich, you don't need to fight it. I'm not like trying to frame you. I am letting you know that it is OK for you to act on this fantasy, because I am gross and so are you." She then places his hand on her breast.

In describing herself as "gross," she is embracing abjection as an identity and inviting him to dwell in that space too. The reaction shot depicts Rich laughing for a long time, and some audience reactions may be aligned with his. Dunham encourages the audience to respond to her as gross by wearing unflattering clothing ensembles that make her seem out of place in her own body. In this episode, she wears a baby doll dress and lingerie, a sexual aesthetic that links the "girl" with adult sexuality through the incongruity of adult women's bodies with childish garments. But in this scene, the cut and striped pattern are unattractive and only seem suitable for a young girl; Hannah looks far from seductive. Amused at her idea that she is making his "fantasies come true," Rich makes Hannah into an abject object in isolation. He asks if she is on drugs and then is entertained by the idea that she throws out in retaliation that she will sue if he does not write her a check. "Hannah," he says, "you barely have the wherewithal to get to work at 10 AM. There's no suing app on your iPhone." In her shame—a shame common to her as she constantly crosses boundaries of the social and normative—she realizes that she has misrecognized the space she inhabits.

Part of her problem is that her abjection often springs from an inability to recognize boundaries; for Hannah, every space is both personal and professional. As an autobiographical writer, public and private blend for her, and she cannot see the distinction. Her inability to recognize boundaries—existing in that in-between characteristic of abjection—make her an abject object to others who want to flee her attempts to draw everyone into an aesthetics of the abject. The office is frequently the location of abjection, with the mise-en-scène of the office simultaneously offering possibility (employment) and undermining it, as the drab enclosed setting produces a feeling of inertia. In one job interview, her rapport with her interviewer is strong: they joke about what they have in common as Brooklynites, and he seems to enjoy her sense of humor. But the interview takes an excruciating turn when she yet again fails to recognize the limits of professional space and attempts to make her interviewer into something gross and dirty. After he says he went to Syracuse University, she says, "I read a statistic that said that Syracuse has the highest incidence of date rape of any university . . . which weirdly went way down the year that you graduated." Her pinky finger plays at the corner of her mouth as an awkward attempt at a cutesy, seductive performance as she continues, "That was just a joke, because I'm saying there was no more date rape. Because they figured out who it was that was doing it. And it was you." As with the previous, tightly shot office scene with her boss, the audience is drawn into a small space we cannot escape, with nowhere to look but at the appalled reaction shots of her interviewer and at Hannah, who yet again misses social cues (figures 3.1 and 3.2). She instantly loses the job opportunity, and he attempts to school her on the reason for her failure: "Maybe you're not used to office environments like this, but, um, jokes about rape or race or incest or any of that kind of stuff is not office-ok."[23]

After a couple of failed jobs, Hannah's boyfriend, Adam, suggests that she may not be suited for a job in a "traditional sense," perhaps casting doubt on her ability to take care of herself. This may be an increasingly common

figures 3.1 & 3.2
Hannah (Lena
Dunham) repels in
a job interview.

theme in the new economy. While the woman's workplace sitcom has often
addressed the themes of sexism and dissatisfaction, a utopic strand that holds
up work as a space to gain freedom and confidence is also important in many
of *Girls'* television predecessors. Mary Richards in *The Mary Tyler Moore Show*
was one of the first to model finding confidence and community at work, and
the four successful protagonists of *Sex and the City*, while often struggling
in romantic relationships, were fairly consistently depicted as being good at
their jobs. One of the distinctions between the precarious-girl comedy and
some other sitcoms produced in this period featuring millennial women is
that the latter, like Mindy Kaling's *The Mindy Project*, depict women who are
professionally competent even if they are romantically awkward.

The professionally competent woman struggling with confusing romantic interests takes a somewhat retro turn in *Girls*. While the millennial male
characters demonstrate narcissism too, they are, like many of the older characters, often the voices of rationality, morality, and, perhaps most importantly in a narrative logic that particularly pathologizes "girls," authenticity.
Hannah's boyfriend, Adam, best illustrates the ways in which male precarity

can even be cast as heroic. Adam is troubled and directionless until he is cast in a Broadway show in season three, but he is still capable of calling attention to how Hannah's embrace of abjection and narcissism is inappropriate. He focuses on the status of her book when her editor and mentor dies, troubles her enabling friendship with her emotionally manipulative friend Jessa, and calls attention to her narcissism in other contexts. In making him the moral voice, Hannah's sexual abjection with Adam—including his urination on her and initial sexual interaction with her in which she is an object whose pleasure is of no concern to him—becomes an acceptable part of being in a relationship. But as opposed to offering an alternative to abjection as ordinary and everyday, the show eventually romanticizes Hannah's abjection as ultimately making her more desirable than a more confident woman would be.

Adam's brief relationship with another woman, Natalia, demonstrates how uncomfortable he is with a woman who refuses an abject subject position. When they first have sex, she tells him what does and does not give her pleasure. He says he likes how clear she is, and she asks, "What other way is there?" This is a dramatic irony given how many times the audience has seen women on the program—particularly Hannah—unable to articulate what they want sexually and otherwise. When Natalia does not see abjection as part of her sexual practice, their relationship unravels. She does not agree to being penetrated from behind while on all fours, having bodily fluids released on her, or being objectified during intercourse. This stands in contrast to the first sex scene on *Girls*, in which Hannah and Adam's sex acts appear similar to a stale porn film. The unflattering camera angles and their performance of rote porn language in flat tones suggest no real desire on her part. At one point, Adam calls Natalia a "dirty little whore," but she stops him to say, "I can like your cock and not be your whore." Her ability to say what she does and does not like during sex seems to disrupt his fantasy; moreover, he is troubled that she asserts herself as an agent and not an object through speech that does not simply reflect back his desires. While Adam's desires are certainly common sexual practices in which many people take pleasure, Natalia's clear resistance to sexual abjection makes her less desirable to Adam.

In some ways, Hannah's pain at failed expectations is a common theme for all ages. Hannah's narcissism, however, results in her constantly attempting to make her abject negotiation with a precarious world the model for others. Others' refusal to be pulled into her world then further isolates her, making her an object of repugnance. Toward the end of season three, she indicts her coworkers at GQ. They are all writers who are on the corporate sponsored "advitorial staff."

When are you going to go from calling yourself a poet to calling yourself a former poet, which is what you actually are. Because you yourself told me you haven't written anything of substance in five years. . . . Am I seriously the only one of us who prides herself on being a truly authentic person? This is tripping me out! . . . I just expect *more* from life.

After this outburst, her supervisor fires her, suggesting that it is not "the place" for her, and by this time we have doubts that there is *any* place for Hannah. Despite her desire for acceptance, she also desires exceptionalism and, of course, dwells in the jouissance that her abjection produces. But her constant attempt to pull others into abjection repels people (including some viewers who do not embrace the excruciating pleasure of viewing the abject) and increases what she simultaneously abhors and embraces as a sign of her exceptionalism.

Since Hannah is so thoroughly rejected by many people, the show does not model abjection as an ideal, but it does suggest that it is an understandable coping strategy in precarious times. Moreover, because the other women on the show are abject to lesser degrees, *Girls* somewhat normalizes this as a characteristic of middle-class white women after college. Dunham and her staff were famously criticized for the absence of diversity in her central cast in the first season and the lack of diversity in representing gentrified Brooklyn. But the affective logic of *Girls* that represents privileged narcissism and sexual abjection would most likely make the inclusion of women of color in this representational schema problematic to these same critics, given representational histories of racialized abjection of Asian, Latina, and African American women. This makes *The Mis-Adventures of Awkward Black Girl* especially worth examining as an outlier and as a text that clearly plays with the abject but in a different way by rejecting the classical Western model.

Black Abjection without White Supremacy

Hannah Horvath takes pride in her abjection as something that sets her apart as an artist, and *Girls* treats abjection as something that many young women experience as a defining part of their identity (at least at the postcollege moment in their lives). *The Mis-Adventures of Awkward Black Girl*, however, treats J's kind of abjection as mostly atypical for the world she inhabits, even as her abjection interpellates the audience. While the abjection on *Girls* centers on a normalization of white female millennial abjection, *Awkward Black*

Girl centers on the dissonance between J's identity and awkwardness as the form that black abjection takes.

As Darieck Scott has argued, abjection is an "inescapable aspect of blackness."[24] It is "a kind of lowering historical cloud" that hovers over black subjects, enveloping them with the oppressive history of "humiliating defeat, a useless history which must be in some way overturned or overcome. To this way of seeing, the past is an obstacle to imagining and building an empowered political position capable of effective liberation politics."[25] Historical depictions of blacks in the West as Other, between animal and human, and the historical subjection of black bodies in slavery and colonialism have made black abjection foundational to the Western black experience. Abjection haunts black bodies as the representational shadow. The black grotesque in comedy—most vividly depicted in the minstrel's black face, bulging eyes, and large mouth; smiling or eating watermelon; moving, ironically, with elegance and skill, so that even black talent is tied to abjection—is embedded in the cultural understanding of what black comedic performance is.

The paths that African Americans have taken to negotiate this history in comedy are varied and overlapping. Some have been forced to take stereotypical roles but have found ways to demonstrate their skill and talents despite the constraints. Comedians have embraced a culturally specific humor that speaks to group experiences, often emerging out of discourses of rage, what Bambi Haggins has called "laughing mad."[26] Some have trod a road that people have read as opportunistically replicating the same stereotypes. Other comedians have embraced an integrative model, eschewing the specificity of black experience or black trauma.[27] One of the challenges is that black abjection is what performers want to escape, but it is so often the grounds for compelling humor. This builds on a tension that Scott articulates: in many black representational histories, the black abject subject is a hero "in disguise," perpetually degraded by but capable of becoming a subject despite—and through—a history of abjection.[28] We might ask, then: How do comedians, who see the comedic potential of abjection, also escape the shadow of black humiliation shaped by white supremacy?

Issa Rae's embrace of black awkwardness as J is one answer to that question. Just as Nussbaum said that *Girls* was "us" (without questioning the limits of that identification), numerous people have pointed to Issa Rae's show as part of a new, unapologetic subculture with which African Americans might identify: "black nerd" culture.[29] A nerd identity in *Awkward Black Girl* takes the form of awkwardness, which is contrary to the "cool" and emotional strength and reserve often associated with African Americans. J's voiceover narration in the first episode states that she is the "two worst things that someone can be, awkward and black." And this experience of being "in between, the ambiguous, the composite," makes this akin to abjection because of the shame that can be experienced because of it.[30] The complexity of affects that make up the awkward are ephemeral—inappropriate speech, bodily movement, social interaction, and emotion. And like abjection, the ever-shifting target of the awkward makes it something that one longs to discard but cannot capture.

Another example of a twenty-first-century show that makes awkwardness the identifying characteristic of its protagonist is the MTV show *Awkward*, about white high-school student Jenna Hamilton's attempts to fit in, but her maladjustment is treated as a normal part of adolescence, a conventional trope of teenage comedies and melodramas. J's awkwardness is not developmental or something she will outgrow but grounded in her African American subject position. Blackness may make J abject, but her particular performance of blackness is *also* a means of rejecting the kind of abjection traditionally linked to blackness. Awkwardness is not something usually associated with abjection, or a synonym for it. The dissonance between awkwardness and blackness, however, puts J in a transitional (and comically transformative) space: she is in between being unrecognizable to others as black and being unassimilable as abject. Thus, *black abjection itself becomes a joke* in *Awkward Black Girl* and a refusal of the categorizations allotted to black people in entertainment (and the world). By embracing awkwardness as the height of black abjection, *Awkward Black Girl* works to provide an alternative, less pathologized framework for reading the black body.

One of the show's mechanisms of depathologizing blackness is refusing to make blackness the sole abject object. J's job at the call center for the diet pill company Gutbusters is abjection in the classic sense as Kristeva defines it, as the weight-loss product that they sell causes people to vomit and experience nausea for a month. The series makes viewing and treating others as abject the norm in people's relationships to one another in the workplace. When the audience is introduced to J's boss in the second episode, viewers discover that she is a white woman who inappropriately presumes an intimacy with black culture, demonstrated by her African dress, cornrowed hair, and speech. When she sees that J has cut off her hair to sport a short, natural Afro, the show presents a montage of her inappropriate comments to J. She asks questions such as, "Girlfriend, how are we going to get cornrows now?"; "What about your boyfriend? He dumped you? Can you hook us up? Just kidding!"; and "It reminds me of pubic hair. Can I touch it?" Her boss's everyday

figure 3.3 J (Issa Rae) rejects her boss.

appropriation is a recognizable, cringe-worthy farcical representation to the audience. Thus, her boss's attempts to make an abject black woman into an object are confounded by J treating her white proprietariness as an object of disgust. J fantasizes about verbalizing her rage at these questions and, in the end, yells "No!" loudly and performs the instinctual drawing back that many black people do when confronted with the request to touch their hair (figure 3.3). The physical expression of disgust—the bodily turn away from the abject—is a constant form of human interaction on the series, complicating the traditional unilateral treatment of the abject. While her employer treats her as the abject black object of the Western gaze, the "Negro" on the other side of the white look, J looks back at her and turns her into an abject object. Abjection goes both ways.

J is an abject object to many others at work, particularly a coworker with whom she had a one-night stand. After a few embarrassing situations when he catches her avoiding him and his calls, he begins to draw back from her at work as if repelled (or perhaps in shame because of her reaction to him). In one scene, he passes her in the hall with an exaggerated and pained grimace on his face, clinging to the wall as if he could disappear into it. He and Nina, J's work nemesis, treat J as a source of disgust, their faces in grimaces, their bodies jerking away from her presence. But the workplace is filled with "types" who repel. J describes them as the "drama queen who never shuts up"; the "loud black bitch"; the "guy who always makes weird noises"; the "space-invading germ chick"; a "multiracial, walking rainbow of racism" who

rebecca wanzo

gets away with offensive comments because nobody knows his identity; and her nemesis, Nina, "the bitch." As most of the cast is black, but none of the typology is particularly associated with blackness, the abjection is not *particularly* raced.

Because almost all the bodies at work repel, work itself becomes an abject object. The web series thus indicts the kinds of jobs that millennials often find themselves occupying, but it also invites the question: Do the abject find themselves in these positions, or do the positions themselves produce abjection? If Hannah's abjection in the workplace was about her attempt to draw others into her abjection, J's is about being surrounded by it and unable to escape. The characters constantly reference being trapped in certain jobs despite (or because of) their undergraduate training. J fantasizes about fleeing her job to work in retail, a dream that quickly turns into a nightmare as she imagines encountering a college classmate who warns her son that this is the outcome of a degree in African American studies. J's love interest, White Jay, runs an anger-management seminar but wants to be an artist. Her best friend, CeCe, constantly uses the word "syndrome" when she diagnoses J's anxieties because she says it makes her feel like she is using her psychology degree.

CeCe's pathologizing of all J's struggles is also indicative of the pathologization of millennials as sick—narcissistic, lazy, directionless, and overmedicated—a pathologization that Dunham's *Girls* does little to disabuse. Yet for all of CeCe's diagnoses, abjection is not individual or purely psychological nor, again, particularly raced. Despite the idiosyncratic nature of what makes people repel in *Awkward Black Girl*, they are all stereotypes that seem to be part of the office setting. If the office was structurally less absurd, the people with whom she works would presumably be different. They are "types" of workers shaped by the abject workplace, but the workplace is also partially abject because of the workers. At the same time, we have little indication that there is work that will not be absurd, although J does hope for at least a slightly less ludicrous work environment. In the logic of the show—and in the logic of the recession—those lowered expectations function as substantial progress.

As with *Girls*, the mise-en-scène of the office is central to showing how the abject subject is constructed by place. The web series references the recession when it demonstrates what people are willing to do to be employed. When J's boss is away and Nina becomes a supervisor, Nina brings in her sorority sisters and stages a black version of the abject hazing rituals attached to pledging fraternities and sororities. The episode is set on Halloween, and

Rae stages it with red lighting and treats the text as a horror film. At one point, Fred, J's crush, is doing push-ups with a box of file folders on his back as one of the sorority sisters yells at him, reminding him that they are in a recession. He does his best but still collapses under the burden of the task and the weight of subjugation.

The theme of the unbearable weight of job searches and the depths to which people will sink to obtain a job is a continual theme in the second season of the web series. When J is in a group interview for a job, and one person gets up and gives a highly dramatic, overwrought speech about how it had been a "goal all of her life" to work at a company that was fairly new, J fantasizes about slapping her and saying, "It's a recession, bitch!" Her anger at being outmaneuvered and outplayed by others is continued in a fantasy about a *Hunger Games* scenario in which a bunch of young people are standing in a circle near a doorway that says "job." They fight to the death, and J picks up a bow and arrow to vanquish opponents. She celebrates until a person she thought had been eliminated hits her on the head and kills her before she walks through the door.

Despite J's fantasies, it is unclear what skill sets she has that could lead to a more productive future. As with Hannah, we're not sure that she has any real skills or talents. In her interviews, J does not perform in a way that would set her apart from other applicants; we have no sense of her abilities or passions (other than an interest in writing very bad, "ratchet" rap lyrics). While the web series ends with J getting a new job and escaping Gutbusters, nothing seems particularly special about J professionally. The series lacks scenes in which she wins something because she is spectacularly good or even succeeds because of her quirkiness. J is quirky and appealing, but that does not suggest any hidden skills that would lead her to a professional future. If some of Hannah's misery is about not yet succeeding in her chosen profession, J still lacks a notion of what that profession would be.

The lack of professional futurity in *Awkward Black Girl* is central to the abjection aesthetic in precarious-girl comedies but quite counter to the normative uplift model of black entertainment, whose creators often see themselves as offering an intervention and contrast with representations more focused on a "gritty realist" urban model that emphasizes crime and poverty.[31] J's mother visits, and her last words to J are "Be somebody!" This phrase is familiar to most African American children who grew up in the late twentieth century. The show continues to riff on this expression in an office scene that suddenly turns, as J's voiceover states, into a "gospel version of *Stomp the Yard*," as a vocal Christian coworker named Sister Mary takes language used

rebecca wanzo

to lift morale and transforms it into a clichéd uplift song, which was featured in a film about the uplift of teenagers of color, *Sister Act 2*: "If you wanna be somebody, you wanna go somewhere, you better wake up and paaaay attention." This parody of uplifting music in black entertainment calls attention to the expected affect of black middle-class representations—even in comedy. Success follows song, or, as her white employer claims, "When you people sing and dance, the world is yours."

The scene exemplifies how the series is attentive to race and racism, but it nonetheless refuses to make white supremacy the primary obstacle in J's middle-class postcollege struggles. Her challenges are consistent with others in a similar class position; these challenges are, of course, also raced, but the affect represented here is what we might call "abjection-lite." The series presents a subject who is also in between: alienating others, stuck, out of place, and distasteful, but not so deeply mired in the muck that audiences cannot celebrate her persona. This is a narrative choice that resists the excessive abjection of blackness in favor of an awkward abject subjectivity that positions J in the tradition of mainstream American sitcoms. And Rae has commented on her desire to see black women in genres often denied them. Much of the media reflexivity of the *Awkward Black Girl* either reworks conventional black representations in film and TV or reimagines black women protagonists in other genres—refusing the narrow sets of roles Hollywood has offered most black actresses.

As the precarious-girl comedy makes abjection both "other" and "everyday," J's blackness makes hypervisible the abjection traditionally central to comedies featuring women, but *Awkward Black Girl* does not depict the explicit sexual abjection that Hannah experiences on *Girls*, which often ends in her humiliation. J is also romantically abject, but this mode of abjection mostly emerges from the disconnect—the awkward and precarious fit—between J's blackness and romance conventions. The dissonance produces the shame. When White Jay asks J out on a date, CeCe schools her in the conventions of "interracial dating." CeCe maps out heterosexual male dating preferences based on racial identity, and she goes through her closet to find racially correct attire for a first date with a white man. J fantasizes about meeting White Jay, evoking the nineties teen comedy *She's All That*. Replicating a well-known scene from that film (in which actress Rachael Leigh Cook has removed her grunge alternative-girl clothes and, to the tune of Sixpence None the Richer's "Kiss Me," walks down the stairs in a sexy red dress, with contacts in place of her usual glasses, to the astonishment of Freddie Prinze Jr.), the same song plays here when J walks down the stairs. White Jay looks up in awe and then watches her take a pratfall in her heels.

The failed romantic fantasy is a characteristic of many women's comedy scenes, always emphasizing the implausibility of the romantic fantasy for real women. The doubleness here is J's awkward blackness, in which the abject black body must be recuperated as a possible real romantic interest for the white hero.[32] If one aspect of Dunham's abjection in *Girls* is sometimes the positioning of her body in ways that construct her as an object and not a subject—and, at times, repugnant even to herself—Rae's "play" with abjection in *Awkward Black Girl* makes "abjection" safe for post-civil-rights babies. This is an abjection that is not governed by traditional stereotypes but that reflects this generation's hybrid status as people who are part of multiracial communities. It is an abjection rooted both in the black community (given the specificity of injurious treatments of black people and the specificity of black culture itself, as referenced in the series) and yet not limited to this (as the series also deploys, for instance, the tradition of out-of-place-ness that is characteristic of the romantic comedy).

At the end of season two of the web series, the audience gets a happy ending. J has left Gutbusters and been reunited with White Jay after they encounter some conflicts in their relationship. He tells her that he loves her, and she responds awkwardly, failing both to give the audience the pleasure of the traditional romantic comedy in which her romantic future would be secured and, moreover, to give herself an escape from her awkwardness. Instead, J's voiceover explicitly states that she cannot escape it and that she is accepting of this. Of course, self-acceptance is good, though her awkwardness will continue to be disruptive to her interpersonal relationships and her work life. J will be fine—but probably not much better than that.

Laughing at Limited Horizons

The racial identity of performers constantly makes a difference in quintessential "American" stories. As Ann duCille eloquently argues in an essay about the "color of class" in media, African Americans are often unimaginable in popular narratives that turn on class identities thoroughly marked as white in the US imaginary.[33] Thus, part of what makes a comparison between *Girls* and *The Mis-Adventures of Awkward Black Girl* so intriguing is that these protagonists are both struggling middle-class college-educated women who often repel others; but if a black woman was depicted as extremely narcissistic, a chronic liar, peed on, calling herself "gross," and not just aimless but professionally incompetent, such a representation would undoubtedly have resulted in accusations of racism far more virulent than Dunham received for

rebecca wanzo

her all-white cast. And yet both shows seem to find something fruitful in not just representing abject women but accepting them.

It may be tempting to read Rae's treatment of abjection as more progressive since she resists Western framings of abject blackness, and *Girls*, at its darkest, depicts an infantilized and unlikable, incompetent woman, but both shows are deeply reflexive representations of women and failure. Typically white women protagonists in US sitcoms inexorably head toward triumph and success. For African Americans, TV roles originally were limited to that of Mammy or Sapphire. On occasion, shows such as *Julia* offered normative representations of the middle class and racial uplift.[34] Thus, part of the work of both shows is to model an aesthetic self-fashioning that speaks not only to the contemporary political moment but to the televised representations of white women and African American women. These women may not, as *The Mary Tyler Moore Show* theme song suggests, "make it after all." Or they will make something of themselves but still be less than others imagined of them—and less than what they imagined for themselves. These new genres of precarity imagine practices of self-fashioning that help disappointed subjects deal with their limited horizons, and abjection seems to be a preferred mode in comedy. But it should not be surprising that even when sharing, to some degree, the same aesthetic mode, the creators Lena Dunham and Issa Rae would craft different jokes about their limited futures. Despite sharing profoundly intertwined national and media histories, African American women and white women's perspectives of their horizons are indelibly shaped by their pasts.

Notes

1   Keidra, "Why I Think *Awkward Black Girl* Is the Future of Television," *Learned Fangirl*, October 16, 2011, http://thelearnedfangirl.com/2011/10/16/why-i -think-awkward-black-girl-is-the-future-of-television/; Richard Majors and Janet Mancini Billson, *Cool Pose: The Dilemmas of Black Manhood in America* (New York: Lexington, 1992).

2   Tom Gliatto and Charlotte Triggs, "Picks and Pans, Main TV," *People*, April 23, 2012, http://www.people.com/archive/picks-and-pans-main-tv-vol-77-no-17 /; Matt Roush, "Weekend TV Review: HBO's *Girls* Rule, *Titanic* Sinks Again, NYC 22," *TV Guide*, April 13, 2012, http://www.tvguide.com/News/Weekend-TV -Review-1046009.aspx.

3   Emily Nussbaum, "It's Different for 'Girls,'" *New York Magazine*, March 25, 2012, http://nymag.com/arts/tv/features/girls-lena-dunham-2012-4/.

4   Kendra James, "Dear Lena Dunham: I Exist," *Racialicious*, April 19, 2012, http:// www.racialicious.com/2012/04/19/dear-lena-dunham-i-exist/; Jessie Daniels,

"Lena Dunham and the Trouble with (White) 'Girls,'" *Racism Review*, April 8, 2014, http://www.racismreview.com/blog/2014/04/08/lena-dunham-white-girls/.

5   Lauren Berlant, *Cruel Optimism* (Durham, NC: Duke University Press, 2007), 201.

6   Kathleen Rowe, *The Unruly Woman: Gender and the Genres of Laughter* (Austin: University of Texas Press, 1995).

7   Lynne Joyrich, "All that Television Allows: TV Melodrama, Postmodernism, and Consumer Culture," *Camera Obscura* 16 (1988): 148; Christine Acham, *Revolution Televised: Prime Time and the Struggle for Black Power* (Minneapolis: University of Minnesota Press, 2004).

8   Darieck Scott, *Extravagant Abjection: Blackness, Power, and Sexuality in the African American Literary Imagination* (New York: NYU Press, 2010), 5.

9   See Bonnie J. Dow, "Femininity and Feminism in Murphy Brown," *Southern Communication Journal* 57, no. 2 (1992): 143–55; and Amanda D. Lotz, "Postfeminist Television Criticism: Rehabilitating Critical Terms and Identifying Postfeminist Attributes," *Feminist Media Studies* 1, no. 1 (2010): 105–21.

10 Susan Douglas, *The Rise of Enlightened Sexism: How Pop Culture Took Us from Girl Power to Girls Gone Wild* (New York: St. Martin's Press, 2011).

11 Hanna Rosin, "The Patriarchy Is Dead," *Slate*, September 11, 2013, http://www.slate.com/articles/double_x/doublex/2013/09/the_end_of_men_why_feminists_won_t_accept_that_things_are_looking_up_for.html; Tami Luhby, "Men Are Disappearing from the Workforce," CNN *Money*, June 19, 2013, http://money.cnn.com/2013/06/19/news/economy/men-workforce/; Amanda Alix, "Why Are Men Disappearing from the Workforce?," *Motley Fool*, February 16, 2014, http://www.fool.com/investing/general/2014/02/16/why-are-men-disappearing-from-the-workforce.aspx.

12 Rich Morin and Paul Taylor, "Who's Been Hardest Hit by the Recession?" *Pew Research Center*, April 23, 2009, http://www.pewsocialtrends.org/2009/04/23/iv-whos-been-hardest-hit-by-the-recession/.

13 In 2009, for the first time more than half of all children born to women under thirty were born outside marriage, a statistic that also troubled people concerned with heterosexual women marrying later in life or not at all, suggesting new shifts in the nexus of economic and marital choices. A number of high-profile popular articles discussed the theme of women disappointed by their romantic options.

14 Berlant, *Cruel Optimism*, 195.

15 John Limon, *Stand-Up Comedy in Theory, or, Abjection in America* (Durham, NC: Duke University Press, 2000), 4.

16 Colin Irvine, "Why *30 Rock* Rocks and *The Office* Needs Some Work: The Role of Time/Space in Contemporary Sitcoms," in *Time in Television Narrative: Exploring Temporality in Twenty-First-Century Programming*, ed. Melissa Ames (Jackson: University Press of Mississippi, 2012), 218–31.

17 Most of these postrecession precarious-girl comedies have been on television because women have greater presence as writers and performers (despite a still profound gender imbalance).

18 Jean Twenge, *Generation Me: Why Today's Young Americans Are More Confident, Assertive, Entitled—and More Miserable than Ever Before* (New York: Simon and Schuster, 2006).

19 Julia Kristeva, *Powers of Horror: An Essay on Abjection*, trans. Leon S. Roudiez (New York: Columbia University Press, 1982), 2.

20 Kristeva, *Powers of Horror*, 9

21 Kristeva, *Powers of Horror*, 9.

22 Sigmund Freud, "On Narcissism," in *The Freud Reader*, ed. Peter Gay (New York: Norton, 1995), 545–61.

23 *Girls*, season 1, episode 2, "Vagina Panic," dir. Lena Dunham, aired April 22, 2012, on HBO.

24 Scott, *Extravagant Abjection*, 4.

25 Scott, *Extravagant Abjection*, 4.

26 Bambi Haggins, *Laughing Mad: The Black Comic Persona In Post-Soul America* (New Brunswick, NJ: Rutgers University Press, 2007).

27 For a broader overview of the history of African American comedy, see Mel Watkins, *On the Real Side: A History of African American Comedy* (New York: Simon and Schuster, 1994).

28 Scott, *Extravagant Abjection*, 5.

29 Clinton Yates, "Donald Glover, Issa Rae, Baratunde Thurston: The Rise of the Black Nerd?" *Washington Post*, November 26, 2012, http://www .washingtonpost.com/blogs/therootdc/post/donald-glover-issa-rae-baratunde -thurston-the-rise-of-the-black-nerd/2012/11/26/7015b27e-37dd-11e2-a263 -foebffed2f15_blog.html.

30 Kristeva, *Powers of Horror*, 4.

31 See Herman Gray, *Watching Race: Television and the Struggle for Blackness* (Minneapolis: University of Minnesota Press, 1995).

32 For a discussion of the constant implausibility of black women as romantic heroines, see Linda Mizejewski, "Queen Latifah, Unruly Women, and the Bodies of Romantic Comedy," *Genders* 46 (2007), http://link.galegroup.com /apps/doc/A179660982/AONE?u=nysl_sc_cornl&sid=AONE&xid=78557985.

33 Ann duCille, "The Colour of Class: Classifying Race in the Popular Imagination," *Social Identities* 7, no. 3 (2001): 409–19.

34 Beretta Smith-Shomade, *Shaded Lives: African American Women and Television* (New Brunswick, NJ: Rutgers University Press, 2002), 13–15.

chapter four

Abject Feminism, Grotesque Comedy, & Apocalyptic Laughter on *Inside Amy Schumer*

maggie hennefeld

In "Acting Off-Camera," a satirical skit from the feminist comedy series *Inside Amy Schumer* (Comedy Central, 2013–), Amy takes a break from the celebrity industry's grueling beauty standards by dabbling in off-screen voice acting for a Hollywood animation film. The characters of her costars, voiced by Megan Fox and Jessica Alba, materialize as hypersexual scantily clad jungle cats—Fox introduces her avatar: "I'm sexy but I also love math." In contrast, Amy's feline persona, Dumpy the Frumpy Meerkat, traipses in with a loud thud: Dumpy is an enormous ogress who shits and belches uncontrollably and has an obscenely exposed vulva in lieu of fashionable wardrobe. When Amy inquires why her meerkat cannot be drawn wearing pants, a slick producer explains that the film's animation was outsourced to Japan, where no one could even imagine fitting pants onto such a large female body. Amy eventually overcomes her initial horror and disgust (when informed of the royalties she'll receive from her overpriced defecating meerkat action figure), but the punch line is clear: there exist two options for women in comedy, *glamorous celebrity* or *grotesque self-abandon* (figure 4.1).

These tensions between celebrity capital and comedic refusal stem from deeper ambivalences endemic to popular feminist media culture: about the legacies of earlier feminist activism, the gender politics of comedic self-

figure 4.1 Amy Schumer dabbles in cartoon voice acting.

deprecation, and the relationship between edgy humor and commoditization (such as Amy's willingness to stomach public humiliation for lavish royalties). The feminist politics of comedies about gender and abjection, I argue, exemplify the shape-shifting aesthetics of twenty-first-century feminisms. I use the term *abject feminism* here to designate the productive ambiguity between individual self-making and collectivist solidarity that has been driving recent feminist politics. A stigmatized signifier of the post-second-wave culture wars of the 1990s and early 2000s, feminism has vividly returned as a popular political movement. Espoused by celebrities from Jennifer Lawrence and Beyoncé to Mindy Kaling and Ariana Grande, the resurgence of feminism as a potent force in the battle to combat gender oppression and systemic discrimination is taking shape overwhelmingly (though not exclusively) through mainstream popular comedy. This is the humorous voice of popular feminism. Struggles over the meaning of intersectional identity are temporarily resolved through jokes about the apparent incongruities between feminism's collective formations and its individualistic, self-making performance.

Whom does feminism represent? The urgency of speaking for all women under the banner of a universal signifier has been repeatedly complicated by revealing the antagonisms between gender and sexuality, race, class, ethnicity, age, ability, education, geography, and myriad other factors. This dissemination of interests across a vast terrain of social issues has given rise to vivid discomfort regarding the ultimate subject of feminism. Whose priorities does the movement favor, and how to aestheticize this contested, unending question?

The *New York Times* weighed in by declaring 2015 to be "The Year We Obsessed over Identity," which *Times* writer Wesley Morris then illustrated with an iconic slideshow of "The 30 Greatest Identity Freakouts of 2015."[1] These include Margaret Cho's impersonation of a North Korean official, Rachel Dolezal's scandalous attempt to pass as a black NAACP leader, Caitlyn Jenner's celebrity transfeminist advocacy, and a handful of anomalous film and television characters (from *Mad Max: Fury Road*, *Trainwreck*, and *Unbreakable Kimmy Schmidt*). The underlying lack of relations among many of the slideshow's examples ironically echoes its larger point: as Morris puts it, "*Who do we think we are?*" (Absent from this list were also the "men's rights" groups and white supremacist trolls gaining influence by appropriating the rhetoric of popular identitarian politics.) To this point, the examples in the slideshow, curated for their iconic singularity, often missed the mark of identity's social symbolization, which the slides were meant to represent in aggregate. For example, what does it mean to be a woman, or to be a woman of color, or even a feminist protagonist in an action genre film, under the terms of one's own making?

I focus my investigation of these questions—really, of the feminist drive to resolve the relations between social collectivity and individualist identity—through a closer look at the gender politics of abject comedy: humorous performances that exaggerate tropes of self-authorization through the abject aesthetics of grotesque bodily exposure and humiliating self-deprecation. I argue here that feminist abject comedy represents a primary site in which twenty-first-century feminisms' contradictory ideals and ambiguous aesthetics are envisioned, articulated, and exhaustively reimagined.

Feminist abject comedies take up long-standing cultural phobias of the female body—particularly its repressed or scrupulously regulated physicality—and mine them for their satirical potentials. For example, in Margaret Cho's stand-up show *I'm the One That I Want*, Cho recounts having diarrhea while stuck in a Los Angeles traffic jam—due to a regimented "persimmon diet" she had been following at the behest of her exploitative ABC television producers in preparation for the filming of her sitcom *All-American Girl* (ABC, 1994–95).[2] In this vein, performers such as Cho, Schumer, Mindy Kaling, Issa Rae, and Lena Dunham frequently intermingle painful experiences of personal abjection (from slapstick sexual violence to gross bodily humiliation) with comedic portrayals of the obscene contradictions between discourses of feminist empowerment and realities of gendered social fragmentation.

maggie hennefeld

For example, on *Girls*, female characters frequently berate one another in self-serving monologues that alternate between compelling manifesto and ludicrous self-caricature. The line between emotional authenticity and satirical mockery becomes cynically blurred and is frequently drawn around the uncertain position of women's bodies in a variety of situations: from half-consenting to violent sex by means of exaggerated, slapstick intercourse (which happens at some point to nearly every character on *Girls*), to broadcasting one's STDs over social media, to the ambivalence of regulating women's bodily appetites and excretions (overeating and dieting, overdosing and cleansing, selling out and staying true, letting it out and holding it in) in a corporate commodified hipster culture. This is precisely the logic of feminist comedy on *Girls*: the ambiguity about whether female sociality, and by extension female bodies, are, in fact, *abject* or *hilarious*. On the show, it is always somewhere in between—if the *Girls'* viewer is frequently unsure whether to laugh or to cry (or both), the object of this laughter and tears is even more unstable: do we laugh *at* the characters and cry *with* them, or are such distinctions in relation to *Girls* entirely useless? Again, this affective ambiguity is repeatedly drawn around the fuzzy position of female figures: self-striving, self-destructing bodies making their way through an explicitly hostile, inherently absurd, obsessively sexual, and confusingly gendered urban landscape.

These tensions between the fabrication of identity and its concrete, carnal materiality take on a lighter tone in the abject feminist "buddy comedy" *Broad City*: a farcical series that (like *Girls*) takes place in 2010s hipster New York City. The feminist politics of Abbi and Ilana's stoner antics hinge on their ability to parlay abject social precarity into absurd physical comedy. For example, Abbi works as a "pube sweeper" at a trendy gym; her roommate's live-in boyfriend, Matty Bevers, constantly eats all her food, neglects to flush the toilet, farts loudly, and generally makes her apartment into an unclean and nauseating space; and as two semiemployed, young urban nonprofessionals living in an obscenely unaffordable city, both Abbi and Ilana must episodically navigate the underbellies of the city's waste economy to make ends meet—from the temporary job market to a remote island postal delivery station and a fetid empty subway car.

Broad City's uncertainty about the dynamic between laughter and abjection—whether laughter displaces abject bodies or embraces them—turns on Abbi and Ilana's own flexible commitment to ratifying the clichés associated with earlier feminist movements. For example, in an episode titled "Feminist Heroes," Abbi and Ilana compare themselves to Amelia Earhart for their virtual "flight around the world," during which they spend several hours on Facebook randomly propositioning assorted social media acquaintances. In another episode, "Hello, Hillary," after being fired from her temp job at a predatory marketing company, Deals, Deals, Deals, Ilana is briefly employed as a fundraiser for Hillary Clinton's presidential campaign. A celebrity cameo by HRC, whom the girls are ecstatic to encounter at the campaign headquarters, offsets Ilana's extreme disappointment to learn that her new dream job is, in fact, entirely unpaid. From *Broad City*'s rejection of the myth of the self-actualizing career woman, to the characters' magnetic attraction to filth and detritus despite their apparent preference for commodity creature comforts (epitomized by Abbi's hoarding of Bed Bath and Beyond coupons), Abbi and Ilana comically fail to reap the benefits of second wave feminism, even while enjoying many of the entitlements achieved by it.

Such comedies about gendered bodily abjection express not affirmative liberation but the profound unsettling of meaning around laughter and its relation to female and feminist social identity. To be funny through one's grotesque bodily difference thereby offers an alternative means for pursuing freedom and belonging in a hypercommodified, image-obsessed, perniciously unstable media environment. Simply put, the glamorous celebrity and the raunchy comedienne are now two sides of the same coin—neither seems viable or even particularly desirable without the fantasy of the other: the ideal self-image and the undisciplined grotesque body.

Abject Feminism and the Unruly Woman

Through her body, her speech, and her laughter, especially in the public sphere, she creates a disruptive spectacle of herself.
—Kathleen Rowe, *The Unruly Woman*

No single figure has been more generative and celebrated among feminist comedy scholars than the unruly woman. *Broad City*'s Abbi and Ilana, as well as Schumer, Cho, and Dunham, are frequently invoked as unruly women, "who laugh too loudly, say things ladies shouldn't . . . fart and burp and poop . . . and refuse taming."[3] The unruly woman, as defined by Kathleen Rowe in *The Unruly Woman* (1995), flaunts her excessive, grotesque body while excreting noisy carnivalesque laughter, and thereby disrupts gendered social norms. Rowe argues that this figure has "the power . . . to challenge social and symbolic systems that would keep women in their place."[4] More grotesque or carnivalesque than truly abject, the unruly woman has been haunted by an imperative to establish her own social relevance. It is always the gendered relations of power that she momentarily disrupts, rather than her material isolation or even existential nausea. Her protest does not have access to the deeper roots of social alienation.

Methodologically, Rowe draws extensively on Mikhail Bakhtin's theory of the carnivalesque, which (like the abject) revels in all that is taboo or unholy. "The unfinished and open body (dying, bringing forth and being born) is not separated from the world by clearly defined boundaries."[5] Similarly, the abject body (*the corpse, the deject, the stray*) further marks *an existential threshold*—at the border of *living* and *being*—"when that subject, weary of fruitless attempts to identify with something on the outside, finds the impossible within; when it finds that the impossible constitutes its very *being*, that it *is* nothing other than abject."[6] The unfinished carnivalesque body, likewise, "is blended with the world, with animals, with objects. . . . It is an incarnation of this world at the absolute lower stratum, as the swallowing up and generating principle, as the bodily grave and bosom."[7] Both concepts, *the abject* and *the carnivalesque*, reside at the place where the body fails to establish its distinction, separation, or autonomy from the rest of the world—as well as from the grotesque materiality that constitutes its own being: the living corpses, messy bodies, and voracious appetites that we all possess and inhabit.

If *abjection* has been the key discourse of feminist horror studies, the *carnivalesque*, not the abject, has been a central stake of feminist comedy studies. A wide range of strong important texts, including Rowe's *Unruly Woman* (1995), Mary Russo's *Female Grotesque* (1994), M. Alison Kibler's *Rank Ladies* (1999), Mary Douglas's *Purity and Danger* (2002), Susan Glenn's *Female Spectacle* (2002), Patricia Mellencamp's *High Anxiety* (1990), and Linda Mizejewski's *Pretty/Funny* (2014) adapt Bakhtin's notion of the carnivalesque for the critical analysis of gender, comedy, and laughter in twentieth- and twenty-first-century media culture.[8] Although the abject as a signifier is often equated with the grotesque in feminist writings on carnivalesque comedy, the idea of abjection (as theorized by Julia Kristeva, Georges Bataille, Maurice Blanchot, Louis-Ferdinand Céline, Hélène Cixous) rarely becomes central or even relevant methodological terrain. In contrast, abjection has represented the privileged discourse for exploring tropes and images of female monstrosity in feminist horror scholarship. Key examples include Barbara Creed's *Monstrous-Feminine* (1993), Carol Clover's *Men, Women, and Chainsaws* (1993), Isabel Pinedo's *Recreational Terror* (1997), as well as more recent works including Tony Magistrale's *Abject Terrors* (2005), Sarah Arnold's *Maternal Horror Film* (2013), and Angela Smith's *Hideous Progeny* (2012).[9]

Abjection, "a border . . . that does not radically cut off the subject from what threatens it," renders women's oozing, uterine, corpse-like, or supernatural bodies as loci for confronting that which simultaneously threatens life and becomes the very condition of possibility for life: the abject.[10] Creed invokes Kristeva: "Abjection by its very nature is ambiguous; it both repels and attracts."[11] Female abjection in horror films, according to scholars such as Creed, Clover, and Linda Williams, functions as a form of objection against the repeated disempowerment and victimization of women. For example, figures such as the "archaic mother," the "femme-castratrice," and the "lesbian succubus" appear to provide the only possible characters in which violence against women can signify more than sheer submission, victimhood, passivity, and subjugation.

Indeed, both discourses—of feminist carnivalesque laughter and of monstrous-feminine horror—attribute a liberatory or subversive power to the grotesque image of women's bodies: whether laughing volubly while gleefully opening all orifices to the people, or shuddering violently while nursing gaping wounds and seeking revenge against psychopathic male perpetrators. If abjection in horror arises from a violent collapse of physical boundaries and erasure of taboos and repressions, in comedy, the grotesque aversion behind laughter follows a very different cultural logic and narrative pattern. In contrast to the *monstrous-feminine*, the *unruly woman* subverts culturally situated prohibitions, rather than primordial or archaic taboos. For example, when Roseanne Barr grabbed her crotch while singing the National Anthem at a San Diego Padres game,[12] or when Lena Dunham overshared with Jimmy Kimmel about her urinary tract infection,[13] the impetus for laughter derived explicitly from the shock of female bodily exposure within inappropriately public social contexts.

Again, even though both feminist comedy studies and feminist horror studies emphasize grotesque female bodies, there remain pointed methodological differences between the two fields. The discourse of abjection, which draws heavily on psychoanalytic theory, tends to center on primordial taboos: mixing blood and milk (e.g., breast milk and menstruation); the forbidden desire for incest; and the destructive drive toward death. In contrast, the carnivalesque, again, focuses on socially and historically situated prohibitions. Women's grotesque embodiment in the comedy genre carries a mandatory social relevance, but the primordial or even the existential remains a persistent limit. Female bodily abhorrence, when made funny, is always assigned a topical or trivialized material context. This imperative social relevance haunts women's grotesque bodily comedy. The fundamental incapacity for

figures 4.2 & 4.3
Female spontaneous
decapitation due to
a peanut allergy.

the female grotesque to become actively abject has been likewise inescapable in critical scholarship on feminism and comedy.

For example, in a skit on *Inside Amy Schumer*, when Schumer's and Parker Posey's heads spontaneously explode as a result of their nut allergies (even though they eat peanuts, which are legumes), this absurdist violence derives not from their underlying existential dread, but from their obsessive fixation on how their salads will be prepared by a trendy New York City restaurant (figures 4.2 and 4.3). (As Rob King suggests in his chapter on Louis C. K. in this volume, such compulsory social relevance has only become a limitation for male comedians in the thick of #MeToo.) Schumer's farcical mockery of cosmopolitan femininity raises more pointed questions about the gender politics of abject comedy. Does the laughing discourse of the female grotesque, in contrast to that of horror, even have access to the ontological or the existential: to the problems of being and existence at the core of abjection?

The mandatory social relevance of grotesque female bodies in comedy, as opposed to their primordial counterparts in horror, sheds light on why feminist comedy theorists have pursued the concept of the carnivalesque over the abject. Again, unlike the monstrous-feminine, the unruly woman disrupts social norms rather than existential taboos. The idea of the unruly woman, however, so central to the social politics of feminist comedy scholarship, is itself an anachronism, sourced from Bakhtin's analysis of medieval folk culture. Bakhtin's theory of the carnivalesque—of a temporary social revolution wherein the liberation of repressed, grotesque bodies becomes empowering for everyone—is utterly singular to the context of medieval folk practices. The history of these carnivalesque rituals must be understood both on their own terms and in productive tension with their updated appropriation by discourses of the unruly woman. It is through the gap between carnival's historicity and its unruly reboot that feminist laughter might at last break free of its grotesque imperative—and become actively, actionably abject.

The Carnivalesque-Grotesque vs. Abject Comedy

Bakhtin's idea of the carnivalesque derives not from his own cultural moment but from medieval folk traditions: the popular feasts and festivals, such as the Feast of Fools and the Feast of the Ass, that provided temporary, unofficially tolerated releases from the rigid hierarchical norms and ecclesiastical rituals that governed medieval life. As Bakhtin writes, "Large medieval cities devoted an average of three months a year to these festivities. The influence of the carnival spirit was irresistible: it made a man renounce his official state as monk, cleric, scholar, and perceive the world in its laughing aspect."[14] The people did not perform carnivals: they *lived in them*—like a pageant without footlights, which "does not acknowledge any distinction between actor and spectator."[15] This total lack of separation between the *laughing body* and the *comic spectacle*—a dual, Janus-faced, joyfully relative, ambivalent experience of all matter and being—strongly resembles the eruption of laughter at the thresholds of abjection. For example, Bakhtin's language evokes Kristeva's idea of abjection as jouissance ("the abject is inaccessible except through jouissance"), as well as Bataille's experiments with laughter as an experience of ecstatic risk and abject incarnation—knowing death within the limits of life.[16] Bakhtin himself, however, emphasizes the historical specificity of this comedic abandon. The carnivalesque provides a release not from the constitutive violence of the psyche, but from the repressive rites and customs of medieval society.[17]

There has been significant debate among comedy scholars about the political potency of the carnivalesque, which is unofficially tolerated by the powers that be and rigorously delimited in both its temporal duration and its spatial location. The carnivalesque represents a temporary social revolution,

maggie hennefeld

but one that might very well contribute to the health of the state more than it undermines or challenges it. Giorgio Agamben cites the carnivalesque as an important example of the "state of exception." He writes, "The secret solidarity between anomie and law comes to light . . . with those periodic feasts (such as . . . the Carnival of the medieval and modern world) that are characterized by unbridled license and the suspension and overturning of normal legal and social hierarchies."[18] In other words, carnival actually affirms rather than challenges the secret basis of the law in its own constitutive exception. The law (whether the symbolic law of the father or the sovereign law of the nation-state) is defined by what is outside it. Arguments such as these drive the main objections to theorizing the carnivalesque as a centerpiece of comedy's subversive politics.[19]

It is not my intention here to challenge these political theories of carnival as intrinsic to the constitutive violence of the law. If anything, I think the *state of exception* question has been a red herring from the real problem with how the carnivalesque often gets applied to modern cultural politics. The aspect of Bakhtin's theory of the *carnivalesque-grotesque* that has received too little attention from comedy scholars turns on its deeply complicated relationship with the genres of *grotesque realism*. This is an absolutely crucial point for Bakhtin in *Rabelais and His World*, and it provides the basis for his central linkage between joyful feasts and the degraded bodily lower stratum (the anus, the vagina, the belly, and so forth). As Bakhtin defines it, "The essential principle of grotesque realism is degradation, that is, the lowering of all that is high, spiritual, ideal, abstract."[20] The grotesque, degraded body itself becomes the locus of carnival's joyful collectivist social politics: "The body and bodily life have here a cosmic and at the same time an all-people's character. . . . The material bodily principle is contained not in the biological individual, not in the bourgeois ego, but in the people, a people who are continually growing and renewed."[21] In other words, the utter lack of abjection associated with this grotesque body in its carnivalesque degradation is absolutely essential to its liberatory politics: to the ambivalent, dual-bodied, joyful experience of collective regeneration that it ignites.

Medieval folk culture, according to Bakhtin, represents the last space in which "the material bodily principle in grotesque realism is offered in its all-popular festive and utopian aspect."[22] After this time, the carnivalesque ceases to function as a mode of life and becomes instead a literary trope. While the carnivalesque easily traverses lived experience and literary representation, Bakhtin is decisive that the meaning of this grotesque body changes radically after the Renaissance. More than any other Renaissance writer, according to Bakhtin, François Rabelais carnivalizes literature in *Gargantua and Pantagruel*.[23] He situates Rabelais's writings in their historical context:

> The bodily lower stratum of grotesque realism still fulfilled its unifying, degrading, uncrowning, and simultaneously regenerating functions. However divided, atomized, individualized were the "private" bodies, Renaissance realism did not cut off the umbilical cord which tied them to the fruitful womb of earth. Bodies could not be considered for themselves; they represented a material bodily whole and therefore transgressed the limits of their isolation. The private and universal were still blended in a contradictory unity. The carnival spirit still reigned in the depths of Renaissance literature.[24]

For example, when the giant Gargantua arrives in Paris, he is so annoyed by the crowds of people in the streets that he literally drowns them in buckets of his own urine by pissing on them from the top of Notre Dame. After this abject flood, the survivors laugh so gaily and uproariously that this, according to Rabelais, is how Paris comes to be named *Par-Ris* (By Laughter). This scene from *Gargantua and Pantagruel* encapsulates the very sense of material bodily connectivity and regeneration through degradation that, Bakhtin argues, "still reigned in the depths of Renaissance literature."[25]

The carnivalesque-grotesque only becomes abject—a site not of ambivalent regeneration but of primordial terror—through the Romantic cult of individualism. This disarticulation between the grotesque body and collective regeneration ("death is included in life") escalates with the aesthetics of modernist alienation and becomes perhaps even more confounding with the slippery pastiche and opportunistic commodification characteristic of late capitalism. In other words, *the grotesque body of late-capitalist comedy can never capture the carnivalesque*, because the collective regeneration of carnival here is always sundered from the grotesque signification of the individual body.

Each culture has its own grotesque system of imagery. Romantic grotesque form conveys an abiding obsession with uncanny figures: lifelike marionettes, tragic dolls, and Satanic bogeymen. For example, in one story from Hoffmann's *Night Pieces* (1816), a man is haunted by his childhood terror of a Sandman who would visit naughty children in their bedrooms at night, gouge out their eyes, and then feed those eyes to his own children, who lived on the moon.[26] As Bakhtin writes, "The world of Romantic grotesque is to a certain extent a terrifying world, alien to man. . . . Something frightening is revealed in that which was habitual and secure."[27] This is why Romanticism becomes largely suspicious of laughter, characterizing the comic by

maggie hennefeld

its cynical irony, its cruel detached mockery, and its potential gateway to demonic possession. This carnivalesque body no longer holds an uncomplicated power to convert terror into something gay and laughable, as in medieval folk culture. (In general, Bakhtin abstains from direct discussion of modernist culture, largely because of the pressures of censorship while writing under Soviet Stalinism.)[28]

The *bodily participation in the potentiality of another world*—crucial to the medieval festival, wherein "old age is pregnant, death is gestation," and so forth—becomes fatally severed: "What remains is nothing but a corpse, old age deprived of pregnancy, equal to itself alone; it is alienated and torn away from the whole in which it had been linked. . . . The result is a broken grotesque figure, the demon of fertility with phallus cut off and belly crushed."[29] In other words, the grotesque body becomes abject only in modernity. Grotesque realism comes to represent an impossible object of inner terror and of overwhelming alienation, which must be evacuated by any means necessary: not least of all through laughter. Bakhtin quotes Wolfgang Kayser's 1957 text *The Grotesque in Art and Literature*: "Laughter combined with bitterness which takes the grotesque form acquires the traits of mockery and cynicism, and finally becomes Satanic."[30] This prevailing form of laughter—as sardonic, ironic, sarcastic, cynical, detached, and even demonic—contrasts sharply with the *joyful laughter* of carnival, which demands absolute bodily participation from every laugher, and thereby brings about perpetual change and social renewal.[31]

I take this detour through the annals of Rabelais to raise questions about how these carnivalesque politics of laughter might signify in present-day media culture. When unruly women make disruptive spectacles of their laughter, their unrepressed sexuality, and their abject bodily excess in twenty-first-century film and media, to what extent are these gleeful transgressions actually carnivalesque? (It is worth noting that this is a different question than whether these images are troubling, ambiguous, or even subversive—I am asking to what extent they are actually carnivalesque.) Another way to pose this question: What kind of relationship do these images coordinate between the grotesque female body and a feminist politics of laughter? While carnival celebrates the grotesque body as a location of joyful renewal and regeneration, the abject emerges from the very impossibility of this carnivalesque rebirth. The abject represents the remainder between the carnivalesque-grotesque and grotesque realism: between the jubilant redemption of bawdy, messy, profane excess and the obsessive exclusion of this excess as traumatic, taboo, and existentially isolating.

Again, the debates about carnivalesque politics—about whether an unofficially tolerated, temporary revolution can have lasting effects on the social—have been distractions from the more important and central issues. Really, it is impossible to know whether temporary liberation can effect lasting, meaningful, political change—and, constitutively, as Carl Schmitt, Agamben, Derrida, and others have argued, political norms operate through exceptional means: by means of the exception.[32] The problem of the carnivalesque, and of its relevance to the present-day politics of laughter, resides in the gap between *grotesque comedy* and *abject aversion*: again, this is the terrain not of the carnivalesque-grotesque but of *abject comedy*.

At the Limits of Feminism: Kristeva's and Schumer's Two Theories of Laughter

The discourse of female sexuality or bodily excess, again, is not liberating or scandalous in itself: this is the fallacy of the unruly woman. Rather, the female grotesque (to invoke Russo's book) on *Inside Amy Schumer* uses antifeminist self-deprecation as a gateway to laughter about the contradictions between collective political insurgency and neoliberal individualist agency. Like many comedians who combat social injustice and sexist misogyny, Amy Schumer often muddies the line between feminist satire and apparently sexist self-deprecation. For example, the variety format of *Inside Amy Schumer* alternates between witty polemical critiques (tackling sexual violence, workplace discrimination, rape culture, and sexist media double standards), and obscene, scathing self-ridicule. For every raunchy anecdote about her pussy in Schumer's stand-up (of which there are many), "the material lower stratum" takes on a broader social emphasis in her television program.

A vagina on *Inside Amy Schumer* is never just a vagina: it ranges from an impossible object of sight gags about rape ("Football Town Nights," "The Trial of Bill Cosby"), to an accumulation of cobwebs in parodies about the terror of female aging ("Last F**kable Day," "Trouble Accepting a Compliment"), to a cosmic alternate universe in a skit about vaginal oral sex ("Hiker Bones"). As Amy's fascinated, bewildered male cunnilinguist declares, upon reemerging from her vagina (with a full beard), "My god! It's full of stars!" This is at least partly why Schumer's grotesque bodily and sexual humor sometimes becomes repetitively gimmicky and borderline misogynistic—especially in her stand-up performances, late night interviews, and various other media appearances.[33]

maggie hennefeld

There exist two key modes of laughter on *Inside Amy Schumer*: aggressive, derisive laughter at the absurdities of structural sexism, and a destabilizing, self-flagellating laughter at the equally oppressive norms of cosmopolitan femininity. For example, in one skit, "Judging Strippers," a group of affluent women at a trendy gym make demeaning comments about female exotic dancers working at a strip club across the street: "That is *so sad*. Oh my god, look at that. Like, what happened? It's like, I wish they could draw their self-worth from something else." The ironic reversal arrives at the end when the gym class instructor enters: "All right bitches! Welcome to Body Pole Punk Class. Let's do it. Get on your poles! Faces down, asses up. Do it! You're all whores!" The gay, male drill sergeant instructor then shouts repeatedly, "Whores! Whores! Whores!" at the all-female class while the women scramble to their respective stripper poles. The ironic structure of this skit mirrors Schumer's "Football Town Nights" parody about the misogynistic rhetoric rampant in men's athletics. In this spoof of the television show *Friday Night Lights*, a controversial high school football coach officially bans his players from raping women, only to give them a subsequent locker room pep talk that metaphorically licenses the very mentality he had prohibited. "Football is not about rape: it's about violently dominating anyone who stands between you and what you want! You've got to get yourself into the mindset that you are gods and you are entitled."

Since Schumer openly celebrates the feminist politics of her comedy—her show was repeatedly declared "the most feminist show on television"—the difference between the "Football Town Nights" coach and the "judging strippers" women is implicitly one of spectator position.[34] Whereas the realities reflected by the antiraping coach's misogynistic speech give license to its incisive feminist satire, the ludicrous premise that these judgmental women would be attending a Body Pole Punk Class provokes a more uncomfortable, introspective experience of laughter. These two modes of comedy, of course, are not mutually exclusive. For example, Amy plays the coach's wife in "Football Town Nights": a bored housewife right out of Betty Friedan's *The Feminine Mystique* (1963), who appears in each scene with an abjectly gigantic, increasingly oversized glass of white wine that eventually threatens to dwarf her entire body.[35]

Both comedic modes—*polemical satire* and *farcical self-deprecation*—spring from pervasive uncertainties about the relationship between women's bodies and comedic violence. When does violence against women become funny? The answer to this question opens onto the show's own address to the present-day ambivalences of popular feminism. *Schumer's* oscillation between hard-hitting satire and self-eviscerating caricature navigates the impasses of popular feminism (for example, between social equity and individual agency) by way of the abject female body. What is the line between the grotesque conventions of gendered comedy and the horrific destabilizing eruption of the abject? In a sense, Schumer's comedy about feminism is not so different from Bakhtin's understanding of grotesque realism: both respond to the confusing separation between inherently grotesque bodies as simultaneous sites of joyful collective liberation and individualizing abject alienation.

Kristeva reflects on precisely this problem in *The Powers of Horror*, in which she names two different kinds of laughter. First, there is the laughter "that place[s] or displace[s] abjection . . . situationist in a sense," as abjection represents foremost a location of utter abandonment at the margins of subjectivity and cultural belonging.[36] The poor rube or debased clown plays foil for marking out the margins of what is desirable: literally that which pertains to desire as an endless, repetitive cycle of object attachment and subject formation. Dumpy the Frumpy Meerkat—with her exposed cartoon vulva, uncontrollable defecation, and one-word vocabulary of "worms!"—epitomizes the abject object of this situationist laughter that "displaces abjection."

Kristeva invokes a second kind of laughter, however, that exceeds this cycle of boundary formation and ritual purgation: "horrified, apocalyptic" laughter. This second laughter shatters the ego in the very gesture of fortifying it. The *horrified, apocalyptic* laughter that *bursts out* or *gushes forth*—"bare, anguished, and as fascinated as it is frightened"—represents a unique collision between comedy and abjection for Kristeva in this text.[37] *Powers of Horror* (1982) and *Black Sun* (1989) both mark Kristeva's general turn away from her abiding interest in Bakhtin—essential to her earlier feminist writings on the social and historical specificity of linguistic structure: "Word, Dialogue, Novel" (1966), "The System and the Speaking Subject" (1975), "Revolution in Poetic Language" (1974).[38] Kristeva's notion of the carnivalesque, which comes up repeatedly in her earlier writings, emphasizes the murderous drama at the heart of this genre, above its uncomplicated joy or social renewal. For example, in "Word, Dialogue, Novel," Kristeva describes the radical transformation of carnivalesque ambivalence in modernist discourse:

> The word "carnivalesque" lends itself to an ambiguity one must avoid. In contemporary society, it generally connotes parody, hence, a strengthening of the law. There is a tendency to blot out the carnival's *dramatic* (murderous, cynical, and revolutionary in the sense of *dialectical transformation*) aspects. . . . The laughter of the carnival is not simply parodic; it is no more comic than tragic; it is both at once, one might say that is *serious*.[39]

maggie hennefeld

Kristeva here perhaps overstates the drama of the carnivalesque's dialectical transformation (parody and murder—or comedy and the consequences of violence—are not mutually exclusive). In *Powers of Horror*, the carnivalesque drama of dialectical transformation is abandoned in favor of notions such as painful jouissance, symbolic defilement, and apocalyptic laughter. Apparently, Kristeva's notion of abject comedy distances itself from the carnivalesque—and from its implicit association with the dialogical bivalence of language. Kristeva's idea of abject comedy instead draws on modernist notions of laughter as the eruption of catastrophe, the sacred, the impossible, the irredeemable, and the unrepresentable or unnamable.

Specifically, Kristeva's definition centers on writings by Bataille, Nietzsche, Freud, and Artaud: abject comedy is not regenerative and renewing, like the carnivalesque of medieval folk culture. Rather, it stages a confrontation with the difference between *being* and *meaning*, between existential survival and intersubjective articulation. As Bataille writes in an essay, "Nietzsche's Laughter," in *The Unfinished System of Nonknowledge*, "I can laugh at the impossible in humanity . . . laughing knowing I am sinking. . . . I no longer hold life to the standard of the impossible in order to escape it, as nature does in tragedy, in Aristotle's theory of catharsis. Zarathustra made laughter *sacred*."[40] According to Bataille, only a laughter that extends from the miserable dregs of abjection has the potential to access *the sacred, the impossible,* or *the unrepresentable* in secular modernity. Like Kristeva, Bataille opposes an apocalyptic eruption of nihilistic laughter with the displacement achieved through catharsis. Similarly, for Kristeva, Céline's laughter of the apocalypse—the laughter that drowns "ideology, thesis, interpretation, mania, collectivity, threat, or hope"—arises from the collapse between the pleasures of meaning and the nonmeaning of being: between laughter and abjection.[41]

In other words, the politics of abject comedy stem from their utter incommensurability. This is no doubt why unruly or grotesque laughter has provided such an appealing framework for feminist comedy theorists. As Russo argues, "The images of the [female] grotesque body are precisely those which are abjected from the bodily canons of classical aesthetics."[42] Key theorists of the comic, from Aristotle and Quintilian to Thomas Hobbes and Henri Bergson, have repeatedly defined laughter as an assertion of cruel or callous superiority over a hapless object of ridicule: the abject deject, who moreover provides a target for the laughing subject's displacement of abjection. The power dynamics of this comic laughter have been emphatically gendered and sexually sadistic: women appear either as fetishistic objects of smutty "blue" humor or as ostracized targets of sexist tendentious humor. Feminist comedy theorists (Rowe, Russo, Mizejewski, Kibler, Rebecca Krefting) have thereby sought to redeem women's objectification by derisive humor through the discourse of female bodily excess: when women's gleeful grotesque self-display performs a reversal of the gendered power dynamics of laughter. Yet, the question remains: To what extent does this use of grotesque bodily comedy—which transgresses the norms of classical femininity—represent a mode of comedic resistance in itself?

When the unruly woman becomes a trope or gimmick (as she clearly has à la Frumpy Dumpy), she functions primarily to demarcate a safe boundary between *filth* (the abject Other) and *defilement* (unbearable contamination). As Kristeva argues, drawing on Mary Douglas's analysis of gender and taboo pestilence in *Purity and Danger*, the collapse between filth and defilement is conventionally (if not constitutively) drawn around the lines of sexual difference. "At the limit, if someone personifies abjection without assurance of purification, it is a woman, 'any woman,' the 'woman as a whole'; as far as he is concerned, man exposes abjection by knowing it, and through that very act purifies it."[43] Yet, rather than embodying that hopeless void of utter abjection (which is of course also racialized as much as it is gendered), popular feminist comedy today springs from the antagonism between laughter's *displacement of abjection* and its *apocalyptic inheritance* of it.

Inside Amy Schumer is exemplary but by no means exceptional: many popular feminist comedies today negotiate between satirizing misogyny and turning the violence of ridicule inward on the self—not just as self-deprecation, but toward the apocalyptic limits of laughter as self-annihilation. This fundamental ambivalence or oscillation between sadistic mockery and masochistic self-violence drives the politics of popular feminist discourse, which increasingly finds expression through the indirect and amorphous forms of laughter and comedy. Again, the *politics of feminist abject comedy* emerge from the antagonisms internal to popular feminist representations: between issues-based polemics and that rising feeling of inner anxiety—suspended between *horror* and *fascination*—that always remains just beyond the limits of coherent knowledge or representation.

Horrified Apocalyptic Laughter
on *Inside Amy Schumer*

Schumer's feminist politics revolves around its tension between displaced laughter and the comedic rising up of a profound inner horror. Such a dialectic between mockery and abjection unfolds in tandem with the show's performance of its own feminism, provoking something more profound, ambivalent, and destabilizing than simple derisive laughter. Beyond isolated modes of lampooning—derisive satire versus abject self-abasement—these comedic antagonisms spring from oscillations internal to the meaning and politics of feminism. An affirmative rights-based polemic (demanding collective protection by a central governing body or juridical authority) clashes with individualistic forms of representation, based on the irreducible complexity of identity as it internalizes the failures of state-administered equity and justice.

The politics of *equality feminism* (frequently associated with the second wave movement) are represented primarily through topical parody and derisive satire on *Inside Amy Schumer*. For examples, *Schumer's* quick-witted, joke-laden segments depict everything from a *Call of Duty* videogame in which playing as the female avatar guarantees being raped, having your character defamed in a military tribunal, and then dishonorably discharged while the assaulter gets off scot-free to a brilliant segment in which Schumer, Tina Fey, and Patricia Arquette celebrate Julia Louis-Dreyfus's "last f**kable day" before the media officially declares her too old for romantic viability (a skit that coincided with headlines that thirty-seven-year-old Maggie Gyllenhaal was no longer young enough to play across from a fifty-five-year old man);[44] to a fantastic segment, "Cool with It," in which Amy accompanies her male coworkers to a strip club and then ends up volunteering to bury the corpse of the exotic dancer whom her colleague had accidentally asphyxiated during kinky foreplay. Amy breaks character midway through digging this secret grave to note, "I'll just be here doing 100 percent of the work even though at work I make 78 cents on the dollar! . . . The Wage Gap for Women: Write to your congressperson today and tell them you're not cool with it. Or just support raising minimum wage. Two-thirds of minimum-wage workers are women."

Albeit in burlesqued form, *Inside Amy Schumer* derives its wider reputation as a heavy-hitting feminist comedy from segments such as these that champion collectivist women's rights by incisively satirizing the misogynistic extremes of heteronormative culture and sexist popular media representations. Further, in these segments, the image of abjection remains more or less unseen, evoked through absurd scenarios and allusive word play but never actually visualized. While we do not behold the decomposing corpse of this abused sex worker, we laugh through the absurd disconnect between professional inequity and antifeminist cultural rationalizations: institutional redress versus, simply, "being cool with it."

As an alternative to this double bind between activist recourse and "post-feminist" denial, *Inside Amy Schumer* frequently represents a different kind of comedy: one that radically internalizes the aggressive ridicule of satire by abandoning the collectivist politics of civil protection and rights-based representation.[45] Leveling its mockery precisely at this postfeminist culture, which at once shirks feminist solidarity while reaping the benefits of equality activism, *Inside Amy Schumer* turns the violence of laughter inward toward the self, provoking a very different experience of comedy and identification, until gendered humor reaches a horrific or even apocalyptic limit.

In one skit, about the cultural taboo of women accepting a compliment, Amy and her friends meet outside Central Park and then exchange and deflect an increasingly bizarre series of pleasantries. With each deflection, the subsequent compliment becomes more and more self-abasing, doubling down on the impossibility for women to accept a nice gesture without supplementing it with horrific aggression and self-violence. For example, Amy congratulates a pregnant friend who frets that she is so old that she might instead give birth to a cobweb by announcing, "I just want to crawl inside your pussy and have you give birth to me!"

The inability of language to articulate an endpoint to the collision between political satire and pathological self-negation frequently erupts, usually in fantastic or uncanny images of violence. In a truly remarkable example, "I'm So Bad," Amy and her friends go around the table confessing to increasingly horrific violent acts under the guise of venting their concerns about having ingested too many calories. "I was cyberbullying my niece on Instagram the other day, and I literally ate like 15 mini-muffins; I'm so bad." "The other morning, when that woman walked off the G. W. Bridge, I didn't do anything to help her; it's because I was chewing my calzone—I'm so bad!" "Yesterday, after I took a smoke machine to the burn unit to see how they'd react, I ate so much General Tso's, they gave me his hat. It looks insane on me." "Shut your dick off, you look amazing in hats and you know this."

Like much of Schumer's comedy, the joke here derives from exaggerating a sexist stereotype to the point of absurdity: that women are so consumed with their personal body image that they become completely desensitized to the horrific escalation of everyday thoughtlessness. After Amy terminates her pregnancy—even though "they literally don't have a term for how late this abortion was"—she is mainly upset that she still seems to be eating for two, displacing an exaggerated ambivalence about maternity and reproductive rights onto her abject engorgement on a bucket of wings and a sixteen-ounce lobster. (A similar dynamic between cosmetic insecurity and horrific irresponsibility drives a season two sketch in which Paul Giamatti, playing a homosexual God, negotiates with Amy about how many third world villagers he would have to blight to cure her of genital herpes—in a zero-sum game of divine punishment.) The women who eventually eviscerate and engorge their male waiter when he asks them if they would like to order any dessert do not abject themselves in a climactic assertion of their feminist liberation. Bodily abjection emphatically fails to resolve the comedic high-wire act between sexist fantasy and misogynistic reality from which the entire sketch proceeds.

Similarly, "Trouble Accepting a Compliment" culminates with extreme ritual suicide when the ladies run into their friend Amanda, who, in passing, mildly accepts a compliment on her new jacket. In response to this woman's acceptance of a compliment, one lady sticks a gun in her mouth and pulls the trigger, while others douse themselves in kerosene, fatally snap their own neck, or stab their friends with various writing implements; meanwhile, Amy hurls herself bodily into oncoming traffic, and the arsonist lights a match igniting a literally explosive display of graphic physical violence. Laughter, here, does not simply displace abjection: although *Schumer* is clearly critiquing women's own complicity in reproducing antifeminist misogyny, the show refrains from offering its viewer an unambiguous ideological position. Neither affirmative feminist advocacy nor antifeminist self-flagellation anchors the point of laughter for *Schumer's* laughing spectator.

Many such skits on *Inside Amy Schumer* take the comedy of female self-abasement to its logical physical conclusion. In one season three sketch, "Bakery in Maine," a group of women share their repressed, violent, and vindictive desires with one another. They attempt to resolve their overwhelming nausea at their conventional responsibilities (such as marriage, work, and parenting) by acting on their deepest desires, which, absurdly, revolve around the fantasy of opening a bakery in rural Maine. One woman muses, "You guys, I love my little Blendolyn DaFoe, but sometimes when *Dora the Explorer* is on again, and they're laughing at literally nothing, I think about tracking down *Dora* creator Valerie Walsh Valdes, *Clockwork Orange*-ing her eyes open, and making her watch a video of my kids singing that lazy, atonal theme song until she cries blood, and then whipping up some homemade jam for my little bakery in Maine." Conjuring a "postfeminist" Sandman (to invoke Bakhtin's discussion of Hoffmann), the joke here juxtaposes horrific violence with obscene normalcy: optically imprisoning a female media producer while taking flight to a rural bakery. As with much of the gendered comedy on this show, the articulation of its feminist politics emerges through the sheer incongruity between violent repressed fantasies and utterly ordinary everyday fixations.

After the one woman insinuates that she'd like to make homemade jam out of *Dora* creator Walsh Valdes's eyeballs, another girlfriend quips, "Jam is my jam!": an idiotically banal pun that weirdly provokes the women to nearly uncontrollable hysterics. At this, Amy comments, "See, women are funny!" invoking a tired debate about gender essentialism and comedic vocation by exposing the systemic violence that underpins it.[46] The polemical question of what it means for women *to be funny* takes on an existential weight as it is forced through word play and grotesque exaggeration to reconcile with the tedium of conventional domesticity, the commodity cultures of parenting, the power imbalances of marriage, and systemic inequality in the professional sphere. Everything comes up, and potentially nothing stays repressed.

Indeed, the central theme of the skit is displacement: from the abjection of desire to the nihilistic absurdity of suffering through all that bullshit in exchange for the freedom to make baked goods in rural New England. As in "Trouble Accepting a Compliment," the compromise between fantasy and conformity unravels at the possibility of desire's actualization: when one friend confesses to having quit her job, divorced her husband, and, in fact, opened a bakery in Maine. This reversal of impossibility literally "petrifies" the women, who spontaneously turn to stone and crumble into dust—which the unburdened homemaker then gleefully collects in a bowl, announcing that her friends' ashes will make delicious scones: "I know! Scones!!" The ladies' fantastic metamorphosis—ossified by the realization that their avowed fantasy is very much within the realm of possibility—explicitly evokes the myth of Medusa: the horrific Gorgon who turns men to stone at the mere sight of her image.[47]

As Kristeva describes her in *The Severed Head*, "Medusa is *abject* as primitive matrix of that archaic nondifferentiation in which there is neither subject nor object, only the sticky, slimy abject."[48] Kristeva compares Medusa to Baubo, the ancient Greek crone who exposed her genitals to the weeping goddess Demeter, thereby provoking Demeter's laughter and stirring her from her mourning and depression. (Baubo's androgyny, in its historical and mythic contexts, epitomizes Kristeva's notion of archaic nondifferentiation.) *Apocalypse*, from the ancient Greek *apo* and *kalupto*, literally meaning "uncovering," "disclosure of knowledge," or "the lifting of a veil or revelation," is a thematic obsession on *Inside Amy Schumer* and the frequent climax of comedic abjection. When the show's apparent social relevance reaches an impasse (as it so often does), comedy crosses the threshold of abjection. Feminist laughter signifies not just disruption or subversion but the nauseating impossibility of ever solidifying these momentary reversals of power. *Schumer's* apocalyptic laughter provokes a simultaneously ecstatic and sickening response, deriving from the mutual contamination between feminist counterculture and antifeminist ideology. This zone of political nondifferentiation is precisely what is at stake for Kristeva in "approaching abjection": the starting point of *The Powers of Horror*.

Kristeva and Schumer perhaps would have much more to say to each other than either would ever realize. While Schumer frequently and jubilantly invokes her personal obsession with her own genitals (once pretending to flash David Letterman in a memorable late night interview), the *chora* (from the Greek *choiros*, meaning both "vulva" and "pig") represents a key figure of abjection for Kristeva.[49] In *The Severed Head*, Kristeva associates the chora with Medusa: "As sexually aroused female, Medusa displays a vulva to which maleficence confers more than phallic power."[50] Instead of provoking laughter through abject exhibitionism, however, *Inside Amy Schumer* turns the decapitated Gorgon's unwatchable abjection on its head by making her speak in plain language. Jokes such as "Jam is my jam!" anticipate the impotence of their own laughter, when these women will become petrified not by taboo obscenity but by their own boring fantasies. As it turns out, the bakery in Maine surpasses even the adultery, infanticide, and evisceration scenarios that the women concoct—one-upping homicidal violence with artisanal cannibalism (again, human ashes are the secret ingredient).

Through its abject escalation of laughter, *Schumer* further colludes with the laughing spectator's own disorienting position in relation to the show's politics—especially its feminism.

The Politics of Feminist Comedy in the Aftermath of Apocalyptic Abjection

In the time since I first wrote this chapter, and since the most recent (though not final) season of *Inside Amy Schumer* aired in summer 2016, popular feminist comedy has grown notably angrier, more nihilistic, and further suspicious of the gendered tropes of self-deprecation. For example, queer stand-up comedian Hannah Gadsby refused to reduce her own experiential trauma to a gimmicky punch line in her viral Netflix special, *Nanette* (2018), which consists of multiple sets not meant to provoke laughter for the audience. With the election of Donald Trump, the rise of #MeToo and Time's Up, and feminist theory's incisive return to Marxist materialism and analyses of class politics, the landscape has again changed.

Inside Amy Schumer remains a formative part of this present-day picture. Popular discourses of abject feminist laughter increasingly attempt to close the gap between reality and representation—between biopolitical violence and critical satire. Rather than bridge the divide, *Schumer*'s antics linger in the void; they exaggerate ad absurdum the unresolvable tensions between satirical laughter as a useful instrument and comedic violence as an apocalyptic, world-shattering rupture. *Schumer* unleashed an extremity of representations: spontaneous combustion, ritual decapitation, and cannibalistic ossification, to name a few instances. Its brand of abject feminist comedy, as I have argued, is a pretext for opening onto a murkier and more destabilizing horizon of affective politics and corporeal refusal.

As feminism seeks a unified voice, and gender searches for a form, images of grotesque or unruly embodiment have become more the norm than the exception. Abject comedy, as an alternating site of liberating laughter and of nihilistic impossibility, provides a fertile terrain for acting out the contradictory meanings and ideals of gender identity and its shape-shifting relationship to feminist politics in the twenty-first century.

Notes

Epigraph: Kathleen Rowe, *The Unruly Woman: Gender and the Genres of Laughter* (Austin: University of Texas Press, 1995), 31.

    Color versions of images in this chapter may be found at http://scalar.usc.edu/works/abjection-incorporated-insert/index.

1 Wesley Morris, "The Year We Obsessed over Identity," *New York Times Sunday Magazine*, October 6, 2015, MM48.

2 George Rush, Joanna Molloy, Marcus Baram, and Marc Malman, "Cho Tells a H'Wood Horror Story," *New York Daily News*, July 18, 1999.

3 Nick Paumgarten, "Id Girls," *New Yorker*, June 23, 2014.

4 Kathleen Rowe, *The Unruly Woman: Gender and the Genres of Laughter* (Austin: University of Texas Press, 1995).

5 Mikhail Bakhtin, *Rabelais and His World*, trans. Hélène Iswolsky (Bloomington: Indiana University Press, 2009), 26–27.

6 Julia Kristeva, *Powers of Horror: An Essay on Abjection*, trans. Leon S. Roudiez (New York: Columbia University Press, 1982), 5.

7 Bakhtin, *Rabelais and His World*, 27.

8 Mary Russo, *The Female Grotesque: Risk, Excess, and Modernity* (New York: Routledge, 1995); M. Alison Kibler, *Rank Ladies: Gender and Cultural Hierarchy in American Vaudeville* (Chapel Hill: University of North Carolina Press, 1999); Mary Douglas, *Purity and Danger: An Analysis of Concepts of Pollution and Taboo* (London: Routledge, 2002); Susan Glenn, *Female Spectacle: The*

Theatrical Roots of Modern Feminism (Cambridge, MA: Harvard University Press, 2002); Patricia Mellencamp, *High Anxiety: Catastrophe, Scandal, Age, and Comedy* (Bloomington: Indiana University Press, 1990); Linda Mizejewski, *Pretty/Funny: Women Comedians and Body Politics* (Austin: University of Texas Press, 2014).

9   Barbara Creed, *Monstrous-Feminine: Film, Feminism, Psychoanalysis* (London: Routledge, 1993); Carol Clover, *Men, Women, and Chainsaws: Gender in the Modern Horror Film* (Princeton, NJ: Princeton University Press, 1993); Isabel Pinedo, *Recreational Terror: Women and the Pleasures of Horror Film Viewing* (New York: State University of New York Press, 1997); Tony Magistrale, *Abject Terrors: Surveying the Modern and Postmodern Horror Film* (New York: Peter Lang, 2005); Sarah Arnold, *Maternal Horror Film: Melodrama and Motherhood* (New York: Palgrave Macmillan, 2013); Angela Smith, *Hideous Progeny: Disability, Eugenics, and Classic Horror Cinema* (New York: Columbia University Press, 2012).

10 Kristeva, *Powers of Horror*, 9.

11 Creed, *Monstrous-Feminine*, 15.

12 Geoff Edgers, "Roseanne on the Day She Shrieked the 'Star-Spangled Banner,' Grabbed Her Crotch, and Earned a Rebuke from President Bush," *Washington Post*, July 23, 2015.

13 Stacey Ritzen, "Allow Lena Dunham to Regale You with This Tale of Getting a UTI in Japan," *Uproxx*, October 9, 2015.

14 Bakhtin, *Rabelais and His World*, 13.

15 Bakhtin, *Rabelais and His World*, 7.

16 Kristeva, *Powers of Horror*, 9.

17 Three of the most vital components of this medieval folk humor include: first, *ritual spectacles* (such as pageants and shows, wherein a mock priest might preside over the wedding between a giant and a donkey); second, *comic verbal compositions* (blasphemous parodies written in Latin or the vernacular); and third, *Billingsgate* (genres of curses, oaths, and blazons meant to defile all that was holy or sacrosanct).

18 Giorgio Agamben, *State of Exception* (Chicago: University of Chicago Press, 2004), 71.

19 In addition to the feminist writers I discuss, several comedy scholars have championed the carnivalesque as a form of counter-politics that survives into modern entertainment culture. Key accounts include Robert Stam, *Subversive Pleasures: Bakhtin, Cultural Criticism, and Film* (Baltimore, MD: Johns Hopkins University Press, 1989); Peter Stallybrass and Allon White, *The Politics and Poetics of Transgression* (Ithaca, NY: Cornell University Press, 1986); and Jonathan Gray, Jeffrey Jones, and Ethan White, eds., *Satire TV: Politics and Comedy in the Post-Network Era* (New York: NYU Press, 2009).

20 Bakhtin, *Rabelais and His World*, 19.

21 Bakhtin, *Rabelais and His World*, 19.

22 Bakhtin, *Rabelais and His World*, 19.

23 François Rabelais, *Gargantua and Pantagruel*, trans. and ed. M. A. Screech (London: Penguin Classics, 2006).

24 Bakhtin, *Rabelais and His World*, 23.

25 Bakhtin, *Rabelais and His World*, 23.

26 E. T. A. Hoffmann, *Tales of Hoffmann* (London: Penguin Classics, 1982). Freud provides an elaborate interpretation of Hoffmann's Sandman tale in his 1919 essay "The Uncanny," in which he argues that the effect of the uncanny derives from the uncertainty in the tale about whether the terrors recounted are purely fantastic or gruesomely real.

27 Bakhtin, *Rabelais and His World*, 39.

28 Although Bakhtin wrote *Rabelais and His World* in 1940, it was not successfully published in Russian until 1965. Even then, its incisive account of comedy's social politics masqueraded under the title "Rabelais and Folk Culture in the Middle Ages and Renaissance."

29 Bakhtin, *Rabelais and His World*, 52, 53.

30 Wolfgang Kayser, *The Grotesque in Art and Literature* (Bloomington: Indiana University Press, 1963); Bakhtin, *Rabelais and His World*, 51.

31 As Hoffmann's character Nathanael in "The Sandman" puts it, "Laugh, I beg you, laugh at me as much as you like! I beg it of you! But, God in Heaven! my hair is standing on end, and it is as if, when I plead with you to laugh at me, I do so in the madness of despair" (*Tales of Hoffmann*, 86). The insurmountable distance between laughing observer and comic victim reflects the madness and alienation that Nathanael suffers in relation to his own memories and subjective experience.

32 See Carl Schmitt, *The Concept of the Political* (New Brunswick, NJ: Rutgers University Press, 1976); Jacques Derrida, *Acts of Religion* (New York: Routledge, 2002).

33 Anne Thériault, "Amy Schumer Isn't as Feminist as the Internet Thinks," *Daily Dot*, June 10, 2015.

34 Megan Garber, "How Comedians Became Public Intellectuals," *Atlantic*, May 28, 2015.

35 Betty Friedan, *The Feminine Mystique* (New York: Norton, 1963).

36 Kristeva, *Powers of Horror*, 8.

37 Kristeva, *Powers of Horror*, 206.

38 Julia Kristeva and Toril Moi, *The Kristeva Reader* (New York: Columbia University Press, 1986).

39 Kristeva and Moi, *The Kristeva Reader*, 50.

40 Georges Bataille and Stuart Kendall, eds., *The Unfinished System of Nonknowledge* (Minneapolis: University of Minnesota Press, 2001), 23.

41 Kristeva, *Powers of Horror*, 206.

42 Russo, *Female Grotesque*, 8.

43 Kristeva, *Powers of Horror*, 85.

44 Ross McDonagh, "Maggie Gyllenhaal, 37, Reveals Her 'Astonishment' after Casting Director Told Her She Was Too Old to Play the Love Interest of a 55-Year-Old Man," *Daily Mail*, May 21, 2015.

45 For a brilliant analysis of Amy Schumer's abject satirical critique of postfeminist ideology, see Jason Middleton, "A Rather Crude Feminism," in "Gender and Comedy," ed. Maggie Hennefeld and Kristen Anderson Wanger, special issue, *Feminist Media Histories* 3, no. 2 (Spring 2017): 120–40.

46 Many feminist comedy scholars (Mizejewski, Krefting, and Joanne Gilbert) and feminist comedians (Tina Fey, Amy Schumer, and Sarah Silverman) have incisively debunked Christopher Hitchens's sexist polemic "Why Women Aren't Funny." *Vanity Fair* also published a feminist response to Hitchens by Alessandra Stanley, "Who Says Women Aren't Funny?" (April 2008). As Fey amusingly scorns Hitchens in her autobiography, *Bossypants* (New York: Little, Brown, 2011), "I don't like Chinese food, but I don't write articles trying to prove it doesn't exist."

47 Anca Parvulescu recuperates Medusa's stony gaze with feminist laughter: "Always-already petrified in our habitual seriousness, we do not need Perseus' mirror to neutralize Medusa's gaze; it is our gaze that needs work, and Medusa's laughter can help us" (107). *Laughter: Notes on a Passion* (Cambridge, MA: MIT Press, 2010).

48 Julia Kristeva, *The Severed Head: Capital Visions* (New York: Columbia University Press, 2012), 31.

49 E. Alex Jung, "Amy Schumer Got to Fluster Letterman One Last Time by Showing Her 'Vagina,'" *Vulture*, April 21, 2015.

50 Kristeva, *Severed Head*, 31.

abject

bodies

humans,

animals,

objects

part II

chapter five

The Animal
& the Animalistic:
China's Late 1950s
Socialist Satirical
Comedy

yiman wang

During the first seventeen years of the People's Republic of China (1949–66), the Chinese film industry and film culture underwent tumultuous transformations due to waves of political campaigns. All of these transformations came to the fore in the vexed fate of satirical comedy. Because of its barbed humor and a hereditary connection to the slapstick comedy practiced in the presocialist era, satirical comedy virtually disappeared in the People's Republic of China between 1949 and 1955, falling victim to the new Communist government's bid for legitimacy through positive propaganda. The return of satirical comedy in 1956 was triggered by the new cultural policy One Hundred Flowers, announced by Mao Zedong on the heels of Nikita Khrushchev's "thaw" in the USSR (1953–64). Under the slogan "Let one hundred flowers bloom; let one hundred schools contend" (*baihua qifang, baijia zhengming*), the One Hundred Flowers campaign encouraged intellectuals and artists to voice their opinions (including criticism of the Communist government).[1] The resulting intellectual and artistic freedom, however, was soon truncated, and the corollary rebirth of satirical comedy was squashed in 1957 when Mao launched the anti-Rightist campaign in June of that year. Film and theater workers who ventured to make films and plays that exposed social problems came under persecution as procapitalist, antiparty "Rightists." Many lost their positions, their films and plays chastised as "poisonous weeds" to be rooted out of the socialist garden.

What was expelled from the socialist body politic constituted the abject. The state-sponsored cleansing of intellectuals, artists, and their works emblematized the new socialist government's struggle to define and shore up its body politic by dictating who and what to include as part of that body politic, or to exclude from it. The undesirable abject was not simply antithetical to the desirable socialist politics, however. Rather, it fundamentally shaped what was desirable. Or, what was abjected enabled the very formation of the socialist body politic. As Georges Bataille argues, the abject (including the disinherited waste population), which the system cannot fully expel, "constitutes the foundations of collective existence."[2] In the context of my study, the abject disinherited waste population (i.e., film and theater workers inherited from China's presocialist republican era) and their works represent the ideological preconditions for the formation of a socialist collective in China, as well as the perpetual Other challenging the coherence of that body politic.

Teetering on the shifting borderline between what was to be included and what was to be excluded in the socialist body politic, the satirical comedy of the 1950s as a film genre met different treatments, first phased out then encouraged, only to be censored once again. The 1950s satirical comedy is a poignant site for tracing the conflicted reconfiguration of socialist China's geopolitical and cultural landscapes. The ideological strife over the border between inclusion and exclusion in the socialist body politic found expression in the binary of humanity and animalism in satirical comedy's diegesis and in its circumscribing discourses. I use animalism here to refer to filmic representations and performances that mimic animal behaviors in ways contrary to a desirable socialist humanity as embodied in a socialist "new human." The exclusion of such abject animalism makes possible the ideological construction of socialist humanity.

In this study, I first outline Western philosophical and Chinese political discourses on laughter, positing the notion of the *socialist laughter doctrine* to highlight the unique practices of laughter management under the socialist ethos. I understand socialist laughter management as a manifestation of Jacques Derrida's concept of hospitality—an aporia whose possibility goes in tandem with its impossibility. I then bring the aporia's logical impasse to bear on two satirical comedies produced during the One Hundred Flowers campaign, *An Unfinished Comedy* (*Meiyou wancheng de xiju*) (dir. Lv Ban,

1957) and *A Nightmare in the Zoo* (*Youyuan jingmeng*) (dir. Shi Lan, 1956). My analysis shows how socialist hospitality (i.e., its production and accommodation of the desirable "new human") was paradoxically predicated on and ultimately undermined by what it aimed to eradicate, namely, abject animalism, along with its crass physical humor, found in satire and in the comedians' performance styles. A key site where animalism plays out is in the comedians' facial expressions, which are rendered grotesque through extreme close-up shots. Such animalist disfiguration resembles what Gilles Deleuze and Félix Guattari describe as *defacialization*, or face erasure, which tears through and subverts socialist humanity, or what they critique as the "abstract machine of faciality"—the power system that overcodes and forecloses nonconformity.[3]

In this light, I argue that, contrary to the state's ideological policing of the borderline between included humanity and excluded animalism, the films reveal an increasing breakdown of this binary through the mediation of a third term—the animal and animality. Thus we encounter a strand of vexed *inter(dis)course* between the animal, the animalistic, and the socialist new human in the late 1950s cultural-political landscape.[4] By unpacking their interactions in the films, my study sheds light on an understudied trope of the human-animal composite as it fumbled its way through these precarious high-socialist politics. I further suggest that the intractable "animal" Other and the animalist specter, unleashed by satirical comedies and their circumscribing discourses, continue to unsettle and haunt socialist projections of ideological purism.

Socialist "Hospitality" and Its Laughter Doctrine

Socialist China in the 1950s unfolded through a series of melodramatic sociopolitical campaigns that aimed to establish a "new" society and a "new" human, counterposed to the perceived persistence of the "old," associated with the feudal and colonial experience in pre-1949 China. In this binary structure, the "old," deemed antithetical to the new body politic, was reduced to the abject and met with ideological cleansing. In other words, the "new" socialist regime performed a Derridean form of "hospitality." By policing the boundaries and setting rules in the house, Derrida argues, authority makes hospitality conditional; that is, guests may enjoy hospitality only on the condition that they follow the host's rules. Such hospitality, premised on the host-guest hierarchy and the production of the Self/Other binary, is not *genuine* hospitality. Nor is genuine hospitality possible, since once hosts relinquish control, they also lose the power to host, hence the obviation of hospitality.[5] Hospitality, therefore, is a quintessential aporia, an impasse or paradox whose conditions of possibility also constitute its conditions of impossibility. Its accommodation of the selected guests entails the exclusion and abjection of the apparent nonguests.

Derrida's theorization of hospitality helps us to understand cultural workers' probationary status in 1950s socialist China. Having established their careers and developed their work styles during the presocialist era in interaction with Western commercial culture, film and other cultural workers were scrutinized and subjected to "thought reform" (*sixiang gaizao*) so that they could be remolded into socialist workers under the new political regime. Mao Zedong's demand for political conformity through the stipulation that literature and arts ought to serve workers, peasants, and soldiers produced intense trepidation and vulnerability in cultural workers, even when they were allowed, or encouraged, to unleash their minds in creative activities.

A specific mechanism to ensure ideological conformity that is of particular relevance to my study is what I call the *socialist laughter doctrine*. This doctrine emerged from the triple-layered sociopolitical management of comedy, of cultural workers' political stances, and of comedians' performance styles, with the goal of ensuring the political propriety of all laughter. While differing from Western theories of laughter significantly, Chinese socialist ideologies share the fundamental understanding of laughter as both physiological and socially divisive, in that it works to separate the Self from the Other, the human from the animal, and those eligible for the dominant system of hospitality from those ineligible.

Western philosophers such as Herbert Spencer, René Descartes, and Immanuel Kant understood laughter as a physical and physiological process that mechanically channeled energy toward release.[6] In mapping machinic physics onto the physiological process of laughter, this strain of theory deploys a Cartesian animal-machine analogy, which implicates humans and thus negates human exceptionalism, rendering it continuous with animality. Different from this view that laughter stems from animality and is released through a quasi-mechanical process, Henri Bergson and Charles Baudelaire believed that the comic and laughter were "strictly human," or an effect of the human recognition of its superiority over the subhuman, including the animal.[7] These theorists all struggled to understand laughter in relation to the human, the animal, and the machinic. Despite their differences, their theories agree that laughter offers disconcerting pleasures that sustain a system hospitable to the insiders, yet exclusive to the outsiders. The fact that the excluded Others are associated with the animal confirms the linkage between animalism and the abject.

In the context of 1950s China, this inclusive-exclusive mechanism of laughter continued to play a pivotal role in constructing a state-endorsed socialist new human. Following the melodramatic Manichean structure of good versus bad, socialist ideologues sought to define what a socialist satire was and how laughter could help consolidate socialist China, which led to the socialist laughter doctrine. This doctrine had its precursor in the theorization and ideological regulation of satire in the thirties and forties, when satirical literature proliferated, oftentimes targeting the governing Nationalist Party and the social ills for which the government was responsible. When writers similarly used satire to expose social problems in the Communist base of Yan'an, Mao Zedong realized that satirical exposés could undermine Communist legitimacy. He launched the three-year Yan'an rectification campaign (*zhengfeng yundong*), starting in February 1942, which included convening an assembly of literary and artistic workers.[8] Mao's talks at this assembly exerted long-term influence on literature and art from the forties through the sixties. Published as "Talks at the Yan'an Forum on Literature and Art," Mao's speeches describe satire as indispensable, yet warn against its abuse, and demand its different usage depending on its target (the enemy, the ally, or the comrade).[9] In post-1949 China, Mao's "Talks" became canonized as directives for literary and artistic creation.

In a 1957 article, "Fengci xiju de yilei" (One type of satirical comedy), an anonymous author criticizes antirevolutionary satire for its exclusive focus on small, inglorious details in life. The author argues that such satire pokes fun indiscriminately, failing to differentiate the beautiful (social progress) from the ugly (social ills), or to take the people's stance on what really marks the line between the good and the bad.[10] This article emblematizes the emergence of a laughter doctrine in the late 1950s. According to this doctrine, any laughter derived from exaggerated caricaturization of the ugly and the negative without a positive counterpart was blasphemous to the new regime and therefore unacceptable. Furthermore, vulgar bodily humor conducive to dehumanization and animalism was in bad taste and associated with pre-1949 slapstick comedy. In this context, the Western physiological understanding of laughter as being associated with animal instincts and machinic processes was recognized only to be denounced. Questions of why people laugh and what purposes laughter serves came to be realigned with socialist and functionalist stipulations of "healthy" laughter.

This intensifying ideological scrutiny (as manifested in the socialist laughter doctrine) made film workers acutely aware of their precarious, probationary position vis-à-vis socialist cinematic pedagogy. Lv Ban, the director of the three most well-known satirical comedies of the late 1950s (including *An Unfinished Comedy*, under study here), illustrates precisely this consciousness of precarity. A well-known actor in 1930s Shanghai, Lv actively participated in Leftist drama and cinema in the resistance against Japanese invasion. In the late 1930s, he went to Yan'an, creating skits that incorporated local folk entertainment formats. After 1949, he participated in making some of the earliest socialist films. In 1956, shortly after Mao's announcement of the One Hundred Flowers policy in February, Lv founded the Spring Comedy Club with other cultural workers. In August, his first satirical comedy, *Before the New Director Arrives* (*Xin juzhang daolai zhiqian*) (1956), based on a successful play, was released by Changchun Film Studio and received critical acclaim. Meanwhile, Lv Ban published an article in *Popular Cinema* (*Dazhong dianying*), the first popular film magazine in socialist China, describing his trepidation and fear of making mistakes, which led to his cautious approach to making satirical comedy in the new political environment.[11]

In early 1957, Changchun Film Studio released Lv's second satirical comedy, *The Man Who Violates the Social Mores* (*Buju xiaojie de ren*). As advised by Zhong Dianfei, an eminent first-generation film critic of the new China, who also initiated this film, Lv avoided "criticizing the social system" and instead focused on small glitches in everyday life.[12] Lv's two comedies stimulated heated discussion, resulting in a special column, "Guochan xijupian bitan" (Thoughts on domestic comedies), published in two issues of *Popular Cinema* in July 1957. Meanwhile, Lv Ban shifted from gingerly testing the water to boldly advocating "director supremacy" (*daoyan zhishang*), arguing that "filmmaking should be determined by the director, independent of the party and administrators."[13] He also believed that "comedy should aim for laughs" and advocated for a film studio dedicated to comedy.[14] He was soon persecuted as a Rightist, and his films were attacked as antiparty "poisonous weeds."

His third comedy in the making, ominously entitled *An Unfinished Comedy* (*Meiyou wancheng de xiju*), was banned. As if anticipating the ill fate of the film, Lv had an officious, dogmatic character in the film articulate a caution against making satire: "A satirical film is very difficult to make. You must be prepared to be beaten down." Later in the film, after watching the first diegetic comic skit performed by Yin Xiucen and Han Langen—the most popular comic duo in pre-1949 Shanghai, the same dogmatist pontificates, "Satire correctly deployed is a cleansing fire. This skit, however, is a rampant fire that burns everything indiscriminately." In the film this dogmatist is named Yi Bangzi, a homonym for *yi bangzi*, or one big stick, caricaturing him as an overbearing ideologue who beats down creative work with one big stick. The film ends with Yi Bangzi being hit on the head accidentally by a big stick and thereupon driven out.

In reality, however, ideologues like Yi Bangzi were already assembling evidence against Lv Ban, labeling him as a Rightist. Such evidence started with Lv's questionable political stance and lifestyle, then spread to include the perceived gimmicky buffoonery and slanderous characterizations in his comedies. By 1958, Lv Ban's attempt to build the genre of satirical comedy in socialist China had been aborted; his career, along with that of the many film workers involved in his films, was terminated.

Abject Animalism in *An Unfinished Comedy*

Lv Ban's three late 1950s satirical comedies all inherited the slapstick traditions and bodily humor deriving from comedians' performances. *An Unfinished Comedy*, in particular, foregrounds bodily humor by casting Han Langen (nicknamed Monkey) and Yin Xiucen—known as the Chinese Laurel and Hardy in pre-1949 Shanghai. By reinvigorating bodily humor, Lv unleashed a spectrum of physiological and affective responses from the audience. The foregrounded bodily and physiological laughter provoked frenzied somaphobic diatribes against corporeality, seen as symptomatic of animalism (opposed to the socialist new human), whether it pertained to the comedians' bodily humor, the audience members' bodily reactions, or the comedy intuitively grasped as a "body genre."[15] In this section, I trace the film's deployment of bodily humor, its presocialist Shanghai lineage, and subsequent somaphobic diatribes. I also identify moments where bodily humor was endorsed for various reasons. Taken together, the purist ideologues equated bodily humor with an abject animalism ineligible for socialist hospitality—only to end up making it constitutive of the very foundation of the socialist body politic.

An Unfinished Comedy takes full advantage of the Yin-Han comedic duo's dramatically contrasting physical appearances (rotund vs. skinny) and their pantomimic performance. The film makes frequent references to Yin's excessive body weight and his bodily functions, which are analogized with his excessive material desires. Shortly after the opening of the film, which shows a Han-Yin reunion in the socialist era, Han compares Yin's rotund body to a "manure factory," twisting the socialist glorification of the "factory" into an abject, profane, animalist, physiological plant. The film then unfolds through three embedded comic skits, each followed by a critique session in which the diegetic audience (including the ideologue Yi Bangzi) are asked to comment on the ideological stance of the skit. These diegetic critique sessions satirize extradiegetic ideological coercion.

In the first skit, "The Death of Manager Zhu," Yin plays the overweight Manager Zhu (a homophone for the Chinese character meaning "pig"), who indulges in luxury items. This skit again consistently emphasizes Yin's heavy body, in sharp contrast to his skinny secretary, played by Han. Seeing himself reflected in a funhouse mirror, Zhu gleefully twists his body and makes faces to generate distorted mirror images. Finding the mirror amusing and conducive to health-inducing laughter, he orders more to be procured from Shanghai and Guangzhou—cities considered more developed in commercial culture than northeast China, where the film is set and shot. Later in this skit, Manager Zhu is mistakenly thought to have been killed during a train trip. Upon his sudden return, he is taken for a ghost, which prompts his secretary to test his body to make sure it is capable of feeling pain and therefore fleshy, vulnerable, and alive. Having proved that he is a living body, Manager Zhu, who seizes every opportunity to gratify his materialist desires, demands an extravagant glass coffin from Shanghai to replace his locally made pine coffin. In this comic skit, the hyperbolic visual presentation of Yin's heavy body and his corporeal desires are associated with his incorrigible Shanghai fetish, as illustrated in the funhouse mirror and the glass coffin, with glass being an icon of modernist glitz, contrary to the down-to-earth agriculture and heavy industry in northeast China.[16]

Similarly, in the film's second comic skit, "The Man Who Likes to Brag," the comic duo's bodily humor is again sutured into past Shanghai vernacular culture—this time through a children's musical, *The Sparrow and the Child* (*Maque yu xiaohai*), written and popularized by Li Jinhui, a musician educator based in Shanghai.[17] Respectively decked out as a fat baby in a bib and a skinny bird wearing a prosthetic beak and wings, Yin and Han comically imitate children's body language while lip syncing a recorded children's vocal performance of *The Sparrow and the Child*. The suturing of the visual (the comedians' adult bodies dressed in a makeshift bib and wings) with the audio (the children's vocal performance) produces an uncanny and elastic incongruity. The clumsy pantomime mocks Yin's character (whose bragging about his singing skills had led others to request performances from the comic duo in the first place). Yet, their farcical pantomimic reenactment of *The Sparrow and the Child* also suggests the lasting power of presocialist Shanghai's vernacular culture. It thereby reinforces the comedians' own well-known Shanghai lineage.

This reinsertion of the most well-known children's musical, the funhouse mirrors, and the macabrely decadent glass coffin—all referencing presocialist Shanghai's popular culture and commercialism—created a poignant tension with post-1949 politics, which called for a clean break with the past. Similarly, the recycling of the comic duo and their bodily humor contradicted the state-enforced thought reform and its socialist laughter doctrine. In relation to the new socialist body politic, the persisting republican-era Shanghai-based commercial culture evokes Bataille's notion of the abject (including the "disinherited waste population") whose disavowal paradoxically undergirds the system of the desirable. Thus, the unruly challenge posed by Lv Ban's *An Unfinished Comedy* consisted in the return of the abject messy history associated with the bodies of the comedians, the audience, and the slapstick comedy genre.

Indeed, slapstick comedy was already a thorn in the flesh of socially conscious commentators during the republican era (1911–49). Oftentimes copying their Western counterparts, early Chinese slapstick comedies felicitously married cinematic techniques of trick shots with comedians' corporeal performance, generating hyperbolic bodily humor through clowning and pantomiming for the camera. By rendering the comedian's body a clumsy yet indestructible exhibitionist spectacle, such visceral bodily humor called attention to dehumanization, or the human-animal-machine contiguity that ensured endless motion, commotion, and emotion.[18] Comedians like Han Langen and Yin Xiucen emerged precisely from such a milieu, explicitly mimicking Hollywood's Laurel-Hardy duo.

Despite the wild popularity of slapstick comedy and bodily humor in China, no Chinese filmic or political discourse has been developed to address comedy's visceral bodily premise seriously, or its agenda of playing for laughs. Instead, commentators sought to rationalize ostensibly senseless humor in sociopolitical terms or dismissed it as retrogressive. If laughter simply offered sensorial pleasure through intestinal massaging and was ultimately useless, as Kant claims, then filmmakers and critics must address a fundamental question: Why make comedy?

The writings of Cai Chusheng before and after 1949 shed a key light on this question and the geopolitical contexts in which it was raised. Cai was a veteran film director and commentator, best known for making left-leaning social exposé films in early 1930s Shanghai. He continued to serve in important official positions after 1949. For Cai, the justification for bodily humor and slapstick comedic relief prior to 1949 was the lowbrow audience's desire for bodily stimulation. This view is best represented in his response to the criticism of his film *Lamb Gone Astray* (*Mitu de gaoyang*), which was released in 1936 to mixed reviews. While applauded for his realistic depiction of homeless children's harsh lives, Cai was also criticized for using satire and comedy—considered incompatible with the film's strong social concerns. In a 1936 interview, Cai responded by citing Charlie Chaplin's widely popular broad comedy. He further argued for the necessarily sensationalized plot devices because of the majority Chinese audience's lowbrow tastes. Instead of putting film on a pedestal and appealing to only 20 percent of the Chinese audience, Cai preferred to make a film that presented only a partially correct worldview, but that would appeal to 100 percent of the audience. For Cai, broad comedy and vulgar bodily humor were the price the filmmaker had to pay to reach a largely undereducated audience with a "deformed" (*jixing*) taste. Guided by this pragmatic strategy, Cai regularly cast the comic duo Han and Yin in his 1930s films, such as Han in *The Song of the Fisherman* (*Yuguang qu*; 1934) and Yin in *Lamb Gone Astray*. The comedians' bodily humor offered temporary relief in the otherwise somber films. That is to say, the comedians' corporeal humor was conditionally "hosted" as comic relief in social exposé films to attract the audience but was ultimately curtailed by the host film's straight-faced house rules (à la Derrida's notion of conditional hospitality).

In the 1950s, Cai, as a carry-over filmmaker and critic, was tentatively hosted by the new political regime, partially thanks to his pre-1949 career of making left-leaning films. He was appointed director of the Arts Committee of the Film Bureau, among other high-ranking official positions. His recruitment by the new regime may have led him to denounce comedy and bodily humor. In a long diatribe against *An Unfinished Comedy*, Cai accused Lv Ban of attempting bourgeois restoration by featuring Han and Yin—the "so-called comedians from the old times," focusing on "box office revenue," and emulating Hollywood comedy.[19] He also criticized Han and Yin for sticking to their "retrogressive tricks" (*laoyitao de yanji*) and resisting thought reform.[20] Cai specifically took issue with Lv's use of animal imagery and metaphors in *An Unfinished Comedy*, including the pig and the bear as embodied by the overweight Yin, and the monkey and the sheep as performed by the skinny Han. He argued that animalism, as suggested by the comedians' clowning of animal behaviors, bestialized new state officials, turning the socialist government into a menagerie similar to old Shanghai's entertainment venues, such as the Great World.[21]

This anxiety about animalism and bestialization reversed a well-known republican-era film star publicity strategy of associating an actor with an animal. The animal trope branded the actors while conjoining commercial discourses on stardom and fandom. One example can be found in the magazine *Dianying xiju* (Film theater; 1936), which features a full-page display of four female stars' heads grafted onto animal bodies (figure 5.1).

They are the heads of Hu Die (aka Butterfly Wu), flanked by butterfly wings; Chen Yanyan (literally Swallow Chen), on a bird body perched on a branch; Tan Ying, trailing a snake body; and Wang Renmei, with a prowling feline body. Entitled "Mingxing dongwu guan," which could mean either the stars' views on animals or stars viewed as animals, human-animal composites were created for humor and delight. Thus, it is unsurprising that Han Langen built his reputation as the awkward-looking "skinny monkey" (*shou pihou*) in the 1930s, which also prompted Cai Chusheng to cast him as Xiaohou (little monkey)—the oppressed and starved younger brother to Xiaomao (little cat, played by Wang Renmei, a singer/dancer turned screen actress nicknamed the wild cat)—in his 1934 social exposé film, *The Song of the Fisherman*.

In socialist China, however, animal tropes (as part of star and fan discourses and animal-celebrity humor) were considered gimmicky, dehumanizing, and guilty of capitalist profiteerism. This led Cai Chusheng to criticize Han's and Yin's so-called animalist acting and bestialization in *An Unfinished Comedy*—an irony considering his own casting of the comic duo in his 1930s films precisely on account of their physical, human-animal humor. Similar disavowal of animal-based bodily humor and pantomimic comedy appeared in Wang Renmei's attack on the film, with significant refocus on its undesirable agitation of the audience's body. In an article "A Lesson for Actors," coauthored with film actor-producer Li Yunong, Wang Renmei criticized Han's and Yin's animalist acting as viscerally repulsive and improperly stimulating the audience physiologically, making the movie unbearably painful to watch.[22] Commenting on the film's opening sequence, where Yin greets Han (both playing themselves) at the Changchun Railway Station for their first reunion after 1949, Wang and Li described the comedians' gamut of exaggerated facial expressions, including squinting eyes, knitting brows, twisting lips, baring teeth, and Han doing his trademark ear twitching (figure 5.2).

They stated that such grotesque gimmicks made viewers shudder, instead of moving them. Like Cai Chusheng, they attributed what they perceived to be vulgar acting to the comedians' entrenched bourgeois sensibilities and failed thought reform.[23] Thus, Wang and Li highlighted the audience's visceral responses only to discount and disavow the comedians' embodied performances as animalist and repulsive.

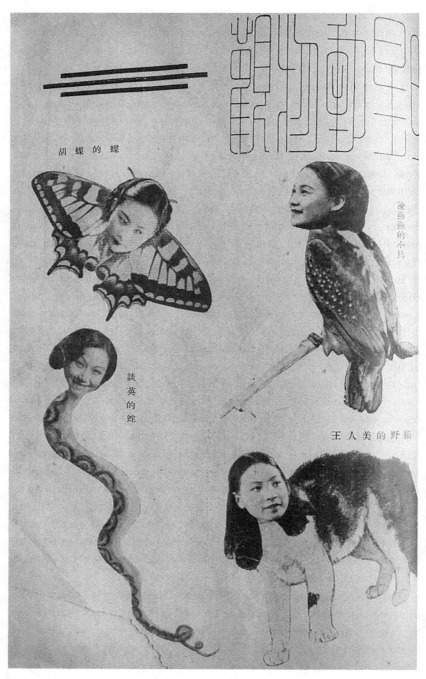

胡蝶的蝶

陳燕燕的小鳥

談英的蛇

王人美的野貓

figure 5.1 Four major actresses' heads grafted onto animals' bodies, as advertised in *Dianying xiju* (Film theater, 1936).

figure 5.2 Han Langen (Chinese Laurel) making faces to the camera in *An Unfinished Comedy*'s train station reunion scene.

The socialist laughter doctrine that drove Wang and Li's diatribe specifically targeted the comedians' facial (as well as bodily) expressions. The goal was to produce what Deleuze and Guattari would describe as the "abstract machine of faciality"—a power mechanism that systemically stipulates fixed meanings and rejects nonconformity and impurity. Such enforced meaning making and disciplining, through the process of faciality, stem from what Deleuze and Guattari call the "despotic assemblage" and the "authoritarian assemblage" that "act through signifiers and act upon souls and subjects."[24] To translate it into the context of the 1950s China, the socialist power assemblage that produced the new human worked through literary, artistic, and political venues *as well as* through various bodily regimes (including approved facial expressions and body language). The laughter doctrine, which strove to align the physical, physiological act of laughing with socialist ideology, facilitated precisely a faciality of conformist laughter to foreclose polyvocal (or polyfacial) semiotics.

The operation of the faciality-inducing laughter doctrine, however, was by no means unchallenged. Despite the somaphobic discourses that abjected bodily humor (including inappropriate facial expressions) as animalism, endorsement of bodily humor recurred periodically. As late as August 1949, a veteran Shanghai director-critic, Shi Dongshan, still advocated for lowbrow comedy in the emerging new China. As director of the Techniques Committee of the Central Film Bureau, Shi argued that Chinese cinema after 1949 would continue to be urban oriented (contrary to Mao Zedong's rural focus). Echoing Cai Chusheng's 1936 interview, Shi stated,

> If the [urban] audience wants to see fast-paced fighting scenes, we will not mind offering such excitement. If the audience is drawn to trick shots, we are happy to meet their desire. If the audience is interested in everyday domestic scenes, we might as well use those as subtle conduits for everyday struggles. *If the audience likes gimmicky farce (or slapstick drama), we could stage it with a couple of funny characters who are fundamentally good, but retain flaws that are not immediately corrigible. Or we might even center the entire farce on such funny caricaturized characters.*[25]

In 1957, in anticipation of *An Unfinished Comedy*, Han and Yin's comeback and reunion aroused much public interest. Media agencies enthusiastically celebrated their long overdue rebirth and reunion after their supposedly successful thought reform. A *People's Daily* article, "Meeting Comedian Yin Xiucen," excitedly announced Yin's return to the screen.[26] The rest of the report foregrounded Yin's rotund physique. Not only did it enable him to elicit belly laughs in a humorous scene in Lv Ban's satirical comedy *The Man Who Violates the Social Mores*, but his post-1949 weight gain (by thirty kilograms) also entitled him to housing on the premises of the Changchun Film Studio (literally being granted hospitality by the state-owned institution) to spare him the trouble of commuting. This special accommodation, according to Yin in the report, contrasted sharply with the "old society" film studio boss who simply exploited his physique. In this report, the author did not hesitate to affirm the public appeal in the socialist era of Yin and Han's bodily humor and forthcoming satirical comedy. Thus, the report skillfully navigated the thin line between entertainment and politics, seeking to make abject bodily humor politically viable again.

Significantly, this report was reprinted in major state-owned newspapers, including *People's Daily*, *Beijing Daily* (*Beijing ribao*), *Workers' Daily* (*Gongren ribao*), and *Liberation Daily* (*Jiefang ribao*), within just a couple of months. With the ideological criticism of *An Unfinished Comedy*, however, the affirmation of bodily humor, slapstick, and satirical comedy was silenced. Not until after the Cultural Revolution (1966–76) would satirical comedy make another comeback. This time, none other than Han Langen himself endorsed a return to slapstick humor. In his 1981 interview with Pang Zhaolin, a Shanghai University professor, Han observed that the pre-1949 audience wanted to see not only comedy (*xiju*), but also farce and slapstick pictures (*huaji pian*).[27] Han stated that a situational comedy made the audience laugh through the actor's humorous dialogue and funny facial expressions, while a farce or slapstick comedy used exaggerated body language to generate bodily humor, as illustrated by Chaplin. Echoing Wang Renmei's intuitive understanding of what Linda Williams would later describe as a "body genre," Han emphasized the physiological effect that an actor's bodily humor could exert on the audience through instigating the latter's physical mimicry.[28] Yet, unlike Wang, who denounced the comedians' slapstick acting and the audience's visceral reaction as abject, Han believed bodily humor catalyzed the audience's "healthy" laughter. His usage of *jiankang* (healthy) could be intentional or inadvertent, referring to both physical health (enhanced by the physiological act of laughing) and a healthy message acceptable to the dominant ideology. The pun was symptomatic of entrenched difficulty *and* a persistent effort to legitimize farce and satirical comedy, to make room for their lowbrow Rabelaisian resistance to ideological control, their deliberate physiological stimulation and manipulation of viewers' bodies, and their perceived derivation from Hollywood comedy.

By persisting on the edge of, and intermittently erupting into, public discourse, unruly comedy, along with abject comedians and their bodily humor, countered the socialist fallacy of dehistoricization. It challenged the purist socialist belief that history could be manipulated and truncated to conform to an artificial telos. It also constituted the limit case against which the ideologues sought to delineate the socialist body politic through the laugher doctrine and the rules of hospitality. In this sense, Lv Ban's *An Unfinished Comedy*, accused of animalist and dehumanizing performance, stands as the abject body in China's socialist film history, simultaneously necessitating the socialist laughter doctrine and exceeding its confines.

Triangulating and Collapsing Animalism, Animality, and Humanity in *A Nightmare in the Zoo*

Unlike *An Unfinished Comedy*, which was actively abjected as the "poisonous weed," the satirical comedy *A Nightmare in the Zoo* (dir. Shi Lan, 1956) achieved box office success yet attracted little political or critical attention, possibly because it was an apparently unproblematic cautionary tale about how to become a socialist new human.[29] Yet, its manifest tripod structure of the desirable socialist new human, benign animality, and abject animalism ultimately collapses because animalism returns to destabilize socialist hospitality.

Produced by the Central Studio of Newsreels and Documentary (*Zhongyang xinwen jilu dianying zhipianchang*), which was founded in July 1953, *A Nightmare in the Zoo* was set and shot in the Beijing Zoo, which originated as the Qing dynasty's Experimental Agricultural Farm, opened to the public in 1908, with animals procured from Germany, and renamed the Beijing Zoo in 1955. The half-hour short film interweaves fiction and documentary, framed by a *xiangsheng* (literally face and voice), or crosstalk performance, featuring two performers' witty verbal bantering about comic situations. These situations emerge from the interweaving of documentary footage of zoo animals with the fictional narrative of a zoo visitor violating regulations and making himself a laughingstock in the process. This hybridized intermedial, metacinematic form indicates the film's multiple agendas: cinematizing the traditional live-action *xiangsheng* (in the opening frame); promoting the newly renamed Beijing Zoo (through documentary footage); and satirizing inappropriate behaviors in public space (in the fictional part). These different registers give rise to multilayered comic appeals, which play the literal animals in the crosstalk/*xiangsheng* performance and the documentary footage against the metaphorical animal in the fictional part.

In the film's opening crosstalk, the two crosstalk/*xiangsheng* performers (Hou Baolin and Guo Qiru) talk about the new hybrid media form, that is, the filming of their own crosstalk performance, and the camera's ability to manipulate the performers' body sizes by zooming in and out. Hou refers to this cinematographic manipulation of physical size as the "science of film." They then switch to the "science of the zoo" (including the construction of the animals' "homes" and the comprehensive care and management of the animals). Hou concludes that the zoo is much better equipped than Guo's home, prompting Guo's evocation of Marx's statement (as interpreted in China) that "humans are also animals, but superior animals" (*gaodeng dongwu*). This opening juxtaposition of human and nonhuman animals prompts the (diegetic) audience to view the main human character in the fictional part and the zoo animals in the documentary footage through a comparative lens for the rest of the film.

In the fictional narrative, a selfish man (played by Hou) tours the zoo, trespassing into the elephants' and tigers' enclosures. His interactions and juxtaposition with the animals cause the other zoo visitors (and the film audience)

figure 5.3 A Nightmare in the Zoo protagonist (Hou Baolin) pressing against the elephant's side to listen to the swallowed harmonica continuing to make sound as it is digested.

to see him as an animal-like and laughable spectacle. While watching the beaver swimming, he annoys other visitors by moving his hands in a swimming gesture. Upon seeing the elephant performing, he walks into the elephant zone to play the harmonica, getting the elephant to dance to his music. The elephant then swallows his harmonica, which continues to make sounds as it is pushed through the elephant's guts (figure 5.3). His crossing of the human-animal borderline puts him in an awkward situation, rendering him an object of public ridicule (in contrast to the well-trained, crowd-pleasing elephant). He lays down on a slate bench, ignoring the "no laying on the bench" sign and getting the back of his jacket printed with stripes of wet paint, which in turn leads a child to confuse him with a zebra.

Finally, he scampers over the rocks to get a better view only to fall into the tiger zone. Attempting to escape, he locks himself into a tiger cage, which literally turns him into an animal on display, provoking the zoo visitors' and film viewers' derision. In all these scenes, the audience (along with the law-abiding zoo visitors) is encouraged to see the human character as a quasi-animal who has bestialized himself by violating zoo regulations, and who therefore deserves abjection by the collective or those recognized as good socialist subjects. In other words, the more the human resembles an animal in his appearance, behavior, and existential situation, the more animalist and abject he becomes.

Interwoven with this narrative is documentary footage that introduces the zoo animals in simple pedagogical terms, showing them enjoying their "scientifically" constructed houses and play zones (featuring imitation trees, climbing structures, and swimming pools, as well as air conditioning and heating) in the now-socialist institution, the Beijing Zoo. As Hou states in the framing crosstalk performance, the zoo is better equipped than the human performers' homes. The pleasing imagery of docile animals in their replica "homes" suggests that they are accepted as legitimate residents of the zoo, and conditional hospitality (à la Derrida) is granted to them in exchange for their toeing the line and remaining in their designated zones. The successful biogovernance in the newly renamed socialist zoo mirrors the socialist governance of reformed, new human subjects. The docile zoo animals, therefore, are presented as quasi-new humans who have transitioned from their past natural habitats to their present zoo "homes." Some of them (such as the elephant) have learned to follow human instructions to sit or dance. By promoting this benign animality as an assimilable form of Otherness—eligible for hospitality in the socialist institution (the Beijing Zoo), the documentary footage complements the socialist discourse of thought reform, reeducation, and elimination of abject dehumanizing animalism.

In satirizing an animalized human trespasser in the narrative, while celebrating the zoo animals' grace and docility in the documentary footage, the film inserts a notion of animality between the dyad of the animalistic and the human. If the abject "old" and the animalistic are associated with the derided human protagonist (as in An Unfinished Comedy), and the "new" and the "human" are embodied by the well-disciplined zoo visitors, then the zoo animals represent benign animality, their contained behaviors rendering them the assimilable Other approximating the quasi-new human. Yet, occupying the slippery middle ground, teetering on the edge of animalism, animality not only mediates but also eventually collapses the human and the animalist, calling into question the socialist biogovernance and its conditions of hospitality.

Hou Baolin, the crosstalk performer who played the trespasser (his first-ever dramatic role), commented on the challenge of acting with animals: "You have to not only do your duty for your own role, but also pay close attention to your animal partner. If the animal loses its temper, neither the actor nor the director could do anything about it."[30] Hou's observation demystifies the image of benign animality, pointing to the unstable line between the human, the animal, and the animalist in the human-animal coperformance. This line eventually breaks down when the human trespasser and the animals briefly share the same frame and are then juxtaposed through rapidly edited close-ups and shot-reverse shots.

Keeping the human character and the animal in the same frame through long shots and long takes enhances the "dramatic and moral value of the episode" and "carries us at once to the heights of cinematographic emotion," according to André Bazin.[31] The "heights of cinematographic emotion" derive from life's precarity writ large, that is, the raw, suspenseful competition in which one's survival comes at the price of another's extinguishment. Through unedited, prolonged coframing, the human and the nonhuman animals' lives are leveled in their equal precarity and contingency. Furthermore, the animal's pressing presence displaces anthropocentrism. Recognizing an animal's conspicuous presence (especially presence through death) in film, Vivian Sobchack argues that the rabbit's death in Renoir's *La Règle du jeu* (1939) "has a 'ferocious reality' that the [human] character's death does not. . . . [It] violently, abruptly, punctuates fictional space with documentary space."[32] Both Bazin and Sobchack emphasize nonhuman animals' ability to unravel the well-choreographed human film by embodying unpredictability and the realm of the real. In exceeding choreographed film language and challenging anthropocentric narratives, the ferociously real animality constitutes the absolute abject Other that shatters the conditions of human order and hospitality.

This abject animality verging on animalism is ostensibly missing in *A Nightmare in the Zoo*, for the animals under the zoo's socialist biogovernance predominantly serve pedagogical and entertainment purposes.[33] The ideological imperative for successful biogovernance, combined with the genre of comedy, eliminates dire contingencies (such as death or any other irreversible accident). Thus, in the few brief long shots where the trespasser and a tiger or a crocodile share the frame, the zoo visitors and the film audience are elicited to experience momentary fear, which quickly yields to laughter at the (safely) transgressive human. This well-managed affective stability forestalls the return of the abject and thereby deters what Bazin describes as the "heights of cinematographic emotion." The displacement of fear by laughter staves off the abject and reinforces the animals' orderly biogovernance (or their benign animality) as well as the broader state politics of the socialist zoo regime.

Nonetheless, the few brief long shots, followed by rapid cuts of extreme reaction close-up shots, do instigate a momentary yet significant glimpse into the abyss of the abject animality turning into animalism, which is not easily disavowed. In the series of extreme close-up shots following the trespasser's fall into a tiger enclosure, we see analogous facial expressions on all three parties (figures 5.4, 5.5, and 5.6)—the law-abiding zoo visitors (the socialist new human), the abject human trespasser (ridiculed for his animalism), and the tiger (animality granted conditional hospitality). Mirroring one another in their intense looks, the initial triad between humanity, animality, and animalism come to encounter *and embody* the same quasi-crisis of the nearly nullified order. The zoo cage dressed up as a hospitable home is visibly crumbling under the pressure of the unexpected abject outburst. To be sure, these intense extreme close-up shots soon yield to stability, as the law-abiding zoo visitors laugh at the human trespasser, while the tiger is safely kept away from the humans. Yet, brief as they are, these close-up shots embody the significant return and eruption of the abject.

If the crowd's choreographed docile laughter in most of the film expresses social conformity, evoking the "abstract machine of faciality" that the socialist laughter doctrine enforces, then the rapidly edited close-ups of the intense facial expressions tear apart such faciality. Like Han's and Yin's exaggerated facial expressions in *An Unfinished Comedy*, which were panned for gimmicky animalism and political retrogression, the analogously distorted faces of the trespasser, the tiger, and the momentarily agitated crowd dismantle socialist faciality by effacing the face. As Deleuze and Guattari put it, "When the face is effaced, when the faciality traits disappear, we can be sure that we have entered another regime, other zones infinitely muter and more imperceptible where subterranean becomings-animal occur, becomings-molecular, nocturnal deterritorializations over-spilling the limits of the signifying system."[34] Such effacement calls attention to subtle yet poignant moments when the authoritative, anthropocentric state ideology dissolves, yielding to new possibilities of meaning making, affect, and politics. In *An Unfinished Comedy* and *A Nightmare in the Zoo*, ostensible face making for the camera becomes face dissolving, and socialist placid faciality is taken over by intense fear, suspense, and ferocity, which distort the faces, rendering them illegible within the socialist episteme, thus converting them into abject animalism. Such abject animalism is not a dwindling residue from the past or from the West to be easily cleansed. It remains the substratum tearing through normative socialist laughing faciality, throwing the body politic and its hospitality into disarray while demanding a different signifying system.

Conclusion: Unleashing Abject Animalism

As the One Hundred Flowers campaign ground to a halt, yielding to the anti-Rightist campaign in June 1957, experiments with satire lost their political legitimacy. Discourses on animals and animalism took on new forms.

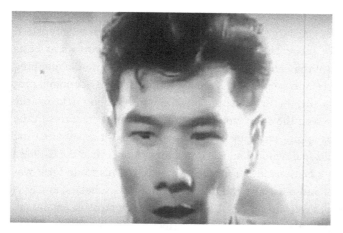

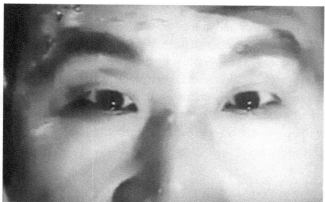

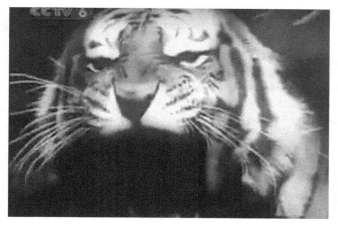

figures 5.4, 5.5, & 5.6 The zoo visitor, the trespasser, and the tiger all manifesting the analogous facial expression of tension and fear.

Literally, a campaign to exterminate four pests—mice, flies, mosquitos, and sparrows—was launched in February 1958, with the sparrows being replaced by cockroaches in 1960. The controversial inclusion of sparrows as pests was symptomatic of the central government's frenzied abjection of anything suspect in the system to guarantee its ideological purity and economic productivity. Symbolically, the Buddhist phrase "niu gui she sheng" (the ox, the demon, the snake, and the spirit, referring to supernatural creatures in the nether world) was appropriated by Mao, who resignified it as supernatural characters in traditional regional operas in his 1955 "A Speech at the Chinese Communist Party's Nationwide Propaganda Meeting." This same term was later used to label and persecute the Rightists, bourgeois scholars, and anybody considered not warranting socialist hospitality, thus creating an animalist outcast group that Bataille elsewhere describes as the abject disinherited waste population.[35]

As the discourses on animals and animalism spilled over from abjecting film workers and films to scapegoating all perceived political adversaries, satirical comedy on the screen was overtaken by black comedy and travesty in everyday life. Short-lived and obscured as 1950s socialist satirical comedy was, it unleashed a category of abject subhuman animalism that continued to haunt and circumscribe the socialist body politic. As such, animalist satiric comedy stands as the necessary abject that fundamentally frames socialist Chinese cinema and politics.

Notes

I would like to thank the editors, especially Maggie Hennefeld, and the reviewers for their helpful suggestions and meticulous editing. All remaining errors are my sole responsibility.

1 For a propagandist description of this campaign and the preceding Communist-initiated political movements, see Lu Dingyi, *Baihua qifang, baijia zhengming, jinian zhengfeng yundong shiwu zhounian* [Let one hundred flowers bloom, let one hundred schools contend: In memory of the fifteenth anniversary of the Yan'an Rectification Campaign] (Nanjing: Jiangsu renmin chubanshe, 1957).

2 Georges Bataille, "Abjection and Miserable Forms," in *More and Less*, ed. Sylvère Lotringer and Chris Kraus, trans. Yvonne Shafir (1934; Brooklyn, NY: Semiotext(e)/Autonomedia, 1999), 8–13, quotation at 10.

3 Gilles Deleuze and Félix Guattari, *A Thousand Plateaus: Capitalism and Schizophrenia*, trans. Brian Massumi (Minneapolis: University of Minnesota Press, 1987), 180.

4   Ackbar Abbas uses the concept of inter(dis)course to understand contemporary Chinese artist Xu Bing's installation/performance piece *A Case Study of Transference*, first performed in Beijing in 1994. Abbas describes the performance as "[c]opulating pigs with writing all over their bodies signify[ing] both intercourse and discourse (however nonsensical)." He states that the hybrid form challenges the audience, rendering the transference ironically impossible yet revelatory. See Ackbar Abbas, "China and the Human: A Visual Dossier," *Social Text* 30, no. 1 (Spring 2012): 91–108. Abbas's analysis of the literally mating pigs, whose bodies are inexplicably inscribed with Romanesque and Sinophonic writings, demonstrates the inevitable copulation between the human (civilization) and the animalist (drive), between the discourse and intercourse. Inter(dis)course, therefore, encapsulates the animalist underpinning of the human, be it socialist or postsocialist (as in Xu Bing's work).

5   Jacques Derrida and Anne Dufourmantelle, *Of Hospitality: Anne Dufourmantelle Invites Jacques Derrida to Respond*, trans. Rachel Bowlby (Stanford: CA: Stanford University Press, 2000), 135, 151–55.

6   Herbert Spencer, "The Physiology of Laughter," in *Illustrations of Universal Progress: A Series of Discussions* (New York: D. Appleton, 1864), 194–209. See Justin E. H. Smith, "Kant on Jokes" (paper presented to the Reflection on Art and Aesthetics Workshop, Montreal, April 9, 2009), http://www.jehsmith .com/philosophy/2009/04/kant-on-jokes.html; Immanuel Kant, *Critique of Judgment*, trans. John H. Bernard (New York: Cosimo, 2007), 134.

7   Henri Bergson, *Laughter: An Essay on the Meaning of Comic*, trans. Fred Rothwell and Cloudesley Brereton (New York: Dover, 2005), 4; Charles Baudelaire, "Of the Essence of Laughter, and Generally of the Comic in the Plastic Arts," in *Baudelaire: Selected Writings on Arts and Artists*, trans. with an introduction by P. E. Charvet (Cambridge: Cambridge University Press, 1981), 148. I thank Maggie Hennefeld for pointing my attention to Baudelaire's essay.

8   See Sun Hengcun, Ma Jing, and Li Jinfeng, *Fengci wenlei yanjiu* [A study of the genre of satire] (Chengdu: Sichuan University Press, 2013).

9   "Zai Yan'an wenyi zuotanhui shang de jianghua" [Talks at the Yan'an Forum on Literature and Art], *Jiefang ribao* [Liberation daily], October 19, 1943.

10 "Fengci xiju de yilei" [One type of satirical comedy], *Dushu yuebao* [Reading monthly], 5 (1957): 11.

11 Lv Ban, "Tantan wo de xinli hua" [My thoughts on making film], *Dazhong dianying* [Popular Cinema] 17 (1956), quoted in Wang Huazhen, "Wei wancheng de xiju: Lv Ban fengci xiju de chuangzuo ji dui qi pipan de shimo" [An Unfinished Comedy: How Lv Ban created his satirical comedies and how they were denounced], *Dianying xinzuo* [New works in cinema] 6 (2009): 44–47, quotation at 45.

12 Xu Fang, "Lv Ban de 'xiju'" [The "comedy" of Lv Ban], *Popular Cinema* 18 (1957); see Wang Huazhen, "Wei wancheng de xiju: Lv Ban fengci xiju de chuangzuo ji dui qi pipan de shimo," 46. Zhong Dianfei did not follow his cau-

tion to Lv, however. In his article "Dianying de luogu" [Drumming up cinema], published in December 1956 in *Wenyi bao* [Literature and art newspaper] and *Wenhui bao* [Mercury newspaper], he asked why the party directive of "arts serving workers, peasants and soldiers" had failed to produce films that really spoke to the audience. He further criticized the bureaucrats' officious control over film and other artistic creation as the root cause for reducing socialist cinema to slogan chanting and cardboard political lectures. This article was soon used to incriminate Zhong, making him a Rightist; criticized in August and September 1957, he was subsequently sent to the labor camp.

13 "Lv Ban shi xiongmeng de dangnei youpai fenzi" [Lv Ban is a ferocious Rightist within the Party], *Popular Cinema* 17 (1957). See Wang Huazhen, "Wei wancheng de xiju: Lv Ban fengci xiju de chuangzuo ji dui qi pipan de shimo," 44.

14 "Lv Ban shi ge fandang daoyan" [Lv Ban is an anti-Party film director], *Renmin ribao* [*People's Daily*], August 20, 1957.

15 I draw on Linda Williams's discussion of the body genre in her article "Film Bodies: Gender, Genre, and Excess," *Film Quarterly* 44, no. 4 (Summer 1991): 2–13.

16 For instance, one of Shanghai's most famous entertainment venues, called the Great World, built in 1917, boasted twelve funhouse mirrors as a major attraction.

17 The musical was first performed in 1921 in Shanghai and soon became a standing repertoire piece popular with Chinese communities in both China and Southeast Asia.

18 From the earliest existing comedy short, *The Love of a Laborer* [*Laogong zhi aiqing*] (1922) to the singular musical comedy, *Scenes of City Life* [*Dushi fengguang*] (1935), to the 1940s urban screwball comedies such as *Long Live the Madame* [*Taitai wansui*] (1947), Chinese comedy followed a similar trajectory as that of Hollywood comedy. Studies have considered their roots in vernacular modernism, their participation in Leftist social critique, and their witty depiction of urban sophisticates' war of the sexes.

19 Cai Chusheng, "You ducao jiude jinxing douzheng—zai *Meiyou wancheng de xiju* taolun dahui shang de zongjie fayan" [Where there is poisonous grass there is struggle—Closing remarks at the forum on *An Unfinished Comedy*], *Zhongguo dianying* [Chinese film], January 1958, 30–42.

20 Cai, "You ducao jiude jinxing douzheng," 33.

21 Cai, "You ducao jiude jinxing douzheng," 34.

22 Wang Renmei and Li Yunong, "Yanyuan de jiaoxun" [A lesson for actors], *Zhongguo dianying* [Chinese film] 3 (1958): 69–70.

23 Criticism of Han Langen and his supposedly gimmicky acting retained from the "old society" was already manifest in 1955, before Mao's official launching of the One Hundred Flowers campaign. In a letter to the editor of *Xiju bao* [Theater newspaper], Yao Lin, a self-identified young viewer, vehemently attacked Han's excessive clowning, ad-lib speech, and lack of makeup as pandering to retrogressive viewers and spreading the capitalist poison. Yao Lin, "Fandui Han Langen de xialiu yanchu" [Speaking against Han Langen's vulgar acting], *Xiju bao* [Theater newspaper] 2 (1955): 25.

24 Deleuze and Guattari, *A Thousand Plateaus*, 180.

25 Shi Dongshan, "Muqian dianying yishu de zuofa" [The current practices of film art], *Renmin ribao* [People's daily], August 7, 1949, emphasis mine.

26 Wang Wenlian, "Huijian xiju yanyuan Yin Xiuceng" [Meeting comedian Yin Xiuceng], *Renmin ribao* [People's daily], February 1957.

27 Pang Zhaolin, "Xiju yingxing Han Langeng de yiyuan" [The last will of comedian star Han Langeng], *Shanghai caifeng* [Shanghai anecdotes] 6 (2015): 55.

28 While Williams excludes comedy from her three "gross" body genres (i.e., pornography, horror, and melodrama), she defines the gross quality of the body genre as "the perception that the body of the spectator is caught up in an almost involuntary mimicry of the emotion or sensation of the body on the screen" ("Film Bodies," 4). This description reiterates Wang Renmei's perception of the bodily humor in Han and Yin's farce and its visceral impact on the audience.

29 Huo Zhuang, "Hou Baolin yu dianying" [Hou Baolin and film], *Dianying yishu* [Film art] 3 (2006): 61. In fact, the film's Chinese title, *Youyuan jingmeng*, literally meaning "an interrupted dream in the garden," is predominantly known as an episode in a sixteenth-century classical drama entitled *The Peony Pavillion* (Mudan ting). It was repeatedly adapted for the stage and was made into a Kunqu opera film in 1959–60, featuring Mei Lanfang, China's most well-known Peking opera performer. This episode later inspired the Taiwan novelist Bai Xianyong's landmark stream-of-consciousness short story of the same title, published in 1966. The 1956 short film has become completely obscured in the shadow of these well-known works of the same title.

30 Hou Baolin, "Wo yan Youyuan jingmeng" [Reflecting upon acting in *A Nightmare in the Zoo*], *Dazhong dianying* [Popular film] 2 (1957): 12–13.

31 André Bazin, *What Is Cinema?* vol. 1, trans. Hugh Gray (Berkeley: University of California Press, 1967), 49.

32 Vivian Sobchack, *Carnal Thoughts: Embodiment and Moving Image Culture* (Berkeley: University of California Press, 2004), 274.

33 In many other comedies produced in the same period, animals, especially livestock, are protected, even privileged, as they represent prosperity and the success of rural development. Two examples are *Falling into the River* [*Luoshui ji*] (dir. Zhou Feng, 1956), and *The Cuckoo Is Singing Again* [*Buguniao you jiao le*] (dir. Huang Zuolin, 1958). In *The Cuckoo Is Singing Again*, a Yorkshire pig awarded to a progressive production team attracts so much attention from the team leader that he neglects the human team members' interests. The film criticizes the team leader for privileging the nonhuman animal over the humans. Yet, it ended up being condemned for advocating individual humans' interests instead of focusing on collective politics.

34 Deleuze and Guattari, *A Thousand Plateaus*, 115.

35 Cheng Boda, "Hengsao yiqie niugui sheshen" [Sweeping away all oxen, demons, snakes, and spirits], *Renmin ribao* [People's daily], June 1, 1966; Bataille, "Abjection and Miserable Forms."

chapter six

Anticolonial Folly & the Reversals of Repatriation

rijuta mehta

And yet a remarkable thing happens in the experience of my fools: from them not only true things, but even sharp reproaches, will be listened to; so that a statement which, if it came from a wise man's mouth, might be a capital offense, coming from a fool gives rise to incredible delight.

—Erasmus, *The Praise of Folly*

God alone knows why the prosecution describes a short story as obscene when it is not even remotely so—if I want to mention a woman's breasts then I will call them a woman's breasts—a woman's breasts can't be called peanuts, or a table, or a shaving razor—though it has to be said that for some people the very existence of women is an obscenity, but what to do of that.

—Saadat Hasan Manto, *Lazzat-e Sang* [The taste of stones]

There is Diogenes' famous gesture, recounted so frequently in Antiquity, of masturbating in public and saying: But why are you scandalized, since masturbation satisfies a need, just as eating does? I eat in public, so why should I not satisfy this need also in public?

—Michel Foucault, *The Courage of Truth*

[After Partition] K. lived on in Pakistan [instead of returning to India like she was pressured to do]. . . . The common description of her was that she was like a dervish whose words had . . . oracular importance. She never moved out without a pistol, is supposed to have shot three intruders who entered her house when she was alone—and wrote reams of mystic poetry.

—Ritu Menon and Kamla Bhasin, *Borders and Boundaries*

Carrying implications of wretchedness and expulsion, abjection is crucial to theories and aesthetics of anticolonialism. In conceptions of freedom articulated by the colonized, abjection functions both as an injury to be redressed and as a mode of identitarianism consolidated through incapacity. Sewn together as negation and validation without the possibility of being only one at a time, abjection is a methodological presupposition in anticolonial thought, an unquestioned convenience by which down-and-out situations enable freedom without actualizing its attainment. In classic anticolonial texts like Aimé Césaire's *Discourse on Colonialism* (1950) and Frantz Fanon's *Black Skin, White Masks* (1952), as well as more recent interventions, such as Andrea Smith's *Conquest: Sexual Violence and American Indian Genocide* (2005) and Katherine McKitrrick's "Mathematics Black Life" (2014), there appears a vital doubleness to the work of abjection: not only does it undergird theories of the split subject who, choking, trembling, and nauseous with anger and self-contempt, disintegrates under the colonial gaze, but abjection also governs political demands for dignity, liberty, equality, and reparations. In anticolonial thought, abjection creates a scenario of freedom akin to the phoenix about to rise from its ashes. For example, the colonized in Fanon's schema tragically lose a corporeal perception of their own, but at the same time, the dazzling poetics of corporeality in *Black Skin, White Masks* resets and rearticulates the abject body beyond the limit set for it by the colonial gaze. Fanon's famous prayer to his body at the end of *Black Skin*—"O my body, make of me always a man who questions"—is an entreaty for an embodied reason that is immanent to abjection, a reason that is always about to be, but not yet, formulated. Abjection is crucial to anticolonialism because it occasions its own breach, offering the possibility of a new future, a new past, and a new human rising from incapacity and injury at any given moment.

In M. K. Gandhi's *Hind Swaraj* (*Indian Home Rule*, 1909), an early dialogue on anticolonial ethics, the colonized fall prey to neocolonialism because they aim merely to replace the white race in its indomitability instead of transforming the very structure of sovereignty that white supremacy imposed on them. To address this knotty problem of colonialism perpetuated by the colonized, Gandhi rethinks sovereignty by turning to self-abjection, rather than indomitability, as an essential precursor and a regular habit for the cultivation of home rule, or national independence. Here, abjection entails the practice of maintaining one's body as wrecked—neither wretched nor prosperous but always in close relation to one's incapacity and privation.[1] Abjection offers the colonized subject the freedom to act contrary to her own immediate self-interest, with the calculation that voluntary self-ruination is a route out of the reversals of the master-slave dialectic, which, Gandhi's concern is, makes everyone a slave to the project of mastery. Gandhi's anticolonialism insists on renouncing "bodily welfare" as a hindrance to truth and freedom. Only an interest in remaining abject leads to the possibility of true freedom in *Hind Swaraj*, a freedom wherein one does not become the master once one breaks the chains of enslavement.[2] The colonizing master is ruined mainly through his disinterest in abjection because, for Gandhi, true freedom lives on through and emerges in relation to abjection. Therefore, surprisingly, a nonrelation to abjection, a nonrelation to privation and incapacity, is the chink in the master's indomitable armor. Only the colonized are primed for true freedom.

Anticolonialism in Fanon and Gandhi legitimizes the colonized as not simply abject but, rather, as the one who *knows* abjection by always being in relation to it. Though "thingified"—borrowing Aimé Césaire's blunt idiom— the colonized is a knowing thing. To that extent, anticolonial thought is the first patent taken out by the colonized on the potentiality of abjection, since abjection and, resultantly, freedom (including the freedom not to do as the master does) are what the master cannot know from his position of mastery. Putting abjection beyond the master's conception is a fundamental move in Gandhi's anticolonialism, a move made to undermine the routine understanding that indomitability is better than incapacity. But tempting as it is either to celebrate or to dismiss this ethical gesture, it is more generative to ask if anticolonialism might have missed the irony of arguing against mastery while holding on to abjection as a calculable option that will produce a general good and true freedom, just not *yet* but at any given moment after right now. If ethics and knowledge based on mastery might always misfire, are not ethics and knowledge based on abjection also susceptible to radical incalculability? The hope and the potential of a good and true freedom are not to be conflated with its actualization, and irony, I would argue, reflects a measure of the distance between them. My essay is not so much a plotting of the ways in which anticolonial thought has used abjection but, rather, a close reading of the turns, crossings, surprises, impasses, interruptions, detours, and reversals that mark anticolonial aesthetics when it attempts to represent the incapacity and injury of the colonized. In the aesthetics of anticolonialism, the figure of irony often runs counter to the theoretical desire to master abjection. Jonathan Lear argues in *A Case for Irony* (2011) that irony is "a form of existence," "a form of not being sure" about what it means to become human.[3] More than a witty turn of phrase, irony, for Lear, taking Kierkegaard's example of Socrates, demonstrates that becoming human is an uncertain adventure, and thus irony makes the human. Drawing on the formal aspect of Lear's argument, I suggest that irony is the form by which uncertainty and incalculability are introduced into abjection, a practice in anticolonial ethics that runs the risk of being as programmable as the master's conception of freedom. Irony operates to upset the assumption that the incapacitated know no mastery and that the master knows no incapacity.

With South Asian independence from British rule through a horrifyingly violent Partition of population and territory (1947), the colonized in South Asia became masters, giving new life to colonialism and giving credence to Gandhi's dire warnings about the misfiring of an anticolonialism based on mastery. But this definite misfiring does not guarantee that an anticolonialism based on abjection will never miss its mark. In fact, it is crucial to understand how freedom appears from the point of view of abjection, and anticolonial aesthetics enables us to understand precisely this. Through an analysis of Saadat Hasan Manto's darkly comic Urdu-language short stories, written in the aftermath of the Partition of India and Pakistan, as well as archival photographs of incapacitated women taken in post-Partition repatriation camps, I argue that irony and abjection are co-constitutive forms in anticolonialism, sometimes working as rivals and other times as allies. In anticolonial aesthetics, irony certainly shows how masterful freedom injures, but more importantly, it also makes us unsure about the purchase abjection has on freedom. Closely reading a few of Manto's frequently anthologized short stories, namely "Thanda Gosht" ("Cold Meat"), "Khol Do" ("Open It"), "Toba Tek Singh," and "Bu" ("Smell"), my chapter demonstrates that abjection is comedy's difference from itself rather than its opposite. The truth-telling persona of licensed lunacy—from the uncertain existence of a Socrates to Erasmian folly to Shakespearean fools—reappears in Manto's anticolonial humanism when injured characters are mobilized to speak truth to power or made to withhold truth vital to power. But the cover of injury is fragile at all times and in all epochs, and Manto's abject comedies landed him in court various times for authoring obscene works.

Unlike theory and literature, photography's representation of abject individuals has laid it open to moral condemnation on the charge of voyeuristic exploitation. Such condemnation implies that the ethical gesture in photography is limited to simply refusing to represent the abject individual on the assumption that her compliance with being photographed is nothing but a sign of her incapacity to act otherwise. Photographs of abject women in transit camps after the Partition, thus, seem like the last place to discover irony, but instead of relegating these photographed subjects to powerlessness, I bring the photos together with voices in autobiography and witness testimony to ask what—if any—acts of freedom we might uncover if we took irony to be a part of photographic language.[4] What surprises do images of incapacitated women hold for us? In the account that follows, irony offers ways to agitate the cry of powerlessness and incapacity, especially the powerlessness of "rescued" women who are captured in these photographs, and comes to the forefront to disrupt both abjection and mastery.

Visualizing Apparent Rape

Anticolonialism is trapped in an impossible logic: the opposition to colonialism becomes the means of its persistence. Independence from British rule through the Partition of India and Pakistan is one such failure of opposition, where the gendered repatriation of populations makes comparable colonial and decolonial states. The Partition was an event that founded the independent states of India and Pakistan in 1947 through the transfer of 14 million people across borders deliberately drawn to segregate Hindus and Muslims. It was characterized by the abduction, rape, and genocide of millions of women of all religions. From 1947 to 1956, women became the targets of militarized "search and rescue operations," so that Hindu and Sikh women in the borderlands were forcibly brought to India and Muslim women to Pakistan. These search and rescue operations were photographed intensively, and the resulting images were housed across state, humanitarian, and photojournalistic archives in the subcontinent, Europe, and America.

What kinds of difference did the camera make to the exchange of women that founded the states of India and Pakistan? What does the medium do with the injury of repatriation? Fanon's notion of "muscular tension," the nervous condition of the native whose latent corporeality of humiliation and anger erupts in fratricidal violence during anticolonial political movements, traverses both abjection and indomitability, activity and passivity, silence and quiet, becoming a useful tool for theorizing the photographic pose of women in the transit camp.

Apparent mass rape emerges in South Asian portrait photography with the repatriation portrait, 1947 onward. It appears as a chorus staged unexceptionally. As Ariella Azoulay has argued in her work in the Israeli/Palestinian context, the "unexceptional" photograph is a good place to think rape. I interpret unexceptionality as a call to reconstruct rape's representation beyond the signs of force and resistance, such as the ripped dress, the scream

figure 6.1 "'Rescued' non-Muslim women who arrived in the Ganga Ram Transit Camp in Lahore in February 1948 from Campbellpore and Kunja refugee camps in Pakistan for evacuation to India under military escort." Photo and caption by Photo Division, Ministry of Information and Broadcasting, Government of India.

off-screen, or the structuring absence of a closed door. A group portrait of "rescue and repatriation" taken at a transit camp hospital in Lahore, Pakistan, is presented to the spectator as the end of the atrocity, rather than a continuation of it (figure 6.1). It shows a group of women and children, huddled together on the hospital terrace, their faces underlit in the bright sunshine of a cold February morning in 1948. A caption describes this group as "rescued" without saying from whom or what. As we look closely at the image, the mysteries multiply if we stop seeing degradation as an endpoint. Why are the rescued subjects on top of a building, exposed to the elements on a freezing morning? How long did they try to shield their eyes in the blinding light? Who are they? These are questions by which one wants to reach some sort of certainty, the aperture by which insight will open. To an extent, it does open, if we turn to the literary genre of autobiography.

In the Gujarati-language memoir *Mool Sootan Ukhdelan* (*Torn from the Roots*, 1982) of Kamla Patel, an Indian humanitarian worker who received a "rescued" group of six hundred women at the transit hospital, she narrates their arrival at length, even if she does not mention a camera or reproduce images in her text. "Their bodies were full of sores, their clothes were dirty and torn, and their hair full of lice. . . . For six months these women had not had any salt. . . . They could take a bath only once in every fifteen days. . . . In the 180-mile truck journey [to the camp], they had been given no drinking water."[5] The feast prepared to welcome the women had to be discarded, for all six hundred of them were dying of starvation and could not digest the rich food. So—the memoir continues—light porridge was cooked in the middle of the night, as the relief workers dealt with more deaths in the group, and the next morning Patel awoke to find that

> not only were all the bathrooms . . . full of excreta, but the entire passage and even some beddings had been soiled. It was impossible to even stand and look at this sight. I began wondering how to solve the problem. The sweepers, who were assigned the task of cleaning up our camp, were hardly enough to cope with this almost gigantic task. . . . I made the women and the children sit out in the sunshine in the large compound of the hospital, as well as its terrace, and requested the Pakistani authorities, for about 10 sweepers to clean up the whole place.[6]

This is presumably when the photograph was taken.

This partial reconstruction shows us that the image of apparent rape in the moment of repatriation reveals a certain blankness in a field beset by the plenitude of violence. This blankness arises from the obscure lives of the women: their faces cannot be matched with accounts of missing and abducted women; their names and narration are gaps. What the photograph shows us visually is this very blankness, an uncommunicative blackout in the sunlight. The photo of apparent rape reveals to us the limit of insight without the renunciation of sight, generating the possibility that more might be rigorously imagined because so little can be certainly known. The limit of insight is different from the refusal of humanitarian workers to probe into "what really happened" to their subjects. The limit of insight represents the turn to the indecipherable and irretrievable in anticolonial critique as a necessary response to structural violence and the mandatory circulation of women. A method of critical speculation is available to the scholar when she reaches the thresholds of archival recovery. In Saidiya Hartman's meditations on black women's lives lost along the transatlantic slave route, what is available is "critical fabulation" along and against the grain of the archive, the method of "narrative restraint, the refusal to fill in the gaps and provide closure" when there is none to be found, and "the imperative to respect" that which exceeds the discoverable.[7] Critical fabulation is thus a narrative conceit of restraint, narration via a performative refusal to narrate. And Hartman declares that she is "unsure if it is possible to salvage an existence from a handful of words" about the murder of a slave girl named Venus. While I agree with Hartman's assessment of irreparable loss in the archive of slavery, the rhetoric of recovery is worrying here because of the theory of language behind it, a theory where irretrievability is a matter of word count. Let us remember the irretrieval of Gayatri Spivak's Bhuvaneswari Bhaduri in "Can the Subaltern Speak?" where Bhaduri, an anticolonial agent, had not only written an entire letter of explanation for her suicide but carried out an act of writing with her menstruating body—all with the hope of making her anticolonialism legible through an abject body. While the distance separating Hartman's Venus and Spivak's Bhaduri is great, each enables us to account for colonized women's hope of being heard under erasure.

In Saadat Hasan Manto's Urdu-language four-page short story "Khol Do" ("Open It"), the geographic exchange of women in Partition unfolds as the displacement of meaning. The narrative climax rests on the exchanged woman who activates the double entendre of the phrase "open it." Sakina, a teenager who is abducted, recovered, apparently gang raped, and recovered again in a comatose state, lies inert and corpse-like on a hospital stretcher when she hears the instruction "open it" and immediately unfastens the drawstrings of her pants. Her action is driven by automatic audio violence, for Sakina cannot see that the doctor examining her, in giving the command "open it" to his orderly, has, in fact, pointed to the closed window to let some air into the hospital. In the doctor's innocuous iteration of a command that Sakina might have heard often during the days of her abduction by the group of her supposed rescuers, the referent is not Sakina but a window: "The window, open it." The corpse-like Sakina, however, taken for dead at the hospital, is attested as living through her automatic movement to unfasten her trousers. The doctor "breaks out in a cold sweat," but her father "exclaims joyously" that his daughter is indeed alive, in the closing line of this gut-wrenching short story. The near total evacuation of sentiment in the characters' and narrator's diegesis until this final flare-up of feeling amplifies the sledgehammer of a conclusion.

In her comatose state, Sakina, the subject whose structural and psychological point of view we never occupy, takes the phrase "open it" at its word.

Irony operates here not by dissimulation but by things being taken at their word in the ground of exchange, by the perfect coherence between the living corpse, her automated muscle memory, and the ears' openness to the spoken phrase "open it." I argue that through the structure of ironic iteration—in the break between what Sakina hears, what is audible and seeable to other characters, and what we read—we recognize the violence of repair as a repetition of the violence of rape. In the double entendre, the reader discovers automated discipline as violent punishment. The difference is that the atrocity this time is not visited directly on Sakina's body but is a medical examination ascertaining life.

The condition of impossibility for Manto's "returned" woman is her scene of retrieval: a scene where the audible spark of rape—"open it"—and the automation of muscular conditioning, of blind obedience, suffice for the father to know that his daughter is alive and returned to him. This scene of retrieval is impossible without the father, but retrieval is also impossible because of him. The text is ironic not only because of the titular, double/mixed-up meaning but also because the father's joyful interpretation of Sakina's denuding gesture demonstrates that her indecipherability unfolds narratively only to be interpreted inappropriately, only to be determined proprietorially as life.

Recent interpretations of "Open It" demand a disambiguation of the denuding gesture—whether Sakina's denuding is intentional, whether she is alive, whether the doctor's reaction verifies rape, whether the father ignores rape. It is true that Sakina's father, in a benevolent fatherly fashion, *apostrophizes* as life, rather than treat as only lifelike, his daughter's blind obedience to a destructive command. But Manto's reader, she who sustains the textual contract of dark humor and cruel irony, is expected to know better than the father: the pleasure of this text comes precisely because the reader is not a dupe like the father, because she can see irony at work. The figure of irony cannot unfold if the reader takes up the position of the father, as Veena Das's reading of "Open It" requires of the reader in its affirmation of life. Sakina's state needs to be undecidable for literary form to unfold.[8] No patriarchal glorification of life—and no anthropological reading of positive homemaking in the wake of annihilation—can retrieve the irretrievability that we confront in "Open It" through the device of the double entendre. Sakina on the stretcher stages not the optimism of woman's life-making, as Veena Das would have it, but the unsentimental margin of irony's work.

In the transit camp, infants were legally dekinned from their mothers. The Central Recovery Operation could pay no heed to blood relations between mother and child because of its focus on restoring patriarchal domestic ties, precisely because the objective was to correct property transactions, not to unravel the kinship crisis brought on by forced dispersion. Yet, in the transit camp, where the nullification of mothers' rights was underway, we find traces of a mother-child photographic genealogy, traces that form a pietà of repatriation.

In figures 6.2, 6.3, and 6.4, taken from the state, photojournalistic and humanitarian archive, women hold their infants quietly in the absence of fathers. Rather undramatically, genealogy is forged without the father, making it possible to emphasize an anticolonialism without patriarchs. The analogy between family and anticolonial state no longer holds up when women assume mothers' rights in the wake of exceptional homelessness, compulsory circulation, and the general law of the father that reorganized entire nation-states. The performance of photographic genealogy forges a space of anticolonial intimacy within the legal terrain of dispossession and mothers' rightslessness.

This pietà of repatriation (figure 6.4) plays with the meaning of rescue and what Hortense Spillers has called the "confusions of consanguinity" that derive from an absent father in the conferral of legitimacy.[9] In the official caption, the word "rescued" is marked off within scare quotes, raising the question of what "rescued" really meant, whether it was a euphemism for rape and/or its redress, the ambiguity demonstrating that even photographic statements made during rescue operations were themselves skeptical about rescue as actual rescue. The unnamed woman, by her frontal pose, looks out of the image, with a half-exposed neonatal infant in her arms, retaining within herself the air of meditative quiet but also the muscular tension of the one who poses. While it echoes conventions of classical iconography, this repatriation portrait of a woman and a neonatal infant together in a transit camp is surprising to encounter within the situation of search and rescue after Partition, when most "rescued" women were forced to leave behind their babies before they were repatriated, on the assumption that babies were the unwanted consequences of rape and were better off with their fathers or in foster homes or orphan refugee camps. The subject of this portrait appears neither conjugal nor virginal, neither committed to anonymity nor desirous of differentiation, but rather in the *hum* of muscular tension. Unlike images of street demonstrators, picketers, boycotters, and hunger strikers, who constituted the classic anticolonial subject of resistance prior to 1947, the repatriation portrait forces a change in the conception of anticolonial action, affiliating such action with quiet. The meditative feminine who acts by being quiet disrupts the dominant understandings of resistance and freedom.

figure 6.2 "Indo-Pakistan Conflict 1948–1950. Indian Bengal, Dhubulia. Refugee camp." Photo and caption by Red Cross.

figure 6.3 Bert Brandt, "Victims of Religious Strife," Delhi, 1947.

figure 6.4 "Photograph taken of 'rescued' non-Muslim woman and child who arrived in the Ganga Ram Transit Camp in Lahore in February 1948 (from Campbellpore and Kunja refugee camps in Pakistan) for evacuation to India under military escort." Photo and caption by Photo Division, Ministry of Information and Broadcasting, Government of India.

"The hum of the portrait"—to use the words of photo theorist Tina Campt, who characterizes the sonic registers of an image through the phrase "quiet photography"—is "neither silent nor inaudible" but necessitates that we ask "at what frequencies do these images become audible or intelligible?"[10] With the repatriation portrait, we might say that only under the disruption of abjection as utter powerlessness does the chorus of "rescued" women become available, not in the loudness of protest or power reversal, not in a lament over incapacity, but in the steady hum of living after and with apparent rape.

The search and rescue operations between 1947 and 1953 were carried out mostly by women humanitarian workers liaising with military evacuation units. A densely packed point-of-view shot (figure 6.5), taken from inside a crowd of men, sets apart Mridula Sarabhai, the head of the recovery operation, principally by the gesture of her open righthand palm. Woman as negotiator between state officials and familial patriarchs keeps out of sight the repatriated women for whom she speaks. Everyone else is so cramped in the small space that they must fold their hands tightly to fit in. The slight luxury of interstitial space between Sarabhai and her framed audience echoes the colonial politics of sexual segregation that made such a photograph, and the very idea of a recovery operation for women, possible in the first place. This is one way to plot the contradictions of a South Asian feminism that was co-opted by the militarized state and of a joint humanitarian operation that resulted in women's nonconsensual repatriation of women.

In an instantly perceivable manner, this image is a diagram of the women's recovery operation, because women, the subjects of Sarabhai's program and the discussion pictured here, are missing in the frame. The existence of this undated and unattributed image also implies that the humanitarian workers, the doctors, or the army men took cameras or camerapersons with them. There is anecdotal evidence in her biography to suggest that photographs were, in fact, taken.[11] The biography has many accounts of Sarabhai rushing out in the midst of a Hindu-Muslim riot, once with a camera, and managing to bring calm to a volatile situation. My contention is that the history of antiracist feminist humanitarianism should not be limited to the situation of search and rescue but should also be recognized as operating wherever a woman disrupts the path of racial-colonial chauvinistic violence.

In the last decade, internet groups and social media websites have started to crowdsource interviews with Partition survivors in a bid to change the narrative. "Reunion," the viral 2013 Google advertisement in which childhood friends separated by Partition are reunited by the ability of their descendants to use the search engine, captured how the popular imagination has

figure 6.5 Mridula Sarabhai with refugees in West Punjab. Date and photographer unknown.

now moved beyond the horror of Partition toward the trope of reunification and reparation between men through their descendants. Today, women of the Partition are being recast as militant rescuers on horseback, as seen in Guneet Singh Bhalla's oral history project documenting the testimonies of Partition survivors:

> One afternoon I interviewed ninety-three-year-old Bhim Sharma in a machine parts shop in Punjab. He recalled the day his village in West Punjab was surrounded by mobs. The entire village was holed up in one house. When hope was nearly lost, three women rode in from behind a hill on horseback. Masked as men with turbans on their heads and straps of ammunition wrapped around their bodies, they caught the mob unawares and lobbed grenades at the leader. He was killed instantly, and the mob dispersed. The women then escorted the villagers to safety.
>
> Months later, and thousands of miles away in California, Kuldip Kaur corroborates Sharma's story, recalling the three women on horseback who defended the caravan she was in when it was being attacked by mobs.[12]

rijuta mehta

This fantastic tale, very satisfying and more than a little thrilling to hear, and, in a rare windfall for research, even corroborated at a diasporic level, transfigures Partition's quarry into combative rescuers / masked anarchists that we cannot help but want. They are masked, they are unidentified, and they galvanize inaccessibility and irretrievability with a vengeance. While the romance of resistance in the archive of apparent mass rape is naturally suspect, this personification of our collective feminist desire, this moment of hurrah that comes without any foreshadowing when we have sunk so deep in the quicksand of horrific misogyny, is indeed a gift that beggars the imagination. Untrammeled by bureaucratic maneuvering, both in the act of freedom and in the researcher's ease of access, the three militant and masked queer feminist rescuers embody the practice of critical fabulation. But this gift does not come at the expense of those acts of freedom that are quieter, that might have to be *read* into the light of day from the invisibility by which they are obscured.

Injury to women results in a breakdown of rescue and in the ascension of the punitive feminine in Saadat Hasan Manto's short story about lust, death, and rape in the Partition, "Thanda Gosht" ("Cold Meat," 1950).[13] After Kulwant Kaur, the spirited but jealous lover of Sikh protagonist Ishar Singh, stabs him in bed with his own dagger, he narrates to her the cause of his sexual impotence: upon abducting and raping a Muslim girl during the Partition, Singh had made the (to him) body-and-soul-numbing discovery that his victim had been as cold as a corpse all along. "Thanda Gosht" does not concern itself with why necrotic rape is worse than rape, but by the end of the short story, which spans all of five pages, Singh is the cold corpse. Manto, a master of quick-and-dirty narrative irony, uses a title that refers both to the summarily dismissed rape victim and to her rapist, Ishar Singh, a Scheherazade-like figure whose end is tied up with the end of the rape story he tells and occurs at the hands of his unsympathetic lover, Kulwant Kaur. The rapist is a victim of the irony of his own words in that his narration about raping a corpse makes him into an abject corpse. At a historical moment of de facto amnesty for rapists in the Partition, it is not coincidental that this text has its rapist bleed to death.

[Kulwant Kaur said,] "If you dare to lie to me, I'll cut you into pieces. Now swear by Waheguru that you weren't with another woman."

Guiltily, Ishar Singh shook his head. Kulwant Kaur lost her head. She snatched the dagger lying in the corner, pulled it out of its scabbard and lunged at Ishar Singh.

Blood began to spurt out of the wounds. Still unsatisfied, Kulwant Kaur began to claw at his face like a mad cat and to curse the nameless woman.[14]

How should a feminist read a male author's plot of female jealously over a male lover who is impotent because he has just returned from raping a corpse of the enemy religion? As the passage cited above confirms, the narrative action is motivated by Kaur's desire for Singh's confession. Doubtless, Manto makes Kaur speak in Singh's voice ("curse the nameless woman") and looks at her through Singh's eyes ("like a mad cat"), but also evident and startling is that Kaur's sexuality is not Singh's prerogative. Rather, it is the other way around. Through the imperative of brevity in "Thanda Gosht," the romance plot, the rape plot, the impotence plot, and the revenge plot converge on two women: Kaur, the green-eyed madwoman, avenges the murder-rape of the unnamed victim. The paternalism of rescue—an illusion enabling the subjugation of women—is wholly exploded in the surreal mise-en-scène of Kulwant Kaur watching Ishar Singh bleed to death without lifting a finger to rescue him. Kaur's quiet nonrescue of Singh is as much an action as the punishment she has meted out. The impotence of the rapist, his failure to reach arousal in a consenting encounter, and the climax with blood spurting out instead of semen establish the co-constitution of irony and abjection. Not only does his death coincide with the closure of his narration of the rape, but the rape produces impotence. The abject corpse of rape reverses into the punitive abjection of the rapist in the aesthetics of repatriation.

To insist on finding only absolute degradation in the photographic and literary representation of repatriated woman is as perverse as fabulating a fiction that bestows freedom and agency on her, and yet, a critical fabulation in the wake of abjection can interrupt the prescribed lure of absolute degradation and enable anticolonial feminism to ask how abjection is not self-identical but entails an imagination and performance of freedom in incalculable ways, different from the promise of a good and true freedom as sought in Gandhi.

The Uses of Folly

Manto's classic short story "Toba Tek Singh," named after the village and birthplace of its protagonist Bishan Singh, portrays the shoring up and the dissolution of masculine subjectivity through the folly of loving one's home more than oneself. A gibe at the project of population removal, the tale is set in a mental asylum in Lahore, where the announcement of territorial remapping causes tragicomic befuddlement in the madmen, who are told that they will be exchanged between the states of India and Pakistan. The premise is that those expelled from society, those who inhabit a parallel dimension of lunacy, are subject to the even greater folly of the sovereign state and its lunatic laws, which make horrific repatriation identical to glorious freedom. Compared to the rest of Manto's oeuvre, this is only a modestly hellish premise. There are no corpses being raped or corpse-like women unfastening their trousers. Ironic discourse in "Toba Tek Singh" vindicates a madman's sovereign performance of inertia as true freedom, a performance that is as potent as it is fragile. Bishan Singh resists repatriation while two nations around him are tottering toward annihilation under unjust dictates. He collapses with a shriek after a night of standing unchallenged "like a Colossus" in no man's land between the territorial boundaries of India and Pakistan. "Toba Tek Singh" stages an aesthetic challenge to the abject space of the frontier through the figure of Bishan the Colossus, who has nothing disintegrable about him but who nonetheless collapses from statuesque exhaustion. Singh's potent gesture of becoming a statue, free from the dubious freedom of nation-state sovereignty, of becoming a master of his own coming or going—his discourse—is a profoundly fragile one since it ends in his own annihilation. Manto's lunatic becomes the Colossus by choosing death instead of abjection but ends as an abject corpse whose wholeness is bound to territorial disintegration by being expelled from both terrains.

The action in "Toba Tek Singh" begins with the joint decision of the two new states to repatriate and commit Hindu and Sikh madmen from Pakistan to mental institutions in India and to bring Muslim madmen from India to mental institutions in Pakistan. If there was any doubt that Manto intended to lampoon the irredeemable insanity of the Partition decision, or make his readers unconsciously condemn their own justification of Partition, it is resolved by the narrative voice and its free indirect style, which feigns ignorance to match the diegetic characters' genuine befuddlement: "Whether this [exchange] was a reasonable or unreasonable idea is difficult to say. . . . As to where Pakistan was located, the inmates knew nothing. That was why both the mad and the partially mad were unable to decide whether they were now in India or in Pakistan. If they were in India, where on earth was Pakistan? And if they were in Pakistan, then how come that until only the other day it was India?"[15]

The ironic discourse of "Toba Tek Singh" includes utterances of many lunatic characters, from inmates to doctors to state agents, as well as a wisely foolish narrative persona who protests the Partition by dropping the reporting clauses when relaying their utterances. Thus framed, ironic discourse provides the reader with an opportunity to see the aesthetic undoing of repatriation's will to abjection, because repatriation, the mark of nation-state freedom as unfreedom, descends into misdirection, displacement, and zany performances of dissent: "One day a Muslim lunatic, while taking his bath, raised the slogan 'Pakistan Zindabad' [Long live Pakistan] with such enthusiasm that he lost his footing and was later found lying on the floor unconscious."[16] Patriotic sloganeering plays out as the classic joke of slipping on a banana peel. The narrator seems to know and weigh ironic reversal well, as more of an observer than a sufferer of it, indicated by the series of insane reaction shots after the announcement of repatriation: one patient takes off all his clothes and runs into the garden stark naked; another climbs a tree and decides to stay there since the tree is neither India nor Pakistan; and so on.

Life goes on, chastened by comic lessons in which the relation to abjection has no lasting denigration of the soul. Manto's outcasts find neither the lofty extravagance of sovereign violence nor the depths of revolting degradation. Buffoonery recues abjection from that which is nauseating to that which is amusingly awkward. Undoubtedly, with "Toba Tek Singh," Manto is not attempting to write abject comedy as merely abject, because when he does write extreme abjection, without irony, as in the short story "Bu" ("Smell"), his writing starts to smell at the level of the sentence.[17] Every aspect of the narrative machinery is made too disgusting to be pleasurable. Narrated from the point of view of a heterosexual young man named Randheer, "Bu" transvalues femininity, race, and the fetish for abjection. Randheer finds the clean and scented "milky-white" body of his well-to-do bride "immensely revolting," "like the sour belches of indigestion. A pathetic, sickly smell. . . . The femininity in her being seemed strangely compressed . . . the way white globs float listlessly in colorless liquid when the milk has gone bad."[18] Randheer desires the abject tribal woman (coded brown) and rejects the powerful bourgeois woman (coded white) as truly abject. The mixed metaphor of white globs in rancid milk combined with the belch of indigestion takes abjection in the postcolonial context away from the question of incapacity and into the realm of capacity. For Randheer, the little horrors of the everyday derive from the possibility of ungoverned female sexuality in the bourgeois rights-bearing woman. The woman in privation holds no power to disgust or horrify Randheer. Rather, ironically, the abject can be located where capacity terrorizes him at the strange intersection of race and gender.

The comic element in Manto's texts, especially in "Bu," often develops out of his own gleeful transgression of the politics of good taste and respectability in Urdu literature, a transgression for which he was brought to court on obscenity charges more than five times in his short life. In "Toba Tek Singh," in contrast, Manto unsettles the comic by never once appearing to transgress the bounds of propriety.[19] Not only did the tale's politics of Colossus-as-phallus escape the charges of "obscenity," "filth," and "uncleanness," but the lunatic's erect body, never explicitly offered or recognized as a statement about sexuality, is presented as a point of unproblematic sympathetic identification for the audience. The madman Singh, who, the narrator tells us, has been standing erect on his feet for fifteen years, on "two swollen legs" in the Lahore asylum, who goes by the name of his village, Toba Tek Singh, ends "like a Colossus," declaring, "This is Toba Tek Singh" in the no man's land.[20] Slyly, Manto inserts the nonserious, apparently irrelevant detail of Singh's unnaturally erect body, using madness as a cover for sexuality. With "Toba Tek Singh," Manto undermines his self-declared ethics of plain speech, his habit of calling a spade a spade, expressed in his famous statement against obscenity (see epigraph), a statement made in favor of using the proper word in the proper place, fearlessly and without shame, because breasts must be called breasts, not peanuts. Much like the public masturbation of cynic Diogenes, who likened ingestion to ejaculation, thus confusing the acceptable orifice with the unacceptable one, Manto's writing is geared toward undercutting the tight association of sex with shame in the public sphere. In "Thanda Gosht" ("Cold Meat"), which was the state censorship machine's favorite target, erections are barely veiled through the simile of trumps in a game of cards, retaining what the censor board would perceive to be gratuitous crassness. In readings of "Toba Tek Singh," however, Singh's near-constant erect verticality has gone unremarked because of the diversion tactic that is anticolonial folly.

The translation of "Toba Tek Singh" from Urdu to English presents the brutal simplicity of repatriation as masculine rapture, mobilizing an economy of erection and release. In translator Khalid Hasan's sonorous English, Bishan Singh becomes "like a Colossus," a dissenting body, an erect column whose passivity is its activity, who rises up out of the frontier and then ends face down. His miraculous conversion to an inert statue, no longer a symptom of "cartographic anxiety,"[21] is a masterfully unusable aesthetic closure for the state policies of expulsion and repatriation. When one goes line by line, there is, of course, no Colossus present in Manto's original Urdu-language text, in which horror and laughter come from his felicity with the apt phrasing of plain words: "Jaise ab koi taqat use wahan sey hata na sakey gi." This translates to an utterance of immobility, "As if, now, no amount of force [feminine] could ever remove him from his place." The immovable Colossus is not there in Manto until Manto is translated to English.

While no translation can hold up the original text's regime of the proper word in the proper place, Khalid Hasan's translations of Manto have come under scathing attack for impropriety, blatant editorial violence, and insensibly unethical disfiguration.[22] Hasan's irreconcilable intimacy with Manto's Urdu text makes it end up in an incorrect albeit innovative place, but Hasan's additions are a mode of errancy in translation that I find attractive and useful for their conflicting investment in the original. The irony of mistranslation is thematized in the madman's delirious gibberish, in which we can detect a mixture of Hindi, Urdu, Persian, English, Punjabi, and Sanskrit: "The porridge of the green gram of the lantern of the un-conscious of the annexe of the thudding and thundering from above."[23] Staying with Khalid Hasan's mistranslated Colossus a little longer, we see that the harder Bishan Singh tries to reach his ancestral home in the village of Toba Tek Singh, the more relentlessly he is drawn back into the catastrophe of repatriation, to the amusement of bureaucratic officials, till a final reversal is achieved in his death. The reversal does not come about through a messianic intervention or humanitarian rescue. Rather, the reversal is embodied in the swollen legs of a dissenting body that has stood erect for fifteen years, a ribald aesthetic measure of the magnitude of resistance, an aesthetics of inert nondeportability to manage the mortality of abject homelessness.[24]

Because Bishan Singh is the Colossus, his name is also the village name Toba Tek Singh; he *lives* in Toba Tek Singh, that is, Toba Tek Singh is where he lives. It is a rapturous end, if there ever was one, like the militant dervish woman renamed K. in real life, the oracle who wrote reams of mystic poetry as a lifelong tactic to survive the abjection of repatriation after she was abducted to Pakistan and refused to be brought back to India because she had put down roots (see epigraph). At the end, Singh is in no man's land *not* because he does not know whether Toba Tek Singh is in Pakistan or in India. He is there because he *does* know that it has been allocated to Pakistan, where he can no longer stay because he is being repatriated to India. After he is told by his deporting officer that Toba Tek Singh is in Pakistan, he refuses to move, even though the bureaucratic machine tries to deceive him into voluntary repatriation: "Many efforts were made to explain to him that Toba Tek Singh had already been moved to India, or would be moved immediately, but had no effect on Bishan Singh."[25] Clearly, the insane man remains unduped but pays for his decision not to move with death and absolute arrest. Colossal finitude, problematic and restrictive though it is in its phallic elevation, is a way to break free of the predetermined script of repatriation that ends in wretchedness and expulsion.[26]

The new sovereign state produced an abject script not only for Manto's comic irony, by naming it "unclean," "filthy," "taboo," and "disgusting" under

rijuta mehta

obscenity law, but also for native subjects, especially the women photographed in repatriation portraits between 1947 and 1956. Rather than dismiss this abject script as an oversimplification of complex literariness, or treat it as an endpoint of photographic spectatorship, I argue for the ever-renewed and incalculable mediation between irony and abjection, such that abjection might lead to some sort of freedom or it might misfire, but it has no more certain purchase on a new and true freedom than mastery does.

From the grounds of circulation and vagrancy of repatriated populations, anticolonialism can be defined as the turn to the fabulated, the incalculable, and the inaccessible in the composition of resistance. Whether it is the militant feminism of a woman playing heroic knight in survivor testimony; or her pose of muscular tension in identification photographs that hum, quietly but audibly, as she is deported; or her headlong rush out of safety into the path of a mob to prevent racially motivated killing; or the literary punishment of rapists at a historical moment of de facto amnesty; or a madman's refusal to be deported and choice to die in the place he already is—such acts and qualities of freedom expose the ultimately inescapable limit of the reigning problematic of anticolonialism, which has precluded our subjects by relegating them to mere and full abjection, and by extension to mere and full calculability.

Notes

Epigraphs: Erasmus, *The Praise of Folly*, trans. Hoyt Hopewell Hudson (1509; Princeton, NJ: Princeton University Press, 2015), 50; Saadat Hasan Manto, *Lazzat-e Sang* [The taste of stones] in *Manto Nama* (Lahore: Sang-e Meel Publications, 1995), 636–37; Michel Foucault, *The Courage of Truth: Lectures at the Collège de France, 1983–1984* (Basingstoke: Palgrave Macmillan, 2012), 171; Ritu Menon and Kamla Bhasin, *Borders and Boundaries: Women in India's Partition* (New Brunswick, NJ: Rutgers University Press, 1998), 96.

1 Giorgio Agamben, *Potentialities: Collected Essays in Philosophy*, ed. and trans. Daniel Heller-Roazen (Stanford, CA: Stanford University Press, 2000), offers an account of potentiality as impotentiality, rather than an opposition to actuality. The relation to one's own incapacity is a key step in his general argument that potentiality also implies not to be or not to do something, in addition to the possibility of being or doing something.

2 On modern civilization's disastrous prioritization of "bodily welfare" over all else, see Mohandas Karamchand Gandhi, *Hind Swaraj* in *Hind Swaraj and Other Writings*, ed. Anthony J. Parel (1909; New York: Cambridge University Press, 2009), 34. See Margaret Bourke-White, *Interview with India: In the Words and Pictures of Margaret Bourke-White* (London: Travel Book Club,

1951), for a gently comic description of the costly security and care-giving mechanisms that had to be put into place every time M. K. Gandhi traveled by third class on the train, or lived in the quarters of caste untouchables, or decided to regulate his diet with many restrictions and fasts. Sarojini Naidu is said to have remarked that it cost a small fortune to keep Gandhi in poverty.

3 Jonathan Lear, *A Case for Irony* (Cambridge, MA: Harvard University Press, 2011), 6.

4 Lilie Chouliaraki, *The Ironic Spectator: Solidarity in the Age of Post-Humanitarianism* (Cambridge: Polity, 2013), tracks the movement of the humanitarian spectator from the politics of pity to the politics of irony over the last few decades.

5 Kamla Patel, *Torn from the Roots: A Partition Memoir* (New Delhi: Women Unlimited, 2005), 84–85.

6 Patel, *Torn from the Roots*, 85.

7 Saidiya Hartman, "Venus in Two Acts," *Small Acts* 12, no. 2 (2008): 1–14.

8 Veena Das, "Language and Body: Transactions in the Construction of Pain," *Daedalus* 125, no. 1 (Winter 1996): 67–91. This is a revised and reinterpreted take on the version in Veena Das and Ashis Nandy, "Violence, Victimage, and the Language of Silence," *Contributions to Indian Sociology* 19, no. 1 (January–June 1985): 177–95.

9 Hortense Spillers, "Mama's Baby, Papa's Maybe: An American Grammar Book," *Diacritics* 17, no. 2 (Summer 1987): 64–81.

10 Tina Campt, *Listening to Images* (Durham, NC: Duke University Press, 2017), 6–25.

11 See Aparna Basu's biography of Mridula Sarabhai, *Mridula Sarabhai: Rebel with a Cause*, Gender Studies Series (Oxford: Oxford University Press, 2005).

12 Sakshi Virmani, "Talking of Tragedy: An Oral History Project on Partition Takes Off," *Outlook Magazine*, October 13, 2014, https://www.outlookindia .com/magazine/story/talking-of-tragedy/292133.

13 Saadat Hasan Manto, "Thanda Gosht" [Cold meat], in *Stories about the Partition of India*, vol. 1, ed. and trans. Alok Bhalla (1950; New Delhi: Indus, HarperCollins, 1994), 91–96.

14 Manto, "Thanda Gosht," 1:94.

15 Saadat Hasan Manto, "Toba Tek Singh," in *The Norton Anthology of World Literature*, vol. F: *The Twentieth Century*, ed. Martin Puchner, trans. Khalid Hasan (1953; New York: Norton, 2012), 729.

16 Manto, "Toba Tek Singh," 730.

17 Manto was ceaselessly inebriated while writing. The fact that he drank himself to death is well known. Manto's abject body and his cynical practice of self-ruination haunt our reading of his works. For a cinematic portrayal, see Sarmad Khoosat's *Manto* (Karachi, Pakistan: A&B Productions, 2015).

18 Saadat Hasan Manto, *Bū* [Smell], trans. Muhammad Umar Memon, *The Annual of Urdu Studies* 27 (2012): 68–73.

19 "Toba Tek Singh" is the most anthologized of Manto's works, appearing frequently on world literature syllabi.

20 The full line in Khalid Hasan's translation reads, "There he stood in no man's land on his swollen legs like a colossus" (734).

21 The phrase is Sankaran Krishna's in "Cartographic Anxiety: Mapping the Body Politic in India," *Alternatives: Global, Local, Political* 19, no. 4 (Fall 1994): 507–21.

22 Alok Bhalla's essay "The Politics of Translation: Manto's Partition Stories and Khalid Hasan's English Version," *Social Scientist* 29, no. 7/8 (July–August 2001): 19–38, excoriates Khalid Hasan, claiming, "Manto survives the translation because his stories are powerful and disturbing. There ought to be, however, a minimum ethic for every translator" (22).

23 There is slippage between various recitations of gibberish in the text. "Lantern" becomes "government of Pakistan," which becomes "government of Toba Tek Singh."

24 See Jacques Derrida on the Colossal in *Truth in Painting*, trans. Geoffrey Bennington and Ian McLeod (Chicago: University of Chicago Press, 1987).

25 Manto, "Toba Tek Singh," 734.

26 A confined madman, Singh has abnegated his right of pater familias, but the specter of his daughter's apparent rape, suspended in the palpable form of an ellipsis, hangs over the ironic discourse: "Your daughter Roop Kaur . . ."—he [Muslim visitor] hesitated—"She is safe too . . . in India." The insinuation is that Bishan Singh's daughter is not or has not been safe. That the visitor is Muslim while the daughter is Sikh is also a significant diegetic fact for a historical moment of interracial violence.

chapter seven

Between Technology & Toy: The Talking Doll as Abject Artifact

meredith a. bak

Since talking dolls were commercially introduced in the nineteenth century, children have anticipated them with high hopes as animate companions promising endless fantasy play. In practice, however, talking dolls are often met with disappointment when their technical limitations fall short of expectations. Edison's phonograph doll, introduced in 1890, promised an exciting union of a traditional toy with new technology, but it proved unsuitable for children's play. Its fragile cylinders scratched easily, resulting in dolls whose voices were screechy and grating. In 1992, a century after Edison's doll, Teen Talk Barbie energized debates on gender stereotypes in toys when she uttered phrases such as "math class is tough," prompting culture-jamming group the Barbie Liberation Organization to switch the voice boxes of talking Barbie and GI Joe dolls and leave them in stores for unwitting customers to purchase.[1] The talking doll's capacity to unnerve and offend gestures to its unique position as an object masquerading as a subject.

Many talking toys have achieved success on the market, such as the classic non-anthropomorphic speaking toy the See 'n Say and talking creatures such as Teddy Ruxpin and Tickle Me Elmo. Yet, when the same voice technologies are embedded in dolls, they acquire an uncanny valence. Maligned on the grounds of both form and content, talking and animate dolls (and ventriloquist dummies) have likewise recurred as menacing televisual and cinematic tropes, central to a robust horror subgenre and appearing in titles such as *Dead of Night* (1945), a 1963 episode of *The Twilight Zone*, the *Child's Play* franchise (1988–), a 1998 episode of *The X-Files*, and *Dead Silence* (2007), to name just a few.[2] In many such examples, dolls hover between subject and object positions, inanimate things meant to be enlivened through the ventriloquist's skill or technological means, or living things, inhabited by (almost invariably) evil spirits. As they invite and resist identification and elude firm classification, talking dolls come to embody the abject. As consumer products, they extend application of the concept of the abject beyond the page and the screen into the material world, where children are encouraged to perform and negotiate their own status as subjects in relation to their playthings. Moreover, as commercial objects and intellectual properties, talking dolls uniquely index the processes of their creation in the form of plastic seams, stamped trademarks, and related documents such as patents.

This chapter traces the talking doll's abject status through an analysis of patent records from the late nineteenth century to the present. Rather than providing a comprehensive, linear account of these toys' development, the following analysis highlights the implementation and modification of several principal technologies to trace recurring problems that inventors have encountered in their attempts to produce and activate dolls' voices while maintaining the verisimilitude assumed to facilitate high play value. Although the technology of the talking doll has changed significantly throughout the form's history, anxieties surrounding the doll have persisted. Pneumatic systems using bellows and valves have historically been well-suited for baby dolls, whose resemblance to infants justifies a vocabulary limited to babbling and short strings of phonemes similar to the words "mama" and "papa." The introduction of the phonograph in the late nineteenth century presented opportunities to expand the doll's vocal repertoire. Early models such as Edison's, equipped with a phonographic cylinder, were capable of playing short recordings such as nursery rhymes. The phonograph would be replaced by magnetic tape by the mid-twentieth century, and eventually, by internet-connected dolls, with "memories" stored in the cloud, which have the capacity to "learn" alongside their young users. Despite the toy's changing technological apparatus, there is a fundamental disjuncture between the doll as an affective plaything and as a technological object. Begging comparison to the child that plays as caregiver (usually mother), but also defined in opposition to her, key to the doll's abject status is the mismatch between its technological interior and its exterior appearance.

This mismatch has heightened stakes because the talking doll is a technology aimed at children—a group perceived as vulnerable and innocent. Since the nineteenth century, the child in the Western context has been imagined as a sentimentalized, fundamentally innocent proto-subject occupying a position that bears an ambivalent relationship to consumer culture, which at once helps to constitute the child as a subject while simultaneously posing a threat to her perceived innocence.[3] Historically marketed to girls, talking dolls encourage traditional nurturing doll play but also often require the child to perform strange, violent, or invasive actions to trigger speech. In so doing, the child is positioned within contradictory terrain, asked to both relinquish and retain emotional attachment to the talking toy. Indeed, as Sianne Ngai asserts, "cute" commodity objects like dolls invite "an unusually intense and yet strangely ambivalent kind of empathy," engaging an ongoing power dynamic to nurture and provide care, but also to abuse and destroy.[4] These conflicting impulses exemplify the "vortex of summons and repulsion" characteristic of the abject.[5]

Consumer panics of varying scales have also erupted in response to the fear that talking dolls might influence the girls playing with them. A string of news stories in 2008 chronicled the alleged discovery of Fisher-Price's Little Mommy Real Loving Baby Cuddle and Coo dolls in Oklahoma and Pennsylvania that reportedly spoke the phrases "Islam is the light" and "Satan is King."[6] Early in 2015, security researchers demonstrated the ease with which the internet-connected My Friend Cayla doll could be "hacked" to speak sexually explicit content.[7] In the wake of a 2000 lawsuit against the makers of talking Teletubby toys that allegedly uttered homophobic epithets and the phrase "bite my butt," one toy store employee noted the range of customer responses to the doll: "Half the people would laugh. Half looked bewildered."[8] The talking doll's liminal status is thus often understood as a vulnerability, foregrounding the perpetual threat of technological malfunction or supernatural or ideological co-optation. Evoking horror and humor, the talking doll has endured as a plaything for more than a century. It fizzles and fails, only to be reborn, always reemerging in ostensibly new and improved forms, though it frequently fails to deliver the promises that precede it. In this chapter I argue that the talking doll represents a site of abjection because it commits to two fundamentally oppositional positions, situated not within but between or across the stable categories of living and dead, animate companion and inanimate thing. Its simultaneous status as affective toy, animated through child's play, and functional technology—an artificially and externally imposed consciousness—sits uneasily with the clear-cut categories and schemata traditionally associated with children's development. These tensions play out in the material form of the dolls themselves, between their lifelike surfaces and technological interiors, facilitating children's play that alternates from tenderness to violence. Because these opposing ideas are staged through the doll's spoken language, Kristeva's theory of abjection provides a fruitful theoretical lens through which to explore their contradictions. Yet the dolls' physical characteristics and the additional linguistic register of patent records also reveal new applications of Kristeva's work in the realms of material culture and intellectual property.

Talking dolls and automata have long been theorized in relation to the uncanny. In Ernst Jentsch's 1906 essay on the subject, he suggests that their uncanniness stems from their imperfect resemblance to living things, which results in a jarring collision between the old and familiar and the new and unknown. Such animate objects destabilize clear-cut categories such as living and dead. Inventors of children's dolls historically endeavored to add speech to the traditional doll form to add another sensory register, thereby making the doll seem *more* real or alive. This added dimension, Jentsch argues, raises the stakes for success or failure: "The finer the mechanism and the truer to nature the formal reproduction, the more strongly will the special effect also make its appearance."[9] Kristeva distinguishes abjection from uncanniness by its heightened violence, likening it to children's refusal of their parents and all that they have been given.[10] As objects that invite their child users (almost always figured as girls) to play at being mothers, talking dolls foster the enactment of the process of maternal abjection, providing the means for them to assert their subjectivity in relation to the doll again and again.

Unlike traditional dolls, which are capable of maintaining a kind of overall coherence (such as a realistic face and limbs and a soft body to invite cuddling), the talking doll commonly exhibits a disjuncture between its representational surface and technological interior. This incongruity begs or dares the child to dismantle it, to get at its interior and see its inner workings, a tendency described by Baudelaire: "The overriding desire of most children is to get at and *see the soul* of their toys. . . . The child twists and turns his toy, scratches it, shakes it, bumps it against the walls, throws it on the ground."[11] This inclination, not to regard the doll at a remove, but relentlessly to handle it, to dismantle it, moves the talking doll from the realm of the uncanny to the abject. After all, as Freud argues in his elaboration and critique of Jentsch's work, children are generally not afraid of their dolls coming to life. On the contrary, they desire it.[12] The various technologies underpinning the doll's voice and the dolls themselves are continually at odds with the dolls' traditional forms, which prompt play that is both tender and terrifying.

Vocal Range: Speech as the Seat of Subjectivity

For Kristeva, speech is a key attribute of subject formation, yet a doll's endowment with a voice—an attempt to bring it to life—is precisely what frequently condemns it to abjection. The interplay between traditional plaything and technological device at work in the talking doll is difficult to observe through material-culture analysis alone, as by the time the doll is manufactured and distributed as a commercial product, it has been assembled, its technology concealed. Patents serve as historically situated evidence of inventors' attempts to wrestle with the problematic relationship between technology and toy. As such, they are a valuable and heretofore under-examined source through which to understand the talking doll's abject status, thereby expanding the concept beyond textual and cinematic analysis into material culture. Concerned primarily with the doll as intellectual property (and therefore linked to the capacity for popularity and profit), patents reveal the incongruity between aesthetics and mechanics as a central preoccupation. With legal imperatives that exhaustively try to articulate the boundaries between the discrete parts that constitute intellectual property, patent language typifies the paternally oriented language of the *symbolic order*, even as the finished doll encourages affective play that recreates the mother-child relationship—one so often characterized as having origins in the prelinguistic. The connection between a young child and a mother, Kelly Oliver writes, is one in which "their bodies physically 'signal' to each other before the onset of language proper, before the mirror stage. Their semiotic relation sets up the onset of language proper."[13] That the doll itself is endowed with speech adds further complexity, as its simulation of human language and cognition is an attempt to reify the primal maternal position, but it does so by employing the very kinds of symbolic language by which the separation of mother and child is initiated.[14]

The two forms of language at play here, the language of the patent and the simulated speech uttered by the doll, bear a complex relationship to each other. Both are gendered, the former associated with the largely masculine makers and inventors of the dolls and the latter feminized, both in the dolls' voices, which were historically recorded by girls and women, and in the identification of girls as the majority of intended users, meant to treat the doll as a child in their care. In this sense, the patent language through which the doll's voice is incarnated functions as a foil to the language uttered by the doll. The incongruity between the doll's speech, meant to animate it and imbue it with subjectivity, and the legal language that lays claim to its technology are

meredith a. bak

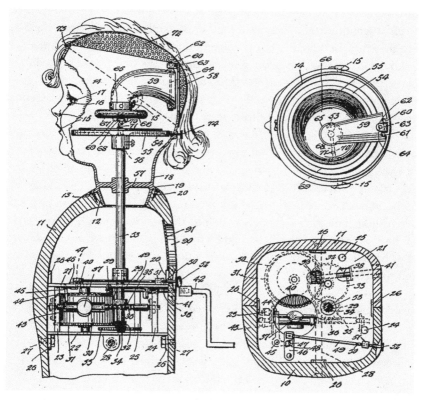

figure 7.1 Christoph Adolf Giebeler-Wanke, diagrams for US Patent 1,325,013 A—Phonetic doll, filed December 16, 1919.

made material in the form of the doll itself. This is exemplified by a tension expressed in a 1919 patent for a "phonetic doll" (figure 7.1), which specified that the doll should be "life-like in appearance and in the production of the human voice, the mechanical parts being so arranged, and the superficial parts being such that the attractiveness and delicateness of the doll are in no way sacrificed."[15]

As the earlier examples suggest, although a talking doll simulates a "speaking being," its voice has been perceived as a site of vulnerability because of the technology that produces it and its susceptibility to ideological co-optation. This vulnerability, in turn, represents a threat to the child. The doll's exterior is meant to mirror the child, to facilitate recognition and invite play, yet it also conceals the technological system housed inside, which, if exposed, has the potential to alienate the child. The voice is central to this complex network of identification, as a technological mechanism housed inside the doll but meant to facilitate its human affect on the surface. As the designers of talking dolls attempt increased realism through the integration of technical parts, they risk falling into what Masahiro Mori calls the *uncanny valley*—the notion that anthropomorphic technologies that strive to achieve extreme verisimilitude in humanoid forms instead often prompt disquiet and even revulsion.[16] Dolls, Scott Eberle writes, are especially susceptible to this kind of criticism; since they, "of all toys, seem to best exemplify the innocence of child's play, we find it particularly unsettling when they betray those expectations."[17] To engage in doll play is to willingly pretend that the doll is an autonomous and animate subject, a pretense carried out through physical activity. Such play is also largely sustained through language, however, both as the child positions herself in relation to the doll (as mother, as confidante) and, literally, as the child narrates her actions and performs one side of an imagined dialogue.

Just like play, language foregrounds a tension between the real and the symbolic. For Kristeva, language is linked with subject formation by its capacity to differentiate the thing from its referent and, in turn, to differentiate the self from others, especially the mother. It "is based on fetishist denial ('I know that, but just the same,' 'the sign is not the thing, but just the same,' etc.)."[18] The talking doll's aesthetics facilitate the same kind of participatory disavowal that makes doll play pleasurable, and its voice is meant to further contribute to this pretense. Yet, integrating the technology necessary for the doll's speech often requires compromises to the doll's function and aesthetics. Thus, while such dolls are engineered to fuel the child's imagination by masquerading as speaking subjects, they often counter their objective in the process. In its simulation of language and cognition, the animate doll can variously appear amusing or terrifying. Both responses, Noël Carroll suggests, "share an overlapping necessary condition insofar as an appropriate object of both states involves the transgression of a category, a concept, a norm, or a commonplace expectation."[19] This is well illustrated by the evil doll Chucky in the *Child's Play* films, whose soft plastic features and cheerful primary-colored costume contrast with his foul language, inappropriate humor, and facility with weapons. Through patent records, the talking doll's fragmented qualities can be observed, revealing playthings that are alarming as well as amusing, and that modify traditional doll play in several important ways.

Technology and Toy: The Talking Doll's Frightening Corporeal Logics

The legal language behind the doll's voice demonstrates inventors' challenges and aspirations—a blueprint of inventors' attempts to imbue the doll with subjectivity. Efforts to integrate speech into a doll's body are often unsuccessful. Voice mechanisms attempt to simulate life and personality but frequently result in arrangements at odds with the flexibility and verisimilitude required for such toys to be successful when handled by children. Various methods, from pneumatic systems to phonographs and electronic technologies, have been employed to make dolls appear to speak. A consideration of the systems responsible for activating and projecting doll speech demonstrates the fraught interplay between aesthetics and technology—an unending tug between unstable subject and object positions that inevitably relegates the doll to abjection.

Always fragmented, the talking doll embodies but often fails to manage the relationship between the aesthetics of its own surfaces and its technological interior. In line with the logic of industrial production, such dolls are always assemblages, comprising numerous component parts fashioned together into the semblance of a complete whole. Within this scheme, speech factors in as an imposition rather than an integral element, a technology developed separately to be incorporated into the doll later. American inventors patenting voice mechanisms for dolls have often relied on limbs and heads from other suppliers, made from materials like bisque and porcelain, historically imported from Germany, and now plastics from China. Dolls' fragmented bodies have been likened to the isolated and alienated bodies of the laborers responsible for producing them.[20] Doll parts appear grotesque in the industrial context, heaped into piles or packaged with systematic efficiency, sliding down chutes and shuddering along conveyor belts to be assembled by machine or hand. Fitting these parts together marks an attempt to conceal the tenuous boundary between surface and interior, to produce a "finished" plaything that resembles a baby, plush creature, or child. The body's surface, writes Laura Ivins-Hulley, is "a key site for negotiating self-coherence and self-autonomy. . . . Skin helps secure corporeal unity, both in terms of physiology and social signification."[21] Yet patents demonstrate how this unity and coherence are perpetually threatened in doll design, exemplifying what Kristeva writes is the root of abjection, that which "disturbs identity, system, order. What does not respect borders, positions, rules. The in-between, the ambiguous, the composite."[22] This clumsy alignment of speech technology and surface aesthetics appears frequently in patents. One 1931 example for a bellows-operated doll featured a chin stuck onto the middle of the doll's face—a separate appendage that clacked in time as the doll emitted sound.[23] Inventors' desires to make convincing mouth movements recurred, as Reem Hilu notes of computerized talking dolls from the 1980s, which emitted synthesized speech accompanied with mechanical "noise," in the form of "clicking" and "grinding," as their mouths were made to open and close.[24]

Prior to voice-activated technology, a doll's speech was initiated via physical means using various inputs to connect the doll's speech to seemingly unrelated parts of its anatomy, in turn forging new corporeal logics. Dolls with pneumatic voice systems, for example, can be made to "cry" or "speak" by being squeezed or tilted on their sides; phonographic models have historically been activated by cranks or pull strings, which wind a motor that will drive the record and set the needle. Reliance on the doll as an anthropomorphic interface has historically resulted in arrangements that detract from, rather than facilitate, conventional doll play. An early patent filed in 1877 (figure 7.2), for example, describes a doll with a reed or kazoo-like structure protruding from its armpit, so that "the doll, when held in the position in which a child is held while being tended or hushed from crying, is placed conveniently for the application of the lips to the mouth of the tube."[25] The child is then meant to blow or speak into the tube to simulate crying or speaking. Other pneumatic systems used reeds as vocal apertures, through which air is driven by plungers and weighted bellows, so that the doll is made to talk by turning or tilting its body.[26] More refined versions allowed the doll to utter multisyllabic cries based on its position, such as one 1929 patent, assigned to the St. Louis Doll and Toy Manufacturing Company, which featured a mechanism that would make the doll speak "papa" when held one way or "ah-ma-ma" if held in another way.[27] These systems gave the child control over not only when the doll spoke but what was uttered, by means of physical manipulation.

Whereas pneumatic systems required concerted physical manipulation to drive air through reeds to produce speech, phonographic dolls were often more delicate, and too much handling risked damaging the speech mechanism, pitting physical play value against the doll's ability to speak. The voice on Edison's metal-bodied phonographic doll was activated by a crank protruding from the doll's back, a kind of prosthetic appendage that gave the doll the appearance of a wind-up automaton. Still relying on phonographic technology seventy-five years later, Mattel engineer John Ryan attempted to improve the design in the company's Chatty Cathy line of dolls with the

meredith a. bak

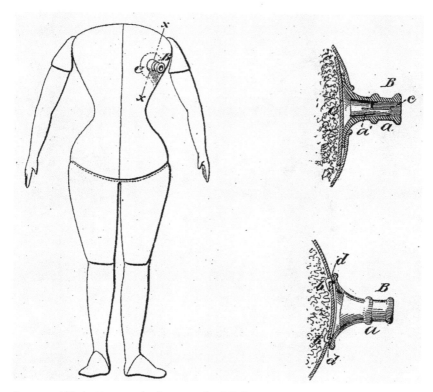

figure 7.2 W. A. Harwood, diagrams for US Patent 189,935 A—Improvement in talking and crying dolls, filed April 24, 1877.

integration of a retractable pull string installed at the base of the doll's neck, known as the "chatty ring" (figure 7.3).[28]

In dolls using these systems, the installation of speech not only came at the cost of the ability to engage in traditional physical doll play, which sometimes includes "careless handling by children," but also, in many instances, foregrounds the fraught relationship between the doll's interior and exterior.[29] These sites—where a metal crank disappears into a doll's back or a retractable string slithers into its neck—showcase the doll's skin as "a fragile container," subject to rupture.[30]

Efforts to mask the instability between the internal and external relied on parts of the doll's body to function as aestheticized technological mechanisms, connecting speech to arms, legs, and heads as a way of "avoiding any apparent manual manipulation of switches."[31] A Mattel patent filed in 1972

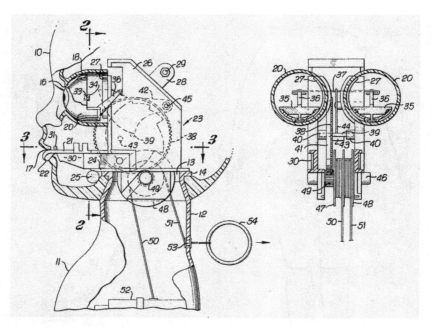

figure 7.3 John Ryan, diagrams for US Patent 3,293,794—Animated talking doll, filed December 27, 1966.

attempted to mitigate the peculiar relationship between the conventional pull-string mechanism and the rest of the doll's body by adding an additional step to triggering the doll's voice. After the pull string winds the record motor, the doll "begins playing only when a child performs a predetermined operation such as pressing a certain location on the toy."[32] The patent's exemplary "predetermined operation" is a kiss from the child user, linking speech to physical affection in a distinct way. Pull-string motors would be replaced by small switches and sensors that could be distributed across the doll's anatomy, a shift that enabled doll makers to require more precise inputs from the child to activate speech and, further, to better conceal the boundary between interior and exterior. One 1987 patent outlines plans for a doll whose speech is voice activated but can additionally be activated by the compression of switches embedded in its eyes, ears, and nose. Touching each part also prompts one of two preprogrammed phrases that relate to that part of the anatomy, such as "that's my nose."[33] Speech is initiated in a 1992 doll by pulling a magnetic hairbrush across its scalp.[34] In each of these instances, efforts

meredith a. bak

to conceal the mechanisms that elicit doll speech make their bodies strange, thereby revealing the abjection inherent in what, on the surface, makes them appear warm and lifelike.

Moreover, just as speech activation has routinely worked against the doll's function and appearance as a living subject, means for playback and amplification have similarly reflected design challenges. Playing and amplifying speech through the doll's mouth has historically proved difficult, hence the common tendency to house the amplifier in the doll's chest, behind a perforated grill. A 1953 patent for a bellows-operated doll proposes to improve this system by forcing the sound up through the base of the doll's neck so that "the necessity for mutilating the body of the doll is obviated, and the sound produced within the doll's body is heard with maximum intensity."[35] As this series of examples demonstrates, inventors' efforts to produce and amplify doll speech have often rendered the doll's body monstrous—a series of pieces through which speech is rerouted and connected to arm, armpit, scalp, neck, and back. The very features designed to make the doll come to life thereby prevent it from appearing and behaving in a lifelike capacity. This disjuncture, in turn, led to the integration of other features to counteract the alienating qualities of the doll's speech, such as moving facial features like bobbing and quivering chins and blinking eyes, designed to synchronize with the doll's voice in a naturalistic, rather than mechanistic, way.[36] As patents map the doll's body, they reveal the tension between interior and exterior and showcase some of the bizarre attempts to create an interface between the two.

Now beyond simple pneumatic systems, phonographs, and even more refined electronic circuitry, contemporary developments in artificial intelligence and speech recognition produce dolls that are allegedly closer than ever to successfully fulfilling their promise as animate playthings. No longer preoccupied solely with the development of a voice, inventors now endeavor to outfit dolls with their own consciousness, and particularly with a semblance of the capacity to remember. For example, Hasbro's My Real Baby (2009) not only contains a voice but actively grows in intelligence alongside its child owner, beginning as an infant with simple cooing and crying and culminating with the impersonation of a toddler capable of emitting short, simple sentences. Like earlier dolls, the toy's instruction manual puts My Real Baby's sophisticated systems into terms commensurate with human development, such as describing the doll as "learning." Despite its sophistication, which links the doll's technical features to more naturalized play practices (for example, it "wakes up" only when stably held on both sides, laughs when bounced or tickled on the soles of its feet, and lets the child know when it's hungry or full), still other features continue the tradition of strange intra- and intercorporeal relationships. For instance, the instruction manual indicates that "the diaper sensing area on her tummy is light sensitive," thus only registering a successful diaper change in bright settings.[37] Unlike the human child, My Real Baby can never "develop" past its toddler stage, but neither does it remain frozen at this moment. Instead, it has a reset button at the base of the neck, which returns it "back to a newborn state so that she 'forgets' all the words she 'learned' and has to start 'learning' them all over again," enacting a loop whereby full maturation is forever forestalled.[38] Given the complex technological structures underlying the doll's surface and their incongruity with its "superficial," or aesthetic, features, it is worth turning further attention to the question of what forms of play such toys engender.

The Subject and Object in Play

The abnormal and surprising anatomical arrangements that negotiate a relationship between the doll's interior and exterior also define the range of actions that a child might undertake with the doll as a plaything. These actions form what Robin Bernstein has described as a thing's "scripts," the material and discursive conditions that outline a thing's intended functions and constitute the range of possible actions that might transgress or run counter to its sanctioned uses.[39] Bernstein's consideration of doll play in nineteenth-century America details the racially inscribed violence girls perpetuated against their dolls. Her examination of Raggedy Ann and her accompanying storybooks, for example, demonstrates how Ann's durable cotton body scripted violent play practices because of its ability to endure more physical abuse than a more fragile doll would.[40] In such violent play, the doll's status seems to oscillate between a position that invites identification and nurturing and another whereby the doll becomes an object available to the child for physical abuse. The doll's ability to be invested with a sense of subjectivity is what makes it an appealing plaything capable of populating a shared fantasy world with the child who mothers it. Yet, as patents for talking dolls frequently predict "careless handling" and "anticipated abuse" by children, the play value gleaned from the doll's aesthetic features clearly needs to be balanced against durability when play takes a violent turn.[41]

Animate toys in literature, Lois Kuznets writes, play on our apprehensions "about what it means to be 'real,'" thus creating a distinct power dynamic between a plaything and its human user, who variously regards the toy as

meredith a. bak

sentient subject and pliant object.[42] Play with such toys, then, takes on new ethical and political dimensions, as the child bears a different relationship and responsibility to a living plaything than she does to a commodity object. Susan Honeyman suggests that "the tendency of postindustrial toy narratives is to idealize passivity by romanticizing the object position," such as when the characters in the *Toy Story* films patiently play dead while awaiting animation by their child owners.[43] In such a formulation, the doll is made available to the child for whatever forms of play the child chooses to enact (often the child pretending to mother the doll), and there is no expectation of reciprocity. Such a dynamic evokes Kristeva's account of the role of the child in relation to the mother: "The child can serve its mother as a token of her own authentication; there is, however, hardly any reason for her to serve as go-between for it to become autonomous and authentic in its turn."[44] The doll's status as a compelling plaything thus hinges on whatever features contribute to its appearance as lifelike, such as its talking apparatus. Simultaneously, however, when those same qualities that seem to endow the doll with subjectivity fail to make the illusion of life complete, they remind the child of her limited ethical obligations to the doll, which is, after all, just a thing.

Yet dolls' representational qualities perpetually complicate this asymmetrical sense of responsibility, at once available as passive objects but resembling living things. Dolls are, writes Eugenia Gonzalez, "perhaps the only consumer products that were not intended to be treated as such. In children's play as in adults' writing about it, dolls are brought to life as fashionable ladies demanding of respect, as children or babies to be coddled or disciplined, and as playmates and confidantes."[45] The endowment of dolls with a voice adds further complication as a concerted effort to provide the child a form of "feedback" as she plays at mothering. Moreover, the complex corporeal designs of talking dolls frequently prove contradictory, often inviting the child to nurture and care for the doll in a traditional manner, but also requiring other forms of interaction to activate the voice mechanisms, creating a slippage between the animated subject and the inanimate object. The integration of technological components in the talking doll simultaneously helps facilitate the illusion of the doll as living companion, but this pretense is often undercut by the requirements and specifications of the technology within, such as the scratchiness of the phonographic cylinder, the need to press its body to activate speech, and the doll's vocabulary—the cultural scripts of a docile, agreeable baby or child.

Children's rough handling of their dolls is a practice documented widely across disciplines, from archaeology to literary analysis.[46] In doll narratives—

stories often narrated by dolls that offer commentary and moral lessons about proper treatment and handling by their human mistresses—the asymmetrical power dynamic between children and the dolls left at their mercy is often reversed. In stories where this trope plays out, Gonzalez suggests, animate dolls come to dominate the girls playing with them, "threaten[ing] to diminish the agency of the girls who were meant to assert themselves in playing with them."[47] In one revenge story published in 1900, the playthings in a toy and sweet shop come to life at night. In the midst of the toys' revelry, a cruel, greedy boy named Bobbie sneaks into the shop to gorge himself on figs. When Bobbie discovers that the toys have come alive, he attempts to evade detection, but the toys discover him hiding behind a barrel. They close in, intending to eat him—payback for his gluttonous habits and mistreatment of others. The talking doll leads the charge, her voice imbuing her with a sense of agency. As the toys close in on Bobbie, the doll commands one of her fellow toys, "Hit him in the stomach and make him speak! . . . He did me that way!"[48]

That the doll exacts revenge not only by forcing the boy to speak, but by triggering that speech by punching him in the stomach draws attention to the violence built into the design of many such dolls. To squeeze, poke, tilt, prod, or hit a doll to make it speak seems fairly routine, but to imagine eliciting speech from a human child in the same manner is disconcerting. Even when playing with the doll as intended, the inputs that variously require the child to tilt, squeeze, pull, press on, or otherwise manipulate the doll to make it speak encourage actions that deviate from the softer, gentler behaviors associated with conventional maternal nurturing behaviors. As the doll resembles a lifelike baby or child and simulates human speech, it invites play that crosses the stable categories of reality and pretend—a voluntary misrecognition that allows the child to engage with and discard the doll at will. Features built into dolls such as auto-shut-offs and power switches anticipate the child's tendency to oscillate between identification and acknowledgment of difference. Such design details foreground the child's position of power in relation to the doll, capable of bringing it "to life" on demand.

Moreover, the disjuncture between a doll's lifelike aesthetic surface and its mechanical inner workings persistently tempts the child to open it up and, as Baudelaire described, explore what makes it work. The curiosity at the heart of such endeavors, however, is frequently interspersed with waves of regret, remorse, and disappointment as children contend with the reality that their toy is not alive, and after the process of disemboweling it, it can no longer even pretend to be so. As a commercial product, the doll is always vulnerable to

meredith a. bak

this kind of destruction or dissection by various stakeholders (ranging from the curious child to the tinkerer or toy engineer). Within doll-collecting communities, the practices of doll repair frequently necessitate dismantling and reconstructing them in various combinations, restoring the doll's voice by attaching its head onto another body, drawing from a reserve of discarded or recycled parts.[49] Among industry competitors, a doll might be "taken to pieces on a sort of operating table, all eyeballs, dismembered limbs, and electronic chips" to see how it works.[50] Likewise, the complete doll, designed to appear seamless, an intact babbling infant or talking child, always contains a roadmap of its own intellectual property, patent numbers stamped into its skin. There is thus an ambivalence and a compulsion toward talking dolls as they at once signify an animate human form and an object available to be disassembled and explored.

Conclusion

Objects that, by their very nature, foreground the instability of the boundaries we rely on to order and structure our experiences can provoke both horror and humor. "Horror," writes Noël Carroll, "is intimately and essentially bound up with the violation, problematization, and transgression of our categories, norms, and concepts." Likewise, he notes, "an essential ingredient of comic amusement is the juxtaposition of incongruous or contrasting objects, events, [and] categories."[51] One might think of the dolls subject to the Barbie Liberation Organization's "surgeries," whose highly gendered exteriors no longer matched the voices issuing from their chests, producing an effect that some found comedic, others horrific. As an assemblage whose interior and surface never quite align, it is perhaps unsurprising that the talking doll has inspired play practices and popular culture products that run the gamut between the murderous Chucky, who—possessed by a serial killer—speaks without batteries, and the angelic baby doll, from whose hollow "lungs" a breathy, bellows-driven "mama" can be forced. These dolls invite analysis from Kristeva's perspective because of their complex performance of language and the mother/child relationship. The dolls themselves, along with their patent archives, are also material and discursive sites that extend Kristeva's formulation, where children encounter and enact the complex knot of emotions associated with abjection, thereby reproducing it in play as part of their own developmental experience.

Honeyman notes that in narratives of animate toys, playthings and their owners are often faced with a hard dilemma: the choice to bring a toy to life or to make it real also requires the forfeiture of the toy's immortality.[52] When a doll is animated via technological means, it similarly becomes subject to a kind of mortality in the form of technological obsolescence, foregrounding the fragility of the subject position in another way. Toys endowed with technological capacities are subject to different temporalities and afterlives than are more traditional playthings. As the toy's limited lifespan reminds children of their own mortality—a potential trauma—it calls to mind Freud's conception of humor as a mechanism to keep emotional pain at bay, whereby the superego obscures the horrific so that the subject can instead experience pleasure commensurate with a childlike perspective.[53] The promise of life, linked to the inevitability of death, thus creates a tension between the romanticized timelessness of the toy and the planned obsolescence of technology—both strategies deployed by the logic of capital. This tension is further entangled with the finitude of childhood, widely considered a period meant to be occupied only fleetingly, then moved through.

The acquisition of language is typically regarded as the catalyst for separation between mother and child, the beginning of the initiation of the subject into the symbolic order. Dolls that talk enact this process with the child in the role of the mother. Yet these dolls' speech, which might offer meaning and structure, has historically been beholden to a logic that privileges not the order and anticipation of human discourse but randomization—a consequence of technological limitation through the twentieth century. Mattel's Chatty Cathy line, for example, featured a phonograph and tone arm that played voice tracks not according to a predetermined sequence but randomly, so that "the doll will in effect talk with or have a conversation with the child playing with the doll, the doll making statements at random which are unexpected and unanticipated just as the sayings of a young child are unpredictable and are identified with the child's personality."[54] In this respect, Chatty Cathy's random speech problematizes readings of language as an initiation into the symbolic order. Here, the conventions of conversation are simulated by mechanization and randomization. The user gains the surprise of not knowing what Cathy will say next but forfeits an overarching belief that Cathy is really endowed with consciousness to listen and respond, instead just looping through a series of open-ended prompts. Contemporary talking dolls, with their "memories" stored in the cloud, attempt to address this shortcoming by relying not on randomization, but on machine learning and algorithmically determined responses.

As it supersedes, convolutes, and problematizes many categories and stable positions we rely on, the talking doll thus perpetually occupies an abject

meredith a. bak

status, at once appearing as a lovable playmate and a repulsive technological monstrosity. Its abjection, traced through industrial and intellectual property history, details an ongoing desire to improve and refine the form—a commitment to it even as it is continuously met with hostility and suspicion. Efforts that persist in its reinvention suggest that it has not been abandoned, largely, perhaps, because of the radical promises inherent in its form—the promises of companionship, personality, and subjectivity, which are rarely realized but omnipresent as possibilities. Perhaps the talking doll also plays on our anxieties that *all* subjects are unstable, untrustworthy as genuine sentient beings against which we define ourselves. It is the disjuncture between the possibility of the toy as subject and the realities of the toy as object that relegate it to an abject position. Kristeva writes, "If the object . . . through its opposition, settles me within the fragile texture of a desire for meaning, which, as a matter of fact, makes me ceaselessly and infinitely homologous to it, what is *abject*, on the contrary, the jettisoned object, is radically excluded and draws me toward the place where meaning collapses."[55] With fissures in its plastic seams that threaten to disclose its inner workings, the talking doll both embodies and perpetuates the dynamic process of abjection. In contrast to the patent language, which seeks to fix and specify the doll's position, the doll as consumer product invites child's play that almost invariably reveals its liminal status. In turn, the child's experiences of these tensions between internal and external, between the timeless affect of the plaything and the planned obsolescence of its interior, become life lessons in their own right.

Notes

1   David Firestone, "While Barbie Talks Tough, G.I. Joe Goes Shopping," *New York Times*, December 31, 1993.

2   "The Ventriloquist's Dummy," *Dead of Night*, directed by Alberto Cavalcanti (London: Ealing Studios, 1945); *The Twilight Zone*, episode 126, "Living Doll," directed by Richard C. Sarafian, aired November 1, 1963, on CBS; *The X-Files*, season 5, episode 10, "Chinga," directed by Kim Manners, aired February 9, 1998, on Fox; *Child's Play*, directed by Tom Holland (Culver City, CA: MGM/ United Artists, 1988); *Child's Play 2*, directed by John Lafia (Universal City, CA: Universal Pictures, 1990); *Child's Play 3*, directed by Jack Bender (Universal City, CA: Universal Pictures, 1991); *Bride of Chucky*, directed by Ronny Yu (Universal City, CA: Universal Pictures, 1998); *Seed of Chucky*, directed by Don Mancini (Universal City, CA: Universal Pictures, 2004); *Curse of Chucky*, directed by Don Mancini (Universal City, CA: Universal Pictures, 2013); *Dead Silence*, directed by James Wan (Universal City, CA: Universal Pictures, 2007).

3   The prototypical child normalized by this discourse of innocence is figured as a white child and the product of middle-class parents. See, for instance, Viviana A. Rotman Zelizer, *Pricing the Priceless Child: The Changing Social Value of Children* (Princeton, NJ: Princeton University Press, 1985); and Henry Jenkins, *The Children's Culture Reader* (New York: NYU Press, 1998).

4   Sianne Ngai, *Our Aesthetic Categories: Zany, Cute, Interesting* (Cambridge, MA: Harvard University Press, 2012), 4, 11.

5   Julia Kristeva, *Powers of Horror: An Essay on Abjection*, trans. Leon S. Roudiez (New York: Columbia University Press, 1982), 1.

6   Matthew Moore. "Talking Fisher-Price Doll Accused of Promoting Islam," *Telegraph* (London), October 13, 2008, http://www.telegraph.co.uk/news/3191347/Talking-Fisher-Price-doll-accused-of-promoting-Islam.html.

7   David Moye, "Talking Doll Cayla Hacked to Spew Filthy Things," *Huffington Post*, February 10, 2015, http://www.huffingtonpost.com/2015/02/09/my-friend-cayla-hacked_n_6647046.html.

8   Todd C. Frankel, "Talking Teletubbie Po Hauled into Court—Woman Files Suit, Saying Doll Spouts Obscenities," *Charleston (WV) Daily Mail*, February 16, 2000, 2A.

9   Ernst Jentsch, "On the Psychology of the Uncanny (1906)," *Angelaki* 2, no. 1 (January 1, 1997): 7–16, quotation on 10.

10 Kristeva, *Powers of Horror*, 5–6.

11 Charles Baudelaire, *The Painter of Modern Life: "Le Peintre de La Vie Moderne" and Other Essays by Charles Baudelaire*, trans. and ed. Jonathan Mayne (London: Phaidon Press, 1964), 202–3.

12 Sigmund Freud, *The Uncanny* (London: Penguin, 2003), 141.

13 Kelly Oliver, *Reading Kristeva: Unraveling the Double-Bind* (Bloomington: Indiana University Press, 1993), 34–35.

14 Deborah Caslav Covino, *Amending the Abject Body: Aesthetic Makeovers in Medicine and Culture* (New York: SUNY Press, 2004), 19–20.

15 Christoph Adolf Giebeler-Wanke, US Patent 1,325,013 A—Phonetic doll, filed December 16, 1919.

16 Scott G. Eberle, "Exploring the Uncanny Valley to Find the Edge of Play," *American Journal of Play* 2, no. 2 (Autumn 2009): 167–94, esp. 176.

17 Eberle, "Exploring the Uncanny Valley," 179.

18 Kristeva, *Powers of Horror*, 37.

19 Noël Carroll, "Horror and Humor," *Journal of Aesthetics and Art Criticism* 57, no. 2 (1999): 145–60, quotation on 154.

20 Eugenia Gonzalez, "'What Remains? An Empty Doll-Case': Deconstruction and Imagination in Victorian Narratives of Doll Production," *Journal of Victorian Culture* 18, no. 3 (September 1, 2013): 335–49, 340; Miriam Formanek-Brunell, *Made to Play House: Dolls and the Commercialization of American Girlhood, 1830–1930* (Baltimore: Johns Hopkins University Press, 1998).

21 Laura Ivins-Hulley, "A Universe of Boundaries: Pixilated Performances in Jan Švankmajer's Food," *Animation* 8, no. 3 (November 1, 2013): 267–82, quotation on 269.

22 Kristeva, *Powers of Horror*, 4.

23 Abe Blaustein, US Patent 1,805,231—Doll, filed May 12, 1931.

24 Reem Hilu, "Girl Talk and Girl Tech," *Velvet Light Trap: A Critical Journal of Film and Television* 78 (Fall 2016): 4–21.

25 W. A. Harwood, US Patent 189,935 A—Improvement in talking and crying dolls, filed April 24, 1877.

26 Frank G. Schneider, US Patent 1,452,527—Voice for dolls, filed May 1, 1923; Fred Evans, US Patent 1,667,107—Talking toy mechanism, filed April 24, 1928.

27 Theodore Hutinkow, US Patent 1,678,222—Doll's voice, filed July 24, 1928; Arthur Petrov, US Patent 1,698,143—Voice mechanism for dolls, filed January 8, 1929.

28 John W. Ryan, US Patent 3,017,187—Multiple speech mechanism, filed January 16, 1962.

29 Charles A. Hunter, US Patent 1,485,137—Talking doll, filed December 6, 1922.

30 Kristeva, *Powers of Horror*, 53.

31 Werner F. Hellman, US Patent 3,162,980 A—Talking doll and the like, filed December 29, 1964.

32 G. Popitt, J. Sargeant, R. Zawistowski, and W. Zeigner, Mattel, Inc., original assignee, US Patent 3,796,284 A—Starting mechanism for toy with phonograph, filed March 10, 1972.

33 James McKeefery, Worlds of Wonder, assignee, US Patent 4,696,653—Speaking toy doll, filed September 29, 1987.

34 Harwood, US Patent 189,935 A—Improvement in talking and crying dolls; Popitt et al., US Patent 3,796,284 A—Starting mechanism for toy with phonograph; David Steele c/o Steele Microsystems, European Patent 19920309008—Talking doll, filed October 2, 1992.

35 Howard Wolfe, US Patent 2,653,412—Sound producing doll, filed September 29, 1953.

36 Blaustein, US Patent 1,805,231—Doll.

37 Hasbro, *My Real Baby*, instruction manual (Pawtucket, RI: Hasbro, 2000), http://www.hasbro.com/common/instruct/MyRealBabyPDF.pdf

38 Hasbro, *My Real Baby* manual.

39 Robin Bernstein, "Dances with Things: Material Culture and the Performance of Race," *Social Text* 27, no. 4 (2009): 67–94, 69.

40 See Robin Bernstein, *Racial Innocence: Performing American Childhood from Slavery to Civil Rights* (New York: NYU Press, 2011).

41 Hunter, US Patent 1,485,137 A—Talking doll; Julius Weih, Ralph Bornn, assignee, Ideal Toy Corp., US Patent 3,230,664 A—Animated crying doll, filed February 6, 1963.

42 Lois R. Kuznets, *When Toys Come Alive: Narratives of Animation, Metamorphosis, and Development* (New Haven, CT: Yale University Press, 1994), 2.

43 Susan Honeyman, "Manufactured Agency and the Playthings Who Dream It for Us," *Children's Literature Association Quarterly* 31, no. 2 (2006): 109–31, 113.

44 Kristeva, *Powers of Horror*, 13.

45 Gonzalez, "'What Remains?,'" 337.

46 See, for instance, Formanek-Brunell, *Made to Play House*; Jane Eva Baxter, *The Archaeology of Childhood: Children, Gender, and Material Culture* (Walnut Creek, CA: Altamira, 2005).

47 Eugenia Gonzalez, "'I Sometimes Think She Is a Spy on All My Actions': Dolls, Girls, and Disciplinary Surveillance in the Nineteenth-Century Doll Tale," *Children's Literature* 39, no. 1 (2011): 33–57, 52.

48 Louis V. Jefferson, "Bobbie's Christmas Eve," *National Magazine* 13, no. 3 (December 1900): 147–50, 149.

49 Bob Pool, "Chatty Cathy Regains Her Voice," *Newark (NJ) Star-Ledger*, June 6, 1997, 23.

50 Gaby Wood, *Edison's Eve: A Magical History of the Quest for Mechanical Life* (New York: Knopf, 2002), xxvi.

51 Carroll, "Horror and Humor," 152–53.

52 Honeyman, "Manufactured Agency," 119.

53 Sigmund Freud, "On Humor," 1927, in *The Standard Edition of the Complete Psychological Works of Sigmund Freud*, vol. 21 (London: Hogarth, 1961), 161–66.

54 John W. Ryan, US Patent 3,082,006—Phonograph tone arm and speaker, filed March 19, 1963.

55 Kristeva, *Powers of Horror*, 1–2.

chapter eight

Absolute Dismemberment: The Burlesque Natural History of Georges Bataille

james leo cahill

It wins its truth only when, in absolute dismemberment [absoluten Zerrissenheit], it finds itself.
—G. W. F. Hegel

Queneau's Dare

Raymond Queneau, writing in homage of his friend and former collaborator Georges Bataille, referred to his texts published in the dissident surrealist journal *Documents* (1929–30) as sketching "a sort of natural history (and consequently dialectical). These are considerations that Bataille, to my knowledge, never subsequently developed, though one finds distant echoes of them in his book on Lascaux."[1] Queneau's description of Bataille's early work as a dialectical natural history has the ring of a dare or surrealist prank to it, suggesting an extension of his "exercises in style" to both his friend's work and a mode of reading it.[2] What uses may come from understanding a strand of Bataille's thought as sketching out a form of natural history, and a dialectical one at that? It does not seem that Queneau had in mind the idea of natural history developed by Frankfurt school thinkers such as Theodor Adorno, who in 1932 summarized the efforts to develop such a practice as "not a synthesis of natural and historical methods, but a change of perspective" that considered both the historical aspects of "nature" and a conception of history attentive to multiple temporalities, both human and nonhuman.[3] A Bataillean iteration of natural history may be conceived as parallel to that outlined by Adorno, in its pursuit of a change of perspective, with the important difference that Bataille treated dialectics with considerable skepticism (even as he wrote his way into them) and worked with a radicalized conception of nature as absolutely contingent, dynamic, and heterogeneous.

This chapter accepts Queneau's dare, in part for the pleasure of trying it, but also for the economy with which it draws together important strands of Bataille's thinking about animality, aesthetics, abjection, and comic laughter, demonstrating their mutual entanglements in his thought, as well as their untimely productivity in an era of accelerated and often frightful metamorphoses, extinctions, exhaustion, and death on a planetary scale. What follows attempts to trace over and fill in some of the principal lines of Bataille's sketch for a natural history. First, it elaborates a Bataillean form of natural history understood as an observational and interpretive practice—a way of looking critically and non-anthropocentrically that is attentive to the non-necessity of what goes by the name "nature" (its contingency), while also refusing to maintain the threshold that separates natural history from anthropology. Second, it considers natural history as a *mode of figuration* and form of "picture thinking" that takes up the natural historian's cutting perspective in a burlesque manner, maintaining the unsublimated presence of abject things and disfiguring properties, and communicating them to the beholder through laughter. Bataille's engagement with dialectics may be understood as threefold: (1) he describes a dialectic of forms between harmony and incongruity, anthropomorphic order and formlessness, that expresses nature's revolt against itself; (2) his natural history develops the differential aspect of the field's empirical inquiries over the typically favored systematic aspects; and (3) he also puts himself into a dialectical relationship with Georg Wilhelm Friedrich Hegel's thought, as the expression of an abject dialectics that prioritizes—and sticks with—the materialist practice of "picture thinking," which Hegel believed philosophical thought had to overcome.

The set of texts Queneau invited Bataille's readers to consider as a dialectical natural history did not appear, at first blush, to have much to do with the traditional objects of natural history—flora, fauna, and milieu—but rather focused on images on ancient coins, old photographs, gnostic practices, juvenile comic strips, human anatomy, and cave painting. The texts predate

Bataille's 1934 essay "Abjection and Miserable Forms," in which he conceptualized abjection as the double movement of expulsion of an object and repulsion by a subject. Abjection refers to the lack of power to avoid the culturally variable and relational grouping of *things* believed to be necessary to cast out—to *abject*—in order to produce and sustain human being.[4] It primarily refers to "things excluded by the body, plus similar elements," but Bataille's concept was also proto-biopolitical (concerned with the control of and investment in the life of populations) and often separate from any physiological necessity or rational reasoning.[5] These texts were often deliberately antagonistic toward philosophical dialectical thinking, even as they developed a complementary method. Bataille's writings from 1929–32 explicitly and hastily dismiss dialectics as a set of "sleights of hand" intended to reduce the violence of antinomies, to smuggle a "rational order" into accounts of nature (such as in Hegel's perceived panlogism), and to maintain a totalizing, idealist system.[6] The Bataille of *Documents* advocated for an intransigent, radical particularism that declassifies or "bring things down in the world" from any lofty idealist perch and separates them from recourse to a transcendental, master signifier.[7] Bataille and Queneau recapitulated these points in "Critique of the Foundations of the Hegelian Dialectic," where they decried the idea that dialectics were a universal, naturally occurring phenomenon rather than a particular expression of lived experience and human class struggle.[8] Nothing, they asserted, appeared more absurd in Hegel's work than the attempt to locate dialectics in nature. This critique was not a turn away from nature as an important field of investigation. Rather it marked a pivot from seeking a dialectics of nature to thinking of nature, and particularly animal life, dialectically. Bataille was interested in a "dialectic of forms" at play in nature and culture that alternated between incongruity and harmony, low and high seductions.[9] Bataille belatedly recognized this approach as more than a simple refutation of Hegel, acknowledging in 1943, "Without Hegel, I would have had to first of all be Hegel" and in 1958, "In a sense, Hegel's thought is the opposite of mine, but I have only discovered this dialectically, or if I can say it thus, in a Hegelian manner."[10]

The seriousness with which Bataille initially took the historical dimension of animal existence stands as one of the most significant distinctions between his and Hegel's projects, though as Queneau notes, this difference brought Bataille's style of argumentation quite close to that of Hegel's.[11] Bataille criticized Hegel's treatment of nature as an undifferentiated totality, where nature exists primarily as "the fall of the idea, a negation, at once a revolt and an *absurdity* [*un non sens*]."[12] In "The Academic Horse," a symptomatic reading of visual designs of Greek and Gallic coins, published in the first issue of *Documents*, Bataille asserted that though it might *appear* that animals lacked the self-conscious agency of humans to deviate from their own nature, they were indeed historical creatures: "It is no less incontestable that this liberty, of which humanity believes itself to be the unique expression, is just as much the reality of an ordinary animal, whose particular form expresses a gratuitous choice between innumerable possibilities."[13] (After Bataille began attending Alexander Kojève's seminars on *Phenomenology* in 1933, his writings underwent a Kojèvean-Hegelian drift, wherein he adapted the view that animals do not have death in the same way humans do—self-consciously—and exist "lost in a global animality to which it offers no opposition."[14]) Bataille did not disagree with the perceived Hegelian position of nature as a revolt—as *revolting* matter—and as nonsense; rather, he thought these perspectives needed to be taken up more radically, claiming that nature's revolt was not against the *idea*, as Hegel would have it, but was "a constant revolt against itself."[15]

If Bataille showed more sympathy toward traditional natural history than he initially did toward dialectics—both were grand systems aimed at the development of universally applicable laws—it was likely because of the broad empirical foundations of the science, which required it to get a little dirty and to work from the bottom up. Taxonomy, to the extent it was a practice of differentiation, was in keeping with Bataille's interests of the moment, though the unifying and categorical elements were, as Rodolphe Gasché notes, "alien" to his practice.[16] The sweeping taxonomic projects of nineteenth-century naturalists coupled exhaustive empirical observation and comparison of the diversity of life forms with the deduction of logic-based scientific laws, whether starting from below, as with the comparative anatomy work of Georges Cuvier, or above, as in the system of Étienne Geoffroy Saint-Hilaire. Cuvier's principle of correlation between part and whole—from the tooth, the whole tiger—devised a method for ingeniously constructing "kingdoms" (vertebrates, invertebrate, and mollusks) from the fragmented remnants of various specimens. Saint-Hilaire, working from an opposite vantage, developed a transcendental explanation of anatomy, wherein each animal could be shown to be a variation of a single platonic design (expressing that a unity of plan existed at a level of totality).[17] Bataille was wary of the potential reduction of the singularities and incongruities of terrestrial existence into artificial taxonomies whose primary purpose was the elevation of human existence in the tradition of Western idealism. But the field provided a frequent source of interesting data and methodological inspiration for his work, even if Bataille often approached the material through what Gasché, in reference to Bataille's relationship to Hegel, conceptualizes as a form of "reverse reading."[18] Bataille's natural history in reverse found its "truth" in a form of "absolute dismemberment," which sought the dissection of entities and the drawing out of inherent incongruities, rather than the imposition of integrities or the construction of totalities at the levels of individual, species, and kingdom. Like a naturalist, Bataille cut apart and dissected his subjects, studying them through wide-ranging and often surprising forms of comparative analysis. Natural history in this context suggests a *way of looking*, a manner of trying to perceive phenomena in and through their incongruities and most significantly ungrounded from the given-ness of man as the teleological endpoint of historical development. This method sought—as he described in his essay "The Human Face," using old photographic portraits as its primary data—"a real negation of the existence of human nature."[19]

Bataille sketched a de-anthropomorphized and non-anthropocentric approach to natural history, which then provided a vantage from which to practice anthropology differently, within a broadened anthro-zoological context that does not conflate the two terms (as occurred in the racial science based on eighteenth- and nineteenth-century taxonomies) but rather holds them in a state of tension that provides an enlarged field of consideration.[20] His work may be understood as smashing the figure of Vitruvian Man— Leonardo da Vinci's perfectly geometrically proportioned diagram of man as the ideal common measure for all things—which he believed delimited modes of inquiry. In "The Deviations of Nature," a brief text on the attractive and stupefying powers of monsters and other anomalous phenomena, which is one of his most explicit statements on natural history (and which summarizes a set of ideas presented across "The Academic Horse," "The Language of Flowers," "The Human Face," and "Base Materialism and Gnosticism," to name a few, which a longer study would engage), Bataille argued that the "impression of aggressive incongruity" and "profound seductiveness" sparked by incongruous visions were simply the most legible and precise expression of a fundamental truth: that nature is nothing *but* deviations from nature, a dialectic of forms that moves between well-proportioned geometric figures and hideous and polluting masses.[21] Any geometric regularity or ideal form, the argument goes, was simply an abstraction premised on (and repressing) a set of irreducible singularities. Bataille used composite photographs by Francis Galton as an example of this idealist reduction of particularity given real form thanks to the truth claims granted to photographic media. Galton's composites—themselves inspired by the extension of natural history taxonomies into racial theories—produced an image of ideal beauty from a multitude of average photographs: "The composite image would thus give a kind of reality to the necessarily beautiful Platonic idea. At the same time, beauty would be at the mercy of a definition as classical as that of the common measure. But each individual form escapes this common measure and is, to a certain degree, a monster."[22] Unlike the teratological atlases of nineteenth-century natural historians, such as the three volumes produced by Saint-Hilaire, which Bataille dismissed as simply replicating rational taxonomic systems with monsters as their subjects, his approach suggests that natural history should be nothing other than a form of teratology without recourse to a normative standard.

"Deviations of Nature" features full-page reproductions of several plates from Nicolas François Regnault and Geneviève de Nangis Regnault's *Les Écarts de la nature, ou recueil des principales monstruosités que la nature produit dans le genre animal* (1775), including a luxuriously rendered classical illustration of "monstrous" conjoined twins whose separate heads meld into a single cherubic face that looks straight at the beholder (figure 8.1). (All the images in the folio insert their human and animal monsters into a similarly classical mise-en-scène, draping them in togas and depicting them subtly gesticulating in a manner that Simon Baker compares to the postures of a stoic philosopher.)[23] In the context of Bataille's article, the image parodies the geometric perfection of Vitruvian Man, the composited beauty of Galton's superimpositions, and dialectical synthesis as uplift, offering a perverse dialectical counterpart, or seductive form, that draws one not toward elevation and transcendence but toward precisely what these figures exclude: a concern for entropic dissemination, base matter, and abject things.[24] Recalling a comment made in relation to a photograph of a provincial wedding in "The Human Face," the image of an impossible face suggests "a juxtaposition of monsters breeding incompatibles."[25] The legend to the plate of the twins, which, like the image itself, went unremarked on by Bataille, reads in part: "The convergence of the two skulls exposes a slit in the middle of the forehead that somewhat resembles female genitalia. They died in birth."[26] The head, seat of reason, and sexual organs, seat of desire but also ejection (of offspring, both wanted and unwanted), occupy the same impossible position, giving (still)birth to a burlesque image. It depicts the human visage as an illusion comprising a composite of heterogeneous monster parts that might otherwise be denied or abjected from the category of human being.

The burlesque refers to a representational practice rooted in grotesque and derisive forms of imitation and caricature, whose main objective is to

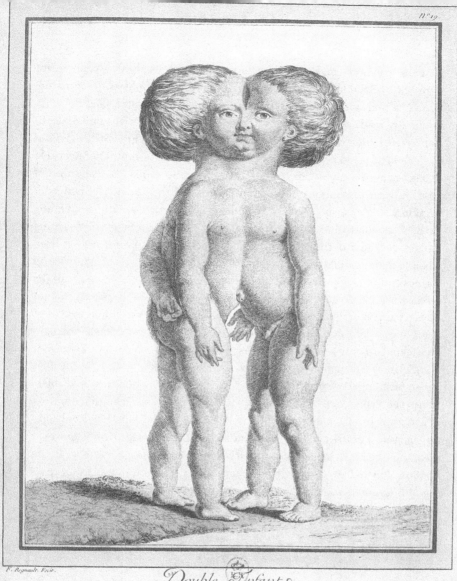

Nº19.

Double Enfant.

Tiré du Cabinet de Mr. Pinson, Chirurgien à Paris.

Ces deux Enfans reunis Sont venus a terme; ils Sont adhérans par les Poitrines et par les Têtes comme on le voit dans le Squelette Nº 2 a les deux Têtes reunies ne forment qu'un Seul Visage, deux Oreilles, une Seule Langue dans la Bouche; un Oesophage, une trachée artere, Ces deux par= ties Se divisent en deux Branches chacune, pour communiquer aux deux Estomacs et aux deux Poitrines; la reunion des deux Crânes offre au milieu du front une fente qui a quelque ressemblance avec la partie genitale d'une Femme, ils Sont Morts en Naissant.

figure 8.1 *Double Enfant (Conjoined Twins)*, color plate, in Nicolas François Regnault and Geneviève de Nangis Regnault's *Les Écarts de la nature, ou recueil des principales monstruosités que la nature produit dans le genre animal* (Paris, 1775). Courtesy of the Bibliothèque Nationale de France.

generate laughter (in French, the term was often used as a synonym for slapstick).[27] Bataille assessed his contribution to philosophy as the introduction of "a philosophy founded on the experience of laughter," and his work frequently reads as a burlesque iteration of natural historians and dialecticians.[28] He believed a burst or explosion of laughter—the French term is *éclat de rire*—incarnated a violent experience, a form of auto-mutilation, capable of shattering the objects of thought as well as the thinker. A condition of possibility for disruptions of old continuities and the creation of new connections, laughter, according to Bataille, was "nature, violently suspending itself."[29] Laughter ventilated whatever it erupted from, momentarily negating the present order of things. This violent suspension manifested a "leap from possible to impossible and from impossible to the possible."[30] Laughter's leap springs from the appearance of an incongruity (what he would later call the unknown): the greater the incongruity, the stronger the impact. Laughter "doesn't affirm or assuage anything," except, perhaps, its own non-necessity. Bataille was determined not to reify or ontologize the experience of laughter's leap: "it's only a leap," not an *Ursprung* (origin) so much as a *Sprungzeit* (springtime).[31] Laughter's springtime may not affirm anything, but it does generate strange "offspring" through its ejections, splits, breaches, and abjections. The experience of laughter is a form of movement, an animation out of and away from a laughing self. Bataille's focus on the experience of laughter suggests a priority for use value, or rather, the *burlesque* (use) *value* over meaning: the bewildering sight of the bulbous red anuses of monkeys in the London Zoo and swollen big toes apparently taught him more than a reading of Bergson's *Laughter: An Essay on the Meaning of the Comic*.[32] Burlesque value refers to the capacity of an image, idea, or situation to produce both a momentary suspension of present terms and an animating leap toward new arrangements.

Picture Thinking

Bataille's "silence" on the burlesque image produced by the convergence of monster parts in the Regnaults' plate, his decision to let the image speak and even scream for itself, corresponded with his approach regarding the montage of visual documents and text in *Documents*. The documents set within the journal retain a quotient of autonomy from the texts they accompany (they are never illustrations in the traditional sense), respecting a resistance to transposition of their material and sensual particularity. He explained his approach to visual documents in "Base Materialism and Gnosticism" as motivated by "the representation of forms in which it is possible to see the image of this base matter that alone, by its incongruity and by an overwhelming lack of respect, permits the intellect to escape from the constraints of idealism. In the same way today certain plastic representations are the expression of an intransigent materialism, of a recourse to everything that compromises the powers that be in matters of form, ridiculing the traditional entities, naively rivaling stupefying scarecrows."[33] The images express a heterogeneous quality through their sensual address that ekphrasis cannot fully capture. The plate of the conjoined twins plays a pivotal role in Bataille's burlesque natural history in developing an element of critical theory abjected from the writing of Hegel, the great philosopher of totality: the problem of "picture thinking" (*Vorstellen/vorstellendes Bewußtsein*).[34] The coming together of the monster parts produces a beatific human visage but also an unexpected appearance of genitalia. Bataille's picture thinking engages an abject dialectics: a dialectical thinking that does not resolve in an overcoming synthesis (*Aufhebung*), but instead maintains a relationship with particularity, materiality, and a sense of life inseparable from what the category of human excludes in order to assert its illusion of integrity. To understand Bataille's practice of picture thinking, it is useful to briefly rehearse Hegel's concept, which largely rests on the problem of clearly defining humans as distinct from animals, the phenomenon of abjection, and the production of burlesque images.

In Hegel's posthumously published lectures on aesthetics, he discourses on the purported threshold between humans and animals through reference to the eighteenth-century Dutch polymath Petrus Camper's "line of beauty" and its relation to Greek sculpture.[35] The line of beauty, as Hegel glosses it, articulates the primary difference between what he refers to as "human face" (*menschlichen Gesichtsbildung*) and "animal profile" (*tierischen Profils*)—as if animals could not even be granted a face, which seems to require animation by *spirit*. This distinction inspires a lengthy passage on the architecture of the animal's head as primarily determined by the mouth and devoration.

> In the formation of the animal head the predominant thing is the mouth, as the tool for chewing, with the upper and lower jaw, the teeth, and the masticatory muscles. The other organs are added to this principal organ as only servants and helpers: the nose especially as sniffing out food, the eye, less important, for spying it. The express prominence of these formations exclusively devoted to natural needs and their satisfaction gives the animal head the appearance of being merely adapted to natural functions without any spiritual or ideal significance. So, after all, we can understand the whole of the animal organism

in light of these tools in the mouth. In other words, the specific kind of food demands a specific structure of the mouth, a special kind of teeth, with which there then most closely correspond the build of the jaws, masticatory muscles, cheek bones, and, in addition, the spine, thigh-bones, hoofs, etc. The animal body serves purely natural purposes and acquires by this dependence on the merely material aspect of nourishment an expression of spiritual absence.[36]

All of animal existence is wrapped up in the muzzle, the combined feature of the mouth, jaw, and nose, "which presses forward as if to get as near as possible to the consumption of food."[37] The line separating animality from beauty, as inscribed in the profile of the head, distinguishes a wholly material existence determined by natural functions and the nourishment an animal takes in (such that their whole structure fulfills the demands of an unreflective consumption) from a human existence defined by self-conscious assertions against nature. Animality exists primarily as a negative ontology in the form of "spiritual absence." The human face, on the contrary, has a structure that incorporates but also subjugates as secondary the animal mouth through the presence of more "ideal" or "theoretical" organs: the upper part of the face and particularly the eyes.[38] The animal and spiritual aspects of the human face are therein mediated by the nose, which still serves the animal imperative of devouring things but operates at one remove from wholly practical activity. For Hegel, the human face is inscribed with *figurative* value (*figure* is French for face or countenance) that separates it from simple animal consumption. (In his lectures on aesthetics, animal consumption is rendered simple, but he complicates it immensely and even allows animals subjectivity and a "real being-for-self" in his reflections on the process of digestion and excretion in animals in *Philosophy of Nature*, which may be summarized by the dictum *cacat ergo est*.)[39]

But figures also posed a problem for Hegel, as he had already made clear in the section of *The Phenomenology of Spirit* (1807) addressed to physiognomy and phrenology. Much of Hegel's concern lay in a critique of the two popular sciences for their violently deterministic and reductive assessment of humanity. The ability to read the character of a person through surface appearances or the shape of his or her bones denies that individual the very dynamism of spirit and character that can only be judged by means of deeds.[40] Donald Phillip Verene argues in an illuminating reading of this section of the *Phenomenology* that these so-called sciences overlooked the power of the mask and the performative ruse: the production of fictions.[41] Hegel believed that, unlike animals, for a human "a bone is nothing *in itself*, much less *his*

james leo cahill

true identity," and the only appropriate response to the reductive diagnosis from a physiognomist or phrenologist is to box their ears and rattle their skulls.[42] Figures, pictures, images all belong to the category of what Gasché summarizes as a "sensible representation of thought," which is necessary but also insufficient: "The image belongs to what discourse allowed to fall by the side in its self-constitution and becoming, what it had to expel in order to achieve transparency."[43] Hegel's *Phenomenology* aims to become a *boneless* endeavor, one that ultimately exceeds or transcends its material supports. Figures cannot be wholly trusted nor systematically interpreted; they must be abjected in service of philosophy's highest callings.

Verene's explication of Hegel's detour into anatomical pseudosciences emphasizes the manner in which the philosopher is setting up a critique of the faulty logic that leads one to believe a clear and definitive line or wholly determinate causal connection may be drawn between individual and environment or between inner life and exterior appearance.[44] The critique of physiognomy and phrenology sets up Hegel's important distinction between representation, or picture thinking (which Verene terms "pictorial consciousness"), and conceptual thought (*Begriff*). Hegel expresses suspicion for the reductive materialism of physiognomy and phrenology. He also believes that thought must ultimately overcome its figurative supports to reach the absolute and infinite. He makes this case for the superiority of pure concept by recourse to a rather striking and burlesque figurative example: the role of the genitals as organs of the basest and most noble functions.

> The *depth*, that spirit drives out from within, but does so only as far as the level of *pictorial consciousness* and then stays on this level, and the *ignorance* of this consciousness, what it is, what it says, is the same linking of high and low that in the living being nature naïvely expresses in linking the organ of its highest perfection, the organ of procreating, and the organ of pissing. The infinite judgment as infinite is the perfection of its own self-comprehended life; but consciousness of the infinite judgment remaining at the pictorial level retains itself as pissing [*Pissen*].[45]

Hegel draws an odd dialectical image, or rather a stalled image of an *abject* dialectics: what proper and progressive dialectics must cast out or abort, but what also risks generating the sort of cutting laughter Bataille describes. Hegel, whom Verene suggests is making a play between *Pissen* and *Wissen* (knowledge), considers picture thinking that is not dialectically animated toward the elevating *Aufhebung* of conceptual thinking to be the equivalent of urination. Picture thinking leaps in the wrong direction, taking form as *pissing*, an animal expression of abject matter. Conceptual thinking, that is to say, proper philosophical thought, is for Hegel something *like* a transcendental ejaculation that disseminates itself into elevated intellectual offspring. In supposedly shedding its reliance on any particular material substrate, conceptual thinking gives (male) birth to and propagates a true philosophy. Pictorial consciousness, picture or figural thinking that does not move beyond its particular material specificity, results in an abject form of thought.

Hegel's pissing also has its unexpected productivities, perverse and monstrous as they may be. In *Philosophy of Nature* (1830), Hegel pursues a lengthy excursus on processes of digestion and excretion in animals. Hegel describes digestion—"the triumph over food"—as a process wherein animals exert a subjectivity and positive relation to the external world by devouring and then "angrily" dealing with the part of the world they have swallowed.[46] In doing so, creatures asserts themselves against that which they have ingested. Digestion and excretion function as processes of affirmative self-differentiation that reproduce something near identical but external to animal. "This real production in which the animal, in repelling itself duplicates itself, is the final stage of animality as such," and this process takes three complementary forms: formal repulsion or excretion (defecation and urination), the constructive instinct (which is a higher form of excretion and an *urform* of the artistic impulse, such as the spider's excretion of its web or a bee's the wax of its hive and the honey therein), and propagation of the species (which is excretion of an even more elevated form).[47] To summarize Hegel's line of thinking, one finds here a view of animal subjectivity as an abject product, a literal abjection of the self, resulting from digestion and excretion. Repulsion, construction, and propagation suggest the progressive dialectical development of this originary act. Amid this lecture, Hegel refers to the evacuated substances of animals as not merely the "heterogeneous, inassimilable matter" of ingested food but composed from "the same ingredients of which the animal organs consist."[48] Urine, he observes, contains elements found in bone, hair, and so on. His point may be taken as double: first that the animal excretes something of its former self in the originary acts of digestion and excretion, but also that even the act of pissing may involve previously unknown forms of generation and overcoming. *Eine fröhliche Pissenschaft.*

So what offspring issue from the conceptual phallus of Hegel's immense philosophical imagination? Among other things, a practice of picture thinking that holds neither suspicion of being seduced as lowly nor undue veneration for idealist conceptualization, but that takes advantage of its suspension or stalling to perform thinking through the particularity of figurative thought. Bataille's natural history offers a most burlesque and virulent strain of picture thinking, but it also opens up a consideration of natural history as a mode of representation in which the abjected matter of picture thinking retains a vital function.

Dismemberment

Naturalists cut up animals. Anatomists and surgeons cut up people. Burlesques are cutups. Bataille's burlesque natural history troubles the distinction between these practices, noting that the thresholds determining human and animal life are not as ironclad as Western tradition would like to insist (hence the need of great philosophers like Hegel to continually return to the problem). Humans are not necessarily exterior to the concerns of natural history as envisioned in Bataille's oeuvre, nor are they its necessary telos. Bataille's burlesque natural history engages in a comical suspension, dissection, and reconfiguration of the human body with an eye for what he calls "disproportion" and "the absence of common measure among various human entities."[49] Through the eye of a natural historian, Bataille disassembles a gross anatomy of anti-idealist evolutionary fables in a series of short articles about big toes, mouths, severed ears, eyes, human faces, and phantasmic organs such as the solar anus, the jesuve, and the pineal eye, producing a vision of bodies as contingently associated parts that are just as likely to express disorder as any "unity of plan." These cuts are, of course, largely of the order of picture thinking conceptualized by Hegel and made into a materialist practice by Bataille.

Bataille does not conflate humans with other animals, nor deny a difference between species, but the threshold between these modes of existence appear to him as far more labile than most humanist thought would admit. In his article "The Big Toe," a classic study of disproportion, Bataille comically observes that the big toe was "the most *human* part of the human body," a statement that simultaneously upends traditions of Western metaphysics that situate humanity in mind and spirit and *animalizes* the rest of the body, suggesting that human corporeality is a relational category rather than a stable ontological fact.[50] The big toe holds this status by its supporting role in orienting human life along a vertical axis and in leading an upright existence but also in its direct, near constant contact with mud, filth, and animal existence—precisely that culturally variable and relational grouping of things believed to be necessary to abject in order to sustain *human* being, though in a highly burlesque manner. Bataille assigns the big toe the task of serving as a corporeal threshold between human and animal life, and as a principal organ for articulating a lacerating, anti-anthropocentric critique of "man" as a stable, self-identical category. The big toe opens his thought onto questions of animal lives and existences. Much human agony emerges from an inflated sense of difference and exceptionalism among human animals, whose upright position nurtures an idealist worldview.

In "Mouth," Bataille elaborates on the significance of structural disposition, positing that the buccal orifice is the "beginning" and "prow" of horizontally oriented animals, as well as the most "alive" and beastly part. With regard to humans, the question of a clear and distinct beginning is a bit more complex because of their upright posture: "It is not even possible to say where he begins [où il commence]."[51] The human mouth plays only a "bestial role" in rare cases of limit experiences, such as extreme terror, hilarity, or ecstasy, when one throws one's head back and the mouth becomes an extension of the spinal column—reassuming the position it occupies in quadrupedal animals who live parallel with the earth. This observation is rooted, for Bataille, in the fundamental importance of the tubelike structural orientation of animals and humans. "It is easy, starting with the worm, to consider ironically an animal, a fish, a monkey, a man, as a tube with two orifices, anal and buccal: the nostrils, the eyes, the ears, the brain represent the complications of the buccal orifices; the penis, the testicles, or the female organs that correspond to them, are the complication of the anal."[52] The posture of humans has altered the primacy of this line of animality and the direct passage from one end of this tube to the other, but this repressed structure still has the capacity, under the right circumstances, to reassert itself and animate one's face and even one's entire body with animal expressions. Bataille's imaginative anatomy places the buccal and anal orifices in a complementary relationship, wherein they perform reversible roles of ingestion and excretion. Laughter is a bodily expression that places these orifices back into an analogous relationship, wherein the sphincter muscles of the mouth act in a similar manner as the sphincter muscles of the anus during defecation. This reorientation made possible by laughter temporarily restores the animal buccal-anal axis and its primal form of expression, which have been made less direct in the architecture of the human body.

As the swollen pivot between animal and human dispositions, the "ignominy" of the big toe has a particularly strong "burlesque value."[53] The raucous laughter inspired by the big toe has the potential to suspend or crack apart

james leo cahill

(by cracking up) the human body. In unpublished notes from around 1930, Bataille posited that laughter occasioned a particular process of abjection:

> When bursts of laughter occur, we must admit that the nervous discharge that would normally have been released by the anus (or by the neighboring sexual organs) is released by the buccal orifice. But in laughter, the excretion ceases to be positively material: it becomes ideological in this sense that the excremental object of spasmodic contractions *is only an image* and not a certain quantity of sperm, urine, blood, or filth. This image can consist of one of the enumerated excrements or one of the excretory organs. It can equally consist of a thing, a person, or an action of a marked excremental character, for example, the fall.[54]

Lacerating laughter, the apex of picture thinking, expresses an abject image that unmakes and remakes the typical orientation of a creature. It temporarily disfigures, defaces, and reconfigures the human face. Laughter redistributes the animal and human relationships within a body. Animals typically "begin" with a mouth and "end" in an anus. These two points, as well as their horizontal relationship with the earth, coordinate their existence. Humans share a vertical orientation common to plants and trees. In "The Big Toe," Bataille refers to the evolution of humans as a development from tree-dwelling apes to essentially becoming mobile trees themselves. These physiological shifts and the relatively unique attitude they have given humans have led them to believe that they are in some genuine way above animals and their material concerns, and thus, "human life is erroneously seen as an elevation."[55] If one cannot say where humans begin, one can at least point to one of their primary points of departure. Bataille refers to the big toe—named, with some irony, *until the very last sentence,* in the general singular ("the") like the phantasmic solar anus, jesuve, and pineal eye—as both "the most *human* part of the human body" and that which keeps humans in touch with their animal brethren because of the *base* position of the toe.[56] It is always in contact with mud, dirt, and everything lowly and of an animal order. Notably, he refers to the foot as an *organ,* suggesting that this appendage finds its precise and vital function in its orchestration of elevating and abasing activities.[57]

The most human part of humans is precisely that which is in continuous touch with the animality and abject matter it wishes to leave behind. The big toe is the base and pedestal on which human erection depends, but this erection exists only as a condition of the big toe's muddy and degrading existence. What is more, big toes and other such body parts—whose corns, blisters, and uncontrollable corporeal functions seem to "independently lead an ignoble life"—are always humiliatingly dragging us back down into that which we imagine ourselves to have escaped and overcome.[58] This condition is profoundly comic. It tells the mythical history of how humanity strives to distance itself from abject things only to continually step in them.

> Since by its physical attitude the human race distances itself *as much as it can* from terrestrial mud—whereas a spasmodic laugh carries joy to its summit each time its purest flight lands man's own arrogance spread-eagle in the mud—one can imagine that a toe, always more or less damaged and humiliating, is psychologically analogous to the brutal fall of a man—in other words, to death. The hideously cadaverous and at the same time loud and proud appearance of the big toe corresponds to this derision and gives a very shrill expression to the disorder of the human body, that product of the violent discord of the organs.[59]

Bataille's study of the big toe and other beasts leads him to conclude that there are two forms of categorically opposed seductiveness: one that leads toward ever greater unities and aspires to light and ideal beauty, and another whose attractive powers draw one toward entropic dispersion into mud, filth, and abject animal matters.[60] The latter is a seductiveness that makes no room for elevating transpositions but that remains at the level of direct material contact and has the effect, as he writes in the concluding sentence, of widening the eyes and opening the mouth to the point of screaming before one of Jacques-André Boiffard's disproportionately large portraits of big toes.[61] "The Big Toe" is, of course, not just concerned with the burlesque but is itself incredibly funny. It aims to performatively produce the very effects it describes, particularly a form of lacerating laughter that inscribes and animates lines of animality in the human face while calling into question the integrity of the body. In the final issue of *Documents*, Bataille muses that few things are more "generally human" than the desire to self-mutilate, to rupture personal homogeneity, to throw oneself "outside the self," and in doing so, to liberate heterogeneous elements or to try to become other than human: absolute dismemberment.[62]

Alteration, Defacement

The burlesque value of picture thinking touches on a key aspect of natural history as a *mode of figuration*, which depicts its subjects through a cutting gaze that does not take human or animal being for granted as givens. As a figural practice, it attempts to maintain contact with the deviations and revolts of Bataille's concept of nature—as well as its revolting contents—in its form. It is a category of *figuration* that materializes and configures what it abjects in the process of coming into existence. Through this practice, it also aims to cut into and cut apart the beholder. The echoes of Bataille's sketch of natural history, according to Queneau, could be detected in his "book on Lascaux" and the birth of art, published in 1955, whose ideas also draw on his writings in *Documents*.[63]

Art, according to the zoo-anthropological fantasies of Bataille's natural history, also springs, like laughter, from abjection. Like the big toe, art marks a point of contact, and even the point of passage, between abject matter, animals, and humans. Reflecting on prehistoric art, such as that found at Lascaux, Trois Frères, and Pech Merle, Bataille sees in it the "miraculous" event by which animals became human through the act of representation. Drawing on Cuvier's principle of correlation of parts, he describes his method of analysis as an attempt to "reconstitute the whole from fragments."[64] One cannot help but suspect the principle of disproportion is once again at play, since these primal images simultaneously efface the human by figuratively emphasizing the animal aspect of being and *disfiguring* the human face, as if trying to recapture something of animal existence in the act of leaving it behind.[65] With the birth of art came the birth of humans as a species that consciously differentiated itself from other animals, and the *work* of art consists in this separation from and visual mourning for the animals that we *no longer* are, or rather no longer *appear* or *think* themselves to be. Figuration entailed the abjection of animals and the simultaneous establishment of a threshold or line tasked with marking and maintaining this separation. The preponderance of hunting scenes, and of scenes of eroticized mutual human and animal destruction, such as in the shaft at Lascaux where a disemboweled bison is pictured alongside a dying man with a bird's head and an erect penis, allegorize this process of a productive double negation. To the extent that the cave paintings may be understood as a form of picture thinking—mental pissing, in Hegel's terms—they eject the animal. Hegelian man "pees" himself into existence, just as animals do, but this time with the phallus rather than the penis. Unlike in the process of animal urination, the phallus produces something qualitatively different: the human, and by virtue of this differentiation, the rest of the animal kingdom too.[66]

Bataille's reflection on the primal act of creation draws on a review essay of G. H. Luquet's *L'Art primitif* (1930), in which Bataille defines so-called primitive art, by which he means a particularly violent form of graphic art—found in the works of early humans, "savages," children, and contemporary artists such as Masson, Miró, and Picasso—as marked by a process of *alteration*.[67] Belonging to an etymological cluster of words—alter, alterity—that signify transformation, deterioration, distortion, falsification, the negative effects of intoxication, as well as difference and othering, *alteration* emphasizes the strong link between art, abject matter, and abjection. Georges Didi-Huberman explains that *alteration* is also a term from philosophy: it is the French rendering for Aristotle's description of the movement of forms and for Hegel's *die Änderung*, or the transformations implicit in becoming.[68] Bataille places this idealist lineage in contact with an unsettling materialism. In a footnote that emphasizes the destructive, contaminating, and even abject aspects of creation, Bataille explains, "The term 'alteration' expresses both a partial decomposition analogous to that of corpses and the passage to a perfectly heterogeneous state corresponding to what the Protestant professor Rudolf Otto calls the 'wholly other' [*tout autre*], which is to say the sacred, realized, for example, in a ghost."[69] Primitive art may be understood as a species of creation through alteration, which holds itself in closer relation to the abject matters cast out in its origin. Bataille distinguishes between primary and secondary processes of alteration, wherein the former refer to the transformations of forms presented—particularly human forms, which are targets of often violent disfigurations—and the latter refer to the transformations of the substrate, wherein a blank piece of paper, a wall, or the back of a classmate's suit are transformed by processes of destructive creation that have a sadistic libidinal charge.[70] Alteration, for Bataille, is always plural and in a sense dialectical, for it sets off a "series of deformations" and "successive destructions" that introduce into the drawing and its substrate a sense of movement that expresses a non-self-identical identity.[71]

A third consideration may be added to Bataille's notion of alteration for the way in which such graphic traces also effect a form of reception. Here Bataille's consideration of laughter and its disfiguring, animal effects comes into communication with the disfiguring effects of a non-anthropocentric alteration in primitive graphic arts, which seeks to decenter the very being it is credited with expressing. In his descriptions of the paintings in Lascaux, Bataille marvels at their tortured or twisted perspectives, which "mingled awkwardness and strength of expression" in the postures of animals and, through skillful use of the curvature of grotto walls, also require torsions and displacements on the part of the beholder.[72]

Bataille recognizes something of this element of an *altering* force in modes of reception of contemporaneous popular culture, such as the anarchic comic strip *Les Pieds nickelés*. "Nickeled feet," a slang term for extraordinarily lazy people, suggests an alteration by contamination wherein the disproportionate and deformed big toe infects and remakes the entire body in a most grotesque form. The strip depicts the amoral misadventures and "delirious laughter of three particularly 'ugly' rogues," Croquignol, Ribouldingue, and Filochard, as they scam suckers out of their money and then quickly eat, drink, and gamble themselves back into penury.[73] *Les Pieds nickelés*'s raison d'être is to bring all forms of loftiness and adult sobriety crashing down to earth with the "formidable sound of smashing dishes" and to provide contradictory evidence to the admonishing refrain of schoolmasters and strict parents everywhere that "life is not a burst of laughter."[74] Bataille casts the three rogues as variations of a modern-day Prometheus tasked with snatching bursts of laughter instead of fire from the gods.[75] The exploits of *Les Pieds nickelés* deliver to children everywhere lessons in the values of burlesque amusements in a "Mexican" sense of the word. Noting the questionably exoticist qualities of his use of "Mexican," Bataille refers to a sense of amusement "always more or less displaced into the most serious domains" and existing as "the most urgent, and certainly, the most terrifying need of human nature" (a formulation he returns to in 1955 through an allusion to the Day of the Dead sequence of Sergei M. Eisenstein's *¡Que Viva Mexico!*, noting that "in present day Mexico it is common to consider death on the same level as amusements").[76] Amusement potentially bursts the body apart in raucous and cutting laughter that dispenses with the comforts of being human in the process. It is a laughter that displaces and *abjects* the subject from him- or herself.

Beyond Seriousness

"Can someone really laugh to death? (The image is bizarre, but I don't have another.)"[77] When Bataille found himself engaged in this bit of picture thinking in 1943, amid global catastrophe, he was in the hiatus period (1930–54) that Queneau provides for considering Bataille as a dialectical natural historian, and that this chapter has extended along a zigzag path of the burlesque. In the shadow of compounding global catastrophes, the question still lingers. In Bataille's burlesque natural history, animals abject themselves into human being through primitive art and laughter. Laughter and primitive art, likewise, by shattering, cutting up, dismembering, and redistributing human being and human parts, may produce a form of self-abjection. Humans left animality by laughing, and we are on the verge of laughing ourselves out of existence through suicidal forms of expenditure. For humans to die of laughter, to merrily cease being human and learn to be otherwise, may be the necessary path to lessening the catastrophes of the present. The stakes are beyond serious, but also beyond seriousness.

Notes

I thank the Camargo Foundation, Jennifer Wild, and Maggie Hennefeld and Nic Sammond. Epigraph: Georg Wilhelm Friedrich Hegel, *Phenomenology of Spirit*, trans. A. V. Miller (New York: Oxford University Press, 1977), 19 (translation slightly modified).

1   Raymond Queneau, "Premières confrontations avec Hegel," "Hommage à Georges Bataille," special issue, *Critique*, no. 195–96 (1963): 698; and Georg Wilhelm Friedrich Hegel, *Werke*, vol. 3, *Phänomenologie des Geistes* (Frankfurt am Main: Suhrkamp, 1986), 36, from here on cited as W3. The "it" refers to Spirit.

2   Raymond Queneau, *Les Exercices de style* (Paris: Gallimard, 1947).

3   Theodor W. Adorno, "The Idea of Natural History," trans. Bob Hullot-Kentor, *Telos: Critical Theory of the Contemporary* 60 (1984): 118. For an examination of the relationship of natural history to surrealism and the Frankfurt school, see my "Cinema's Natural History," *Journal of Cinema and Media Studies*, 58, no. 2 (Winter 2019): 152–57.

4   Georges Bataille, "L'abjection et les formes misérables," in *Oeuvres complètes*, vol. 2 (Paris: Gallimard, 1970), 219; and Bataille, "Abjection and Miserable Forms," in *More and Less*, ed. Sylvère Lotringer and Chris Kraus, trans. Yvonne Shafir (1934; New York: Semiotext(e), 2000), 10.

5   Bataille, notes for "L'abjection et les formes misérables," 437.

6   See Georges Bataille's "Le Cheval académique," *Documents* 1 (1929): 27–31; Bataille, "Figure Humaine," *Documents* 4 (1929): 194–201, esp. 196–97; Bataille, "Le Bas matérialisme et la gnose," *Documents* 1 (1930): 1–8; and Bataille, "Les Écarts de la nature," *Documents* 2 (1930): 79–82.

7   See Georges Bataille, "Formless," in *Visions of Excess: Selected Writings, 1927–1939*, ed. and trans. Allan Stoekl (Minneapolis: University of Minnesota Press, 1985), 31; and Bataille, "Informe," *Documents* 7 (1929): 382.

8   Georges Bataille and Raymond Queneau, "Critique of the Foundations of the Hegelian Dialectic," in *Visions of Excess*, 105–15; and Bataille, *Oeuvres complètes*, vol. 1 (Paris: Gallimard, 1970), 277–90.

9   Georges Bataille, "The Deviations of Nature," in *Visions of Excess*, 55; and Bataille, "Les Écarts de la nature," 79.

10 Georges Bataille, *Guilty*, trans. Bruce Boone (Venice, CA: Lapis Press, 1988), 108 (translation slightly modified); Bataille, *Oeuvres complètes*, vol. 5 (Paris: Gallimard, 1973), 353; and Bataille, "Notice Autobiographique," in *Oeuvres complètes*, vol. 7 (Paris: Gallimard, 1976), 615.

11 Queneau, "Premières confrontations avec Hegel," 694.

12 Bataille and Queneau, "Critique," 107; and Bataille, *Oeuvres complètes*, 1:279.

13 Georges Bataille, "The Academic Horse," in *Undercover Surrealism: Georges Bataille and Documents*, ed. Dawn Ades and Simon Baker (Cambridge, MA: MIT Press, 2007), 237; and Bataille, "Le Cheval académique," 27.

14 Georges Bataille, "Hegel, Death, and Sacrifice," trans. Jonathan Strauss, "On Bataille," special issue, *Yale French Studies* 78 (1990): 15; and Bataille, *Oeuvres complètes*, vol. 12 (Paris: Gallimard, 1988), 332.

15 Bataille, "The Academic Horse," 238.

16 Rodolphe Gasché, *Georges Bataille: Phenomenology and Phantasmatology*, trans. Roland Vésgö (Stanford, CA: Stanford University Press, 2012), 109.

17 See Georges Cuvier, *Discours sur les révolutions de la surface du globe*, 6th ed. (Paris: Edmond D'Ocagne, 1830), 97–102; and Étienne Geoffroy Saint-Hilaire, *Philosophie Anatomique* (Paris: Méquignon-Marvis, 1818), xxxvi.

18 Gasché, *Georges Bataille*, xviii.

19 Bataille, "Figure Humaine," 96; Bataille, "The Human Face," in *Encyclopaedia Acephalica*, ed. Robert Lebel and Isabelle Waldberg (London: Atlas Press, 1995), 101.

20 Georges Didi-Huberman refers to Bataille's work in *Documents* as engaging a de-anthropomorphism of knowledge and a laceration of an "anthropocentrism of form." See *La ressemblance informe: Ou le gai savoir visuel selon Georges Bataille* (Paris: Macula, 1995), 37–38.

21 Bataille, "The Deviations of Nature," 55.

22 Bataille, "The Deviations of Nature," 55.

23 Simon Baker, "Human Figures," in Bataille, *Undercover Surrealism*, 189.

24 Bataille, "The Deviations of Nature," 53–56.

25 Bataille, "The Human Face," 102.

26 Bataille, "Les Écarts de la nature," 81.

27 See the entries for burlesque in the *Oxford English Dictionary* and in *Grand Robert de la Lange française*.

28 Georges Bataille, "Nonknowledge, Laughter, and Tears," in *The Unfinished System of Nonknowledge*, ed. Stuart Kendall, trans. Michelle Kendall and Stuart Kendall (Minneapolis: University of Minnesota Press, 2001), 138; and Bataille, *Oeuvres complètes*, vol. 8 (Paris: Gallimard, 1976), 220.

29 Bataille, *Guilty*, 103.

30 Bataille, *Guilty*, 101.

31 Bataille, *Guilty*.

32 Bataille, "The Jesuve," in *Visions of Excess*, 75–76; Bataille, *Oeuvres complètes*, 2:16–20; and Bataille, "Nonknowledge, Laughter and Tears," 139.

33 Bataille, "Base Materialism and Gnosticism," in *Visions of Excess*, 51.

34 I am indebted to Georges Didi-Huberman's examination of the montage practices and "visual gay science" of *Documents* in *La ressemblance informe*; and Anne Nesbet's *Savage Junctures: Sergei Eisenstein and the Shape of Thinking* (London: O. B. Taurus, 2003), esp. 85–92. Nesbet's formulation of Eisenstein as practicing a form of Hegelian picture thinking as *philosophy* and not, as Hegel would have it, its failure, does not explicitly engage with Bataille but

has been immeasurably helpful in allowing me to clarify and reconsider Bataille's relation to Hegel.

35 Georg Wilhelm Friedrich Hegel, *Aesthetics: Lectures on Fine Art*, vol. 2, trans. T. M. Knox (New York: Oxford University Press, 1975), 728; and Hegel, *Werke*, vol. 14, *Vorlesungen über die Ästhetik II* (Frankfurt am Main: Suhrkamp, 1986), 383–85, from here on cited as w14.

36 Hegel, *Aesthetics*, 728; Hegel, w14, 384–85.

37 Hegel, *Aesthetics*, 728; Hegel, w14, 384–85.

38 Hegel, *Aesthetics*, 728–729; Hegel, w14, 384–85.

39 Georg Wilhelm Friedrich Hegel, *Philosophy of Nature*, trans. A. V. Miller (New York: Oxford University Press, 2004), 394–406, quotations on 404; and *Werke*, vol. 9, *Enzyklopädie der philosophischen Wissenschaften im Grundrisse (1830)*, book 2, *Die Naturphilosophie* (Frankfurt am Main: Suhrkamp, 1986), 491, from here on cited as w9.

40 Hegel, *Phenomenology of Spirit*, 193–94.

41 Donald Phillip Verene, *Hegel's Recollection: A Study of Images in the Phenomenology of Spirit* (Albany: State University of New York Press, 1985), 83.

42 Hegel, *Phenomenology of Spirit*, 205; Hegel, w3, 256–57.

43 Gasché, *Georges Bataille*, 111–12.

44 Verene, *Hegel's Recollection*, 82.

45 Verene, *Hegel's Recollection*, 87. Verene corrects Miller's more tepid translation of Hegel's *Pissen* as "urination," in Hegel, *Phenomenology of Spirit*, 210; Hegel, w3, 262. Hegel returns to and in fact compounds this image in *Philosophy of Nature*, 404, and in w9, 492, noting, "In many animals the organs of excretion and the genitals, the highest and lowest parts in the animal organization[,] are intimately connected."

46 Hegel, *Philosophy of Nature*, 404. He uses "angry" and "anger" (*Zorn*) to describe digestion on 397 and 403, and in Hegel, w9, 483, 489.

47 Hegel, *Philosophy of Nature*, 404, 406–9; Hegel, w9, 491, 493–97.

48 Hegel, *Philosophy of Nature*, 405–6; Hegel, w9, 493. Although Hegel uses the adjective *heterogenen* (heterogeneous) in these lectures, in this instance, the adjective he uses is *fremdartige*, which suggests something strange or alien.

49 Bataille, "The Human Face," 102.

50 Georges Bataille, "Le Gros Orteil," *Documents* 6 (1929): 297–302; Bataille, "The Big Toe," in *Visions of Excess*, 20–23.

51 Georges Bataille, "Bouche," *Documents* 5 (1930): 299; Bataille, "Mouth," in *Visions of Excess*, 60.

52 Georges Bataille, "L'œil pinéal," in *Oeuvres complètes*, 2:33; and Bataille, "The Pineal Eye," in *Visions of Excess*, 88–89.

53 Bataille, "Big Toe," 22, 23.

54 Georges Bataille, "La valeur d'usage de D. A. F. de Sade (2)," in *Oeuvres complètes*, 2:71 (emphasis added).

55 Bataille, "Big Toe," 20.

56 Bataille, "Big Toe."

57 Bataille, "Big Toe," 21.

58 Bataille, "Big Toe," 22.

59 Bataille, "Big Toe," 22.

60 Bataille, "Big Toe," 22–23.

61 Bataille, "Big Toe."

62 Georges Bataille, "La mutilation sacrifidelle et l'oreille coupée de Vincent Van Gogh," *Documents* 8 (1930): 451–60; Bataille, "Sacrificial Mutilation and the Severed Ear of Vincent Van Gogh," in *Visions of Excess*, 68, 69, 70.

63 Georges Bataille, *Prehistoric Painting: Lascaux, or the Birth of Art*, trans. Austryn Wainhouse (Geneva: Skira, 1955); Bataille, *Oeuvres complètes*, vol. 9 (Paris: Gallimard, 1979).

64 Bataille, *Prehistoric Painting*, 37.

65 Bataille, *Prehistoric Painting*, 114–15.

66 In making this generalized distinction between man and all animals (as an undifferentiated category), Bataille strays from the almost impossible, anti-idealist practice of radical singularity thinking that he pursued in his *Documents*-era writings.

67 Georges Bataille, "L'Art primitif," *Documents* 7 (1930): 392; Bataille, "Primitive Art," in *The Cradle of Humanity: Prehistoric Art and Culture*, ed. and introduced by Stuart Kendall, trans. Michelle Kendall and Stuart Kendall (New York: Zone, 2009), 40. See also Didi-Huberman, *La ressemblance informe*, 252–68.

68 Didi-Huberman, *La ressemblance informe*, 262.

69 Bataille, "Primitive Art," 193n3.

70 Bataille, "Primitive Art," 41.

71 Bataille, "Primitive Art."

72 Bataille, *Prehistoric Painting*, 111.

73 Georges Bataille, "Les Pieds nickelés," *Documents* 4 (1930): 215. Louis Forton, the creator of *Les Pieds nickelés*, originally intended to call his strip *Les Pieds salles* (The filthy feet) but his publishers, the Offenstadt brothers, thought that was too lurid and suggested appropriating the title of a play by Tristan Bernard instead. See Jean Tulard, *Les Pieds nickelés de Louis Forton (1908–1934)* (Paris: Armand Colin, 2008), 40.

74 Bataille, "Les Pieds nickelés," 215–16.

75 Bataille, "Les Pieds nickelés," 216.

76 Bataille, "Les Pieds nickelés"; Bataille, "Hegel, Death, and Sacrifice," 24–25. See also Sergei Eisenstein's drawings made in Mexico in the early 1930s, which also proceed by comic routes to the most serious and amusing subjects.

77 Bataille, *Guilty*, 103; Bataille, *Oeuvres complètes*, 5:346. For one answer, see Maggie Hennefeld, "Death from Laughter, Female Hysteria, and Early Cinema," *Differences* 27, no. 3 (2016): 45–92.

chapter nine

Why, an Abject Art

mark mulroney

MY MOTHER WAS BORN IN 1945. SHE IS BLONDE, FIVE-FEET FOUR-INCHES TALL: SHE LIKE MEXICAN PIZZAS AND COUNTRY SONGS ABOUT AMERICA'S GREATNESS. WHEN I EXHIBIT MY WORK IT IS NOT UNCOMMON TO FIND MY MOTHER AT THE OPENING RECEPTION STATIONED IN FRONT OF ONE OF THE MORE GRAPHIC PIECES, PERHAPS A COMIC DRAWING OF A TEENAGER TIED TO A TREE WITH AN ABSURDLY OVERSIZED ERECTION THAT HE CAN'T QUITE HANDLE. MY MOTHER WILL STAND IN FRONT OF THE DRAWING AND OFFER AN APOLOGY TO ANYONE WHOSE ATTENTION SHE CAN GRAB. "I DON'T KNOW WHAT HAPPENED," SHE'LL SAY, "HE REALLY HAD A VERY NORMAL CHILDHOOD." A CHILDHOOD FULL OF BOREDOM, ADVENTURE, PUNISHMENT, TERROR, TEAM SPORTS, MYSTERY, BIRTHDAY PARTIES, FIGHTING, CLIMBING, HOLE-DIGGING, LYING, AND MY ATTEMPT, ONE SUMMER, TO BUILD A GO-KART OUT OF AN OLD SKATEBOARD AND SOME SCRAP WOOD. I WAS WELL FED, KEPT WARM, GIVEN BOOKS AND A BASEBALL GLOVE, OFFERED ENCOURAGEMENT AND BOUNDARIES, AND PROVIDED WITH A SAFE PLACE TO EAT CEREAL.

WHILE MY PARENTS DID EVERYTHING GOOD PARENTS SHOULD DO, THERE WAS ONE THING THAT THEY DIDN'T DO. THEY DIDN'T TALK ABOUT SEX, EVER. THE PRIESTS AND NUNS IN CATHOLIC SCHOOL DIDN'T HELP PROVIDE MUCH INSIGHT EITHER. ALL I KNEW WAS THAT THERE WERE SOME MAGAZINES UNDER THE MATTRESS ON MY DAD'S SIDE OF THE BED, AND THAT I COULDN'T WAIT FOR MY PARENTS TO LEAVE SO I COULD SNEAK INTO THEIR ROOM AND GET ANOTHER CHANCE TO LIFT THE MATTRESS AND TAKE A LOOK AT ALL THOSE NAKED LADIES.

WHEN I WAS EIGHT YEARS OLD MY PARENTS GAVE ME A BOOK TITLED "WHAT'S HAPPENING TO ME?" IT WAS WRITTEN BY PETER MAYLE AND ILLUSTRATED BY ARTHUR ROBBINS. THE BOOK WAS INTENDED TO SERVE AS A GUIDE TO PUBERTY. IT CONSISTED OF FIFTY-SIX PAGES OF CARTOON DRAWINGS THAT CONFUSED ME AND WORDS THAT I DIDN'T UNDERSTAND LIKE ORGASM, MASTURBATION, CIRCUMCISION, AND OVARIES. THE BOOK WAS DIVIDED INTO SEVENTEEN SECTIONS, EACH OF WHICH WAS MEANT TO COVER A DIFFERENT ASPECT OF PUBERTY. THE SECTIONS HAD CLEVER HEADINGS LIKE "WHY AM I GETTING HAIRY?" OR "WHY IS MY CHEST GETTING BUMPY?" AND THE CORRESPONDING DRAWINGS DEPICTED THINGS LIKE A NAKED BLONDE GIRL LOOKING AT HER BROWN PUBES WITH A CONFUSED LOOK ON HER FACE WONDERING WHY THE HAIR ON HER HEAD DIDN'T MATCH THE HAIR ON HER VAGINA.

MOST OF THE DRAWINGS WERE KIND OF
FUNNY, SOME WERE CONFUSING, OTHERS
WERE DULL; BUT TWO IMAGES WERE
TRULY HORRIFYING.

THE FIRST WAS
OF A GIANT
SPERM DRAWN IN
A WHIMSICAL
STYLE PERFECT
FOR A HALLMARK
CARD. HE WAS
THE COLOR OF
BUBBLEGUM AND
HAD A CARTOON
FACE. HIS ROUND
FLESHY BODY
ALMOST FILLED
THE WHOLE PAGE.
HE WAS LOOKING
UP, TWIDDLING
HIS THUMBS, AND
WHISTLING. THE
CAPTION NEXT TO
HIM READ,
"SPERM CAN'T DO
VERY MUCH
EXCEPT SIT
AROUND UNTIL
YOU GET AN
ERECTION."

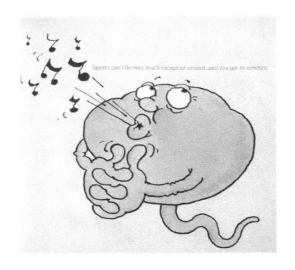

I DIDN'T KNOW WHAT TO MAKE OF THIS
DRAWING: DID SPERM HAVE EYEBALLS, A
MOUTH, ARMS? I KNEW WHAT A SPERM WHALE
WAS AND THAT THEY WERE LARGE SO I THOUGHT
THIS WHISTLING SPERM MUST ALSO BE LARGE.
AND SINCE IT WAS KIND OF FLESH COLORED, I
THOUGHT IT MUST BE LIKE AN ORGAN THAT
LIVED INSIDE OF ME.

*THE SECOND IMAGE IN THE BOOK THAT I
FOUND VERY DISTURBING SHOWED TWO BOYS
IN THE SHOWER LOOKING AT EACH OTHER'S
PENISES. THE CAPTION READ, "THE
GENTLEMAN ON THE LEFT IS CIRCUMCISED,
HIS FRIEND ISN'T."*

The gentleman on the left is circumcised. His friend isn't.

I DIDN'T KNOW WHAT "CIRCUMCISED" MEANT
AND I DIDN'T NOTICE THAT THEIR PENISES
LOOKED DIFFERENT, SO THIS LEFT ME
WONDERING: WHAT IS CIRCUMCISION? WHY ARE
THESE BOYS SHOWERING TOGETHER? IS IT
REALLY OK TO LOOK AT ANOTHER BOY'S PENIS?
AND WHAT ROLE DOES THAT GIANT WHISTLING
SPERM PLAY IN THIS WHOLE NAKED,
STARING-AT-EACH-OTHER-IN-THE-SHOWER SCENE?
MY EIGHT-YEAR-OLD IMAGINATION BEGAN TO
STITCH TOGETHER A NARRATIVE THAT WOULD
HELP ME MAKE SENSE OF THIS BOOK THAT MY
MOTHER AND FATHER HAD GIVEN TO ME WITHOUT
ANY EXPLANATION.

mark mulroney

HERE IS WHAT I CAME UP WITH: IF I EVER TAKE A SHOWER WITH
ANOTHER BOY AND I LOOK AT HIS PENIS, A GIANT WHISTLING SPERM
WILL POP OUT OF MY SIDE, FALL TO THE FLOOR, AND LOOK UP AT ME
WHISTLING. I CONCLUDED THAT WAS HOW YOU KNEW THAT YOU HAD
BECOME A MAN. I RECALL BELIEVING MY EXPLANATION MADE SENSE,
BUT ALSO REALIZING THAT I STILL DID NOT HAVE ALL THE ANSWERS.
WHAT HAPPENS TO YOU AFTER THE SPERM POPS OUT? DOES YOUR SKIN
JUST SEAL ITSELF UP AND HEAL INSTANTLY LIKE WOLVERINE?

I HAD BEEN
TO THE BEACH
AND SEEN
LOTS OF MEN
WITH THEIR
SHIRTS OFF
AND NEVER
SAW A SCAR
THAT
INDICATED
WHERE THEIR
WHISTLING
SPERM HAD
POPPED OUT,
SO I
CONCLUDED
THAT THIS
TRANSITION
INTO MANHOOD
MUST NOT
LEAVE A
SCAR.

THE OVERALL LESSON THAT I LEARNED
WAS THAT I WAS NEVER, EVER GOING TO
SHOWER WITH ANY OTHER BOYS NO MATTER
WHAT. IF THAT WHISTLING SPERM WANTED
OUT OF ME HE WAS GOING TO HAVE TO
GET A KNIFE BECAUSE I WASN'T GOING
TO LOOK AT SOME OTHER KID'S WET
WIENER AND GET EMBARRASSED IN THE
SHOWER. ABSURD AS THIS SOUNDS, I
FOLLOWED THIS LESSON WELL INTO HIGH
SCHOOL. FRESHMAN YEAR I FAKED A
BROKEN ARM TO GET OUT OF P.E. CLASS
BECAUSE I KNEW I WOULD HAVE BEEN
FORCED TO SHOWER WITH THE OTHER
BOYS. INSTEAD OF PLAYING SPORTS,
GETTING SWEATY AND SHOWERING WITH MY
CLASSMATES, I SPENT P.E. ALONE,
CLEANING UP THE FOOTBALL LOCKER
ROOM.

CATHOLIC SCHOOL OFFERED ME ABOUT AS MUCH USEFUL GUIDANCE ON SEX
AS THAT BOOK THAT MY PARENTS GAVE ME. WHAT I GOT FROM THE CLERGY
WAS THAT NO MATTER WHAT YOU DO OR THINK YOU ARE A SINNER AND SEX
IS WRONG AND DIRTY AND SHOULD BE AVOIDED EXCEPT WITHIN A
HETEROSEXUAL MARRIAGE AND FOR THE PURPOSE OF HAVING A BABY. WE
HAD A POSTER UP IN MY NINTH GRADE HOMEROOM THAT SHOWED A HAPPY
YOUNG BOY KNEELING DOWN, PETTING HIS DOG, WITH A CAPTION THAT
READ, "PET YOUR DOG, NOT YOUR DATE."

DURING MY SOPHOMORE YEAR WE HAD TO WATCH A VERY GRAPHIC VIDEO OF A *REAL ABORTION*. WE SAW EVERYTHING INCLUDING A DISMEMBERED FETUS. MY CLASSMATE GABRIEL FAINTED AND SLID OUR OF HIS DESK AND ONTO THE LINOLEUM FLOOR.

THEN THERE WAS FATHER ROBERT'S
MASTURBATION SPEECH. HE WAS
OUR NEW TESTAMENT INSTRUCTOR
AND HE TOLD US THAT AS A YOUNG
BOY HE WAS A CHRONIC
MASTURBATOR AND THAT HE
OVERCAME HIS AFFLICTION WITH
SELF-DISCIPLINE AND A LOT OF
PRAYER. HE ALSO INSTITUTED AN
IN-CLASS WARNING SYSTEM HE
CALLED, "SKIRT ALERT!"
WHENEVER A GIRL IN THE CLASS
HAD HER LEGS OPEN AND HE COULD
SEE HER UNDERWEAR HE'D SHOUT
"SKIRT ALERT!" AND ALL THE
GIRLS WOULD QUICKLY CLOSE
THEIR LEGS. FATHER ROBERT'S
CLASSROOM WAS ALSO WHERE YOU'D
SPEND AN HOUR AFTER CLASS IF
YOU HAD TO SERVE DETENTION. I
SPENT A LOT OF TIME IN FATHER
ROBERT'S CLASSROOM EITHER
LISTENING TO HIM TALK ABOUT
HIS MASTURBATION HABITS OR
SITTING QUIETLY WITH MY FACE
FORWARD AND HANDS FOLDED ON
TOP OF THE DESK.

BETWEEN MY PARENTS RELEGATING ALL EXPLANATIONS OF SEX TO THIS ONE BOOK AND THE CATHOLIC CHURCH'S LITANY OF SINS I WAS ILL-PREPARED FOR PUBERTY AND THE NIGHTLY SERIES OF LINEN CHANGES THAT FOLLOWED. I HAD NO IDEA HOW TO RELATE TO MY OWN BODY EITHER EMOTIONALLY OR PHYSICALLY MUCH LESS THAT OF ANOTHER PERSON. SEX WASN'T JUST A JUMBLED MESS OF FLUIDS, LIMBS, AND APOLOGIES: IT COULD ALSO SEND YOU TO HELL.

FROM A VERY EARLY AGE, I KNEW OF THE INEVITABILITY OF DEATH AND THE RISK OF GOING TO HELL. STARTING IN FIRST GRADE, WE WERE TAUGHT THE STORIES OF ALL THE RIGHTEOUS CATHOLIC MARTYRS. THE ONLY TIME SISTER PIUS WOULD EVER EXPRESS ANY JOY WAS WHEN SHE WOULD TELL STORIES ABOUT THE LIVES OF MARTYRS. SHE WOULD DESCRIBE IN VIVID DETAIL HOW SAINT BARTHOLOMEW'S SKIN WAS FLAYED OFF OF HIS BODY WHILE HE WAS STILL BREATHING. A HORRIFIC DEATH WAS WORTH IT, WE WERE TOLD, BECAUSE THEN YOU'D GET TO SPEND ETERNITY WITH JESUS AND, MOREOVER, YOUR DEATH WOULD BE COMMEMORATED WITH A HOLY CARD THAT WOULD BE CARRIED IN THE WALLETS OF GOOD CATHOLICS EVERYWHERE.

I WAS EDUCATED IN AN ENVIRONMENT IN WHICH A TORTURED AND BEATEN MAN WAS IN THE FRONT OF EVERY CLASSROOM. A MAN THAT WAS NAILED TO A CROSS AND LEFT TO DIE. HIS BODY IN A STATE OF ECSTATIC AGONY, EVERY CUT CARVED WITH CARE, EVERY DROP OF BLOOD FULL, ROUND, AND WET. SURE HE WAS DEAD, BUT HE WAS ALSO VERY SEXY. AT HIS FEET WATCHING HIM WAS HIS OWN MOTHER, WEEPING, HANDS CLASPED IN GRIEF.

Color versions of images in this chapter may be found at http://scalar.usc.edu /works/abjection-incorporated-insert/index.

Why, an Abject Art

abject

aesthetics

structure,

form,

system

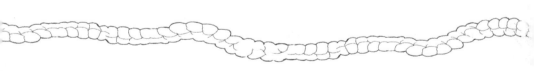

part III

chapter ten

A Matter of Fluids: EC Comics & the Vernacular Abject

nicholas sammond

Now, I am become Death, the destroyer of worlds.
—J. Robert Oppenheimer, *The Decision to Drop the Bomb*

Was the Parthenon worth the sufferings of a single slave? Is it possible to write poetry after Auschwitz? The question has been countered: when the horror of reality tends to become total and blocks political action, where else than in the radical imagination, as refusal of reality, can the rebellion, and its uncompromised goals, be remembered? But today, are the images and their realization still the domain of "illusory" art?
—Herbert Marcuse, *An Essay on Liberation*

The May 1954 cover of EC Comics' *Mad* magazine features the bust of a lone "woman," drawn by the artist Basil Wolverton (figure 10.1). To describe the figure as simply a woman would be inaccurate and misleading. She is a grotesque. Her hair and eyebrows appear to be made of spaghetti or wet straw. Her nose is a snout or a double-barreled penis. Her bloodshot eyes protrude; the epicanthic folds are fatty. Her skin is pocked, and the pox on her face erupt with either hair or pus. Her veined and cracked teeth protrude from

figure 10.1 Cover of the May 1954 issue of EC Comics' *Mad* magazine.

pitted gums, and her tongue looks like 10-grit sandpaper. A simple string of pearls adorns her neck.

The magazine's inside cover offers an explanation, if one were needed. A full-page "advertisement" for *Mad* declares "BEWARE OF IMITATIONS!" and places the same cover side by side with that of the May 18, 1953, issue of *Life* magazine (figure 10.2). The *Life* cover features an attractive young woman; the accompanying text identifies her as a student of opera from Indiana. A caption below the two images warns of imitations, of "filthy unAmerican swipes of *Mad* magazine," the joke, of course, being that it is Wolverton who is parodying the *Life* cover. Below that caption, the magazine offers a test for determining which is genuine: roll up both magazines and smoke them. *Mad* will only "set your head on fire"; *Life* will blow your head off.

It would be reasonable to read these instructions as offhand references to an emerging drug counterculture. (Howard Becker published his "Becoming a Marihuana User" in November 1953; the issue also coincides roughly with the rise of the Beats.) Yet given the age and disposition of *Mad*'s artists and editors, it is just as likely a reference to a joke-shop exploding cigar.[1] Regardless of its inspiration, the gag as a whole could easily be dismissed as juvenile satire, an offhand gibe at popular journalism and a misogynistic jab at postwar female empowerment. But the juvenilia of the joke, and of *Mad* and other "off-color" comic books of the 1940s and 1950s, also expresses an objection to the breezy performance of confidence, the exuberant celebration of the power of possibility in the postwar, easy-credit economy represented by the opera student's sunny smile.

Mad's response to *Life* follows a logic that extends from the central place of abjection in wartime cultural and social life—less than a decade after World War II and now framed by a very new Cold War—which entailed the forceful production of boundaries between a sovereign and just self (as patriot) and an execrable and loathsome Other/enemy, a threat to that self and to the society within which it operated. This abjecting operated not only at the level of representation during the war, through grotesquely offensive propaganda aimed at Axis enemies[2] but also and more profoundly in constant reminders of the gruesome and bloody deaths that were the inevitable result of mechanized combat. This carnage became even more profoundly present with the firebombing of Dresden and the dropping of atomic bombs on Hiroshima and Nagasaki, ostensibly defensive maneuvers that produced slaughter on an entirely new scale. So, if *Life*'s sunny forward look was an act of repression, *Mad*'s response, and those of dozens of other horror, crime, and romance imprints of the fifties, were refusals of that repression—not unlike those by Otto

figure 10.2 Inside cover of the May 1954 issue of *Mad* magazine.

Dix or George Grosz following the nightmare of World War I. Dix and Grosz performed their outrage through graphic depictions of the abjected bodies of mutilated veterans trolling through the Weimar demimonde, often linking sex and death in a single image.[3] Like Dix or Grosz, the artists who produced *Mad* and Cold War pulp comics expressed discomfort with the resumption of an unexamined "normal" life by depicting human bodies generally, but particularly women's bodies, as sites of both erotic fascination and corporeal discomfort and disgust.

Yet where Dix and Grosz had plumbed the Weimar underworld for the abject, comic-book artists in the Cold War era located abjection in everyday life, as the dark side of normal, middle-class, and middle-American whiteness, in the white body generally, and often in women's bodies. An idealized femininity was integral to the Cold War "politics of containment," a fantasy of a well-ordered, rational, and harmonious society as a bulwark against Communist subversion. Comic-book artists and writers, an almost exclusively male group, responded to that repressive fantasy through vernacular images of the abject, and often by abjecting women's bodies in particular.[4] That graphic misogyny, whether intentional or not, represents an explicit performance, a graphic correlate to the implicit violence of the Cold War's containment through gender. Where properly gendered bodies were expected to perform a happy normativity, the anxious and the abject revealed (and sometimes reveled in) the costs of failing to do so.

As Anne McClintock has noted, abjection "hovers on the threshold of the body and the body politic," and in a society organized at least in part through the operations of biopower—the operation of state power through the regulation of the relationship between body and self—parsing the relation between the two becomes very important.[5] In this instance, comic artists' juvenile abreaction when faced with an ideal femininity—creating grotesque and excessive parodies of the actual corporeality of women's bodies—mobilizes abjection as a profoundly ambivalent objection. That parody is simultaneously misogynist in its reaction to the fluid productions of actual bodies and politically resistant when invoking that reaction as a protest against repressive normativity. Following Judith Butler (in a very different context), it becomes possible to understand abjection, usually considered an operation important in the regulation of gendered normativity, as a key site for calling into question that normativity, and the larger social, cultural, and political forces that inform it.[6] Producing and regulating legible gender difference was a central Cold War domestic project, as much championed by the liberal left as by the center and right. The vernacular abject refusal of liberal efforts to regulate social relations through gender—however juvenile—is a site for beginning a counter-history of popular understandings of Cold War conformism as politically conservative.

In Cold War neo-Freudianism—a simplification of psychoanalytic theory that imagined deploying Freud in day-to-day interactions between lay individuals—a common thread was the restoration of a femininity that had been deformed by the absence of male domestic authority during World War II. This idea was espoused by child-rearing guru Benjamin Spock and deployed in the domesticated cultural anthropology of Margaret Mead and in pseudoscientific antifeminist jeremiads by the likes of Philip Wylie. The inherent misogyny of projects to restore that proper femininity fell most heavily on women's bodies in the form of a simultaneous celebration and circumscription of femininity, the body compressed by girdles and accentuated by poodle skirts and angora sweaters. Pulp grotesques of that ideal feminine body, and larger vernacular graphic critiques of the regulation of corporeal and affective existence in the Cold War, gave form and shape to the violence underlying that project. Postwar pulp comics in general, and *Mad* in particular, expressed an adolescent discomfort and dis-ease with bodies and affects, and often mobilized women's bodies to express that discomfort. That abject objection found its material base through that which had been abjected in the process of regulation: in nonnormative bodies and attitudes that were criticized, undermined, and cast aside in the service of an ideal domestic body politic. Pulp vernacular media were considered at best lowbrow, infantile, and disposable; at worst, they were impediments to the proper development of youth and to the embrace of mature social relations in adults. This chapter considers whether the juvenilia of *Mad* and of postwar romance, crime, and horror comics were a form of graphic dissent, of resistance to arguments in popular Cold War psychology, sociology, and developmental theory about how to produce a healthy body politic through the regulation of individual bodies and affects.

It is worthwhile to consider what it means to call comics generally, or *Mad* in particular, "juvenile." An accounting of comic-book readership in the early 1940s noted that "95 percent of children aged eight to eleven and 84 percent of children 12 to seventeen read comics, while 35 percent of adults aged eighteen to thirty did the same."[7] At first blush, the proportionately higher number of child readers seems to confirm the perception that comic books represent a childish form of entertainment. Yet more than a third of midcentury adult Americans *also* read comics and found some meaning, and some pleasure, in the pathos of juvenilia; in its uneasy relationship to sex, death, and the body (the fixations of adolescent experience); and in their material production: blood, semen, mucus, putrescence, and so on—the touchstones of abjection.

The horrors of World War II—wartime deprivation, the Holocaust, the siege of Stalingrad, the firebombing of Dresden and Tokyo, and finally the atomic bombings of Hiroshima and Nagasaki—formed a backdrop to the childhoods of the men and women (though primarily men) who produced and consumed these comics. This was especially true for veterans who had to reintegrate into a peacetime society whose burgeoning economy resulted from that conflict. Following the war, applied psychology and sociology flourished in the United States, much of it taking shape in response to the trauma of wartime experience, both in battle and at home.[8] That reaction was inflected by encounters with totalitarianism and authoritarianism during the war and in the growing Cold War, most famously articulated in Theodor Adorno's *The Authoritarian Personality* and Hannah Arendt's *The Origins of Totalitarianism*, but also promulgated in academic and popular arguments for harmonizing and adjusting—two key terms from the period—the individual's relationship to social and institutional life.[9] Pulp comics, which often linked horror, humor, and discomfort to abject bodies, were called out in some psychological literature of the era, not just as potential corruptors of youth, but as impediments to the harmonization project.

By 1954, these criticisms led to hearings in the US Senate, spurring the comics industry to promulgate the Comics Code, which regulated the content and images of comics in much the same way the Production Code had done for movies earlier in the century.[10] Of its many stipulations, including banning the words "horror" and "terror" in titles, the code informed its adherents that all "scenes of horror, excessive bloodshed, gory or gruesome crimes, depravity, lust, sadism, masochism shall not be permitted."[11] In essence, it demanded the abjection of the abject—the casting off from the body politic those elements that threatened its stability and coherence. (In part for this reason, EC Comics publisher William Gaines converted *Mad*, a comic book created in 1952, to magazine format in 1955. As a magazine rather than a comic book, it was not subject to the Comics Code.)[12]

Calls for censorship and the industry's response of self-censorship were based on a neo-Freudian fantasy of the vulnerability of youth as fragile persons in formation, only recently beginning to become gendered subjects following their infantile separation from the mother, the very process of abjection. Children in need of protection from vernacular literature stood in for greater anxieties around the regulation of identity, linking the individual body to the body politic through the repression of exposure to the abject.[13] Pulp images became objects of censure, potential disruptors of a harmony and adjustment based in social regulation. As Sara Ahmed notes in *The Cultural Politics of Emotion* (2004), "When thinking about how bodies become objects of disgust, we can see that disgust is crucial to power relations. . . . The relation between disgust and power is evident when we consider the spatiality of disgust . . . disgust at 'that which is below' functions to maintain the power relations between above and below, through which 'aboveness' and 'belowness' become properties of particular bodies, objects, and spaces."[14] In the psychoanalytic telling of harmonization, just as the individual child achieved subject status by abjecting bodily products associated with an intimate relation to the mother (and to "belowness"), so the body politic had to repress abjected material to establish proper relations between itself and its component parts. The underlying tensions that informed such arguments about harmonizing postwar American society through the individual play out in Wolverton's reworking of the *Life* magazine cover. The gentle smile of a midwestern art student becomes the tongue-wagging leer of the "Beautiful Girl of the Month," a figure who seems to be happily putrefying before the reader's eyes. The subhead reveals that she "Reads *Mad*," hinting that being a *Mad* reader is somehow the perverse complement to being a "Coed Opera Student from Indiana." Both women seem content with their lot in life, even though one appears to be a living corpse. Or, for the sake of argument here, Wolverton's cover girl is happier living openly as a corpse.

This morbid glee is repeated in a section that Wolverton also drew in the same issue, a series of portraits of typical *Mad* readers (figure 10.3). The opening caption of the section announces "[Here] are views of what we, the editors of *Mad*, believe to be a cross-section of the people who read *Mad*! . . . [W]hile you wander through the following pages, smirking, guffawing, and retching at what you see . . . pause a moment! The face you're retching at might be your own!" Each of the six portraits is monstrous in its own way. All suggest horrible deformity, not unlike the kind commonly imagined in vernacular horror films of the time as resulting from exposure to atomic radiation. Some have extra eyes, ears, and limbs; holes where none should be; and odd unexplained glands. All of them—including "The Young *Mad* Reader" (an ax murderer), "The Student *Mad* Reader" (a straight-A college student made a drooling idiot by reading *Mad*), "The Elderly Mad Reader" (who reclaims his libido after reading *Mad*), and "The Female Reader" (unable to attract boys until she subscribes to *Mad*)—appear approximately human . . . except for "The Critical *Mad* Reader," a demon standing like

figure 10.3 *Top left*, the typical *Mad* reader, according to artist Basil Wolverton; *top right*, the critical *Mad* reader; *middle and bottom*, other *Mad* readers.

Shiva on the back of a bawling infant, desperately shredding the child's copy of *Mad*. This final *Mad* reader is monstrous and perverse. A poke at the alarmist reactions to comic books in the late 1940s and early 1950s, he satirizes the censorious reader, who, attempting to protect innocent youth, actually crushes them, converting the loving maternal embrace into the suppression of free will.

For Julia Kristeva, "The abject is related to perversion." It gives shape and substance to the very thing it denies, and it is perverse "because it neither gives up nor assumes a prohibition, a rule, or a law; but turns them aside, misleads, corrupts; uses them . . . the better to deny them."[15] Yet what *Mad* attempted in its self-parody was not equivalent to the individual act of abjection that Kristeva describes. Beyond that singular taunt to the critical reader, the portrait gallery as a whole signals the magazine's relationship to its audience, as do its letters pages and editorial comments, which often mock the magazine itself. The gallery celebrates its readers as malcontents and outsiders, as defective—if not prior to reading *Mad*, then certainly after. That the magazine, via Wolverton, chose to celebrate its readers (and itself) as monstrous points to its efforts to mobilize a shared abjection in resistance to conformist norms. This anticipates sociologist Paul Goodman's bitter 1956 complaint (ventriloquizing an imagined disaffected youth) that "a man is a fool to work to pay installments on a useless refrigerator for his wife, that the movies, TV, and the Book-of-the-Month Club are beneath contempt, but the Luce publications make you sick to the stomach."[16]

One of the premier Luce publications was, of course, *Life* magazine, and nausea was a perfectly (un)reasonable response to its place in the ongoing operations of social abjection and the regulation of the body politic. The norms described by Goodman signal an exclusionary ethos in and of themselves, an effort to name that which properly marks the social subject. To call your flagship publications *Time* and *Life* is nothing less than to lay claim to the absolute center, the interior of American cultural identity. To reject those publications, to be physically revolted by them, was in turn to claim in that social abjection a self that embraced, through its nausea, being of the abject. Glossing Sianne Ngai's discussion of the operations of disgust, Anne Tyler notes that if we accept abjection as "symptomatic of wider social relations of power, we can begin to ascertain why disgust might be attributed to particular bodies. Disgust is political."[17] That disgust is the collective rejection of the aberrant, the abjecting of difference. At the same time, though, the "paradox of subjectivation," Butler argues, "is precisely that the subject who would resist such norms is itself enabled, if not produced, by such norms."[18] One can,

nicholas sammond

if one actively chooses, at least attempt to turn normative disgust back on itself, to celebrate one's own abjection as an objection.

To be nauseated, then, by one's own production as a good social subject is an invitation to identify with that which is abjected: to refer to comics as juvenilia, then, is not to belittle them. As a figure, the juvenile stands in an abject relation to the social order of which it is not yet fully a part, but from which it is not entirely excluded. The stereotypical adolescent affect—alienated, uneasy with sex, death, and bodies themselves—is a twentieth-century response to getting along, conforming, being one of the crowd, crossing over from the realm of the child into the realm of the adult. Yet Goodman's disgusted response wasn't simply to a narrow, conformist Cold War society in general, but to his colleagues on the liberal left who imagined that advances in psychology and sociology could gradually erase the traumas of the previous decade through a combination of individual therapy and enlightened social policy. Here nausea blends with laughter, a guttural response to being named against one's will. Speaking to the individual's experience of abjection, Kristeva argues that "the braided horror and fascination that bespeaks the incompleteness of the speaking being . . . because it is heard as a narcissistic crisis on the outskirts of the feminine, shows up with a comic gleam the religious and political pretensions that attempt to give meaning to the human adventure. For, facing abjection, meaning has only a scored, rejected, ab-jected meaning—a comical one."[19]

At the individual level, the social engineering that Goodman and others rejected was playing out foremost in child development. In the wildly popular neo-Freudian "child-centered" approach to child rearing promoted by Spock, who had worked with Mead at the New School for Social Research and the New York Psychoanalytic Institute, the child's socialization, eventual happiness, and well-being sprang from its relationship with its parents, especially its mother. None of the Cold War neo-Freudians approached this dyadic relationship in the terms that Kristeva outlines in *Powers of Horror*. Yet Kristeva's sense of the abject as arising from and deeply rooted in the moment when the ego forms around rejecting the mother—accepting the Paternal Signifier and vomiting up the superego with which it will do battle for the rest of its existence—offers an apt lens through which to view the personalized models of adjustment and social control against which *Mad* and others formed their vernacular and abject objection. Yet the intimacy of Kristeva's model, its deferral or diminution of the social to the linguistic and the cultural, suggests an insufficient theoretical architecture when one tries to scale up from the individual to the social and political body, to understand the seeming abject abreaction to modes of "belongingness" found in 1950s vernacular print media.

The abject, for Kristeva, is derived from and, once expelled, opposed to the body, marked by its fluid excesses: blood (especially menstrual blood), urine, feces, and oral, nasal, genital, and rectal mucins. These excreta do not signal that discrete *I*; instead they speak of the ooze from which we spring (and which spurts forth from us) and to which we inevitably return. And they do so in guttural tones. Abjection is the horror of horror, of the void created between the self and its necessary other, and for Kristeva it is always productive: "In abjection, revolt is completely within being. Within the being of language. Contrary to hysteria, which brings about, ignores, or seduces the symbolic but does not produce it, the subject of abjection is eminently productive of culture. Its symptom is the rejection and re-construction of languages."[20] But "productive of culture" is a rather vague formulation. Is this "culture" in the narrow sense of Kultur, the Frankfurt school's celebration of a bourgeois art that through contemplation produces alienation from mercantile and bureaucratic existence? Or is this culture as in the psychosexual wound, the entry into the symbolic, around which our taboos form and are policed? For Kristeva, it is the latter, culture in the Mosaic sense of the Paternal Signifier, taking shape as the child separates from the mother, entering into the discourse of that signifier. "If language, like culture," she says, "sets up a separation and, starting with discrete ele-ments, concatenates an order, it does so precisely by repressing maternal authority and the corporeal mapping that abuts against them." Kristeva ar-gues that this repressed maternal authority informs the myths and rites that govern the boundary between the nonsignifying body and the symbolic order: "It is then appropriate to ask what happens to such a repressed item when the legal, phallic, linguistic symbolic establishment does not carry out the separation in radical fashion—or else, more basically, when the speaking being attempts to think through its advent in order better to es-tablish its effectiveness."[21]

If, however, for the producers and consumers of pulp comics, abjecting produced a clear boundary between self and other by naming the self in re-lation to that which it casts off—shit, piss, snot, menses, and so on—then dwelling on the abject (rather than disavowing it) provided an avenue toward rejecting an ideal self produced by a seemingly corrupt symbolic order. The abject objection, though necessarily inarticulate, slipped away from the con-trol mechanism. That which was meant to be abjected to produce the good self, the one that could harmonize with others, was scraped off the floor and

nicholas sammond

reclaimed as an abjection celebrated as an ill-adjusted exception to liberal conformism.

This approach to the abject is more suited to Georges Bataille than to Kristeva. In "Abjection and Miserable Forms" (1934), Bataille describes abjection as a relation between the social and the individual.[22] The abject, he argues, may indeed be located in things disgusting, putrid, and vile, but this does not mean that abjection as rite of passage into sovereign subjectivation, as Kristeva describes, is open equally to all. "The abjection of a human being is even negative in the formal sense of the word," Bataille says, "because it has at its origin an absence: it is simply the inability to assume with sufficient force the imperative act of excluding abject things (which constitutes the foundation of collective existence)." Helpless infants dwell in the abject because they have not yet learned to clean themselves, have not yet even learned the difference between the self and that which must be washed away. The poor, though, cannot escape abjection in their living conditions because they are actively oppressed. "Filth, snot and vermin are enough to render an infant vile," he continues. "His personal nature is not responsible for it, only the negligence or helplessness of those raising it."[23] The child not cleaned by its parent remains abject; the poor and immiserated are abject because they are actively abjured—they become the abject material itself, the dirty, shabby unwashed masses that define the sovereign subjects who pity them or simply abjure them altogether.

Abjection is the process of casting off that which is of us but is not us, and in the process attempting to draw a bright line around ourselves as subjects. While Bataille discusses the abject as it arises in the mother-child relation, he makes a distinction between things that are abject or disgusting and the sadistic pleasure one may take in the process by which those things are held, repressed, or oppressed. Contrasting anal erotism and anal sadism, he claims that when one takes pleasure in withholding one's shit, the shit is not the cause of the pleasure, the *withholding* is. The abjected thing is required for the sadistic social act of withholding or barring it. The oppressor must designate that which is oppressed, that which must be cast out of or held at a distance from a social body always in danger of defilement. For Bataille, social abjection requires a larger sovereign body, and the abjectly poor, sick, or despised represent that which is cast off to secure the integrity and well-being of that larger sovereign body. The miserable, he argues, once evoked pity and a sense of care. Now, that pity has given way to disgust, and to be miserable, to be immiserated, is to be abject, worthy of being cast out from sovereign society. "In the final analysis," he suggests, "oppressors must be reduced to sovereignty in its individual form; [while] on the contrary, the oppressed are formed out of the amorphous and immense mass of the wretched population."[24] We are all subject to the Paternal Signifier, but some are more subject than others; though none may occupy the ground on which that signifier sits, some may guard the gate. In the collective acts of buying and selling comics—the commercial colloquy through which the commodity condenses the relations of the moment—the embrace of graphic abjection offered an alternative vernacular discourse to those of adjustment, containment, and conformity.

Abjection First, Then Adjustment

Spasms and vomiting protect me. I use them throughout my life, in my repugnance—the intermittent retching that will distance me from, and allow me to avoid, objects and extreme situations that I experience as menacing and dangerous: defilement, sewage, sordidness, the ignominy of compromise, in-between states, betrayal. Fascination and rejection at the same time, abjection is the jolt that leads me into the abject but also separates me from it.
—Julia Kristeva, *Hatred and Forgiveness*

Abject is a term so capacious that it risks beggaring its own utility. It easily accommodates the status of noun, adjective, and verb because, in its immensity, it evades the boundary between subject and object, the self and its necessary other, even as it defines that boundary. Although reports from the Kinsey Institute in 1948 and 1953 challenged reductive understandings of male and female sexuality as complementary and opposed, popular discourse remained firmly rooted in perpetuating a clear gender binary, and the majority of postwar psychological practice encouraged the stabilization of gender roles that had been purportedly disrupted during World War II. Cold War technologies of the subject worked to anticipate exceptions to binary conceptions of self/ other and correct them accordingly. Many postwar American social scientists argued for social engineering at the micro scale, approaching first the formation of the subject in infancy and childhood, and then that subject's relationship to its peer groups, as a means of softly regulating society. William H. Whyte, in his critical overview of the period, *The Organization Man* (1956), grouped such regimes of adjustment under the label the "Social Ethic." Whyte defined the Social Ethic as that "contemporary body of thought which makes morally legitimate the pressures of society against the individual. Its major propositions are three: a belief in the group as the source of creativity; a belief

nicholas sammond

in 'belongingness' as the ultimate need of the individual; and a belief in the application of science to achieve the belongingness."[25] The term *belongingness* (which Whyte borrowed from the sociologist and Industrial Workers of the World apostate Frank Tannenbaum), like Stephen Colbert's "truthiness," captures the ethos of adjustment and conformism in the 1950s (Whyte also coined the term *groupthink*, in 1952).[26] Whyte located the Social Ethic's roots in the work of Veblen, Dewey, and Beard. Its promulgators, such as the industrial psychologist Elton Mayo and Tannenbaum, he termed "social engineers" responsible for creating the pernicious field of "human relations." Finally, he referred to subjects formed through the Social Ethic as "organization men." The proponents of social control through adjustment to which Whyte was reacting—such as Mead, Spock, Gregory Bateson, Erik Erikson, and Erich Fromm—had their roots in and around the New School for Social Research and in neo-Freudian approaches to social and political life.

Indeed, so popular was neo-Freudianism during and after the war that it also gave voice to reactionary fantasies of control, such as Philip Wylie's *Generation of Vipers* (1943) and Ferdinand Lundberg and Marynia Farnham's *Modern Woman: The Lost Sex* (1947), each of which argued for the subjugation and redomestication of women as absolutely necessary for restoring social harmony. Even Goodman, quoted above, who otherwise staked a position to the left, participated in this abreaction, making clear that the ennui, existential dread, and rebelliousness that he found in postwar *male* youth was specifically gendered: "I say 'young men and boys' rather than the 'young people' because the problems I want to discuss in this book belong primarily, in our society, to the boys: how to be useful and make something of oneself. A girl does not have to, she is not expected to, 'make something' of herself. Her career does not have to be self-justifying, for she will have children, like any other natural or creative act."[27] According to Goodman, boys in the wartime and postwar United States were "growing up absurd" not simply because (in the accepted wisdom) the wartime absence of men had feminized social and cultural life. More than that, he argued, the systems of adjustment and harmonization put forward by wartime and Cold War social architects seemed to organize a previously masculine and individualized American social life under the banner of an inherently feminized groupthink, or what Erik Erikson referred to as "momism."[28] This anxiousness surrounding maternal authority and its undermining of individuality found expression in a range of popular books that argued for the social regulation of gender by disciplining motherhood. Some of these, including *Modern Woman: The Lost Sex* and Erikson's *Childhood and Society* (1950), invoked Freud to argue against a nascent feminism, or against women's autonomy more generally. Robert Lindner's *Rebel without a Cause* (1953 [1944])—to which the 1955 movie bears only a passing resemblance—located the origins of sociopathic behavior in bad mothering and urged a reinvestment in (male) individualism as a remedy. In *Must You Conform?* (1956), Lindner parodied the social imperative to adjust and accommodate:

> You must adjust. . . . This is the motto inscribed on the walls of every nursery, and the processes that break the spirit are initiated there. In birth begins conformity. Slowly and subtly, the infant is shaped to the prevailing pattern, his needs for love and care turned against him as weapons to enforce submission. Uniqueness, individuality, difference—these are viewed with horror, even shame; at the very least, they are treated like diseases, and a regiment of specialists are available today to "cure" the child who will not or cannot conform. . . . Does he contradict Spock?—Get the telephone number of the nearest child analyst! Is he unhappy? maladjusted? lonely? too noisy? too quiet? too slow? too fast?[29]

The model of this social engineering began with the infant and child: regulate the psychosexual matrix of developing individuals and they will have a better chance of becoming happy, healthy, and productive Americans.

This regulation was meant to be achieved through introjected (unconsciously absorbed) group norms and a desire to please others. In 1950, David Riesman (along with Reuel Denney and Nathan Glazer) termed the herd mentality of the new mass society "other direction." "What was common to all other-directeds," they said,

> is that their contemporaries are the source of direction for the individual—either those that know him or those with whom he is indirectly acquainted, through friends and through the mass media. This source is of course "internalized" in the sense that dependence on it for guidance in life is implanted early. The goals toward which the other-directed person strives shift with that guidance: it is only the process of striving itself and the process of paying close attention to the signals from others that remain unaltered throughout life.[30]

Like Whyte, Riesman somewhat nostalgically contrasted the other-directed character with its predecessor, the more individualistic and self-contained "inner-directed" type (Whyte's contrast was between Max Weber's Protestant ethic and the Social Ethic). While both Whyte and Riesman conceded that there was no going back, both valorized the bygone days of an American individualism they saw gradually replaced by a more anxious, uncertain, and docile American society.

The common conception of cultural life in the postwar United States is of a time in which intense political conservatism and anticommunist paranoia inspired social conformity and aesthetic debasement. That image isn't without some merit, but it lacks nuance. If we understand conservatism not as a political stance associated with a reactionary Right, but as a cautious fear of ideological excess of any kind, developed in reaction to the American encounter with fascism and with Stalinism, then the word *conservative* also describes most of the Cold War intellectual center-Left. The devotion to adjustment and social harmony fueled the social-scientific aspects of the Macy Conferences on cybernetics and society, as well as the strong reaction of social critics such as Riesman, Whyte, Lindner, and others, such as Dwight Macdonald and Vance Packard, to what they perceived as a passive acceptance of authority.[31] Herein lies an irony. The mechanisms of adjustment invoked and deployed in the postwar period were meant to avoid repeating the horrors of the Holocaust or Dresden, or to serve as a balm for the shattered souls who had fought at Normandy or Guadalcanal or Okinawa and had come back damaged. They attempted to do so not by suppressing extremes or differences, but by *regulating* them. The ideal society of the Cold War era was meant to anticipate extremes and to locate a normative middle ground that was not imposed but derived from a freely willed if not innate desire to belong. This brave new world would be rational, self-correcting, and interconnected, but somehow free of the ideological extremes that had produced Nazism and Stalinism, which had also relied heavily on systematized social control.

Most of the mechanisms of an imagined gentler postwar social control were human, but many were meant to be applied institutionally. Businesses, governments, and schools added a layer of bureaucracy concerned with harmony, adjustment, and the goal of happiness. First larger corporations, and then smaller ones, added human relations (as opposed to personnel or hiring) offices, which were staffed when possible by professionals with degrees in psychology, psychiatry, and social work. Government offices also engaged in human relations practices in hiring and promotion, and in prophylactic personality testing. Compulsory public schools, rapidly expanding to meet a growing baby-boom population sheltered by stricter child-welfare and child-labor laws (which favored white children), added guidance counselors to their staffs. And so on: to give a few examples, the Myers-Briggs Type Indicator was created in 1944 and standardized in 1956; the Thurstone Temperament Schedule, developed in the 1930s, was adopted as a personnel tool in the 1950s; the Rorschach test was developed in the 1920s to diagnose schizophrenia, but by 1939 it had been converted to a projective personality test, which became so popular after the war that it was parodied in popular culture; and the Thematic Apperception Test, also developed in the 1930s, became increasingly popular in the postwar years for dealing with maladjusted individuals, from schoolchildren to neurotic World War II vets. (Whyte, determined to operationalize his distaste for the Social Ethic, actually ended *The Organization Man* with a chapter titled "How to Cheat on Personality Tests.")[32]

The publishers, authors, and readers of *Mad* magazine, dedicated as it was (and is) to parodying and satirizing the offensive mundanity of the same middlebrow mass culture that had spawned it, performed an ambivalence to belonging expressed through the abject. Throughout the fifties and sixties, *Mad* became increasingly putrescent, more oozy and fly-specked, reveling in its bad taste, ever concerned with the outrage of the moment. *Mad* may have more fully embraced abjection in its comic mode, but it was not alone. In the most grotesque of the horror comics, especially EC's *Tales from the Crypt* (1950–55), the abject was ever present. Ooze bubbled in fetid cauldrons and in the strings of saliva that curtained the mouths of the narrators Crypt Keeper, Vault Keeper, and Old Witch, as well as the victims in their tales (figure 10.4).

In horror titles not under the EC imprint, the abject found its expression more indirectly, through heavy ink lines and abrupt shifts in the color palette. In "The Cloak" (*Black Magic* 2, December 1950), for instance, the face of a man realizing that he wears a cloak made by Satan turns a stark red against a vivid yellow background, appearing like blood floating in urine. The title panel for "Union with the Dead" (*Black Magic* 6, August 1951) features a transfusion between a man and a skeleton. The man's arm appears that of a "normal" white person; his blood seems appropriately red; the skeleton, however, is a putrescent green, seeming well beyond the aid of a transfusion. The cover of *My Romantic Adventures* 50 (October 1954) offers up the screaming face of an insane woman howling her desire through asylum bars, her face an acid green (see figure 10.4). In instances such as these, the abject appears through a crack in a world out of joint, signaled obliquely through instability in color and line.

The abject was redoubled in the poor registration of cheap pulp comics, in which shading didn't always remain within the lines. That vernacular sloppiness, that indifferent failure of the machine, evokes an abject rejection of the tidy processes of individuation then being engineered in social theory, ones which focused on the sovereign to which Kristeva attended. "The border has become an object," Kristeva claims, before asking, "How can I be without

figure 10.4 *Top left,* cover of the March 1954 issue of EC Comics' *The Vault of Horror,* featuring the Crypt Keeper, Vault Keeper, and the Old Witch; *top right,* cover of the October 1954 issue of *My Romantic Adventures; bottom,* images of insanity and dissolution in romance and horror comics.

border? That elsewhere that I imagine beyond the present, or that I hallucinate so that I might, in a present time, speak to you[,] conceive of you—it is now here, jetted, abjected, into 'my' world. . . . Abject. It is something rejected from which one does not part, from which one does not protect oneself as from an object."[33] Even at the levels of layout and graphic representation, the pulp comics defied at a mundane level the regulation of boundaries as the marker of a stable self.

Neurosis, a postwar dramatic staple in horror and romance comics alike, often served as either a precipitating factor in a crisis or a motivation for sudden outbursts of erratic and dangerous behavior. In "I Fell for a Commie" (*Love Secrets* 32, August 1953), the protagonist wonders of her pinko boyfriend, "Perhaps the war embittered Tom like this. . . . I must be patient! One day he'll come to his senses . . . *he must!*" Tormented by the language of communist brainwashing, she becomes convinced that her own lover will kill her, only to find out in the eleventh hour that he's a double agent and she is saved, both from the red menace *and* from loneliness. In "I Talked with My Dead Wife!" (*Strange World of Your Dreams* 1, August 1951), a man dreams that his dead wife gives him instructions on how to heal his dying daughter; in the dream, her multiplied and multicolored hands claw at him as he screams in terror. The same young woman who howled out from the cover of *Romantic Adventures* 50 appeared inside, driven insane by her domineering mother (a classic trope of postwar misogyny and of "momism"); in the depths of her madness, her dreams explode the bounds of the panel, and a thick, spiky red line, as in an EKG, overlays the howling faces of her mother and her lover. A similar fate befalls the young protagonist of "Slave to Despair" (*Romantic Secrets* 22, September 1951). Ditching her sane and sensible boyfriend for an underworld lowlife, she is gradually seduced by swing music, alcohol, and finally drugs. Taking a pill, she stumbles onto the dance floor, and her world gives way to a nightmare, a sea of noses and eyeballs, a narcissistic fragmentation and multiplication of herself.

Luckily for her, she is rescued by her good egg of a boyfriend, and this represents an important difference between the majority of romance and horror comics and the EC brand in its heyday of the early 1950s. The plots of many romance and horror comics were predictable and tame, cautionary tales in which evil is punished and good eventually rewarded, in which true love vanquishes all. Eschewing EC's Beat-era irreverence, even before the institution of the Comics Code Authority in 1954, these comics usually hewed to a narrow path of melodramatic certainty. Yet even in the tamest of comics, a tension between the written word, the plot, and the images on the page remained an avenue through which an abject objection might appear—and to which comics' critics responded. Life in the vernacular had neither the aesthetic pretensions of high art nor the narrow psychological realism favored by much postwar middlebrow literature and drama. Instead, it plowed the furrows of the banal, offering in the mundane and repetitive themes of love, sex, and death a riotous rebellion against a postwar project that could only imagine—amidst nuclear escalation, the violent repression of civil rights, and the promulgation of a control society—a deathless fantasy of love in the service of the future. And if the soft technologies of adjustment didn't work, in 1955 the tranquilizer Miltown (meprobamate) went on the market, initiating a trend toward treating minor psychological issues, such as neuroses, with pharmaceuticals, through which the neurotic or the maladjusted could adjust and belong.

That practice, as Grace Slick put it in 1966, of "feed[ing] your head" marks a good moment to return, briefly, to the Wolverton images. In the *Life* magazine cover that *Mad* parodies, a beautiful young woman smiles confidently but warmly at the reader, while the text in the corner announces that, inside, "General Van Fleet Tells How We Can Win in Korea" (this, only two months before that war ended in less than a victory for the United States). The background is blurred, but one can almost make out the word *Parsifal* behind the opera singing "coed" from Indiana. The woman on the *Mad* cover also smiles at the reader, though the smile is somewhere between a leer and the gaping grin of a panting dog. Where the *Life* cover highlights a general, *Mad* announces "Humor in a Jugular Vein," verbally doubling down on the abjection in the image. The photo-montaged background behind the woman is urban, probably New York City, and in no way iconic—there is no Empire State or Chrysler Building to identify the skyline, only nondescript edifices topped by water towers. On the inside cover, the side-by-side comparison of the original *Life* cover and its *Mad* parody graphically disavows Henry Luce. The publisher promised to encapsulate or deliver *Time* itself, and *Life*, but, according to Goodman, evoked a nausea not unlike that experienced by Sartre's Antoine Roquentin—a deeply existential disquietude that, in the case of the *Mad* reader, ends in self-annihilation. After he lights up an issue of *Mad*, he puffs on an issue of *Life*, which emits a mushroom cloud and blows his head off.

He should have rejected the mundane and the middlebrow, the desperate reaffirmation of the repressive Cold War matrix of belonging and adjustment, that *Life* represented.[34] Kristeva sees in that sheltering network of control a flimsy cover for the abject—the horrific forces of bodily life and death so present in the war and so profoundly repressed after—that which had been abjected, cast out to secure the dulcet harmonies of postwar domesticity. Having lost faith in that "One Master Signifier," she complains bitterly, "We prefer to foresee or seduce; to plan ahead, promise a recovery, or esthetize; to provide social security or make art not too far removed from the level of the media." Rejecting the abject as the price of a secure selfhood, Kristeva argues, each and every one of us settles for less, for the mundane and unremarkable, the good enough. Because, she continues, "who, I ask you, would agree to call himself abject, subject of or subject to abjection?"[35] The easier and safer path, one littered with Holocaust dead and charred bodies at Hiroshima, was to yield to sovereign regulation by what Whyte called the Organization and Marcuse called the System or the Establishment. Better that than to become subject to abjection, to the illusion of sovereignty. Except that some chose the abject as an objection to that sovereignty, to the rationalization of everyday life, of relations between people, of intercourse.

Conclusion

Writing on the abject and eroticism in 1962, Bataille celebrated the futility of the romantic gesture, its unintentional evocation of the abject: "We are discontinuous beings, individuals who perish in isolation in the midst of an incomprehensible adventure, but we yearn for our lost continuity. We find the state of affairs that binds us to our random and ephemeral individuality hard to bear. Along with our tormenting desire that this evanescent thing should last, there stands our obsession with a primal continuity linking us with everything that is."[36] Death, putrescence, rot, decay: those are what charge our animal eroticism, our fierce desire for the other. The *furshlugginer* zanies who graced the pages of *Mad* magazine or the passionate, desperate, and excessive characters that howled their way through romance and horror comics were kin to Allen Ginsberg's saints, who in "Howl," among their many, many abject acts, "walked all night with their shoes full of blood on the snowbank docks / . . . [and] who cooked rotten animals lung heart feet tail borsht & tortillas dreaming of the pure vegetable kingdom."[37] Both voiced an objection to the bland surface of what we now equally blandly call the "midcentury modern," the images and sentiments that Roy Lichtenstein would so blithely and indifferently parody in his large canvases. Bataille found passion rising in the tension between sex and death, appearing because "reproduction leads to the discontinuity of beings, but brings into play their continuity; that is to say, it is intimately linked with death. . . . [D]eath is to be identified with continuity, and both of these concepts are equally fascinating. This fascination is the dominant element in eroticism."[38] That tension between the continuity and discontinuity of human existence—that miasma of sex, reproduction, and death—was and is graphically represented in comics, in the sequential yet separated arrays of panels that adorn each page, in the serial and series nature of the stories.[39] That the ultimately bland and, by today's standards, inoffensive pulp offerings of vernacular sequential art could arouse such fear and anxiety as to inspire US Senate hearings in 1954, and lead to the resulting self-censorship of the Comics Code, speaks less to the horrors depicted in the pulps themselves and more to the profound yet repressed anxieties surrounding a reproductive boom intimately interwoven with the Cold War project. The baby boom was nothing less than an orgy waged on the doorsteps of the charnel houses of World War II, and one that willfully ignored the impending doom of nuclear war. The public secret of the futile absurdity of duck-and-cover drills in schools, for instance, speaks to this desperation, this pathetic admixture of hope and terror. In the face of the repressed abject, treating comics as obscene seems laughable. "Stripping naked," Bataille argued, "is the decisive action. . . . Nakedness offers a contrast to self-possession, to discontinuous existence, [and our bodies] . . . open out to a state of continuity through secret channels that give us a feeling of obscenity. Obscenity is our name for the uneasiness which upsets the physical state associated with self-possession, with the possession of a recognised and stable individuality."[40] This was obscenity as virtue, and unease as presence. Seven years later, Herbert Marcuse would echo Bataille's early claims about abjection as a social act, saying of obscenity,

> This society is obscene in producing and indecently exposing a stifling abundance of wares while depriving its victims abroad of the necessities of life; obscene in stuffing itself and its garbage cans while poisoning and burning the scarce foodstuffs in the fields of its aggression; obscene in the words and smiles of its politicians and entertainers; in its prayers, in its ignorance, and in the wisdom of its kept intellectuals. . . . Obscene is not the picture of a naked woman who exposes her pubic hair but that of a fully clad general who exposes his medals rewarded in a war of aggression.[41]

The ribald excess and irreverence of *Mad*, or the graphic excesses of *Black Magic* or *Love Secrets*, had little to do with Marcuse's fantasy of the potentially liberatory power of naked hippies—except in that both spoke as an abject objection, a spitting back into the face of the body politic all that it had rejected in the name of progress, and to the repression of the horrors of a war so recently passed. Marcuse refused the Vietnam War, and a permanent state of war that sought to protect a rapidly reproducing population through the doctrine of mutually assured destruction, or, as it would come to be known, MAD.

Notes

Epigraphs: J. Robert Oppenheimer, interviewed about the Trinity atomic bomb test on July 16, 1945, in *The Decision to Drop the Bomb*, television documentary directed by Fred Freed and Len Giovannitti, aired January 5, 1965, on NBC; Herbert Marcuse, *An Essay on Liberation* (Boston: Beacon, 1969), 44–45; Julia Kristeva, *Hatred and Forgiveness* (New York: Columbia University Press, 2010), 185.

    Color versions of images in this chapter may be found at http://scalar.usc .edu/works/abjection-incorporated-insert/index.

1 Howard Becker, "Becoming a Marihuana User," *American Journal of Sociology* 59, no. 3 (November 1953): 235–42.

2 See, for instance, *Tokio Jokio* (Los Angeles, CA: Warner Brothers, 1943) or *Bugs Bunny Nips the Nips* (Los Angeles, CA: Warner Brothers, 1944).

3 See, for instance, Dix's *Metropolis* (1928).

4 See Elaine Tyler May, *Homeward Bound: American Families in the Cold War Era* (New York: Basic Books, 1988), for a discussion of domesticity, femininity, and the politics of containment.

5 Anne McClintock, *Imperial Leather: Race, Gender, and Sexuality in the Colonial Context* (New York: Routledge, 1995), 72.

6 Judith Butler, *Bodies That Matter: On the Discursive Limits of "Sex"* (New York: Routledge, 1993).

7 Bart Beaty, *Frederic Wertham and the Critique of Mass Culture* (Jackson: University Press of Mississippi, 2005), 106.

8 See Ellen Herman, *The Romance of American Psychology: Political Culture in the Age of Experts* (Berkeley: University of California Press, 1995), chaps. 3–5.

9 Theodor W. Adorno, Else Frenkel-Brunswik, Daniel J. Levinson, and Nevitt Sanford, *The Authoritarian Personality* (New York: Harper, 1950); Hannah Arendt, *The Origins of Totalitarianism* (New York: Harcourt, Brace, 1951).

10 See Amy Kiste Nyberg, *Seal of Approval: The History of the Comics Code* (Jackson: University Press of Mississippi, 1998); and Beaty, *Fredric Wertham*.

11 Nyberg, *Seal of Approval*, 167.

12 Histories of *Mad* differ on whether the switch happened to retain editor Harvey Kurtzman, or to evade the code. Regardless of intent, the latter was achieved. See Bill Schelly, *Harvey Kurtzman: The Man Who Created MAD and Revolutionized Humor in America* (Seattle: Fantagraphic Books, 2014).

13 See Nicholas Sammond, *Babes in Tomorrowland: Walt Disney and the Making of the American Child, 1930–1960* (Durham, NC: Duke University Press, 2005), 247–99.

14 Sara Ahmed, *The Cultural Politics of Emotion* (New York: Routledge, 2004), 88.

15 Julia Kristeva, *Powers of Horror: An Essay on Abjection*, trans. Leon S. Roudiez (New York: Columbia University Press, 1982), 15.

16 Paul Goodman, *Growing Up Absurd: Problems of Youth in the Organized System* (New York: Random House, 1960), ix–x.

17 Imogen Tyler, *Revolting Subjects: Social Abjection and Resistance in Neoliberal Britain* (London: Zed Books, 2013), 23–24.

18 Butler, *Bodies That Matter*, xxiii.

19 Kristeva, *Powers of Horror*, 209.

20 Kristeva, *Powers of Horror*, 45.

21 Kristeva, *Powers of Horror*, 72–73.

22 To be sure, in *Powers of Horror*, Kristeva also invokes the anthropological, albeit via the colonial subject V. S. Naipaul, and in an equally colonialist register (see 74–75).

23 Georges Bataille, "Abjection and Miserable Forms," *More and Less*, ed. Sylvere Lotringer, trans. Yvonne Shafir (1934; Cambridge, MA: MIT Press, 1993), 10.

24 Bataille, "Abjection and Miserable Forms," 9.

25 William H. Whyte Jr., *The Organization Man* (New York: Simon and Schuster, 1956), 7.

26 Frank Tannenbaum, *A Philosophy of Labor* (New York: Knopf, 1951); William Whyte, "The Corporation and the Wife," *Fortune*, November 1951; and Whyte, "The Wives of Management," *Fortune*, October 1951.

27 Goodman, *Growing Up Absurd*, 13.

28 Erik Erikson, *Childhood and Society* (New York: Norton, 1950), 32–35.

29 Robert Lindner, *Must You Conform?* (New York: Rinehart, 1956), 167–68.

30 David Riesman, Reuel Denney, and Nathan Glazer, *The Lonely Crowd: A Study of the Changing American Character* (New Haven, CT: Yale University Press, 1950), 22.

31 See Fred Turner, *The Democratic Surround: Multimedia and American Liberalism from World War II to the Psychedelic Sixties* (Chicago: University of Chicago Press, 2013), 160–61.

32 See Anne Anastasi, *Psychological Testing*, 4th ed. (New York: Macmillan, 1976).

33 Kristeva, *Powers of Horror*, 4.

34 On contemporary invocations of the middlebrow, see Russell Lynes, *The Tastemakers* (New York: Harper, 1954). See also Dwight Macdonald and John Summers, eds., *Masscult and Midcult: Essays against the American Grain* (New York: NYRB Classics, 2011).

35 Kristeva, *Powers of Horror*, 209.

36 Georges Bataille, *Erotism: Death and Sensuality* (1962; San Francisco: City Lights, 1986), 15.

37 *Furshlugginer* is a Yiddishism popularized by Harvey Kurtzman in *Mad* in the 1950s; it translates, roughly, as "crazy" or "out of one's head." Space does not permit a more detailed discussion of the portmanteaux of *Mad* magazine. Allen Ginsberg, "Howl" 1955–56, in *Collected Poems, 1947–1980* (New

York: HarperPerennial, 2001), http://www.poetryfoundation.org/poem
/179381.

38 Bataille, *Erotism*, 13.
39 Scott McCloud, *Understanding Comics: The Invisible Art* (New York: Harper-
Collins, 1993), esp. chap. 3.
40 Bataille, *Erotism*, 17
41 Marcuse, *An Essay on Liberation*, 7–8.

nicholas sammond

chapter eleven

Spit * Light * Spunk: Larry Clark, an Aesthetic of Frankness

eugenie brinkema

To reject the social injunction can be accomplished by means of that form of silence, which consists in saying things *simply*.
—Roland Barthes, preface to *Tricks*

*   *   *

There is this kind of spit that is fibroid, nearly veined. Eggy coarsened syrup—more mucin glue than water; more sputum's pus than salts.

*   *   *

There is this kind of spunk that is mushy, thin, and pale. Nubilous and barely yellowed—sort of spore, rather sweet, more humid foam than dew. Turned milk toned the wash of dying white flowers. It recalls *De Generatione Animalium*, that moment Aristotle dubs all semen cooked, concocted blood.

*   *   *

There is this kind of light that goes black or dark or blank. Smacking creamy rustles, belatedly revealed to comprise four lips diagonally chewing each other, the oral sloshing grinding a juncture between two adolescent faces. Blanching light behind and to the right of the figures produces stark zones of illumination: blocked at the farthest reach, the girl's stringy hair recedes into an opaque field that comprises the left foreground third of the frame; to its right, faint color sculpts the symmetrical profiles—shadowed, angled, partial—in their consumptive oral apparatus. The opening osculations of *Kids*: a pumpjack's nodding reciprocities meets Jan Svankmajer's *Passionate Dialogue*.

* * *

Always a matter of what you can and cannot get to come out of your mouth. You cannot get that taste out of your mouth . . . (all that *that* that sticks in the teeth).

* * *

And now the boy, postvirgin fuck, posteulogy to the virgin, wipes down his sweaty chest, rolls the railing in the pristine house and orally discharges; the camera, in following it down, renders loosened slaver a form of vertical measure, lets it give the reach of space and time.

* * *

The punctuation of absorbed sucking, if rhythmic, is also an alternating, interrupted unconcealment of the texture of skin: a forehead, slightly pocked and stippled with sweat; a neck, razor burned and slightly scabby; each field of flesh given by the aesthetic juncture of two bodies' movements *with* each other in the midst of a light *from* somewhere. Behind this radiant limning, its diffused unfocused wash, all detail lost amidst fat folds of melting tongues, the hard edge of each skull separated and detached from the ambient space— directly the result of the formal decision to shoot against the light for the duration of the sucking. By the time the image finally reveals the bodies in full, their youth, their intertwining stems, the camera has gone over to the side of the source of light, blocked the window, and here now reveals all the detail of context—architectural, chronological, sociological—the inscription of the image reducing those planes to a flat, even, contrastless hue.

* * *

Under the breath: It hurts. *Repeat.*

* * *

eugenie brinkema

There is no glory in this suffering; it is not an ode: it opens up only onto idiocy.
—Julia Kristeva, *Powers of Horror*

It is a critical commonplace to assert that photographer and filmmaker Larry Clark's oeuvre is obsessed with figures of abjection. His books of photography, *Tulsa* (1971) and *Teenage Lust: An Autobiography* (1983), and films like *Kids* (1995), *Another Day in Paradise* (1998), *Bully* (2001), *Ken Park* (2002), *Wassup Rockers* (2005), *Marfa Girl* (2012), *The Smell of Us* (2014), and the short "Impaled" on the anthology *Destricted* (2006), have been described with alarming consistency in relation to a tropology clustered around his visual interest in icons of disgust: stringy spit, teeth-catching sperm, and streams of malt-yellowed piss in *Kids*; fetishistically pursued bad odors (armpit sniffing, day-ripened toes) and scabby knees in *The Smell of Us*; pockmarks; the lilt of spent cum; toilet bowls oiled with puke's starchy bister; the unclean in the form of contagious disease; the soft abominations of moral apathy; all things in bad taste, what wastes, the distaste; "Human beings caught flush with their animality," as Kristeva figures Céline's abjection, "wallowing in their vomit, as if to come closer to what is essential . . . beyond all 'fancies': violence, blood, and death."[1] Or, alternately, the work's four-decade-long focus on discarded subcultural communities—largely of teenagers, those who are high, wandering, skating, knifed, lost, spanked, messy fucking, clit ignorant, fingered-pussy smelling-sharing, infected, depressed, bored, sick, dizzy, ignored, unconscious, border living, N_2O whipping, reeking, raping, raped, dead—has engendered a parallel, equally sizable critical body that emphasizes his investment in social abjection, reading his work as thematizing political conditions of exclusion, disparagement, cruelty toward and marginalization of these vulnerable-terrible adolescent subjects, the fragile social limits Kristeva voices as "inseparable, contaminated, condemned, at the boundary of what is assimilable, thinkable: abject."[2] In other words, Clark's work is read as invested in either abject things and fluids or abjected peoples and populations (and one might say abjection reaches its crisis point precisely when abjected peoples are taken for abject things).

But these different reading strategies are impoverished in the very same way.

Their importation and repetition of the canon of *signs* of abjection, hierarchizing the dirty and ontologizing "defilement, sewage, and muck," participates in the well-worn, even worn-out, critical tendency to misread abjection—what Kristeva dubs "a 'something' that I do not recognize as a thing"—as a something critics recognize precisely as a set of *things*. This move takes abjection for the abject, regards abjection as a cluster of definable qualities and items instead of as a structure of the unassimilable, a misreading about which I have written elsewhere.[3] The clear insistence from the outset of *Pouvoirs de l'horreur (Powers of Horror)*—literally from the outset; the first chapter is titled "Ni sujet ni objet"—that "L'abject n'est pas un objet en face de moi" requires a relinquishment of the easy ascription of abjection to things presented to the eye and mind, thrown in the path of the subject as a nameable, precise sensual content, the definite article of *that* sticky load, or *this* maimed corpus. Nor, however, are we in the realm of metaphor, of allegory; any critical approach that takes abjection for subcultural exclusion also fails to attend to the formal rigor of Kristeva's account, takes what disturbs social order and rigor, what is cast off in the logics of the social, and, in essence, *symbolizes* precisely where poststructuralism locates a resistance to, or outside of, or extremity in relation to, the symbolic. In *The Forms of the Affects*, I dwell on the consequences of ignoring the structural component to abjection and mistakenly fixating on the ob-jects of ab-jection, pausing abjection's thrownness and reifying it into nameable bad things, so I will not repeat that critique here. Suffice it to say, however, Kristeva's account of abjection does not taxonomize abject icons so much as focus on a structure of infinite destructuring: "What disturbs identity, system, order. What does not respect borders, positions, rules. The in-between, the ambiguous, the composite."[4] The push-me-pull-you route of abjection involves a radical exclusion and expulsion that simultaneously pulls the subject "toward the place where meaning collapses."[5] Kristeva's formulation of the structure—"I abject *myself* within the same motion through which 'I' claim to establish *myself*"—emphasizes the role of motility in abjection, the shedding absorbing energy in which the self is dependent for its coherence on continually if incompletely ejected aspects of self.[6]

Kristeva is adamant that the abject "is not an ob-ject" but rather "revolts of being" that figure in spasms, which opens up speculative potential for other modes of brutal expulsion—including aesthetic instances. Put another way, once abjection is named as a structure that ejects what is tolerable or thinkable to a system while nevertheless retaining the ejected material as seductive, we can see how the two critical approaches to Clark's corpus exclude a third possibility. On the one hand, his work is taken as abject by being so visually frank, obsessed with abject things (exposing in close-up that spit, this spunk); on the other hand, it is taken as being narratively frank (exposing unflinchingly that subculture, this brutal loser) by focusing on abjected figures. But a third way is made available by moving past listable abjected things or

eugenie brinkema

figures, looking instead to abjection as *process*. That reading goes like this: Clark's work engages an aesthetic of frankness that itself abjects visual complexity in the image. Its abjection is a matter of how the photographs and films engage light and line, proportion and diagrammatic arrangement, and has nothing whatsoever to do with spit, spunk, skin, things, bodies, objects. My argument is that Clark's formal investment in sparenesses, the specificity of his framed relation between foreground and background, his use of light, his intermedial interlocutors, are misread as the mere means for the documentation of what is taken in advance to be degraded, humbled, lowered, low. His aesthetic language is (mis)taken as an alibi for a forthrightness in the presentation *of* the abject, in other words, a frankness that serves the abject. As Richard Benjamin expresses this kind of hierarchy: "Dispassionate realism manifests itself on screen as an eerie, aloof, but wry tone that doesn't recoil from abjection and violence. . . . Thematically, the teenage bodies in *Kids* appear in revolting and repulsive ways."[7] Abjection in this critical tradition is figured as master, frankness taken for its privileged tool (its favorite, if unfree, servant).

Alongside the doubled claim for his work's bond to an impoverished notion of abjection, the terms (usually as valuation, occasionally disparagement) "frank," "direct," "sincere," "honest," "open," "raw," "authentic" liberally pepper the popular and scholarly catalog on Clark. His photographs are discussed in the same if distinction-collapsing breath uttering a canon of the contemporary explicit: Richard Prince, Nan Goldin, Richard Kern; his films often take the epithet *pornographic, pedophilic* (a careful *quasi*-sometimes appended).[8]

*   *   *

An arbitrary but telling inventory: of *Tulsa*—"*frank* depictions of sex, drugs and other vices of a certain rarely clothed subset of American youth"; "*honest, blatant* and often shocking portrait style"; "it *unflinchingly* depicted a dirty white trash landscape with the *matter-of-factness* that comes when one is so deeply involved in the scene"; "These are pictures that shimmer with a ferocious *honesty*"; of *Kids*—it portrayed "urban youth so *honestly* and *openly* that it came off as criminally obscene"; "a visual style that looks so uncompromisingly *authentic* that its semblance of realism immediately raises questions"; "the *frankness*, brutality, and scatology with which Telly has sex with young girls and describes them typifies the film's other dialogue and events"; "that these two kids are so unglamorous serves to enhance their *authenticity*";

and "Clark's intrusively voyeuristic view of these kids is also carefully stage-managed to ensure a '*truthful*' and '*authentic*' portrayal."[9] Emphasis mine: *honestly*.

* * *

The conventional assumption of the sincerity and rawness of Clark's work is parasitic, in part, on his own working method—shooting his familiars in *Tulsa* ("It was the way I was living. I just happened to have my camera and be photographing my friends. It was totally innocent; there was no purpose to the photographs"); living among and befriending the untrained adolescents then cast in films like *Kids*, *Marfa Girl*, and *The Smell of Us*; and collaborating with nineteen-year-old Harmony Korine, often presumed to have "authentically" documented his daily goings on when he wrote the script for *Kids*. Korine tells the story that in planning *Ken Park*, "Larry wanted to see five things. He wrote them down in red ink on a napkin. He said, 'Turn these into a movie.' So it would be like 'Kid jerks off while being strangled,' or 'Kid in his underwear stabs his grandparents.' It was like that."[10] This mythology of Clark's brutal realism and the supposed spontaneity and authenticity of his work is as problematic for its reliance on a naïve heuristic of authorial intention as is the simplified deployment of "abjection" discussed above. (In addition, it is a ferociously manufactured sentiment; *Kids*, for example, was a rigorously scripted, produced, and composed film.[11])

In stark contrast to these previous approaches, my interest here is in arguing for abjection's notion of downcasting, lowering, and casting off to describe a formal language of uncluttered openness, sincerity, simplification, and clarification, a brutalizing of visual language by paring down to a radical program of exclusion (of detail, ornament, context, and metanarratives [for a cultural declension, for a moral centeredness now lost]). My argument, then, should be regarded an aesthetic apologetic (in the sense of a spirited defense) of exactly what Henry Giroux finds so noxious in Clark's work:

> Failing to come to grips with considerations of politics, power, and ideology, Clark avoids serious questions regarding how the viewer can account for the simultaneous aggression and powerlessness portrayed by teenagers in *Kids*. . . . Lacking depth and detail, the teenagers who inhabit Clark's film are one-dimensional to the point of caricature. . . . Clark's attempt to let the film speak for itself results in a stylized aesthetic of violence that renders the reality

of violence voyeuristic, spectacular and utterly personal rather than social and political.[12]

This formal process of degrading and wearing down visual composition—structuring the texts through what I call *an aesthetics of frankness*—opens up a field for thinking about the status of the body not as the expressive ground for signs of the abject but as the site of a decomposed framing, which itself should be regarded as casting off aesthetic and semiotic complexity. The extremity of this simplicity—in scenes of injection, infection, brutality, pornography, and decay—constitutes the grounds of Clark's openness, irreducibly linked to a promise of truth in the image, *not for what* it displays but for how it visually excludes, how it formally expels possibilities for visual complexity.

Regarding the abject as a formal strategy of renouncing ornamentation and affirming frankness destabilizes the operative division between the comic and the violent on which this collection is founded—not least because my approach dismisses claims for abjection's bond to dissolutions of subjectivity, affective disturbances, or the corporeal expressivities of either horror or laughter. The grounds for my insistence in this chapter on abjection as a formal problematic, however, is found within canonical accounts of abjection—as when Kristeva writes of Célinian laughter in relation to a "comedy of abjection," emphasizing the "trans-syntactic inscription of emotion" in the structure of "lines pitted with blank spaces." Opposing figural or representational topoi of abjection with the formality of its logic, she details an alternative logic at work: "Descriptions of absurdity, stupidity, violence, sorrow, moral and physical degeneracy locate them [emotions], as a result, and *also in formal fashion [formellement aussi]*, in that interspace between abjection and fascination signaled by Célinian exclamations."[13] Apocalyptic laughter is figured here not as an expression of affect but as an exclamation of literary structure itself—the emphasis on the *outness* of the call, the *exteriority* of its cry. Likewise, the material substrate of Clark's work—skin, light, movement, framing, language—abjects the ornamental in favor of a frankness that *also in a formal fashion* abjects as an aesthetic practice, and not as a signifying one.

The aesthetic of frankness is avowed equally by the form of Clark's work and diegetically by figures of artists who follow negative aesthetic prohibitions on complexity within his oeuvre. The titular figure of *Marfa Girl* says of her art residency, her study of nudes, that since arriving in West Texas "the landscape inspired me to strip things down to the bare essentials. I find it more beautiful, less distracting." Named in relation to the place where she is temporary, contingent, an arrived (eventually to depart) visitor, she is less character than figure for the aesthetic process of peeling down to the bare, dismantling and divesting the image of ostentation, complication. She is co-extensive with the drive to make forms that are *less distracting*.

In *Ken Park*, Tate, introduced in the film through the antiphrasal short-hand of "insane, but smart," grabs a bathroom sash, ties it around his neck and then to the door, and chokes himself while jerking off, spit bubbling and collecting in a foamed corner of his mouth, avowing a growing tension until out-displayed by the elongated ejaculate that drips, glistens off his penis; he gives slack to the noose, *and all the while* wearing a shirt printed with the aesthetic mantra of Clark's corpus: *Keep it simple*. As, indeed, Clark's aesthetic and the autoerotic as praxis both do—simplified, self-referring, stimulation deployed within one single system. If a wry nod toward the accusation that his work is nothing but gratuitous self-pleasuring, or a rejoinder to the praise that his work is nothing but authentic self-portraiture, the autoritratto of autoeroticism is framed under the sign of an aesthetic injunction: while you believe this is what (all) I do, I believe in keeping it simple.

What is ultimately abjected—rejected, expelled—from the visual universe of Clark's texts is a dissembling in relation to violence, an overt ornamentation that would evade a sincerity of form adequate to a clarity of the presentational (*s.v.* "simplicity," that which ever risks opening up only onto idiocy).

* * *

Frank, which is to say *free*—which is, rather, to have initially said, in medieval Latin, *Francus*, for the Frankish Gauls gave full and free rights only to those who were designated as belonging to the dominant social ethnic group, which is to say who conquered, which is to say, importantly, those who were neither slave nor serf nor prisoner nor captive, who retained the right to come and go; who were unencumbered, free of debt, absent obligation, at liberty to do all the many things "free from restraint or impediment; unrestricted, un-checked,"[14] which, in turn, by the fourteenth century, turned into a different kind of freedom. In place of this freedom *from*—a negative condition of *not* being subject *to*, of being exempt *from*—frank comes to mean generatively, affirmatively free, to be liberal, generous, lavish in giving of one's bounty, and from that material givingness what becomes, by the sixteenth century, outspoken, vocally open, offering up a plainness of speech, directness, forthrightness, even sincerity. One cannot expunge the word's bond to freedom, but nor is the etymological landscape navigable: on the one hand, immunity; on the other, the authentic, loyal, true. From the negative self-determined

eugenie brinkema

right to be free of constraint, then from the negative self-limitation of being what fails to engage in concealment, by modernity the *frank* signals the positive duty to unconcealment that will later be dubbed the unreserved stance of candor, what undisguises as an affirmative practice of discourse—infinite negative freedom, obliteration of all interference or obstacle; infinite positive obligation toward disclosure, the drive to bring forth the unhiddenness of truth.

Mikhail Bakhtin, in describing "the problem that all Renaissance literature was trying to solve, namely, to find forms that would make possible and would justify the most extreme freedom and frankness of thought and speech," emphasizes that frankness was not to be understood

> in a narrowly subjective sense as "sincerity," the "soul's truth," or "intimacy." The Renaissance concept of frankness was far more serious; it meant a completely loud, marketplace frankness that concerned everyone. Thought and speech had to be placed under such conditions that the world could expose its other side: the side that was hidden, that nobody talked about, that did not fit the words and forms of prevailing philosophy. . . . Thought and word were searching for a new reality beyond the visible horizon of official philosophy.[15]

*   *   *

Cf. authenticity: a matter of authority; Gr. *authentikos*, original, genuine, acting on one's own (auto-), one who does a thing oneself (a master); cf. direct: straight (as in a line); L. *directus*, *dirigere*, to set straight or guide; cf. sincerity: genuineness, purity; L. *sinceritatem*, soundness, wholeness; *sincerus*, what is clean, what remains uninjured.[16] That one who is sincere might ever remain uninjured is an open question (wound?) for Clark.

*   *   *

Frankness, neither sincerity nor authenticity nor directness, takes a much stronger form, far closer to what Foucault figures in his 1983 "Discourse and Truth" seminar as *parrhesia*, what he dubs in the first lecture "free speech." The *parrhesiastes* "is the one who uses *parrhesia*, i.e., the one who speaks the truth." Like the positive obligations within frankness, Foucault etymologically locates in *parrhesiazesthai* the notion of "to say everything": the one who thusly speaks "does not hide anything, but opens his heart and mind completely to other people through discourse."[17] Our speaker of catalogical excess possesses an avowedly antirhetorical mouth, eschewing the canon of techniques that manipulate judgment through seduction—which, recall, is Aristotle's formal definition of rhetoric: "the faculty of observing in any given case the available means of persuasion," a capacious and general faculty involving "the power of observing the means of persuasion on almost any subject presented to us."[18] This durable, ancient philosophical opposition between parrhesia and rhetoric extends beyond device and figure to the entire field, potentially, of aesthetic and discursive adornment. For example, Foucault locates in Seneca "the idea that personal conversations are the best vehicle for frank speaking and truth-telling insofar as one can dispense, in such conversations, with the need for rhetorical devices and ornamentation."[19] In place of rhetoric's luring, camouflaged mousetrap talk, Foucault teaches that "the *parrhesiastes* uses the most direct words and forms of expression he can find." Crucially, the evasion of rhetoric involves a move away from the mediating judgments of the audience—"Whereas rhetoric provides the speaker with technical devices to help him prevail upon the minds of his audience, . . . in *parrhesia*, the *parrhesiastes* acts on other people's minds by showing them as directly as possible what he actually believes."[20]

This negative refraining from rhetorical supplementarity involves a positive disposition to say "what is true because he *knows* that it *is* true." This, in Foucault's genealogy of the concept, involves a great risk to the speaker; indeed, "if there is a kind of 'proof' of the sincerity of the *parrhesiastes*, it is his *courage*."[21] Such a loquacious jester speaks something dangerous to himself. A tension is inherent to that notion of risk: to have the courage to speak implies that the speaker is the one who is not normatively free to speak. So, wandering, exiled, provocative Diogenes voluntarily and quite riskily infuriates the king with his words, his wit, but a tyrant cannot use this mode of speech, has no Other from which any consequential threat might emanate. (Plutarch's *Life of Alexander* reports one of the better cracks: Alexander the Great, upon finding the famous cynic basking outdoors in the light, asked if he might do any favor for the philosopher, to which Diogenes replied some version of "Yes—get out of my sun.") Foucault summarizes the generality of the parrhesia system as

> a kind of verbal activity where the speaker has a specific relation to truth through frankness, a certain relationship to his own life through danger, a certain type of relation to himself or other people through criticism (self-criticism or criticism of other people), and a specific relation to moral law through freedom and

eugenie brinkema

duty. More precisely, parrhesia is a verbal activity in which a speaker expresses his personal relationship to truth, and risks his life because he recognizes truth-telling as a duty to improve or help other people (as well as himself).[22]

The question, then, is what would a *parrhesiastic aesthetic* involve, formally? One obvious deployment would be to regard the notion of risk integral to Foucault's account as a kind of inscriptive risk to an artist in a specific histori-cal context. Not unlike Stanley Cavell's account of passionate utterance, of "speech as confrontation, as demanding, as owed, . . . each instance of which directs, and risks, if not costs, blood," this would hew closer to a kind of underground, Third, or otherwise risky cinematic utterance, and is emphati-cally *not* what an aesthetic of frankness suggests.[23] Instead, the parrhesiastic risk is not just harm (what is paid in blood): it also risks its own degraded *form*; its risk is reflexive, is inscribed within its own potential. For there is a bad and a good form of classical parrhesia, in which the former, pejorative sense, Foucault says, "consists in saying any- or everything one has in mind without qualification," and the positive sense of risking danger to speak the truth described above. To fail to fall to the bad side—in which the rigor of silence would have been preferable to speech for its own sake—requires that the risk of the spoken truth demands its speaking.

Thus, an aesthetic of frankness confronts something closer to stupidity, what chances its own internal sense of admitting, in addition to the uncon-cealment of truth, a blathering exposure of one's outspokenness, which for all its candid, blunt form speaks freely in the face of the risk of being unwanted, obscene, absurd, excessive, glib, wasteful, waste. In place of a rhetoric of per-suasion, a *parrhesiastic aesthetic* eschews the manipulation of affect to modu-late judgment; shapes and structures itself around something other than the aims of metanarrative, interpretation, seduction, or implorement; fails to make a claim for how the listener to speech (audience to text) ought to feel about or regard the frankness of this speech; and ultimately is indifferent to the use to which such speech might be put, instead unconcealing the work's own eschewing of rhetorical figuration. And it says something dangerous to itself in the process, always also risking exposure as asinine, inane—silly, merely dirty, even foolish, vacant, pointless trash. Fucking waste of time. Fucking around. Bullshit. Whatever. Nothing, nothing at all.

In Clark's photographs and films, a studied abjection of rhetorical devices, by which I mean allegory, critique, context, and ornamentation, destabilizes the possibilities for critique by excluding a diagrammatic position for meta-language. Perversely, in light of the critical party line on Clark with which

I began, the abjecting of disguise, metaphor, and complexity impossibilizes the taking of abject signs for a meaningful elicitation of affect (arousal, disgust, horror, embarrassment). If the division between rhetoric and parrhesia ultimately breaks down over the course of Foucault's lectures, if frankness in the genealogy becomes itself a rhetorical figure, nevertheless it remains different from other figures in that it "is the zero degree of those rhetorical figures which intensify the emotions of the audience."[24] Though neither Plato nor Seneca, Quintilian nor Foucault, cast it in this specific linguistic light, parrhesia is thus opposed to the elicitation of affect as something intensified via rhetorical figure; it remains what is not "simulated or artfully designed," instead retaining its affinities with the unconcealment of truth, which takes a disinterested relation to (all) possibilities for how it might be read.

Or consider a slightly different term for abjecting metalanguages, what Barthes would call the *neutral*, what is neither/nor (*La Critique ni-ni*). (Clark's abjection: neither material nor social.) Barthes's oeuvre plays with multiple terms that devastate criticism—the neutral, but also excess; the third meaning; surface; pleasure; love; joy. As he writes in his preface to Camus's *Tricks*, "Our period interprets a great deal, but Renaud Camus's narratives are neutral, they do not participate in the game of interpretation. They are surfaces without shadows, *without ulterior motives*."[25] Though for Barthes, writing is what permits the purity of an utterance immune to the "cunning tangle of concealed intentions" belonging to speech, for Clark, the conditions of destabilizing and unornamenting the photographic and cinematic image are what refuse the ludic pleasures of the hermeneutic. Haecceitic cinema: each image is its thisness, its hereness, its nowness; the image alone *on its own*, *without ulterior motive*, merely is (*what* it is). Spit. Light. Spunk. If Barthes finds in *Tricks* a haiku-like "asceticism of form (which cuts short the desire to interpret) and a hedonism so serene that all we can say about pleasure is that *it is there* (which is also the contrary of Interpretation)," if the privileged form of sexual practice in Camus is "banal, impoverished, doomed to repetition," and this impoverishment "disproportionate to the wonder of the pleasure" thus afforded, it is the spare economy, the subtlety, the repetitions and failure of deep conveyance, the rejection of claims for being a chronicle, a full and thorough accounting, a scientific, erotic, or otherwise sustained meditation on a community, the deliberately inadequate, even the *politeness* of the writing that makes it so, that renders the form of the work akin to the trick itself: "an intensity, which passes without regret."[26]

Or, as Camus puts it, his book attempts to "utter sexuality . . . calmly. Or, as the writer Duvert would say: *innocently*."[27] Or, as Clark put it in an interview with Gus Van Sant, to compose the image without purpose, without plan, with *purity*.[28]

* * *

What is to be made of a signature shot of Clark's photographic and cinematic work—more durable than junk, froth, cum, crotch, wheels, weed, silhouette—of a figure, usually two, often three, sometimes many, bathed in light, sometimes the thin water of fluorescence, sometimes the warming tonality of an aubade, usually naked, or partially undressed, and entangled, limbs locked, postures bent, but always calm, simple, blank, innocent, and *asleep*?

* * *

"A certain type of awakening: the white, neutral awakening: for a few seconds, whatever Care one felt when one went to sleep, pure moment of Carelessness, forgetfulness of evil, vice in its purest state, kind of clear joy in C major; then the earlier Care falls upon you like a great black bird: the day begins."[29] *Jesus Fucking Christ, what just happened?*

* * *

There is no true sleep in Clark's films until it descends on *all*. Barthes: "Form of this sleep utopia: to sleep together"; "sleep: the very act of trust."[30] Perhaps it arrives first; sleep is what has been happening at the opening of *Another Day in Paradise* to and for the naked, nuzzled (and such young) bodies. It names an innocence, a frankness, which is to say a truthfulness of the repose it displays, always bound to the unconcealment of a plane of skin on the unclothed chest: as in *David Keith Asleep* (1975; in *Teenage Lust*, where it is titled *Teenager Asleep, Oklahoma City*). Or consider the final fourteen-minute sequence of *Kids*, inaugurated when Jennie wanders away from the strobing primary colors of the club, leaves the green pallor of the hall and steps into, over, and on the cluster of crashed bodies littering the apartment floor in off-kilter angles and rhizomatic derangements (the permutations of crossed legs, arms, resting heads seeming contingent, arbitrary, therefore potentially infinite)—nothing but a slow falling to sleep of disparate figures: a brokenhearted, still-wasted Jennie, too late to stop Telly's in-progress defloration; a final holdout in a roaming Casper, who drinks liquor bottle backwash, spies Telly and Darcy tangled, inert, then fucks an unconscious therefore pliable

Jennie on the lightly squeaking sofa next to an inverted shirtless child. She remains asleep, her body converted to the vitality of her limp calves, a flopping hand, the body's branches supported entirely by the thrusting grunter holding them, resituating them when they fail to keep the fold. A black screen, over which one still hears Casper's breathing labor, and then the grayed waking light of New York street scenes: tai chi in the park, a drowsing body lilting against the wall that was its night's support. Unlike the classic city film of the twenties and thirties, your Vertov, your Ruttmann, the real protagonist of *Kids* is not the metropolis, with its rhythms and cycles, but light studied and exposed, studying and exposing. We know the time from this light, this light as the firstness of a different day than the previous one.

Kids opens and closes with black screens over which the sounds of sex avow something is happening that was just or will be revealed, and the morning light to which each black screen cuts bookends the film. The careful distribution of light, its studied composition, its use in symmetrical forms in addition to the various depths of field shaped through natural and highly aestheticized artificial lighting in Clark's shots, distributed over multiple works and over the course of each work, gives the lie to claims for the spontaneity and unfettered realism ascribed to Clark. Intersecting, slightly overexposed Telly-virgin limbs in pale early light with a turned-off lamp on the right edge of the frame (*the aubade*), one minute into the film, is mirrored in a complementary shot, an hour and fifteen minutes later, with the same darkened silhouettes, though this time a new virgin is saying it hurts on the left, and now Telly's on the right, and the far left reach of the frame finds a turned-on lamp (*the eulogy*—by now we know the HIV-infecting deathliness this fuck may bring). These inversions of light unconceal the subtle difference between the two voiceovers, bonded but modified like the light in each defloration frame: Initially, Telly intones, "Virgins, I love them." In the end, "Fucking is what I love. Take that away from me and I really got nothing." The amative target shifts from a plural noun to a gerund, from partner to activity, from unsullied target to its ruining work, the name for inviolate chastity substituted with what grammatically devastates, is incompatible with, the previous placeholder in the grammar of declaring what exactly it is that one loves. The closing praise undoes the grounds of praise in the opening line, thus praising nothing so much as the form of negation and erasure that the film *is*.

Inversion of the romantic bromide: *You always love the one you hurt.*

* * *

eugenie brinkema

In the newness of this new light, Casper's final words close the film. Leaning forward into the silhouette formed by the light behind him, framed centrally, white sofa and pale naked chest glowing with luminescent blankness: "Jesus Christ, what happened?"

Barthes praises a "belatedness in understanding," offering that "if I had to create a god, I would lend him a 'slow understanding': a kind of drip-by-drip understanding of problems. People who understand quickly frighten me."[31]

A quick reading of Casper's closing query turns Clark into a banal moralist.

Slow understanding regards the light instead.

*   *   *

Kids more generally is a formal study of frank illumination. It is neither bodies nor the polis but light whose integrity is declared only to be devastated: what outlines the forms of bodies to suddenly be bleached to blankness; what flashes, interrupts, and strobes the destabilized, wasted, and crying. Light no longer unconceals the give and measure, the angles and planes of the (any) body; it supplants the body, directs the eye to itself above all. Light's frankness insinuates. For in the midst of the careful framings, these studies of light, Clark lets horizontal movement destroy the composition of his image, not once as though in an edited wipe, one shot replaced by another from the side, but continually. Rushing movements of objects intercede between camera and subject again and again, perpetually positing a visual subject only to obliterate it, treating the image as disposable, temporary, contingent, fragile, what is there so that it might be disturbed. Adrian Martin rightly identifies the key to Clark's camera—in its restless relation to bodies—as movement: "His films offer a continuously mobile, almost cubist form of portraiture, the kind that is only possible in cinema. His sensitively hand-held camera never ceases sculpting the flesh, tracing the gestures."[32] But there is also another, specifically luminosity-disturbing dimension to this movement that imposes itself, interposes itself between the static framed images and the camera showing them—the unrelenting, accelerated movement of things, periodic but unpredictable, usually trucks or buses, large enough to ruin the entire reach of the frame, interrupting and slitting the unfettered flow of light around and amid objects.

*   *   *

Ken Park's Tate—the self-choking, self-fucking bearer of the aesthetic mantra to "Keep it simple"—voices the reflexivity that functions as the work's linguistic frankness. "I'll tell you exactly how I did it," a promise to the spectator in anticipation of his splattered vicious murder of his grandparents. This is precisely how, compositionally and linguistically, Clark's work works: his image tells you, exactly, how the things you are seeing done were done. Not politically, ethically, contextually, but flatly, descriptively: "I stabbed her in the breast." Words redouble the image, showing the same flat descriptive fact: the breast, being stabbed. Words redouble words, uncanny for their eschewal of euphemism, synonym, variation, veiling. In *Bully*, the opening phone sex monotone, "I want you to suck my big dick," the unimpeachably clear declaration of erotic exchange, becomes the antirhetorical thrust of the film, commuting the directness of speech from erotics to ethics. Repeatedly in that film, characters eschew the analogical fecundity of language, degrading all possibles in figuration to insistently, repetitively, exhaustingly (and exhaustedly) declare the conceit of the film. Ali says to a boyfriend, "I've got to go down to Fort Lauderdale to help my friend Lisa kill this asshole named Bobby." Lisa, glistening midfuck, pauses to say to Marty the single needlessly sayable declaration—for he is the other of her stated subject pronoun—"We killed a guy"; Lisa, again, to the bystander Claudia, "We killed Bobby. We killed him. He's dead. We did it." The refusal to vary, to find or create a synonym, makes the language of the act blunt, frank—but not economical. It wastes language by degrading its capacity to modify itself for the sake of an appearance of difference, of variation as ornamentation of what is being named, in a way reminiscent of Winfried Menninghaus's description of Kafka's "frankness that effaces itself and passes over into a peculiar sort of style-born 'amnesia,' with a literalness that produces precisely unreadability."[33] Contrast with this the invented term for the arcade game played by characters in *Bully*, in which one can "fatalize" another, fatalizing being closer to fetalizing, a form of Mortal Kombat's worse-than-death finishing-move humiliation, babality, which turns one's opponent into an infant. The dimension of fatality is thereby doubly erased and becomes equivalent to a nascent starting over, deploying invented language not only to vary but to deceive. In the non-new media universe of Clark's diegesis, language does precisely the opposite: it unconceals that it *refuses* to deceive. There is no question that *Macbeth* is one of the main interlocutors for *Bully*, and the omnipresence of the early modern blood, its imagining presaging the consuming guilt of conscience, is here rendered, or rather returned to, actual blood. "There's blood on my fucking shoe," says Lisa, but it is not an imaginary prompt to hysteria. For the image shows that there *is*. What this strategy unconceals is precisely a refusal of cloaked, cloaking language. Recall at this point Foucault's parrhesia, which "consists in saying any- or everything one has in mind without qualification." This blood is not a metaphor. Nor is it Godard's aestheticization of the famous "Ce n'est pas du sang, c'est du rouge." It doesn't *matter* if a stain is red or blood; it is no more violent if blood, no more aestheticized if red. It is instead, merely, resolutely, *there*. On her fucking shoe.

Consider then Clark's 1980 black-and-white photograph from *Teenage Lust*, captioned, which is to say grounded with specificity and opacity by the narrative pacing, *They Met a Girl on Acid in Bryant Park at 6 am and Took Her Home* (figure 11.1). The photograph has been described in the conventional language of the abject as unsettling and frank. One such account details "a guy on top of a girl, who looks to be whacked out of her brain. . . . It's hard to imagine how or why Clark found his way into these rooms with his Leica, but the resulting images are nightmarish. They're *stark* and Clark is unwilling to draw any conclusion about the worlds he gravitates towards."[34] Ignored here is the rigorous formal composition of the image, which consists of three strong vertical bands—a naked man from belly to feet, his erection intruding from the left; a woman's splayed thighs and calves centering the image, her feet exceeding the frame and thus her body giving form to the measure of the height of the image; and a mirror and beam of fluorescent light to the right, across which cuts the central horizontal disruption of a naked man shown in his entire length intersecting with these registers. The grid thus formed comes to its origin point in the crossing of the bodies, the metonymy for which are buttocks obliterating where the man's extension meets and enters the girl. Her face, illegible in its anamorphic angle in the real, is open mouthed and differently illegible in the mirror—the one too blank to seem possibly reflected in the other, which is inverted and seemingly ecstatic—and if the diagonal composition were not sufficient, the eye is drawn to move between the two versions of the girl on acid's face through the bookended black-and-white density of the man's reflected hat cum concentric circles. The eye does more than that. When it starts at the lower left origin to follow the strong visual line of the calves up to the upper-right corner to land at the girl's face, when the eye reads left to right, when the eye follows the graphic imperative thusly, vision literally traces a thrusting motion into the diagrammatic space of the wasted girl. This eye follows the impulsive energy of the man's lower half to enter her, and with some quickness, and with some force, over and over again.

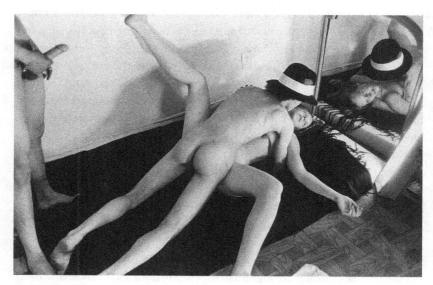

figure 11.1 Larry Clark, *They Met a Girl on Acid in Bryant Park at 6 AM and Took Her Home*, 1980; gelatin silver print, 1981.

The caption's specificity about the encounter that was the precondition for this choreography—of line and light, circle and curve, bodies upright or splayed or bent, fucking or waiting or opened—offers neither a moralist's shaming nor a hermeneutic guide to the legibility of the girl's doubled face, as though indexing the blank quality of Kristeva's Célinian "laughing apocalypse": "the ultimate form of a secular attitude without morality, without judgment, without hope."[35] What the caption declares merely is that *this* meeting, *that* park, *that* hour, *this* girl, *the* taking home, is a singular certain something that happened and that can be unconcealed just so.

Clark's films liberally deploy sexual dysphemisms—in the opening monologue of *Kids*, in the ode to the virgin, that abstraction is praised for "no loose as a goose pussy, no skank"; in *Ken Park*, Shawn's intimate panegyric on his girlfriend's mother, whom he has fucked, has eaten out, is that she and her daughter "have the same pussy smell." Its effect, however, is not to reestablish a hierarchy between the unoffensive and disparaging. The works are equally suspicious of euphemism and attentive to the nuances of the signifier, as in Ruby's insistence in *Kids* that "there's a difference between making love, having sex, and fucking," wherein the first is framed as sweet and slow, the second affectively anemic, and the latter deferred to the onomatopoetic explosive

Boom, Boom, Boom. Dysphemism is often taken as restoring a frankness purportedly lost to polite euphonias—take, as a classic example, Bakhtin's account: "Unofficial (unprintable) argot also varied in force. Every age has its own norms of official speech and propriety. And every age has its own type of words and expressions that are given as a signal to speak freely, to call things by their own names, without any mental restrictions and euphemisms. The use of these colloquialisms created the atmosphere of frankness, inspired certain attitudes, a certain unofficial view of the world."[36] But radically diverging from any such stance, Clark's films are more likely to find euphemistic and dysphemistic speech equally burdensome for their restriction in relation to bald descriptive capacities.

When Jennie and Ruby visit a clinic to get an AIDS test—Jennie ostensibly only keeping the latter company, though it is her test, her one time with Telly, that will ultimately sign positively—Jennie's eyes scan, and the camera cuts to and follows, a poster of identical, save for chromatic alternations and doubled rings, cartoonish representations of flattened unused condoms, each one bearing a different name. From left to right across the four-by-five grid: "Balloon / Jimmy Hat / Shower Curtain / French Letter / Diving Suit / Rubber / Goody Bag / Pro / Glove / Cover / Joy Bag / Envelope / Night Cap / Raincoat / Sheath / Jacket / Scumbag / Dreadnought / Sling / Thing." Consider this poster a mise en abyme instruction in the linguistic workings across *Kids*: the euphemistic (Joy Bag), the dysphemistic (Scumbag), flattened out in their repetitive candy colors and ending with the flat declaration of the inanimate material object that a condom fundamentally *is*—neither life saving nor joy enhancing nor infected juice containing, but just another brute thing, just like any other thing, every thing of which could take the dumb yet accurate final printed denomination of *Thing*.

In place of the indirection of (all) figurative language, obscene or circumlocuting, Clark's films put in their stead this privileged deployment of direct, flat descriptive speech, unclad and disrobed of connotation. In *Kids*, amid "faggot!" screaming and black-body brutalizing in Washington Square Park, one hears the simplified pedagogy of blunt making that takes the form of a series of fractured imperatives, each accompanied by a close-up performance of the advice to an absent but observing individuum: "Break it; scrape it; lick it; dump it; smoke it." An ethical point of exception in *Kids*, declared often in criticism to be the patronizing apogee of the film's focus on white youth—when Casper gives money to a change-requesting man on the subway—is never discussed in relation to the linguistic form it privileges. A black man, all torso to the lower ribs, visibly consisting solely of this trunk and pushing himself along on a questionably balanced skateboard, shaking a cup of change, sings in a repetitive antecedent-consequent phraseology, "I have no legs. I have no legs." Though the film comprises vignettes that turn on bodies, their fluids, their crossing and wasting, it also periodically pauses on scenes that can only be regarded as aesthetically instructive in relation to a frank use of language. Like the condom poster, the camera places itself in sympathy with the careful study of this legless figure, and like the slow vertical scan of the poster, it takes an autonomous interest in excess of the diegetic alibi for its attention. The camera sets itself low on the ground, compositionally leveling with and centering on the red train car door that will open and reveal his body, and over the scene's duration of exactly sixty seconds is the repetition of the brute declaration of precisely what is unavoidably visible about the corporeal form put on display. Such a redundancy between word and image implies not just unnecessariness, but also shows the inutility of the word when faced with the presentational avowals of the body. And yet, these words that might be omitted are emphatically not. They display no new information about the body in the frame nor engagement in the rhetorical persuasions opposed to parrhesia; rather, this statement of visible fact puts on display precisely the words' absence of context, lost ornamentation, and nonpresent imploration. These words abject the totality of the figurative in language. They are in turn figured as a juncture of vulnerability between the protagonists and the partitioned, broken body, as though only such a disconcertingly true, unadorned, complexity-abjecting claim could function as an ethical punctum.

*   *   *

"Was Adam a hard birth? Did he not want to come out? Did he want to stay inside you? Did you have to have an episiotomy? When you have an episiotomy, the vaginal canal is about this close to the anus." Tom's questions to Adam's mother at the beginning of *Marfa Girl*, violent because of their specificity, their presencing of the correct language to describe the anatomical query, precisely cast off the conventional failure to deploy the correctness of language in relation to (this part of, this reality of) the body.

Any part of, any reality of the body becomes a celebration of arbitrariness and neutrality: neither meaningful nor meaningless, neither privileged nor necessarily marginal. In Clark's photographic and cinematic work, every part of the body abjects each claim that might be made *for* it.

As though making a mockery of Jean Epstein's fetishization of the close-up of the face, with its photogenic promise of moral enhancement, in *Bully*, the camera is as apt to linger on the stubble and exterior crease of the labia, slightly folded, nicely fatty, delicately arcing toward hip. Both labia and face are equally available to Clark's camera, equally studied and then moved past, but neither is privileged for a bond to interiority or intimacy. Neither makes sense; neither is sublated to the revelatory realm of meaning—meaning that, as Jean-Luc Nancy defines it, is "the element in which there can be significations, interpretations, representation."[37] In Clark's aesthetic system, neither labia nor face fulfill any directive to answer a question of or for critique. Like violence and fucking, both are fundamentally *uneventful*.

The aesthetic of frankness takes as its ultimate target a *meaningful* relation to the body: but not to reassert the unvarnished presentation of corporeality as the sign of an unfurling truth. In abjecting ornamental, rhetorical, visual, and narrative complexity, a positive aesthetic of frankness makes the body the bearer of the *risk* of truth. The body is not the canvas for candor; it is instead the site of the abjuration of the figurative. Bodies become the ground of truth, yet not as unmediated things. Instead, the body becomes the gesture of undisplaying simulation, withdrawing the ornamentality, the figurativeness, the taken-for-signs horizon of what passes as a false frankness of thought.[38] At the extreme reach of frankness, Clark deploys the body to reveal precisely the shortcoming of the prevailing assumption that the stuff of the corpus can be converted, put to use, for signs of something that does not simultaneously threaten to withdraw. Kristeva's abject, when one lets its banal signs recede, assumes a relation to Barthes's *ni-ni*: "The abject is perverse because it neither gives up nor assumes a prohibition, a rule, or a law; but turns them aside, misleads, corrupts; uses them, takes advantage of them, the better to deny them. It kills in the name of life."[39] The double burden of frankness is its negative withdrawal from servitude, reticence, and silence, as well as its simultaneous positive obligation to bequeathment, disclosure, and saying all. Abjection is the name that neither celebrates nor condemns this law of speaking truth, even in the wake of its foundational risk: that its voicing will be unwanted in a brute divulgation that goes too far—a noise ever risking censure as empty, shallow, or obscene. Instead, the abject is the structural corruption and strategic use of the body *for* metalanguages—of ethics, politics, the social, the moralizing, the pedagogical, the allegorical, the meaningful—the better to deny them all.

Notes

Epigraphs: Roland Barthes, preface to *Tricks*, by Renaud Camus, trans. Richard Howard (New York: St. Martin's Press, 1981), vii; Julia Kristeva, *Powers of Horror: An Essay on Abjection*, trans. Leon S. Roudiez (New York: Columbia University Press, 1982), 147.

1   Kristeva, *Powers of Horror*, 147. Any reading that takes fluids as abject, what becomes waste through the transformation of movement from inside to outside the body (ex-pelled, ex-pressed), is particularly bound to Clark's interest in spit, following the logic whereby, as the psychologist Gordon Allport figures it, "that which is spit out can never remain the same again"; it becomes "not-me." Allport continues: "How very intimate (propriate) the bodily sense is can be seen by performing a little experiment in your imagination. Think first of swallowing the saliva in your mouth, or do so. Then imagine expectorating it into a tumbler and drinking it! What seemed natural and 'mine' suddenly becomes disgusting and alien." Gordon Willard Allport, *Becoming: Basic Considerations for a Psychology of Personality* (New Haven, CT: Yale University Press, 1955), 43.

2   Kristeva, *Powers of Horror*, 18. An example of the socially abjected approach to Clark's work, making reference to his "background as a photo-essayist concerned with immortalizing gritty, 'realistic' representations of desperate, disenfranchised youth trapped at society's margins," can be found in Nicholas Rombes, *New Punk Cinema* (Edinburgh: Edinburgh University Press, 2005), 49. Richard Benjamin brings together these three conventional strands of the abject—disgusting tropes related to bodily functions; marginalized and compromised identities; and the moral abomination for which these two malignities stand—in what he dubs "youth apocalypse films": "The films are obsessed with a scatological adolescent body, one that is violated but also disruptive. In these films, the young body literally erupts or is pulverized. The white youths depicted are pathologically violent and shockingly indifferent to the present or future. Indeed, their very identity formation as white youths is *predicated* on the pursuit of pathological violence and ecstasy." Richard Benjamin, "The Sense of an Ending: Youth Apocalypse Films," *Journal of Film and Video* 56, no. 4 (Winter 2004): 34.

3   See my discussion of Kristeva's theory of abjection in relation to film-theoretical treatments of disgust in Eugenie Brinkema, *The Forms of the Affects* (Durham, NC: Duke University Press, 2014), 133–41.

4   Kristeva, *Powers of Horror*, 4.

5   Kristeva, *Powers of Horror*, 2.

6   Kristeva, *Powers of Horror*, 3.

7   Benjamin, "Sense of an Ending," 41. See the same logic in Jesse Engdahl and Jim Hosney, "Review: *Kids*," *Film Quarterly* 49, no. 2 (Winter 1995–96): 41–44: "The camera rests on the faces of *Kids*' 'real' teens, probing, revealing, betraying all that is beautiful, ugly, attractive, repulsive, alluring, and repugnant."

8 For a situating of Clark among contemporary photographers of the marginal, see Julian Stallabrass, "What's in a Face? Blankness and Significance in Contemporary Art Photography," *October* 122 (Fall 2007): 73. One can easily locate numerous claims for Clark's ostensibly pornographic or pedophilic leanings; for example, for the former, notable also for its blanket rejection of pleasure in Clark's work, see Peter Bradshaw, *"The Smell of Us: Review,"* *Guardian* (London), August 31, 2014: "This film is joyless, passionless, humourless, incurious about real people's real lives. There is no energy or verve, just the compulsive persistence of the porn addict." Or Sudhir Mahadevan, "'Perfect Childhoods': Larry Clark Puts Boys Onscreen," in *Where the Boys Are: Cinemas of Masculinity and Youth,* ed. Murray Pomerance and Frances Gateward (Detroit, MI: Wayne State University Press, 2005), 98: "Clark's films seem to depart from the genre of the teenpic and move toward sexploitation and the *pornographic.*" For the latter, see Daniel Mudie Cunningham, "Larry Clark: Trashing the White American Dream," *Film Journal,* no. 8.

9 Quotations 1 and 2—Ralph Gibson, "Larry Clark," *Interview,* October 2010, 110–15, https://www.interviewmagazine.com/art/larry-clark; 3—Cunningham, "Larry Clark," n.p.; 4—Dick Cheverton's review of *Tulsa,* printed on the back cover of the Grove Press edition, "A Devastating Portrait of an American Tragedy," *Detroit* (MI) *Free Press,* November 7, 1971: "This is not a picture book that will lie quietly and without protest on coffee tables. Nor is this book easy to pick up, confront, challenge. For this is a collection of photographs that assail, lacerate, devastate. And ultimately indict. These are pictures that shimmer with a ferocious honesty"; 5—Gibson, "Larry Clark"; 6—Janet Maslin, "Growing Up Troubled, in Terrifying Ways," *New York Times,* July 21, 1995, C1, C5; 7—Benjamin "Sense of an Ending," 38; 8—Engdahl and Hosney, "Review: *Kids,*" 42; 9—Cunningham, "Larry Clark," n.p.

10 Eric Kohn, "Nashville, Harmony's House, Present Day, Part I," *Harmony Korine: Interviews,* ed. Eric Kohn (Jackson: University Press of Mississippi, 2015), 14.

11 According to coproducer of *Kids* Christine Vachon, despite the illusion of documentary authenticity, *Kids* "was scheduled, it was scripted, it was location managed, and it was production designed." Christine Vachon with David Edelstein, *Shooting to Kill* (New York: Spike Books, 1998), 178.

12 Henry Giroux, "Media Panics and the War Against 'Kids': Larry Clark and the Politics of Diminished Hope," in *Breaking in to the Movies: Film and the Culture of Politics* (Malden, MA: Blackwell, 2002), 182.

13 Kristeva, *Powers of Horror,* 204.

14 *Oxford English Dictionary,* 2nd ed. (1989), s.v. "frank."

15 Mikhail Bakhtin, *Rabelais and His World,* trans. Hélène Iswolsky (Bloomington: Indiana University Press, 1984), 271.

16 *Oxford English Dictionary,* 2nd ed. (1989), s.vv. "authentic," "direct," "sincere."

17 Michel Foucault, *Fearless Speech*, ed. Joseph Pearson, from the transcribed "Discourse and Truth" lectures given at the University of California at Berkeley in fall 1983 (Los Angeles: Semiotext(e), 2001), 12.

18 Aristotle, *Rhetorica* (*Rhetoric*), in *The Basic Works of Aristotle*, ed. Richard McKeon, trans. W. Rhys Roberts (New York: Random House, 1941), bk. 1, ch. 2, 1329.

19 Foucault, *Fearless Speech*, 21.

20 Foucault, *Fearless Speech*, 12.

21 Foucault, *Fearless Speech*, 15.

22 Foucault, *Fearless Speech*, 19.

23 Stanley Cavell, "Performative and Passionate Utterance," in *Philosophy the Day after Tomorrow* (Cambridge, MA: Belknap Press, 2005), 187.

24 Foucault, *Fearless Speech*, 21.

25 Barthes, preface, viii.

26 Barthes, preface, viii, x.

27 Renaud Camus, foreword to *Tricks*, xi.

28 Clark: "I just happened to have my camera and be photographing my friends. It was totally innocent; there was no purpose to the photographs. There was a purity to them that wasn't planned; it was realism." Larry Clark, interview by Gus Van Sant, "Larry Clark: Shockmaker," *Interview Magazine*, July 1995, http://www.harmony-korine.com/paper/int/lc/shockmaker.html.

29 Roland Barthes, "Sleep," session of March 4, 1978, in *The Neutral: Lecture Course at the Collège de France (1977–1978)*, trans. Rosalind Krauss and Denis Hollier (New York: Columbia University Press, 2005), 37. For a different but resonant account of sleep—and one that returns to the question of saliva with a noted difference—see John Paul Ricco, "Drool: Liquid Fore-speech of the Fore-scene," *Scapegoat* 5 (Summer/Autumn 2013): 234–41.

30 Barthes, "Sleep," 40, 41.

31 Barthes, "Sleep," 37.

32 Adrian Martin, "A Larry Clark Portrait," *16:9* 3, no. 13 (September 2005), 11.

33 Winfried Menninghaus, *Disgust: The Theory and History of a Strong Sensation*, trans. Howard Eiland and Joel Golb (Albany: State University of New York Press, 2003), 280.

34 Lynn Hirschberg, "What's the Matter with Kids Today?," *New York Magazine* 23 (June 5, 1995): 38. Emphasis added.

35 Kristeva, *Powers of Horror*, 206.

36 Bakhtin, *Rabelais and His World*, 188.

37 Jean-Luc Nancy, *L'oubli de la philosophie* (Paris: Galilée, 1986) 90–91; this translation is from Christopher Fynsk, foreword to *The Inoperative Community*, ed. Peter Connor, trans. Peter Connor, Lisa Garbus, Michael Holland, and Simona Sawhney (Minneapolis: University of Minnesota Press, 1991) 26, 154.

38 Lyotard's compelling section on frankness, "Franchise," in *Que peindre?* likewise links it to withdrawal—or, rather, moving in the opposite conceptual

direction, he positions frankness as what an antiornamentality in the image is withdrawn toward/into. One rushes away from scenario and toward/into frankness "at the extremes of the intrigue, simple presentation, the frankness of the here and now, revealed by god's shortcoming." Jean-François Lyotard, *Que peindre?* [What to paint?], ed. Herman Parret, trans. Antony Hudek, Vlad Ionescu, and Peter W. Milne (Leuven: Leuven University Press, 2012), 235; see also Jean-François Lyotard, interview, *Cultural Politics* 9, no. 2 (2013): 212–18. Like Foucault, who will find in parrhesia an opposition to rhetoric, Lyotard figures Valerio Adami's frankness as what involves none of the hindrance of intrigue (French, "intrigue": plot, scenario, puzzle, situation, story), but rather a formal purity of withdrawing into line.

39   Kristeva, *Powers of Horror*, 15.

chapter twelve

A Series of Ugly Feelings: Fabulation & Abjection in Shōjo Manga

thomas lamarre

Hatta Ayuko's popular manga series *Wolf Girl and Black Prince* (*Ookami shōjo to kuro ōji*), which began serialization in 2011 in a monthly manga magazine targeted to girls ages twelve to seventeen, opens with a scene of abjection. A sixteen-year-old girl, in her first year of high school, agrees to serve as a dog for a boy in the same class, in exchange for him agreeing to pretend to be her boyfriend. Publicly, then, they appear as boyfriend and girlfriend, while privately they are dog and master. He calls her "wolf girl," implying she is in need of domestication, while she comes to see him as the "black prince," because, although he appears to the world to be a shining prince, she experiences the dark cruelty beneath the handsome surface. Such a scenario resonates with Kristeva's theory of abjection, as Barbara Creed describes it: "to explore the different ways in which abjection, as a source of horror, works within patriarchal societies, as a means of separating the human from the non-human and the fully constituted subject from the partially formed subject."[1] Relegated to the position of a wild animal to be domesticated, the girl appears to be abjected, expelled from the realm of fully constituted human subjects.

But how is a dialogue to be constructed between Kristeva's theory of abjection and the world of shōjo manga, or "comics for girls"? Initially at least, the major obstacle to dialogue appears to be the difference in genre. Hatta's *Wolf Girl* might be best described as romantic comedy, light hearted, and even frivolous, while Kristeva's *Powers of Horror* has usually been applied to works that dwell on grotesque, exorbitant, horrifying moments, such as the horror film. Yet, contrary to generic expectations, laughter and abjection intersect within Kristeva's account. She notes, "Laughing is a way of placing or displacing abjection."[2] Conversely, beneath the smiling surface of romantic comedies like *Wolf Girl* run strong undercurrents of irritability, frustration, anxiety, and even loathing.

Yet a more fundamental problem arises: if the process of constructing a site of mutual encounter does not address the genuine differences between abjection theory and shōjo manga, differences in how they are situated in both the academy and the marketplace, then nothing will have happened. Kristeva's theory is sometimes expanded to comprise new objects from non-European locations. Its increase in capacity augments its aura of authority and sophistication, while the theory remains unchallenged. Kristeva's work encourages such a gesture. An aggressively Eurocentric stance runs throughout her work, most evident in her account of Chinese women.[3] Yet, I do not wish to dwell on Kristeva's Eurocentrism as such. Dwelling on it risks reinforcing a binary opposition between the West and the non-West, feeding reality back into the metaphysical construction of the West.[4] I propose to address a more central problem: her assumptions about subject formation and psychic sovereignty.

Kristeva writes at the outset, "The abject only has one quality of the object—that of being opposed to I."[5] Evidently, she intends to move beyond an account of the subject based on a binary opposition between the subject and the object, which invariably tends to naturalize the subject's mastery over the object, because its sovereignty is presumed in advance. In contrast, Kristeva aims to problematize the sovereign subject, to examine the formation of its (symbolic) mastery. Her account then moves in two directions.

On the one hand, when she challenges the naturalness of the sovereign subject, her notion of the abject potentially activates the materiality of objects, for the abject is above all a materiality that resists containment— bursting forth, seeping out, spilling, overflowing materially and affectively. This move may prove resonant with recent trends dubbed "new materialisms," which strive to liberate objects from inert, passive objecthood, and to imagine the affective and material agency of objects.[6] On the other hand, because she insists on opposing the abject to the subject, clearly the containment of the abject is not really a matter of bodies and objects at all: it is all about the subject, modeled on sovereignty and patriarchy. Material flows may exceed or escape the body, but the paternal subject captures them successfully, using them to shore up its sovereignty.

This is why her theory of affect often presents an impasse for feminism. Barbara Creed remarks, "The problem with Kristeva's theory, particularly for feminists, is that she never makes clear her position on the oppression of women. Her theory moves uneasily between explanation of, and justification for, the formation of human societies based on the subordination of women."[7] In other words, Kristeva's theory of the abject seems to pose a challenge to the sovereignty of the subject—especially to the sovereignty of men over women. Yet it does not grant much force of becoming to the abject: the abject feminine remains subjected to (because subjectified by) the sovereign masculine (patriarch).

The first movement of Kristeva's theory interests me, but disentangling it from the second movement is no easy matter. I thus propose a different kind of encounter between theory and object. The first question is, what kind of object is this *Wolf Girl* series? Serialized manga are nondiscrete objects, very different from the discrete, bounded textual objects on which Kristeva's theory depends, such as novels and the Bible, which invite a tortured metaphysics of the book. Instead of looking at shōjo manga through the lens of Kristeva's theory of abjection, I aim to let her theory *pass through* girls' comics. In subsequent sections, I work through *Wolf Girl* as a *prism*, to refract, disperse, and transform her theory.

Serialization and Fabulation

Serialized manga are difficult to grasp as a whole. It is difficult to decide, for instance, whether they should be considered a serial mode (a story with multiple chapters) or a series (a collection of standalone stories with some common thread). They hover between these two possibilities because of the way in which they are published. The bulk of popular serialized manga start out with an inaugural chapter in one of many manga magazines. *Shūkan Shōnen Jyanpu* (aka *Shōnen Jump*, or Weekly boys jump) is the best known, for the global success of manga such as *One Piece*, *Naruto*, *Hunter × Hunter*, and *Gintama* has led to international adaptations of *Shōnen Jump*. But there are scores of other manga magazines targeted to different demographics, such as *Māgaretto* (*Margaret*), a manga magazine for girls six to twelve, currently published biweekly by the same publishing house as *Shōnen Jump*, Shūeisha. Hatta's *Wolf Girl* series began serialization in 2011 in *Bessatsu Māgaretto*, a monthly magazine spinoff from *Margaret*, targeted to girls and young women

figure 12.1
The cover of the monthly manga magazine *Bessatsu Māgaretto* (*Betsuma*) for October 2014, featuring Kyōya and Eri of *Wolf Girl and Black Prince*, as well as advertising a "bonus feature" DVD, which includes an animated episode of the series not included in the televised anime series.

ages twelve to seventeen (figure 12.1). As readers outgrow the six-to-twelve children's demographic, these magazines often launch spinoffs targeted to somewhat older readers. *Wolf Girl* appears monthly, in chapters or episodes of approximately forty to forty-five pages.

Printed on cheap newsprint and sold inexpensively to increase readership, these weekly, biweekly, and monthly manga magazines are often sold at a loss for the publisher. Big publishing houses benefit in another way: they use readers' response forms to determine which manga will remain in serialization. Each manga within a magazine thus vies with other manga in the same magazine. To continue in serialization, the inaugural chapter, like a pilot episode, has to attract readers' attention, and the subsequent three or four episodes have to hold that attention, gradually garnering a group of loyal readers. While the publishers may not reap profits from the manga magazines, they have established a readership, which is worth a good deal. Put bluntly, this is an attention economy in which readers' attention is bought and sold across markets, but that attention must first be delimited and gathered (primitive accumulation or expropriation).

These conditions of serialization might seem to favor the serial mode, in which the lure to continue reading comes from a desire to know what happens next in the story. It is not, however, so simple as that. Manga magazines are usually thrown away after reading, and although older copies are sometimes found lying around noodle shops or cafés to peruse while waiting for a meal or lingering over coffee, readers may easily miss a week or two. Some readers may not pick up the story until it is well under way. Also, at any point within the serialization, new readers appear who cannot be expected to have read the first chapter or chapters. To accommodate such discontinuous modes of reading, serialized manga have departed from the serial and moved toward a series mode: each chapter or episode must to some degree stand alone and must give a sense of the whole series. The *Wolf Girl* series began to include an inset table of characters in each new chapter, to let new readers or intermittent readers know who was who.

The tendency toward the series mode is repeated and reinforced in three other registers. First, when manga are serialized over many years, they often resort to story arcs, a series of chapters presenting a continuous story. Within an arc, the manga adopts the serial mode. But across arcs, the manga tips toward the series mode. Even the *Wolf Girl* series, which at the time of this writing has reached only about fifty-four chapters, has small story arcs of varying length: a series of three or four chapters deals with the heroine's relation with an old friend who becomes obsessed with getting her to break up with the Black Prince; a chapter or two focuses on a stalker pursuing the Wolf Girl's best friend. If the series continues its run, the first fifty-odd volumes may be retroactively cast as the high school years, to contrast with the coming chapters on the university years.

Second, when a serialized manga proves popular, it will be published in the *tankōbon*, or trade paperback, format. With publication of the paperback, publishers begin to see greater profits. The *Wolf Girl* series moved quickly into the *tankōbon* format: the first volume was published in 2011, within the first year of the manga serialization (figure 12.2). A new volume, comprising about four chapters, has appeared roughly every four months. At the time of this writing about fourteen paperbacks are in circulation. The book format omits the advertisements from the magazine format, usually while adding bonus materials, such as messages from the creators or other ancillary or supplementary features. The paperback allows for a new kind of continuous reading, but it also introduces a new kind of discontinuity: when the reader has finished

オオカミ少女と黒王子

WOLF GIRL
&
BLACK PRINCE

① 八田鮎子

Mc

figure 12.2
The cover of the first paperback volume of *Wolf Girl and Black Prince* manga series, featuring Kyōya.

the volume, she must either wait for the next volume (usually a delay of some months), or turn to the magazine format. Fans of a particular manga commonly follow the magazine serialization and purchase the books. The book format also tends to broaden the readership, attracting new readers to the magazine serialization. More kinds of readers begin to skip in and out of the series.

Third, manga whose popularity leads to paperback publication often make the leap into television, often in *anime* format. Generally speaking, a certain number of paperback volumes must be published to provide enough material (a stock of attention) for an animated television series. With some eight to ten paperback volumes in print, *Wolf Girl* reached critical mass for an anime series, and twelve episodes began airing in 2014 (figure 12.3). Because the anime adaptation marks the moment when a manga series really begins to generate significant profits and attention, publishers and studios have developed a number of different strategies for multimedia franchising. Hatta's *Wolf*

figure 12.3
An image of Eri and Kyōya
frequently used to promote
the manga and anime,
and later restaged with the
human actors to promote a
live-action movie, with fan
overtranslations.

Girl manga series has also spawned (1) a drama CD in 2013; (2) an OAD (original animation disc) bundled with the twelfth volume of the manga series in 2015 (featuring the adaptation of a manga episode not treated in the anime series); and (3) a live-action movie in May 2016. This pattern of transmedial serialization, in which the anime series presents the big commercial leap forward, is one of the most robust patterns for what is commonly called *media mix* in the Japanese context. While the transmedial serialization of manga mobilizes various media forms, including toys, music, drama CDs, live-action films, animated films, console videogames, mobile phone games, literature, and voice actress albums, to name a few, the adaptation of a manga series into an anime series usually provides the linchpin for the media mix.

Multimedia franchising increases the tendency toward the series mode, raising the series effect to a higher power, intensifying it. The anime format diverges from the manga at the level of story, covering only a portion of the manga series, presenting a side story, or changing the manga story to suit a

thomas lamarre

broader audience (home television viewers) with somewhat different expectations. It also diverges in its mode of address, material conventions, tonality, and affective appeal. The anime must at once stand alone as a serial form and feel like it is part of the series, now a multimedia series. Likewise, each new media "instance"—drama CD, OAD, live-action film—heightens the awareness of the series-ness of the serialized manga. Gradually, serialized manga have taken on the feel of anime, as if to anticipate their adaptation, while anime series often evoke the feel of manga.[8]

Serialized manga, then, present an intimate entanglement of the serial mode and the series mode, which results in a distinctive experience of the relation between part and whole at the level of story: a sense of the whole is always implicated in each of the parts, while each part tends to operate somewhat autonomously but still as part of a whole. The manga series is not like the television sitcom with its standalone episodes; nor is it like a graphic novel, with its drive for narrative or subjective closure. It thus poses a general challenge to one of the most familiar ways of understanding the relation of part to whole—narrative unity, or totality. Needless to say, narrative unity is a complex matter, not merely an end or closure. Even if the end or closure never arrives, it might be construed as operating "under erasure," introducing a sense of unity at a subjective level, acting where it is not. Yet the very distinction between story and narrative entails some profound assumptions that have been widely challenged in the context of serialized manga.

Structural and formal analyses of narrative, that is, narratology, begin with a structural or formal distinction between the *what* and *how* of narrative: between what is told (a series of events) and how it is told (narrative discourse), between *fabula* and *syuzhet* (or subject) in Russian formalism, or more simply, between story and narrative discourse.[9] Several commentators have signaled the key problem of this approach: it subordinates story to narrative discourse, and fabula to subject. It introduces a bias toward discursive or subjective enclosure, turning story into a *subjectified object*.

Japanese manga writer, editor, and critic Ōtsuka Eiji has repeatedly taken issue with this bias in the context of multimedia serialization. He argues that multimedia serialization presents a situation in which consumers encounter "small narratives" (*monogatari*) that function as parts to be assembled and understood within a "large narrative." Although not presented directly, the large narrative imparts a sense of overall unity to the serial components, to each of the media instances. Ōtsuka calls this narrative unity a world.[10] His notion of a small narrative is thus analogous to that of fabula, while his large narrative is like the subjective and narrative discursiveness evoked in narratology. Yet his transformation of the notion of large narrative into "world" makes clear that narrative can no longer be assumed to provide closure or subjective enclosure.

Azuma Hiroki expanded on Ōtsuka's insights and challenged the framework of narrative itself. He writes of the end of "grand narratives," highlighting the postmodern rise of a database structure through which consumers make their own little stories, and nothing but little stories.[11] Azuma has insistently argued that multimedia series thus do not lend themselves to a formal analysis, in which story is subordinated to narrative; nor do they lend themselves to a Lacanian style of analysis, in which the semiotic is subordinated to (or organized by) the symbolic. In this respect, Azuma's account recalls Derrida's challenge to the subjective privilege accorded to narrative within narratology. In his challenge, Derrida stressed the autonomy of story (or *fabula*) from narrative (or *syuzhet*), imagining a nonhierarchical relation in which each story would be a part of others, at once larger and smaller than itself, yet without subjective or narrative subordination of each distinctive part to any other.[12]

Ōtsuka, Azuma, and Derrida, albeit for different reasons, call attention to the liberation of story from narrative, granting new autonomy to fabula, to processes of fabulation. Ōtsuka and Azuma link this liberation of story directly to the material conditions in which each media instance is always already inhabited by other media instances, in multiple formats. As such, the manga series with its multimedia world cannot be construed as a subjectified object, that is, an object subordinated to its eventual subjective or discursive enclosure. The manga series, then, is a weird object, not like an object at all in the traditional sense. It entails a nondiscrete mode of existence.

The nondiscrete mode poses pragmatic challenges for the study of manga. Where exactly are the limits for a manga series? Not only are popular manga series notoriously vast and unruly, but ancillary media refuse to remain strictly ancillary: the anime adaptation, for instance, might be ruled out, but then it is so much a part of the business model and the consumer experience of the manga that it appears to permeate the "manga proper" in advance. Likewise, the drama CDs in the *Wolf Girl* series consist largely of voice actors reading the manga dialogue, and yet, for the sake of clarity, even as you are invited to read along with the manga, the order of certain story elements is altered. Fans also create versions in which the manga pages are cut and edited to match the story flow of the drama CDs. It is practically impossible to hold a manga series apart from its various media instances, and to subordinate these latter to the status of "ancillary" production. Manga series are always already multimedia series.

thomas lamarre

The nondiscrete series mode of existence also has subjective implications. Because it places emphasis on fabula and practices of fabulation, it tends to undermine subjective and discursive enclosure, precisely what is presumed in Kristeva's theory of abjection. As such, when scenarios of abjection appear, we cannot be content with interpreting the abject entirely in terms of opposition to the subject that is generative of the subject or transgression of sovereignty that is generative of patriarchy. Needless to say, the series mode implies some kind of unity and thus subjectivity, a material-affective continuum. In the next section, I trace the contours of that continuum by following the fault lines that arise between Kristeva's theory of abjection and the scenarios of abjection occurring in the *Wolf Girl* series. I am looking for the pattern of diffraction that appears as Kristeva's theory passes through the prism of shōjo manga.

Abjection

The *Wolf Girl* series draws its vibe from the initial transformation of Shinohara Erika (aka Eri) into a dog at the hands of Sata Kyōya, the young man who takes advantage of her desperate situation. Eri lies to her two new girlfriends, Tachibana Marin and Tezuka Aki, claiming to have a boyfriend. When Marin and Aki demand to see evidence of him, Eri opportunistically snaps a cell phone shot of a suitably attractive boy. Her gambit backfires, however, when she shows the photo to Marin and Aki, who recognize him as a student in the same school, in the same grade (but a different classroom). They find it hard to believe that the cute but nonetheless average Eri has snagged the handsome prince, Sata Kyōya, who has large numbers of pretty girls swooning around him, vying for his attention. When Eri, in a second moment of desperation, explains the situation to Kyōya, he agrees to pretend to be her boyfriend—on one condition. She must agree to be his dog. Kyōya commands her to spin in a circle and bark three times, then rewards her with a pat on the head, as if domesticating her wildness. Apparently in all innocence, Eri has chosen a popular and attractive boy who harbors a cruel and sadistic streak.

This scenario presents an almost paradigmatic example of abjection. The young woman is not transformed into an object, that is, objectified. She is denied the status of subject, expelled from the domain of fully constituted humans, transformed into a nonperson. It provides a reminder of what is at stake in Kristeva. In Kristeva's account, the abject is in the same position as Lacan's partial object, or fetish (aka *objet petit a*). Kristeva turns to abjection to emphasize the forces of repulsion at work in partial objects, arguing that

Lacan's approach tends to privilege forces of attraction (fetishistic idealization). Abjection is both a psychic mechanism and a social technology. Forces of psychic repulsion are prolonged and stabilized within practices that effectively clear out or ritually purify a social field.

Anne Carson's *Eros the Bittersweet* furnishes a good point of contrast. Carson explores how a host of negative feelings comes to populate romance, ranging from anxiety to anguish, from doubt to paranoia, and maybe even hatred. For Carson, the emergence of such negative feelings may be understood by reference to the object, the beloved, the object of desire. She sums it up this way: "The Greek word *eros* denotes 'want,' 'lack,' 'desire for that which is missing.' The lover wants what he does not have. It is by definition impossible for him to have what he wants if, as soon as it is had, it is no longer wanting. This is more than wordplay. There is a dilemma within *eros* that has been thought crucial by thinkers from Sappho to the present day."[13] In effect, Carson adopts a perspective analogous to that of narratology: she describes the subjectification of the object. The beloved object, because missing, because desired, transforms the lover into the subject of desire, which affords some manner of existential and subjective enclosure, akin to the sovereign hold of narrative over story.

For Kristeva, such an account of desire relies too much on forces of attraction, hence her emphasis on forces of repulsion. Instead of a play on the presence and absence of the object (for the subject) as in Carson's account of eros, Kristeva insists that the object is resolutely expelled, rejected. Indeed Kristeva goes so far as to say, "There are lives not sustained by *desire*, as desire is always for objects."[14]

Philosophically speaking, Kristeva's definition of desire as being "always for objects" may seem unwarranted and somewhat rash, for she seems to rule out the ways in which desire is productive—and there are, after all, philosophical precedents, beginning with Kant, for conceiving desire as productive of objects, instead of merely for objects.[15] Nonetheless, when she focuses on the interactions between partial objects and partial subjects, Kristeva's theory of abjection clears the way to consider the relation between "subjectless desire" (to use Foucault's turn of phrase) and nonobjectlike objects (nonpassive, noninert objects; agential objects), and to take seriously the productivity of desire (even if she oddly presents it as a nondesire). What is at stake for her is a desire that is not for *preexisting* objects. In this respect, her theory feels more in tune with the *Wolf Girl* series than the more traditional subject-centered and narrative-focused account of Carson, especially in its focus on how forces of repulsion are constitutive of a social field.

thomas lamarre

Like many other shōjo manga, the social field of the *Wolf Girl* series is high school. It offers an experience of the highly codified, fully administered, and even arbitrarily regimented practices of school life. In fact, the series presents Eri's desire for a boyfriend in terms of a desire not for an object but to impress her two new girlfriends, Marin and Aki. Eri explains the situation to her longtime friend, Sanda Ayumi (aka San-chan): in high school, you have to make a little group of friends, right away, on the first day, or you won't have a social life, and once you have committed to them, that's that. If they reject you, you won't be welcomed into another group; everyone will shun you— and that's the end of your social life at school.

Eri's explanation brings to the surface the social pressures implicit in high school life for girls. Specifically, it calls attention to how forces of repulsion play a primary role in the clearing out of the social space in which high school romance may take place. Striking is the implication that these social formations are arbitrary and empty. It isn't important whether Eri actually likes Marin and Aki (although in the series, they do indeed become her friends). The codified practices of high school society force Eri into inventing a boyfriend, and Eri's way of getting a boyfriend is arbitrary: she randomly snaps a photo of a seemingly suitable boy. Underlying such apparently desperate behavior are forces of repulsion: a girl without a boyfriend is abject, and then, to keep her boyfriend, a girl may need to play abject. Acting like a girl appears less as a matter of objectification (becoming an object of the male gaze; forces of attraction) than as a matter of abjection (becoming expelled from the domain of fully constituted subjects; forces of repulsion).

In contrast with Kristeva's account, however, the abject is here not opposed to the subject, to a position of psychic mastery or sovereignty. Although Eri's doglike abjection is repeatedly evoked to define the feel of the series, Kyōya is not positioned as the sovereign subject, even though dubbed the Black Prince. The series lingers on his beauty, styling him in a highly feminized manner, as the beautiful boy (*bishōnen*), as if an object for the female gaze. The cover illustration frequently features Kyōya alone, idealizing his attractiveness (see again figure 12.2). He does not entirely become a fetish object, however. Advertisements stress his cruelty and sadism: "the strange attractiveness of the sadistic boy." Other promotional images show Kyōya patting Eri on the head like a dog (as in the poster for the upcoming movie; figure 12.4), holding her in a stylishly brusque manner, or seductively entering her space as if to kiss her. Still, Kyōya does not occupy the place of the subject. He avoids company, prefers to be alone, and does not act directly on

figure 12.4
The handbill and poster image promoting the live-action movie version of *Wolf Girl and Black Prince*.

his feelings. He fits Kristeva's definition of the deject: "The one by whom the abject exists is thus a *deject* who places (himself), *separates* (himself), situates (himself), and therefore *strays* instead of getting his bearings, desiring, belonging, or refusing. Situationist in a sense, and not without laughter—since laughing is a way of placing or displacing abjection."[16]

The *Wolf Girl* series dwells on a coupling: abject girl and deject boy. Initially the deject (Kyōya) functions to place and displace abjection (of Eri). The frequent images of Kyōya patting Eri on the head like a dog capture this relation, as does the third common image used to define the series: Eri sporting cute little wolf ears, somewhat sulkily or even abashedly, and Kyōya looking mischievously beautiful, rakish, with his black cape and crown (see figure 12.3). The two stand apart, as if at once drawn to each other and at odds, in combination of repulsion and attraction. What holds together repulsion (abjection) and attraction (fetishistic idealization) is a force of dejection, embodied in laughter or comedy. On the surface, the *Wolf Girl* series is light hearted and cheerful, bubbly and euphoric, and yet, as Kristeva reminds us, laughter may function to place or displace abjection—a force of repulsion driving bubbles to the frothy surface.

What merits closer attention, then, is how abjection is displaced. Interestingly enough, in *Wolf Girl*, once the abject-deject couple emerges, the abjection initially placed on Eri is gradually displaced onto weak-willed boys. Three scenarios are noteworthy. First, Eri befriends Yū Kusakabe, a shy, feminine-looking, thoroughly abject boy, whom Kyōya continually dismisses as a coward. Yet Kusakabe's friendship with Eri transforms him, awakening an inner strength, allowing him to stand up to Kyōya and to defend Eri. Second, there is Kamiya Nozomi, whose weakness takes a different form: he is always playing the field, flirting with any number of girls, collecting addresses, setting up multiple dates, and generally using his looks and charm to attract as much female attention as possible. As it turns out, however, in the episode in which he suddenly declares his love for San-chan, he does not really love her at all. He wishes to ruin her budding romance with Kyōya's buddy Hibiya Takeru, because Kamiya is afraid of being left on his own, left out of the growing circle of stable couples. His is another kind of cowardice.

Finally, Terasaki Kōichi (aka Terapon) has remained fixated on winning Eri's love since middle school. When she takes a part-time job at a video rental store, she reconnects with him and begins to confide in him about her difficulties with Kyōya. Terapon tries to take advantage of the situation, but when he is not able to destroy Eri's love for Kyōya, he forces himself on her, violently. As the threat of physical violence escalates, Kyōya steps in and thrashes Terapon.

In these three instances, weak-willed boys are abjected, and yet when we look for the subject to which the abject is opposed, we find the couple, Eri and Kyōya. Ideals for male-female coupling (something like the heterosexual matrix, to use Judith Butler's term) are acting where Kristeva situates the sovereign subject, that is, the patriarch. Kristeva's theory thus brings us to a critical impasse. We might stick to the psychoanalytic turn, arguing that the authoritative law of the father is at work behind the heterosexual matrix. Aspects of *Wolf Girl* are in keeping with this sort of argument: the series sometimes implies that what girls really need (and want) are boys who will care for them, but in a manly way: a boy who fusses over a girl, giving in to her every whim, may not be one who will truly care for her, that is, protect her. Kyōya thus proves to be the ideal boyfriend, precisely because the coldness behind his beautiful countenance is inseparable from a masculine will to protect what is his, physically if need be. Although no one adopts the position of the sovereign subject, we might conclude that everything is ordered by degree of affinity with patriarchal authority.

This line of argumentation nonetheless brings us to another impasse, because we have to narrow the scope of inquiry so dramatically, focusing only on moments when subject positions appear clearly defined, and limiting discussion to moments of cathartic release of emotional and physical energy, when someone is actively rejected. We introduce a bias toward subjective enclosure, assuming that all stories are intent on becoming discrete, bounded, subjectified, metaphysical objects, each akin to the Bible or the modern novel. The sovereign power of the subject becomes our default point of reference, and sovereign power becomes the default for thinking about diverse practices. Sovereign power is imposed on the social field, as if it is the only social fact. In response to such an impasse, the challenge is to take both "subjectless power" and "objectless feelings" into account.

Sianne Ngai's account of "ugly feelings" provides a perfect counterpoint. For Ngai, ugly feelings are also "objectless feelings," because they are not directed toward objects. Such feelings function more like moods or tones, permeating and saturating situations, or suffusing works of literature or art, to impart an overall tone, a distinct set of gradations of complexity. Objectless feelings may be said to be subjectless, too. They are neither projected from the subject toward an object, nor introjected, that is, trapped within a subject in the derived form of sovereign interiority. Also, in contrast to Kristeva's focus on canonical, cathartic emotions, objectless feelings are "explicitly amoral and noncathartic" feelings, such as irritation, disgust, envy, "offering no satisfactions of virtue, however oblique, nor any therapeutic or purifying release."[17] Ngai stresses how difficult it is to determine whether ugly feelings are resistant or acquiescent in political terms, precisely because they are not object-oriented or subject-projected.

The tone of the *Wolf Girl* series presents a similar challenge. After a few chapters in which Eri and Kyōya play dog and master, Eri demands a "normalization" of their relationship, and they drop the dog scenario to become girlfriend and boyfriend. Eri then has fairly conventional expectations for dating; she wants to go on memorable outings with Kyōya. With her usual sense of optimism and euphoria, she drags him out to various popular sites for lovers. Kyōya's response to her wishes is irritation, and he so frequently uses the expression *ira-ira* (irritating) that it becomes something of a refrain for the series. Kyōya's response is objective and logical, hence his irritation: If we simply want to spend time together, he asks, what does it matter what we do, or where we go? Why not stay at home?

Kyōya irritation is not directed at Eri nor at himself but at both of them and neither. Irritation is directed at the entire situation of romance, particularly its commercialized aspects. In response to Kyōya's irritation, in this early stage of their romance, Eri cycles from euphoria to dejection with each date. Gradually, she comes to appreciate his irritation and even to share it. As they both come to channel their maniac highs and lows into irritation, they discover a feeling in common, an affective tone that combines attraction and repulsion, which characterizes their proximity and distance throughout the series—irritation.

Irritation differs from both eros and abjection in that it has neither object nor subject. The feelings of irritation run deeper (and loom larger) than the dark erotic longing for an absent object (à la Carson) or the repulsion or abjection of what cannot be contained within the subject (à la Kristeva). Romance in the *Wolf Girl* series becomes a matter of learning how to live with irritation, how to manage it, how to love with it. The conclusion might be that this series recasts romance as a kind of labor, in a manner reminiscent of the conventional wisdom that a relationship takes hard work: you have to work at your interactions with your partner. Yet this purifying, morally tinged interpretation is complicated by the fact that these ugly feelings of irritation do not have an object; they cannot be directed at others. In this sense, irritation is, to repeat Ngai's terms, explicitly *non*cathartic. Irritation does not appear virtuous, nor does it offer a purifying release. Rather than being directed at something or someone, such feelings follow a situation, at once hovering over it, coursing under it, running through it.

Ngai frequently evokes Theodor Adorno's paradigm of fully administered society when she wishes to situate ugly feelings. But ugly feelings neither contest the fully administered society nor bow down to it. They thus situate us on very different politico-aesthetic terrain than Kristeva's theory of abjection. Instead of a politics of sovereignty, they are oriented toward a politics of administration or regulation. Instead of the aesthetics of narrative enclosure, ugly feelings arise alongside processes of fabulation. Still, as the example of *Wolf Girl* attests, objectless feelings preclude neither abjection nor intense erotic longing. They affectively uproot and resituate these more cathartic emotions. And so, by way of conclusion, I propose to draw together the insights of the prior two sections—on serialization, fabulation and abjection—to consider some of the politico-aesthetic implications of the *Wolf Girl* series.

Practices of Self

We have now seen manga series from both sides: first by asking what kind of object a manga series is, considering its material, concrete, objective face, then by turning to the subjective or affective side, considering romantic longing, abjection, and irritation. The terms *objective* and *subjective* are misleading, however, if construed in terms of an absolute divide between mind and matter. An additional gloss is now useful: *form of expression* and *form of content*, which clearly indicate that both sides entail form (as well as substance).

In the *Wolf Girl* series, on the subjective side, the transformation of a girl into a dog plays an integral role in the series' form of expression. This scene of abjection sets the story in motion, serves as a constant point of reference for subsequent developments, and provides iconic imagery for the series. When the *Wolf Girl* series stages its scenes of abjection, it flirts with patriarchal power. Kristeva's theory thus proves useful in teasing out the initial asymmetries at work between the abject-girl Eri and deject-boy Kyōya. Ultimately, however, in part because the series is, after all, closer to romantic comedy than modernist fiction, the abject does not stand in opposition to the subject. As is obvious in the relationship between Eri and Kyōya, the abject-deject relation is functional (combative), relative, and reversible. Although abjection enables dramatic scenarios, it avoids the cathartic emotions stressed in Kristeva's account. Its subjective technology does not mesh neatly with the psychoanalytic mechanisms in Kristeva's account, in which forces of repulsion shore up the sovereignty of the subject and purify the social field in quasi-religious or ritualistic forms of patriarchy. The *Wolf Girl* series points toward a different kind of social technology and thus a different formation of power, more akin to the ugly feelings and regulatory power brought to the fore in Ngai's account.

The action within *Wolf Girl* revolves around high school, and this setting provides additional insight into the form of expression. The series does not focus much on classrooms, teachers, or other institutional features of high school. It gravitates toward interstices (chatting between classes, roaming the halls, meeting after school, texting) and rites of passage (dating, graduation ceremonies, school outings). This tendency to inhabit interstices, temporally punctuated by festive events, is a kind of social technology, seen from the subjective side. If we turn to the objective side of manga series, to the form of content, we gain greater insight into the concrete material orientations affecting and informing this subjective, psychosocial technology.

Because manga serialization involves highly discontinuous modes of reading, allowing for a variety of reading rhythms and orders, it encourages a process of fabulation in which each part of the manga series must at once function as *a* whole and impart a sense of *the* whole, to allow readers to enter into the series at almost any point. Each chapter or episode of the series is at once indefinite and definite: it is *a* story; it is *the* story. The basic units of composition evoke a similar problematic. Each panel, when you peruse it, is a whole, and yet it is a part of the whole of the page, even as the page, the whole, is felt within the panel, the part. This is why Thierry Groensten aptly considers layout to be the integral art of comics. The layout is neither panel nor page; it is the relation between them. It is at once global and partial. This form of content (layout) encourages certain reading practices.

On the one hand, popular manga series move quickly and invite rapid scan-like reading, and yet readers also dwell on details; they linger where the whole of the series feels condensed into a part (as do advertisements). Readers will read back and forth through the series, sometimes repeatedly, as if to refresh the sense of the whole in the parts, which may vanish under the forward movement of a quick read. On the other hand, the use of generic conventions in widely circulated manga magazines may make series feel formulaic. Such conventions also make manga accessible, open to interaction or participation. Manga readers are prone to draw characters, pen little stories and scenarios, or engage in other kinds of interaction—to dress like characters (cosplay), for example. Reading practices thus temporally unfold along the paradoxical flipping between whole and part, doubling the processes of fabulation.

But how does this form of content affect abjection, the subjective side?

The form of content is decidedly weaker than the form of expression. Creators work over the form of content. Even where it is reinforced and consolidated through generic conventions, they apply creative pressure to it, carving out a form. Although their degree of input varies, creators run the gamut from writers, illustrators, editors, inkers, designers, readers, and others who creatively work on the manga series. Much as a woodworker follows and works with the grain, manga creators work with layouts to compose across panels and pages, shaping their manga series by applying pressure to the continuous flipping of whole and part in various registers. At this site of encounter, the play between definite and indefinite articles (there is *a* story; there is *the* story) turns toward the demonstrative article: *this* manga series, *this* experience of the whole that is generated by *this* flow of semiotic elements in which the whole is present, even definite, and yet somehow imperceptible, indefinite. Such a flow brings us into the realm of an affective tonality that is always in the making. As the manga series takes on form, it implies virtual unity. This virtual unity affects the scenarios of abjection in the *Wolf Girl* series.

The *Wolf Girl* creator, Hatta Ayuko, largely follows shōjo manga conventions, which intensify the whole-part paradox in specific ways. Lines and layouts are generally clear, and forms are well defined; the occasional rough scribble in the margins or on the edges of images tends to reinforce the overall sense of clarity and orderliness of the format. The orientations for eye movement across the page are bold and unambiguous, allowing readers to scan quickly over the panels. Simply put, shōjo manga follow formal order, an ordering of forms. This ordering of forms does not lead to closure, however, because of the use of open frames and unfinished edges: each panel seems to open into others, as do the pages, and the various techniques for rendering speech and thoughts (squares, ovals, unenclosed type, scrawled handwriting) make the boundaries between unvoiced and voiced thoughts malleable and porous. As they move between part and whole, shōjo manga produce an oscillation between the orderly and unfinished, generating a distinctive sort of open system.

When shōjo manga fuse panel and page, opening into full-page and double-page layouts, one of the prominent visual conventions is the scattering of elements, fluttering petals, twinkling lights, swirling snowflakes, falling leaves, which sweep up other visual and verbal elements, fusing the orderly and open. Such a gesture stands in stark contrast to the preferred way of fusing page and panel in shōnen manga, or "boys' comics": incisive motion lines in which the thrust of a blade, the sweep of a sword, the force of a punch overwhelm the panel lines, allowing lines to explode across the page, even as they coalesce around a duel or combat. In sum, serial manga composition tends toward different kinds of vortices as a sort of limit experience of the paradoxical relation of page and panel.

Although the force of this form of content is weaker than convention and creation, it affects the overall situation for any form of "subjective" expression such as abjection. This is why abjection in *Wolf Girl* points not so much toward the subject and patriarchy as toward objectless feelings, participatory culture, and regulatory, fully administered systems. It forces a reconsideration of the implicit form of content in Kristeva's theory: the bounded book, which entails exegesis and extends into rites of purification.

The combination of orderliness and openness in shōjo manga make for a conundrum: How are forms of psychosocial friction to be situated in this apparently frictionless field? In the *Wolf Girl* series, friction is introduced through the process of fabulation. Take the first chapter. It opens with Eri's fabrication of a boyfriend. But that story is soon broken off by another story, and so Eri has to resume her tall tale differently: she snaps Kyōya's photo, but now her story becomes another story, which in turn is broken off by Kyōya's story, which is then broken off by San-chan's story, and so forth. In quick succession, even within the first chapter, the manga series offers a series of tales without any narrative closure or subjective enclosure. Yet a feeling of friction arises where one story disrupts another. Eri cannot move forward with her story because of Kyōya's story, then San-chan's story, then Marin's and Aki's stories.

Such friction, arising especially where Eri's stories break off Kyōya's stories (and vice versa), underpins the affective tone for this process of fabulation: irritation. The nondiscrete object takes on a singular feel. A world without narrative unity or discursive enclosure becomes experienced through irritation's singular impersonal tone. The images used to promote the *Wolf Girl* series prolong this singular tone: the icy beauty of the sadistic boy, irritating in its combination of attraction and repulsion; his desirable yet irritatingly brusque affection; and the would-be lovers in a standoff, attracted to each other yet unable to bridge the gap, irritable. The series may take up or digress into various subjective and discursive modalities (such as abjection or erotic longing), provided the scenarios of abjection or longing are situated within and experienced through the objectless feeling of irritation. But what does irritation do?

Niklas Luhmann provides some insight in his account of the self-organizing propensity of modern communications and information systems. He writes, "The system presupposes itself as a self-produced irritation, without being accessible through its own operations, and then sets about transforming irritation into information, which it produces for society (and for itself in society)."[18] Irritation, then, may be taken as a sort of noise produced by the system, which becomes necessary to its operations, even though it is not accessible to them. The operation of the system produces noise as well as signals, but this "excess" noise is not antithetical or oppositional to the production and circulation of signals; on the contrary, noise introduces a feedback effect that allows for the conveyance of signals as information.

Irritation relates to abjection in a similar fashion. Irritation is not antithetical to abjection. Its apparently excess noise generates a feedback effect that allows for the conveyance of abjection, as information for the series, hence the prevalence of abjection in ads and iconic imagery for *Wolf Girl*.

Irritation is also the noise whose amplified feedback makes the *Wolf Girl* series into a self-organizing multimedia franchise system. But what are its social implications?

Terms like *self-organizing* and *self-propagating* are sometimes (mistakenly) thought to imply functioning without human agency or intervention. As Ngai indicates, however, the problem is not a lack of human agency or even of human activity. The problem lies in the difficulty such terms present for our understanding of political resistance and social intervention. The same is true of objectless feelings in *Wolf Girl*: irritation spurs a great deal of human activity and agency, but these do not map neatly in terms of sovereign power, that is, "power over" (domination) and resistance to it. Although irritation is not directed at objects or others, it is not entirely passive: it may be directed at itself, and at oneself. Irritation thus folds back on itself to produce a kind of self-organizing system, as Luhmann remarks, but at the level of the self. It implies a folding of the self onto the self, what Foucault calls "practices of self" (*techniques de soi*).[19] It is not foremost a matter of power over others and subjection to others. The relation to self is primary, and the relation to others passes through it. Thus, in *Wolf Girl*, both abjection and romance are folded into practices of self. Chapter 32 provides a prime example.[20]

Eri has been gaining weight, becoming decidedly plump. Because she is unable to curb her appetite, Kyōya intervenes to help her recover her willpower. Eri assumes that Kyōya is intent on helping her curb her appetite because he is embarrassed by how she looks. Kyōya claims not to mind whether Eri gains weight or not. What concern him are her feelings of inadequacy. Eri emerges triumphant, slimming down, no longer feeling the pressure of a constant desire to eat. In this chapter, what promises to be a classic scenario of abjection—the expulsion of the abject feminine (fat girls)—turns out to be more concerned with practices of self. Kyōya does not function in the place of the other but becomes an accomplice to Eri's self-cultivation. Ultimately, in fact, it is consumption, desire for objects, that proves irritating. Eri's sense of self, then, is not grounded in being abjected or in abjecting others. She channels an objectless ugly feeling to ensure that objects and subjects no longer affect her in the first place. Similarly, in the longer arc of the series, Eri chooses to go to college to become an artist, regardless of her parents' wishes and Kyōya's feelings. Patriarchal attitudes remain a concern, but they are addressed at the level of practices of self.

The practices of self that are associated with objectless feelings are not more liberatory or more enslaving than the cathartic quasi-sacral mechanisms of abjection. They imply different latitudes of power and freedom. In *Wolf Girl*, they appear stretched across two formations. On the one hand, they appear consonant with Adorno's take on a fully administered society and Foucault's account of disciplinary society: practices of self may produce self-disciplining subjects who incorporate administrative procedures, mentally and physically. On the other hand, they may be linked to the entrepreneurial self who acts on self-satisfaction, or self-productive consumption. Indeed, high school in *Wolf Girl* is a site of both disciplinization (segmenting students for the workplace) and self-productive consumption (making students into demographic niches for the market). Between these two formations, other practices of self, with potentially better degrees of freedom, promise to emerge around affect and objectless feelings: self-transformation, self-cultivation, self-fabulation. In any event, when scenarios of abjection are passed through the prism of a nondiscrete object like the *Wolf Girl* series, another field of power emerges, based on practices of self, which encourages us to reconsider Kristeva's metaphysical fascination with Western patriarchy, inviting an encounter with social practices of reading alongside modernist exegeses.

Notes

Color versions of images in this chapter may be found at http://scalar.usc .edu/works/abjection-incorporated-insert/index.

1   Barbara Creed, "Horror and the Monstrous-Feminine: An Imaginary Abjection," in *Horror: The Film Reader*, ed. Mark Jancovich (New York: Routledge, 2002), 68.

2   Julia Kristeva, *Powers of Horror: An Essay on Abjection*, trans. Leon S. Roudiez (New York: Columbia University Press, 1982), 8.

3   Julia Kristeva, *About Chinese Women*, trans. Anita Barrows (London: M. Boyars, 1986).

4   Rey Chow, "Introduction: On Chineseness as a Theoretical Problem," *boundary 2*, 25, no. 3 (1998): 1–24.

5   Kristeva, *Powers of Horror*, 1.

6   See, for instance, the contributions to Diana Coole and Samantha Frost, eds., *New Materialisms: Ontology, Agency, and Politics* (Durham, NC: Duke University Press, 2010); and Jane Bennett, *Vibrant Matter: A Political Ecology of Things* (Durham, NC: Duke University Press, 2009).

7   Creed, "Horror and the Monstrous-Feminine," 92.

8   In *Mikkī no shoshiki: Sengo manga no senjika kigen* (Tokyo: Kadokawa shoten, 2013), Ōtsuka Eiji addresses the ways in which anime conventions have permeated manga.

9   See H. Porter Abbott, *The Cambridge Introduction to Narrative* (Cambridge: Cambridge University Press, 2008).

10 Ōtsuka Eiji, "World and Variation: The Reproduction and Consumption of Narrative," trans. Marc Steinberg, *Mechademia* 5 (2010): 99–116.

11 In the first of two books on the "animalized postmodern," *Otaku: Japan's Database Animals* (Minneapolis: University of Minnesota Press, 2009), Azuma Hiroki addresses the two-tiered structure of database consumption; in the second volume, *Gēmu teki riarizumu no tanjō: Dōbutsuka suru posutomodan 2* (Tokyo: Kōdansha, 2007), he shifts to metanarrative.

12 Jacques Derrida, "Living On," in *Deconstruction and Criticism*, ed. Harold Bloom (New York: Continuum, 1979), 62–142.

13 Anne Carson, *Eros the Bittersweet* (Normal, IL: Dalkey Archive, 1998), 112.

14 Kristeva, *Powers of Horror*, 6.

15 Daniel Smith, "The Inverse Side of Structure: Zizek on Deleuze on Lacan," *Criticism* 46, no. 4 (2004): 635–50. Smith writes, the "fundamental thesis of *Anti-Oedipus* is a stronger variant of Kant's claim; Kant pushed to his necessary conclusion: 'If desire produces, its product is real,' and not merely a fantasy" (641).

16 Kristeva, *Powers of Horror*, 8.

17 Sianne Ngai, *Ugly Feelings* (Cambridge, MA: Harvard University Press, 2004), 6.

18 Niklas Luhmann, *The Reality of Mass Media*, trans. Kathleen Cross (Stanford, CA: Stanford University Press, 2000), 11–12.

19 Foucault's phrase "techniques de soi" was translated as "technologies of the self" in the context of his 1982 seminar at the University of Vermont. See Michel Foucault, *Technologies of the Self: A Seminar with Michel Foucault* (Amherst: University of Massachusetts Press, 1988). Here I translate the phrase as "practices of self," which is in keeping with his emphasis on practices and on the construction of self (*de soi*) rather than action on a preexisting self, the self (*du soi*).

20 Chapter 32 appears in Hatta Ayuko, *Ookami shōjo to kuro ōji: 9* (Tōkyō: Shūeisha, 2014).

chapter thirteen

Powers of Comedy, or, The Abject Dialectics of *Louie*

rob king

Pioneer/Pariah

"I'm crouched in a dining room in Washington Heights, watching a man get ready to masturbate," writes TV critic Emily Nussbaum. "Louis C. K., the stand-up comic who is the star and creator of the FX sitcom *Louie*, slumps in an orange lounge chair. His knees are spread, his pants pushed down to his ankles."[1]

Perhaps you know where this is headed, but you are being misled. First by Nussbaum, because, as she will soon reveal, the scene she is describing is precisely a *scene*, being rehearsed by C. K. in character as part of the filming of his celebrated show *Louie* (2010–15).[2] Next by me, because the article is not from 2017, the year of C. K.'s career-derailing scandal, but from 2011— one year *before* the now-defunct blog *Gawker* published a blind item detailing an incident in which an unnamed male stand-up comedian masturbated in front of two female comics in an Aspen hotel room, and six years before the bombshell *New York Times* report of November 9, 2017, that confirmed the rumors as part of a pattern of sexual misconduct on C. K.'s part.[3] But the third and final subterfuge belongs, of course, to C. K. himself, who, in his infamous confession the day after that report ("These stories are true") effectively reached back to invert Nussbaum's own inversion and reveal the unfunny reality behind what, on set, had been staged as comedy.[4]

Perhaps this is why the confirmation of those rumors was greeted with such a sense of critical betrayal, as though what C. K. had all along been miming as comedy had suddenly become legible as an alibi for its own truth. "We knew [C. K.] was someone who liked to masturbate, whose sexuality, like much of the rest of his personality, was performative—we knew it because he told us," observed Kathryn VanArendonk for *Vulture*. And yet, she continued, C. K.'s acclaimed show *Louie* "was seen as a brilliant artistic *transformation* of himself. It promised us he was seeing himself clearly, and he was making a joke about who he was. We believed him."[5] Writing in *Variety* two days after the *Times* report, critic Sonia Saraiya similarly captured the confusion with which the terms of C. K.'s misconduct traced too precisely over the terms of the show's acclaim. "I couldn't have been more wrong," she wrote of an earlier encomium in which she had celebrated *Louie*'s "performed self-awareness" and "uncomfortable relationship with sex." "Or at least, I was right in the marginal sense that I thought that's what was happening."[6]

But to borrow the critic's formulation, what exactly *had* those of us who were fans of the show "thought was happening"? And in what "marginal sense" had we been right all along? The critical gauntlet here is not the odious one of trying to see beyond the scandal to reclaim what can be salvaged, but rather to consider what it might mean that acclamation and condemnation paradoxically devolved around alternate versions of the same master image—a man jerking off with his pants around his ankles, variously rendered as (comedic) representation or (toxic) reality. More paradoxical still is the fact that both versions have "truth" on their side, at least in the sense that they imply very different mobilizations of the idea of "truth in comedy," with which C. K.'s career had long been associated. The myth of C. K.'s ascent to comedic superstardom had, by the time of the scandal, long been told as a passage from his youthful identity as an absurdist Boston stand-up toward a more mature identity as a comedic "truth teller," working in the mode of abject self-confession. (As critic Jesse David Fox put it: "The tale about Louis C. K. went as follows: He was a struggling absurdist until he decided to (1) create a new hour-long set every year, and (2) make his act more personal.")[7] Early praise for *Louie* was cut from the same cloth: *Louie*, it was said, represented "the next stage in the evolution of the TV sitcom" by reshaping the format into what C. K. described as "autobiographic fiction."[8] Self-exposure, it seems, was the engine of his comedic art. And yet, with the revelation of sexual misconduct, the "truthfulness" that had once worked to confirm that artistry backfired into a different kind of truth—a real/unperformed truth—that C. K.'s artistry was now seen to have camouflaged. "At any given moment, he is working on two levels," wrote *Slate* critic Katy Waldman, days after the scandal broke. "Declaring himself a terrible person is his *shtick*. And this shtick—broadcasting his faults and his desire to improve in the same transmission—allows him to hint that he possesses secret layers of decency, even if, humbly, he pretends not to see them. . . . [His stand-up] absolv[es] him of toxicity by spotlighting his hyperconsciousness of it."[9] Or, as Willa Paskin put it on the same website, *Louie* was "propaganda for Louis C. K.'s decency."[10] Few bodies of comedic work have so carefully laid a snare for their own creator's misdeeds.

Had C. K. indeed been deceiving us all along? I am not particularly fond of the literalism of this inference, above all because it simplifies abjection by reading its self-dramatization as purely other-directed, as though, in confessing to those "fragile states where man strays on the territories of the animal" (Kristeva), C. K. only ever wanted to convince *us* otherwise.[11] Confessing to one's own faults in no way contradicts a real belief in the fantasy of one's own decency, and evasiveness can of course be a trick one plays on (and for) one's sense of self. What the scandal revealed, rather, was the legibility of C. K.'s career and comedy as a series of negotiations within the scene of his compulsions—that is, as a series of efforts precisely to dodge and to discharge their abjecting force—whether sheepishly confessed to in the exculpatory camouflage of a comic monologue or aggressively channeled into the emboldening jouissance of sexual exposure. What I seek to do in this chapter is to locate these negotiations within the text of *Louie*, to approach its comedy as *itself a system for surmounting abject states of being*. Reading the show like this not only challenges many of the received narratives about the frameworks of C. K.'s creativity; it might also transform our intuitions about how abjection induces humor in the first place.

Stand-Up/Short Films

Over the course of its five-season run, *Louie* set new standards of authorship for the American sitcom. At once a prestigious and a popular success, the show drew early industry attention for its so-called "Louie deal," whereby FX agreed to wire C. K. $300,000 per episode, to use as he saw fit.[12] This radically auteurist model—allowing C. K. to make all decisions as star, director, writer, editor, and executive producer—soon inspired other networks to sponsor similar exercises in comedic autonomy. *Variety* identified C. K. in 2012 as the crest in a new "wave of multihyphenate types who are bringing an auteur sensibility" to the sitcom—a wave that would grow to include Lena

Dunham (in HBO's *Girls*, 2012–17) and Marc Maron (in IFC's *Maron*, 2013–16). More recently, that list has expanded to include Aziz Ansari and Alan Yang (in Netflix's *Master of None*, 2015–) and Tig Notaro (in the C. K.–produced *One Mississippi*, 2015–17).[13] (It would be remiss not to note the karmic irony whereby Notaro deliberately inserted a story arc into *One Mississippi*'s second season that drew renewed attention to C. K.'s then still-rumored misdeeds.) Critics meanwhile heralded C. K. for revolutionizing the modern sitcom. *Louie*, it was said, "exploded" the sitcom format by inaugurating a "post-sitcom era."[14] Yet, for all the critical ink spent celebrating the show's originality, there remained a puzzling lacuna: for what is striking is how vaguely substantiated these critical celebrations of the show's uniqueness tended to be, as though the invocation of C. K.'s authorial control could stand as sufficient proof of an originality that, in consequence, went unspecified.

A similar problem haunted assessments of C. K.'s stand-up persona, which, as we have already had cause to note, clung tenaciously to a single narrative: once upon a time, it was said, C. K. was an absurdist Boston stand-up whose routines involved addressing crowds in dolphin talk and discussing the history of circular chessboards; subsequently, he found his "voice" by drawing on his "life experience."[15] The unanimity on this point was as though derived from a single press release. In 2011, *Rolling Stone* described how C. K.'s "daffy side . . . [took] a back seat to . . . more personal material"; that same year, the *New York Times* explained how his "boldly absurdist streak . . . faded as his work became . . . frankly personal"; three years later, comedy website *Splitsider* trotted out the same talking point, noting how C. K. "threw out" the absurdist proclivities of his early stand-up and began to "discover his voice—a man frustratingly learning how to be a father."[16] Within this narrative, absurdity was denigrated as a stage prior to maturity, with fatherhood the agreed-on turning point in C. K.'s comedic bildungsroman, a life event that brought him both an abundant source of new comic material and crossover success. "Having kids, you don't escape from it," C. K. acknowledged, discussing the impact of fatherhood on his comedy. "It's a big, stressful, exhilarating, real-life thing. And it's permanent. You have to grow up."[17] Yet the trajectory proposed here, this coming-of-age tale from youthful absurdism to adult confessional, was hardly distinctive: it was simply a variant of the basic mythos of the male stand-up artist who, in biography after biography, graduates from "mere" joke teller to truth teller, whether his name be Carlin, Pryor, Hicks, whoever—such that what was posited as C. K.'s specificity was in fact complicit with a more generalized ideology of the American stand-up tradition.[18]

I want, then, to begin my take on *Louie* by proposing two principles that have the merit of dislodging this stubbornly entrenched narrative of C. K.'s evolution as simply a matter of personal revelation comedy. The first insists simply that any archaeology of *Louie*'s humor attend to a pair of derivations: one being his career as a stand-up comedian (explicitly referenced in the stand-up sequences that would typically bookend segments within each of the show's episodes); the other his underacknowledged work as a maker of short films, most of which were shot on sixteen millimeter in the 1990s and featured friends from New York's comedy scene of the time (Todd Barry, Laura Kightlinger, Amy Poehler, Rick Shapiro, and others). During the years of his great acclaim, these two derivations did not hold their respective weight in critical discussions of C. K., which tended to posit his stand-up as the baseline framework for his comic creativity. It was, after all, through his stand-up that C. K. first achieved breakout success, so that for many, C. K. was inevitably a stand-up comedian first and everything else second. To the extent, moreover, that his other, non-stand-up creative work was even discussed during this period, those discussions were generally drawn to a cultish revisiting of his critical failures—to what the *New York Times* described as his "shamefully underrated" first attempt at a sitcom, *Lucky Louie* (2006–7); to his disastrously reviewed major-studio directing debut, *Pootie Tang* (2001), which Paramount wrested from him in postproduction; as well as to his debut feature, *Tomorrow Night* (1998), which had languished unseen since a four-day run in Los Angeles until C. K. made it available for digital download on his website in 2014.[19] All these projects were eagerly reclaimed by critics and fans eager to parade their superior discernment over previous negative assessments—to invoke what *Pootie Tang* might have been without studio interference, or how HBO executives were confused by *Lucky Louie*, and so on—while the short films were simply not conspicuous enough to have invited this kind of critical outbidding.

The fact remains, however, that the shorts constitute some of C. K.'s earliest successes, notably "Caesar's Salad" (1990), which netted him the Silver Plaque at the Chicago Film Festival, and "Ice Cream" (1992), which played at Sundance and won the Aspen Shortfest. More so than any of his earlier projects, C. K. repeatedly cited these and other short films as templates for his approach to *Louie*. In interviews, he often referred to stand-up *and* the short film as models for *Louie*'s distinctly modular narrative—whereby episodes would consist of discrete, consecutively arranged ministories, typically two per episode—describing the show in one instance as a "short-film anthology," in another as "like a stand-up set," in which segments are often only tangentially related.[20]

My second principle is that each of C. K.'s creative models for *Louie* corresponds to a different mode of humor. To take stand-up first: as theorist John Limon has argued, the main trunk of the American stand-up tradition has been predicated on the comedian's staging of their own abjection—the comedic presentation of the embarrassed self, an on-stage psychic worrying of those aspects of the self that are obnoxious to one's sense of identity. "What is stood up in stand-up comedy is abjection," Limon writes. "Stand-up makes vertical (or ventral) what should be horizontal (or dorsal). . . . All a stand-up's life feels abject to him or her, and stand-ups try to escape it by staging it as an act."[21] To the extent that this designates a kind of first-person comedy, then the common critical narrative of C. K.'s career path was at least partly correct: ever since the breakout HBO specials, the mode of abject self-presentation indeed came to play a central role in C. K.'s stand-up, which regularly included material like an account of a spousal handjob that was "the saddest thing that ever happened in America" or his attempt to take sexual inventory of his "old hanging balls."[22] And there was, further, a straight line leading from such self-deprecating themes to his sitcom, which similarly staged what the comedian described as "train-wreck" scenarios mirroring "what my life feels like."[23]

If we turn to his short films, though, we have to reckon with a different modality; and this is where the limitations of the critical consensus on C. K.'s comedy become apparent, for C. K.'s many short films operated unwaveringly within the realm of *absurdism*. The film he most commonly cited as an influence—the film that showed him "you can do anything you want, even if it doesn't make any sense"—was Robert Downey Sr.'s *Putney Swope* (1969), whose non-sequitur-laden commercial parodies need to be seen as part of the lineage leading to *Louie*.[24] Short films, C. K. once noted, are ideal for experimentation since they're freed from expectations of both logical plausibility and narrative continuity: "[They] don't have the weight of a feature where every moment has to serve the entire film. If you have a weird little idea you can go out and make a short film about it."[25] His own shorts offer proof of concept, for, at their best, they elaborate "weird little ideas" whose implications are relentlessly explored to their absurdist conclusions. "Ice Cream," for instance, focuses on a young couple who, for increasingly bizarre reasons, are burdened with a stream of unintended pregnancies and their correspondingly bizarre strategies for disposing of the resulting children. "Hello There" (1995), one of several shorts C. K. directed for Howie Mandel's *Sunny Skies* series (1995), posits a class of office workers who communicate only through prerecorded cassette tapes and explores the consequences when playback goes awry. His last short prior to *Louie*, titled "Louis C. K. Says the Darndest

rob king

Things to Kids," which he posted on YouTube in 2008, simply inverts the Bill Cosby premise to show a young girl's reaction to C. K. talking about diarrhea. An early adopter of YouTube as a platform for his short films (other YouTube originals include "Jimmy Carter Builds a House" [2006] and "Louis C. K. Learns about the Catholic Church" [2007]), C. K. was perhaps poised to become one of the website's first comedian auteurs. Instead, his deal with FX harnessed those auteurist energies to the creative paradigms of quality television.

Abjection/Absurdism

Two trajectories, then: stand-up and the short film. And, corresponding to these, two modalities: abjection versus absurdism. What I want to propose is that it is in the dialectic *between* these modes that the comedic work of *Louie* is located. Thus, rather than marking a linear evolution from absurdism to autobiography, the singularity of C. K.'s show was in developing a system that fused this Janus-faced inheritance, relating absurdism to abjection in such a way as to assign the former function and meaning vis-à-vis the latter. But that dialectic can in turn clarify what C. K.'s comedy might have shared with his acts of masturbatory flashing. For it was not just in the impulse to self-exposure, actual or performed, that his comedy buttressed the scandal, but, beyond that, in the endeavor to reverse abjection's degrading charge into something more galvanizing—to channel onanistic compulsion into commandeering display, say, or to convert self-deprecating humor into absurdist flights of fancy. Before any of that can come into focus, though, a conceptual gloss will help better cast into relief the distinction between the modalities in question.

Of particular utility here is Gilles Deleuze's early study *The Logic of Sense* (1969)—a work that is very much that of the "structuralist" pre-Guattari Deleuze, still under the influence of Lacan and psychoanalysis—in which the philosopher defines two opposed trajectories for what he calls "humor." The first trajectory is the conventional one that insists on the corporeal groundedness of all meaning, the sudden switch that reveals language and thought not to be grounded in the abstract realm of ideas but rather in the body. Such a trajectory denies the possibility of what Deleuze calls *signification* (where propositions and statements refer to ideas, concepts, etc.) in favor of *monstration* (where propositions refer to material states of affairs, to bodies and the qualities and quantities thereof). "The important thing [for this form of humor] . . . is to find quickly something to designate, to eat, or to break, which would replace the signification (the Idea) that you have been invited to look for. . . . This exercise, which consists in substituting designations, monstrations, consumptions, and pure destructions for significations, requires an odd inspiration—that one know how to 'descend.'"[26] Here, of course, we find the classic gestures of slapstick, in which material reality deflates our lofty ideals in the form of a belch or a banana peel—the gesture that reveals nobility's concrete grounding in the form of a top-hatted gent clumsily falling into a muddy puddle. But it is also here that we encounter the aforementioned abject mode of comedy with which the modern stand-up tradition is associated. For what happens in abjection is that the process of humor circles around on itself to achieve first-person articulation: the classic triadic joke structure posited by Freud, involving joke teller, butt of the joke, and joke audience, shifts formally into a dyadic register, whereby the joke teller becomes their own butt (so to speak).[27] And what the comedian consequently presents for their audience is an insistence on materiality that now targets the comedian's own selfhood. What is staged by the stand-up comedian is an experience of the self that can no longer pretend to the status of a Cartesian ego, floating freely above the fray of the material world, but is instead entirely absorbed into concrete situations of embodied humiliation and excrementality. From his 2010 special *Hilarious*, C. K.'s "sexual inventory" routine (touched on above) offers a model distillation of the trope, in which the comedian beholds himself in a mirror not as a fantasy of bodily integrity, as per Lacan's mirror stage, but as a series of fragmented body parts that fantasy ordinarily serves to mask.

> The other day I was like "OK, take a sexual inventory right here. What have you got left?" You know. And I took off my clothes, and I stood in the mirror. And I looked in the mirror, like a full-length mirror, naked. . . . And I'm looking at myself and here's the problem: that I didn't even wear down evenly. Like, different parts of my body are like older than others. Like, my dick and balls don't even match each other. Like, my balls are *older* than me. I swear to god: I'm forty-one, my balls are like seventy-two. They're really old and they just kind of hang there. (*audience laughs*) They just hang there. They look like they're being rescued by a helicopter from a mountain. (*audience laughs*) . . . And then my dick is like *happy, shiny, young looking*. My penis is like a young twenty-one-year-old guy walking around with these two old guys following him. . . . And at some point I have to show this shit to some poor unfortunate woman who has to see this fucked-up package of mine. I don't know. Like, I'll tuck my balls between my legs. "I don't have balls. I just have a penis. Is that OK?"[28]

The routine here accomplishes the dynamic of abjection by detaching bodily organs from the fantasy of an ego ideal that would integrate them, and, in so doing, decomposes the very possibility of symbolization into a purely corporeal state of affairs. Put another way, there can be no phallus in abject humor that is not unpacked into its concrete truth as a "fucked-up package," just as there can be no sexual relation that is not hollowed out into a drive to "show this shit."

Thus, whether in the familiar slapstick trope of the muddy puddle or in the more modern first-person style of abjection, what defines humor in Deleuze's first sense is a trajectory of descent; it moves from heights to depths, repudiates symbol and signification, and in their place finds only states of affairs and arrangements of bodies. Yet against this metaphysics of depth, Deleuze posits a radically alternative trajectory for humor—which, according to him, offers a "way out" of the conventional comedic insistence on materiality, and which I want to posit as a working definition of absurdism.[29] In place of a comic epistemology that would resolve the dualism of ideas versus things in favor of the latter, this second trajectory instead skates dexterously between these poles, maintaining the tension between them; it refuses to come to any mooring, either in a concrete state of affairs or in the abstract realm of concepts and signification. Rather, the adventure of such humor is to play out across "the surface where there is no longer anything to denote or even [any idea] to signify, but where pure sense is produced."[30] Useful as a demonstration of the dynamic is another routine of C. K.'s, in which his daughter's repeated "why" pushes sense to the point of its untethering, stretched to the place at which it begins to spread out in a state of pure play.

> This is my daughter the other day, she's like: "Papa, why can't we go outside?" "Well, 'cause it's raining." "Why?" "Well, water's coming out of the sky." "Why?" "Because it was in a cloud." "Why?" "Well, clouds form when there's vapor." (audience laughs) "Why?" "I don't know. I don't know any more things. Those are all the things I know." "Why?" "'Cause I'm stupid. I'm stupid." "Why?" "Well, because I didn't pay attention in school, OK? I went to school but I didn't listen in class." "Why?" "Because I was high all the time. I smoked too much pot." "Why?" "Because my parents didn't give me no guidance. They didn't give a shit." "Why?" "Because they fucked in a car and then had me. And they resented me for taking their youth." "Why?" "Because they had bad morals. They just had no compass." "Why?" "Because *they* had shitty parents. It just keeps going like that." "Why?" "Because fuck it, we're alone in the universe. Nobody gives a shit about us."

I'm going to stop here to be polite to you for a second. But this goes on for like hours and hours, and it gets so weird and abstract. At the end it's like: "Why?" "Well, because some things *are* and some things are *not.*" (*audience laughs*) "Why?" "Because things that are not can't be." (*audience laughs*) "Why?" "Because then (*yelling*) nothing wouldn't be! You can't have fucking nothing isn't! Everything is!" "Why?" "Because if nothing wasn't there'd be all kinds of shit that we don't—like giant ants with top hats dancing around! There's no room for all that shit!"[31]

This can provide a working model of the dynamic of absurdism that I am proposing—a refutation of the possibilities of monstration that equally remains without a signification. The pressure of the child's questioning forces the father to become a kind of unwilling Lewis Carroll, whose bid to ground sense in a seemingly concrete state of affairs (a world where "some things are and some things are not") swerves off course: words begin autonomously to generate new forms of sense (a world in which "nothing wouldn't be") that no longer refer to a possible state of being or stable concept, but instead open the doors through which ludic imaginings begin to crowd ("giant ants with top hats").

Lewis Carroll is a central reference point throughout Deleuze's study, where he comes to stand as the archetype of this art of the surface, of the generative play of language that unleashes sense from any reference to the world of things ("'Twas brillig, and the slithy toves," etc.).[32] As Deleuze quotes Carroll, "Plain superficiality is the character of speech."[33] But Carroll is not the only relevant literary example here, and if we turn now to Julia Kristeva's landmark essay on abjection, we find a similar "art of the surface" being discussed in relation to the modernist prose of James Joyce and Louis-Ferdinand Céline, whose headlong streaming of words ("the rhetoric of the pure signifier, of music in letter") is interpreted as a mode of psychic defense, as a verbal communication that "discloses the abject" as that which modernism seeks to keep at bay.[34] A key example for Kristeva is the soliloquy of Molly Bloom in Joyce's *Ulysses* (1922), in which Molly's disgust at male sexuality "breaks out" with an abjection that the surface flow of her words nonetheless defends against, transforming her phobic reaction into the register of a kind of verbal music, the pure signifier of "music in letter" here encountered as "the only way out."[35] In a commentary on Kristeva, stand-up theorist John Limon has suggested that there might be a role for comedy here, too—specifically for witty forms of verbal humor and puns that exemplify the headlong linguistic nimbleness that Kristeva associates with Molly's speech ("travelling at top speed over an untouched and untouchable abyss [of abjection], of which, on occasion, only the affect shows up"), and that would thus similarly defer abjection by finding respite in the surface becoming of sense.[36]

We seem to find in Molly Bloom an echo of C. K.'s scandal, only in a way that, per Limon's gloss, unexpectedly places C. K. on both sides of that scene, both the bearer of the sexuality that, exposed, "breaks out" abjection *and* the source of the comic nonsense that would guard against it—a crucial clue for understanding the dialectics of humor that inform *Louie*. But it would be a mistake, before taking that leap, to assume from our examples that absurdism must lie solely on the side of the signifier—as a matter of Carrollian neologisms or of C. K.'s play with double negatives, for instance—for there is also an absurdism that pertains to fictive situations and the dynamic of their unfolding. Again, Deleuze provides the model for such an understanding, this time in one of his later texts, "Bartleby; or, The Formula," which describes the narrative operations of Melville's 1853 short story in a fashion strikingly similar to Deleuze's earlier discussion of Carroll's wordplay. Here, Melville's tale is approached as the working out of what Deleuze terms a "formula," which, like the model of absurdism proposed above, similarly performs a dual opposition—that is, a refusal to side with either monstration or signification as the destination of sense. Thus "Bartleby" is to be understood *not* as a text describing a state of affairs (here, a fictive one) *nor* as symbolizing some meaning about the human condition; rather, it is the working out or performance of a formula (the scrivener's "I prefer not to") that, pursued to its conclusion, collapses the representational system of literary fiction, of causes and their effects, behaviors and their motivations.[37] Bartleby's inexplicable refusal is less the negation of a specific content—there is no particular thing he is "against" that would define him as a plausible character—than it is the performance of the abstract concept of refusal as such; and it is less a narratively symbolic act than the engine that collapses the fiction's ability to symbolize at all, leaving the reader only with the unanswerable conundrum of a character who chooses to not act, to the point of his own starvation.

The most fully realized of C. K.'s short films operate precisely on this terrain: a blatantly implausible narrative premise is proposed, the inferable consequences of which are then carefully pursued. Take "Ice Cream" as an example. What if a woman were to continue to bear children, despite neither her nor her partner wanting any? Even so unassuming a premise shows itself to involve two representational conundrums that progressively leverage the film's world into a step-by-step alteration of known reality. First, why would the woman keep getting pregnant anyway—especially since, after the first unintended pregnancy, the couple refrains from intercourse? The second child is conceived when the husband's brother sleeps with the wife; the third by immaculate conception. Second, what do they do with the children? The firstborn is left on the street; the second is given to a magician to make disappear. The divine child, however, is not so easily disposed of. In the film's final sequence, his parents place the infant on a mechanical pony ride on a derelict sidewalk—another abandonment?—only to be immediately killed in a kind of deus ex machina retribution when an out-of-control car mounts the sidewalk. A mariachi band appears out of nowhere and commences to sing a morning greeting to the now-orphaned child.

The modes of reasoning that govern this form of humor, I am suggesting, proceed from a conditional premise (What if?) that establishes a state of exception to our expectations of known reality, and they preserve an absolute fidelity to the terms of that exception. Since it is inherent in the premise that the woman continually bears children, then the expectations of reality and representation must bend to sustain the respective premise. What is essential to an understanding of absurdism, then, is to see it not as itself a representational form, but as a mode of the unfolding of sense that does violence to representational forms; not as itself a representation, but as the positing of a premise that enables sense to wriggle free of the structuring conventions of representation. We might, loosely, want to speak of absurdism in this fictive sense as a type of fantasy, but only with the necessary caveat that it is the *opposite* of the kind of fantasy that, per Lacan, seeks security in the signifying relations of the Symbolic order. Where fantasy, *stricto sensu*, aspires to mount its defense in the rough ground of social identifications and meanings, absurdism simply keeps running.

Thought/Reality

The absurdist is thus one who refuses to allow sense to come to rest within states of affairs or ideas, who refuses to deflate and refuses to mean, neither clown nor satirist, and, as such, fits not at all with stand-up's standard mythology of the true comedian as "truth teller." No doubt there is a basic historicist interest, then, in the fact that one of the preeminent stand-up comedians of the new millennium emerged from this counter-tradition. Yet, whereas the same might be said of, say, Steve Martin in the seventies, C. K.'s distinction in this respect lies in the legibility of his absurdist proclivities as a *correlate* of the more conventionalized abject mode.

We can get a preliminary read on all this if we look first to parallel developments in C. K.'s stand-up around the time of *Louie*'s inception. In a wonderful review of C. K.'s *Live at the Beacon Theater* stand-up special (2011), *New York Times* comedy critic Jason Zinoman noted how C. K. was beginning to move "the playing field of his stories from the real world to the goings-on inside his head."

> You can . . . see this change in the difference between his . . . HBO sitcom, "Lucky Louie," which presented the grim financial challenges and unglamorous sex life of a working-class dad, and his current FX hit, "Louie," a more freewheeling production whose lingering close-ups and dream sequences signal a more subjective perspective. . . . [His comedy now] hinge[s] on elaborate set pieces in which experiences rooted in the real world are jumping-off points for the overheated dramas of his imagination.[38]

This is astute, and it points to the basic principle that came to govern C. K.'s comedy in the years following his mainstream breakout: namely, that the absurdism of his earlier work—far from being abandoned, as the dominant narrative of his career would have it—was instead relocated as, in great part, an interior mode. This is not to discount the number of "real world" absurdities that pepper the text of *Louie*, but to point to C. K.'s general tendency during these years to naturalize absurdism by locating it inside his head as a kind of coping mechanism for abjection, an interiorized response to selfhood's mortification. In his stand-up, this was evident in the spectacular revenge fantasies with which he would respond to real-world grievance—in the 2011 Beacon Theater special, for instance, when his dream of punishing a boy who has bullied his daughter unfurls a bizarre vertigo of sexual humiliation and revenge. First, he fantasizes seducing the bully's mother and then never calling her: "I'm gonna fuck your mum and not call her too. I'm gonna ruin her summer. I'm gonna fuck your mum *twice* and then never call her." But the absurdist move occurs when the same formula (sex as weapon of humiliation) extends over lines of gender and sexual identification to target the father.

> And I don't know about your dad, because he ran out on you. But I'm gonna find him, I'm gonna turn myself gay, and I'm gonna fuck him too. I'm gonna fuck him, and I'm gonna suck his dick so good that he just has to change his whole life. And I'm gonna move into a place with him in the Village for a couple of months, and totally—he'll cut off ties to all his life and start wearing cutoffs that are really tight, and he'll just—and then I'll go to some Christian turn-you-not-gay place, and I'll come back and go, "What's wrong with you, faggot?" and

make him feel bad inside, like, What has he done? (*long pause, audience laughter*) Well, you gotta protect your kids, you know. You gotta look out for them.[39]

Is this really absurdism? The impetus to, as it were, psychologize absurdism, to depict it *as thought*, in fact contravenes our earlier definition by assigning absurdism a defined place in relation to the logic of monstration (albeit here a relation of exteriority, insofar as the described events are marked as purely ideational, existing "outside" material states of affairs). It is thus possible methodologically to identify two levels of absurdism between which C. K.'s comedy has shuttled: an absurdism that limits itself to an interior sphere, which it shares with fantasy, and an absurdism proper for which the absurd thing "really" happens, as it were. The passage from C. K.'s short film work to his mainstream success might thus be said to have hinged on the displacement of the latter in favor of the former—albeit a displacement that would prove only temporary.

At any rate, this same interiorization characterizes the early seasons of the FX show where, as in the Beacon Theater example, absurdism registers primarily as a fantasized response to external aggravation. An example would be season two's sixth episode, "Subway/Pamela," when Louie luxuriates in the daydream of a good deed preposterously well rewarded. The real-world aggravation here will be familiar to New York straphangers: a subway seat in which some strange liquid has mysteriously pooled. The sequence begins with a series of shot-reverse shot structures and panning movements tracing the passengers' gazes at the offending puddle: first Louie, then a middle-aged woman, then an attractive young female, and finally a forty-something man—all are seen in turn staring in disgusted stupor at the brown liquid (figures 13.1 and 13.2). Returning to a close-up of Louie, the sequence cuts from his gaze to the seat and then back to him, his eyes now downturned, conveying thought. At this point, the daydream sequence commences, its beginning marked by a jump cut within the same close-up, suddenly switched to black and white. A soft, stumbling musical theme on cello and pizzicato viola accompanies the action, now in slightly dreamlike slow motion. Still held in the same close-up, Louie stands—the camera moving with him—and removes his sweater, which he uses to mop up the liquid. Shot-reverse shot structures return, only now, Louie holds the gaze of the passengers. The middle-aged woman stands up and caresses Louie's face, each character framed from the other's point of view so that both Louie and the woman look into the camera "at" one another (figures 13.3 and 13.4). The middle-aged man stands up approvingly to fist-bump Louie, the exchange of glances again

figures 13.1, 13.2, 13.3, & 13.4 Shot–reverse shot structures in *Louie*, "Subway/Pamela," directed by Louis C. K., 2011. Louie's abject gaze upon filth is answered in his daydream by the admiring gazes of other passengers.

punctuated by point of view (this time, just Louie's). Finally, the attractive woman stands up in front of Louie before descending out of frame to blow him, while the rest of the car's passengers gather behind smiling and nodding. A group of subway passengers bound only by their disgusted gaze at a filthy puddle has been inverted into a utopic community bound by their admiring gaze at Louie himself.

But what has also been inverted here is nothing less than abjection itself. Here, my analysis can link again to Kristeva's *Powers of Horror*, for it is to Kristeva that we owe an understanding of abjection as a kind of decentering and collapse of subjecthood. Abjection, as she quotes Bataille, is "the inability [of a subject] to . . . exclude abject things," that is, to assume the ego's strength of will to keep at bay a filth from which one thought to separate one's self.[40] In this sense, Kristeva associates abjection with a kind of "narcissism in crisis," a self-disenfranchisement that occurs when one can no longer repress what lies across "the border of my condition as a living being"; "these bodily fluids, this defilement, this shit," everything "I permanently thrust aside in order to live."[41] The danger filth symbolizes to the subject is the impossibility of maintaining the borders on which subjecthood depends: here is this filth that lies outside me, but which cannot be fully Other to me, or this corpse that beseeches me with the temptation of a nonexistence, of becoming a cadaver. But the answer of Louie's daydream is to rescue him from this abject spiral, to restore fantastically the ego's fixity by setting his subjecthood "in place," centered by the spokes of the passengers' eyelines circling admiringly around him.

Is this how C. K. imagines subjecthood's restoration? Namely, that he be appreciatively beheld even—especially—in the public enactment of that which might otherwise risk shame or embarrassment (or scandal)? Yet, if so, absurdism can no longer be considered abjection's obverse, as it would be within Deleuze's system, but, transformed into a daydream, it becomes a component of abjection's psychic and affective logic. Absurdism, qua fantasy, has been functionalized in relation to what Kristeva describes as abjection's "vortex of summons and repulsion."[42] The abject temptation to give oneself over to filth and defilement, Kristeva suggests, can always ricochet back, boomerang-like; desire, tempted by what sickens it, can snap back in protective retreat. The point then is that, in *Louie*, absurdist fantasy *is* the boomerang; it is an interiorized response to an externalized abjection that seeks to sublate it in thought, to find refuge in an absurdist imaginary that galvanizes the self against the sickening lure of abject states of affairs and filthy objects.

rob king

Women/Children

We do not necessarily require the lens of C. K.'s scandal to see a kind of onan-ism here, a closed circle of auto-affection in which abjection gets answered for in the self-pleasuring of absurdist reverie. We might even speak of a kind of "auto-absurdism" here, only with the caveat that the analogy with the scan-dal doesn't quite fit: the circle was not, after all, so tightly closed in those events, where the scene of C. K.'s masturbation required the physical pres-ence of women as props for the workings of his sexual drive. But might this not, then, be the appropriate moment to raise the question of the role of *other people* within the dynamics of C. K.'s comedy? That is, to consider those situa-tions in *Louie* in which absurdist pleasure requires other people to participate in its orbit? After all, if abjection might felicitously be described as a "phobic narcissism" (Kristeva), then there is reason surely to suspect that an orienta-tion to others might similarly play a part in breaking its spell.[43]

Consider, for instance, the relationship accorded most centrality within prescandal accounts of C. K.'s comedy: the one with his children. The con-sensus narrative of C. K.'s career posited his children as the catalyst behind his autobiographical turn; more accurately, though, they should be seen as a further strategy for generating psychic escape routes into the absurd, only this time through detours into his *children's* thought processes. As he ex-plained in an NPR interview in 2011, "Kids do that . . . thing where they take you into a wilderness in your head—like 'What is going on with this kid right now?'"[44] Here absurdism remains as an interior mode, that is, as thought, only now it is located in the thought of *another*, of a child. In a segment from his 2010 special *Hilarious*, for instance, his three-year-old daughter insists that Fig Newtons are in fact called *Pig* Newtons. The child's petulant con-trariness establishes the (lightly) absurdist premise—pork-based cookies— from which C. K. struggles to rescue her by restoring thought to its material grounding. "How do you fuck with me on this? You're three, and I'm forty-one. What are the odds that you're right and I'm wrong? What are the sheer odds of that? And take a bite of the cookie. Does it taste like a pork cookie, motherfucker? I don't think so. Why would they call it a Pig Newton? Oh, it tastes like figs. Fucking interesting that, isn't it?"[45] (It is likely that this event inspired C. K. to name his production company Pig Newton; but it is also conceivable that it and the company name are entirely fabricated allu-sions to Lewis Carroll's *Alice's Adventures in Wonderland* [1865]. Alice's first encounter with the riddling Cheshire Cat involves the exact same rhyming pun—"Did you say pig, or fig?" the cat asks—so that we might think of C. K.

here as Alice, struggling in the wonderland/wilderness of his daughter's Cheshire Cat–like provocations.)[46]

The polarity of humor in this case has obviously been reversed from our earlier examples: the trajectory is not to find respite in the flight of an absurdist imagination, but rather, like Alice, to try vainly to cut absurdism off at the pass by restoring sense to the material logic of monstration (where sense refers to things). In other instances, however, C. K. more willingly follows his children down the rabbit hole. A key example comes early in *Louie's* third season (2012), in an episode that begins with Louie's children sharing knock-knock jokes with their father over breakfast. The jokes begin innocuously enough ("Knock, knock." "Who's there?" "Moo." "Moo who?" "I didn't know you were crying, cow") but quickly veer into surrealist territory ("Knock, knock." "Who's there?" "Painter." "Painter who?" "The painter who painted both of you as mermaids, but instead of being underwater, it's pee-pee"). In a subsequent stand-up sequence, Louie unpacks the absurdist pleasures of children's joke telling.

> My daughter told me a joke the other day. She tells great jokes. They're not like anybody else's jokes. That's why I like them. I've been doing comedy for twenty-five years. I know every joke. Even if I haven't heard it, you start telling me a joke, and I know how it's going to work. But her jokes, I have no idea what's going to happen. I have no idea.
>
> This is the joke she told me the other day. She said: "Who didn't let the gorilla into the ballet?" . . . Already I love this joke. I *love* this joke. I have *not* heard this joke. This is a new joke for me. (*audience laughs*) "Who didn't let the gorilla into the ballet?" And I said "Who?" and she said "Just the people who are in charge of that decision." (*audience laughs*) Just the folks who make that assessment. Their judgment was that it wasn't a good idea to let him in."
>
> I *love* this joke because I picture it. The whole story's in my head. People going into a ballet theater, and the gorilla's just trying to text and not make eye contact. Just trying to go in. It's cool. And then somebody, "Err, no no no no no. You. No, no. Yeah, you. Yes, the gorilla. I'm talking to the gorilla." "Why not, man?" (*as gorilla*) "'Cause you're a gorilla. I don't even have to say anything." "Don't I get any credit for talking and wanting to go to a ballet?" (*audience laughs*) "Doesn't that buy me any credibility?" "No, man. It's a long show. It's three hours. You're not going to—I'm telling you, you're not going to make it. You're okay now, but halfway through you're going to start pounding on people. That's just the way you are, man. I ain't

gonna get burned like that again. Gorilla kills everyone in the ballet once, shame on the gorilla." (*audience laughs*)[47]

It was Freud who first formalized the relation between humor and childhood: humor, he argued, works to overcome the adult inhibition against play, allowing us momentarily to return to the euphoria of childhood, "a period of life in which we were accustomed to deal with our psychical work in general with a small expenditure of energy," and when, in consequence, "we had no need of humor to make us feel happy in our life."[48] C. K.'s children should, then, be seen not simply as markers in his passage to comedic maturity, but also as a pathway opening onto the euphoric absurdities of a child's thought, sometimes followed, sometimes refused. The dialectic of parenthood as one of C. K.'s richest comic themes thus lies in the choices that parenthood allows thought to take. One can choose the "responsible" adult path; that is, one can battle against a child's nonsensical imaginings by referring them to actual states of affairs and correcting them (Fig Newtons, not Pig Newtons). Or one can instead arrogate to one's self the terms of a child's imaginings, taking them as an absurdist formula, a springboard for leapfrogging abjection's "powers of horror" and the psychic expenditure that adult subjectivity imposes.

Yet what is permitted to a spirit of childlike play becomes more discomfiting when applied across lines of gender. This was particularly apparent in *Louie*'s third season, whose major arc revolved around Louie's dread of aloneness and his pursuit of partnership with a series of women. Within the show's guest-star paradigm, C. K. began assigning his female leads—Maria Bamford, Melissa Leo, Parker Posey, Chloë Sevigny—the burden of an unfathomable eccentricity that either alienates Louie and reinforces his abjection (Bamford, Leo, Sevigny) or promises a kind of redemption (Posey). The difficulty, though, was not simply that the show's women thereby became "either crazy or scary or crazy-scary," as a *Slate* season summary put it.[49] More important is how women and children seem thereby to serve the same function for C. K., each alike as forces of an eccentricity that Louie either resists and tries vainly to *make into sense* or welcomes as absurdist salve.

With women, the tipping point between these alternatives is sex; specifically—and with exceptional disingenuity given subsequent revelations—Louie's discovery in women of a solipsistic drive that refuses to acknowledge him as anything but a term of their genital pleasure. The Bamford character mocks Louie's postcoital invitation to have dinner with him and his children; the Leo character physically assaults him to satisfy her thousand-dollar bet that he'll lick her asshole; the Sevigny character mortifies Louie by bringing herself to orgasm while sitting with him at a coffee shop. If the Parker Posey character, Liz, stands out from this pattern, it is not only because the issue of sex never transpires, but also, beyond this, because of the way *her own* abjection is brought into play alongside Louie's, thereby permitting something closer to an eventual mutuality. An oddball bookstore clerk whom Louie dates across a diptych of episodes (four and five), Liz manifests eccentricity not as an expression of the sex drive but as a defense mechanism for warding off what for Kristeva is the "utmost" in abjection—namely, the temptation of one's own corpse, of "death infecting life."[50] The date thus begins with Liz's confession of her own "becoming corpse," a horrifying account of teenage cancer that spreads out abjection before Louie:

> Beating that disease wore me down to seventy pounds. I had no hair. My teeth fell out. I was wearing dentures by the time I was fifteen. . . . I'd be puking, and [my mom] would be kneeling next to me on the bathroom floor sobbing. I'm literally puking chemo-vomit into a toilet and patting my poor mother on the back trying to comfort her. . . . When you go to hell and back, and you literally see death come right into your face like this (*brings hand to face*), it turns you into a little gray skeleton.[51]

But, as the rest of the episode reveals, her response has been to sublate the temptation of her own "little gray skeleton" by creatively forcing the world into absurdist permutations. The date thereby becomes a series of challenges for Louie as Posey's character turns her energies onto him, treating him as reluctant putty for her creative refashionings: she takes him into the changing room of a thrift store and makes him put on a dress; she tricks him into believing that her birth name is "tape recorder"; she takes him to Russ and Daughters to binge on herrings; she convinces him to book a homeless man into a hotel room for the night. Finally, she leads him to the roof of a skyscraper and invites him to sit on the edge with her. Louie's response is panicked refusal, pleading with her to step back and join him. Liz replies by returning to the temptation of one's own corpse: the risk, she explains, is not in standing on the edge of a tall building but in wanting to jump. "The only way I'd fall is if I jumped. That's why you're afraid to come over here. Because a tiny part of you wants to jump. Because it would be so easy. But I don't want to jump, so I'm not afraid. . . . I'm having too good of a time."

Both Liz and Louie might be thought of as "corpse-adjacent" in this moment, only with a marked difference in the temporality of that relation: for Liz, her corpse lies in the past of her illness (at least for now, for she will

rob king

figures 13.5 & 13.6
Liz (Parker Posey)
models self-repair
for Louie. *Louie,*
"Daddy's Girlfriend,
Pt. 2," directed by
Louis C. K., 2012.

unexpectedly die in the season finale), its temptation successfully locked away by an absurdist creativity that continually produces new capacities for being in the world; for Louie, his "becoming corpse" is the fear of his future, as envisioned in a later episode's dream sequence of his solitary and decrepit older self, sitting in a shabby armchair and eating pinwheel cookies. What is permitted in the space of that difference is an improbable pedagogy in abjection, conveyed here in a series of tremulous close-ups worthy of the ending to *City Lights* (1931): Liz models for Louie an absurdist style of self-repair that magics away the impetus to self-annihilation, here figured in the dread temptation of a rooftop leap; Louie, in turn, achieves a beatific understanding that similarly places that disintegrative pulsion on hold, instead converted outward into a relation to another that finally opens onto the terrain of love (figures 13.5 and 13.6). As Jacques-Alain Miller comments in a gloss on Lacan, "To take a person, a whole person as an object, is not the role of the drive, it leads us to introduce love."[52] What is romanticized on the rooftop is nothing less than the transcendence of a mode of relation that, in treating women's presence as a prop for his compulsions, would bring C. K.'s career crashing down.

Potentiality/Actuality

One consequence of the windfall of sexual misconduct revelations in the fall of 2017 was the emergence of an unexpected subgenre of entertainment journalism; namely, the apology review, in which the apologies (or nonapologies) of high-profile men were subject to fine-grained textual exegesis in the effort to telegraph what men needed to understand about issues of consent and culpability. Coming after the dreadfully low bar set by Harvey Weinstein's and Kevin Spacey's evasive mea culpas, C. K.'s received a more mixed reception, in which palpable relief at some much-needed honesty ("These stories are true") coexisted with distaste for the self-aggrandizement with which the comedian framed the power dynamics of misconduct ("The power I had over these women is that they admired me").[53] Rather than contribute to these readings, however, I want to start my conclusion to this essay by attending to another odd matter of wording—specifically, the curious fashion in which C. K. had earlier denied those rumors whenever they were brought up. The comedian's repudiations had been less a matter of "I didn't do that" than, in his own words, "It's not *real*," or "That's nothing to me. That's not *real*," as though the "truth" of his deeds was to be arbitrated less by the deeds themselves than by a kind of discursive relativism that would conjure with their "reality," or as though he owned the ability—and the right—to bestow reality or unreality onto the rumored events by controlling the discourse about them. As he put it in an interview at a screening of *I Love You, Daddy* (2017) at the Toronto International Film Festival, "If you actually participate in a rumor, you make it bigger and you make it real."[54] (And might not the opening to his eventual confession—"These stories are true"—then be read less as welcome honesty than as a trace of that same sense of ownership over the terms of the stories' reality?)

The obvious bad faith here would barely warrant further mention were it not for the way this kind of magical thinking had already become embedded as a formal strategy of his comedy. For what does it mean that something that has happened can nonetheless be thought of as "unreal"? And what happens, conversely, when the unreal thing is in fact what happens? These paradoxes—in which the fact of an event's happening is somehow coupled with a sense of its deniability, its reality strangely questionable—constitute the framework of C. K.'s ongoing experimentation in the later seasons of *Louie*. For, if there was one thing that differentiated the comedic strategies of the show's fourth and fifth seasons from what had preceded them, it was precisely C. K.'s willingness to treat absurdism in this fashion—no longer just as that "second-level" absurdism that circumscribes itself as thought/interiority, but as an impossible something that nonetheless "happens" within the show's world, squeezed out onto the terrain of (narrative) reality. What was described, with reference to the show's final seasons, as C. K.'s "art house phase" might, from the perspective of the scandal, instead be assessed as the gaslighter's paradox: that the fact of something's happening is no guarantee that it will be counted as real.[55]

A distinction needs to be made here between individuated moments of unexplained implausibility that might loosely be thought of as absurdist and the fuller sense of absurdism that involves the application of a formula whose unfolding undermines the representational system of a narrative. The former were a feature of the show ever since the pilot episode (2010), which ends when Louie's blind date flees his embrace by means of a conveniently nearby helicopter. But only following the third season did C. K. begin to give rein to the latter consistently, thus bringing the show full circle with the comic principles of his early short films. The cold open to season four's first episode ("Back") programmatically asserts the new direction. As it begins, Louie is awakened by the noise of garbage collectors loudly hurling trash into the truck. But what next transpires is an apparently real-world materialization of Louie's groggy confusion, in which the garbage collectors now intentionally target their uproar against him, breaking through the windows of Louie's room, jumping around on his bed, crashing garbage can lids together, a kind of uninvited private performance of *Stomp*. Is any of this actually happening, or is it merely the thought of a disturbed sleeper? The depicted events are somewhat recoverable to the latter possibility. It was, after all, a favored directorial device of C. K. to indifferentiate *how* something is perceived from *what* is perceived; that is, to treat a subjective perception "objectively," as though the perceived property belonged to the external world.[56] Other examples cannot, however, be so safely contained. Unquestionably the most extended illustration would be the hurricane story arc—threaded through the fourth season's six "Elevator" episodes—in which "hurricane Jasmine Forsyth" claims the lives of twelve million Floridians and LeBron James, but mostly LeBron James. The more revealing instance, however, predates that season: the ending to season three's eighth episode, "Dad," which thus constitutes something of an early harbinger of C. K.'s more emboldened approach. From the outset, the episode's narrative world is disorientingly off-kilter. Louie has a dispute at an electronics store and is brought into the back office to watch himself on security camera footage—only the "himself" on the monitor is, in one shot, obviously not played by C. K. Next, Louie receives a phone call from his "Uncle Ex" (F. Murray Abraham), who arranges to meet him in the Old World grandeur of Manhattan's Russian Tea Room, strangely empty, and instructs him to visit his estranged father in Boston. From this point on, the "real world" of the narrative fiction begins unaccountably to take shape from Louie's escalating anxieties as he journeys to his father's home. We learn nothing about the reason for the visit, nor about what impels Louie to accede to an instruction against which his own self revolts; what we get instead are scenes from a journey that allegorize the mechanistic nihilism of his abjection as a series of vehicles dragging him tauntingly toward his father. On the flight to Boston, the attendant unaccountably announces over the intercom: "We are making our final descent into Logan Airport in Boston, where your father lives." Driving in a rental car, the GPS scolds him in measured computer tones: "You missed the turn to your father's house. Why are you being such a little pussy about this? He's your father. It's not like he touched your dick or something."[57]

Again, is any of this "actually happening" or is it just thought? Here, the alternative is sustained to the point of its inapplicability, for, as the extraordinary final sequence reveals, it is in the nature of absurdism proper that such discriminations—which are in any case possible only within the logic of monstration—no longer operate. Arriving at the front door of his father's residence, Louie rings the bell but, before the door can be opened, panics and flees. The flight begins with Louie sprinting away on foot but then inexplicably switches to a new series of vehicles, this time corresponding to the logic of wish fulfillment: an upmarket three-wheeled motorbike, then a slick speedboat, each of which Louie simply chances on, jumps onto, and happens to be able to operate (figures 13.7–13.9).[58] The fabric of narrative reality, which early in the episode drew color from Louie's impending panic, has now been decisively and mysteriously transformed to accommodate his desire to escape, such that we find not a dialectic between externalized abjection and fantasized response, but something more like a *materialized fantasy*, in which Louie and the world around him become possessed of a crazy excess in which the unreal thing "happens," in which he keeps on finding new and better ways to make his getaway. The self-destructive trajectory of his abjection—impelling him toward a confrontation from which subjecthood rebels—is flung magically into reverse, into a trajectory of desire that will send him finally out into the ocean, isolated in joyous solitude. The episode's final images thus constitute nothing less than a negative image of utopia that locates Louie somehow "outside" the world, far out at sea and bobbing on the waves, where he throws his head back and laughs. In

figures 13.7, 13.8, & 13.9
Louie makes his
precipitous escape
from his father, first
on foot, then on
a three-wheeled
motorbike, then on
a speedboat. *Louie*,
"Dad," directed by
Louis C. K., 2012.

such instances, a bridge has been built to another logic of absurdism, different from our foregoing examples: absurdism is no longer the imaginary refuge that wards off the subjective threat of abjection; rather, it becomes the potentiality that lurks behind actuality, an unexpectedly transformative power through which the world becomes responsive to Louie's desire to escape. Such an absurdism is no longer the unleashing of a force of sense that *separates itself from* any reference to material states of affairs; rather, it is a possibility that *turns on to* states of affairs and alters them. Only at this higher power does absurdism register not simply as a comedic respite, but in fact as the force of abjection's vanquishing: sense is no longer constrained to existing states of affairs, as it is in abjection, but instead forces them into new shapes.

Here, I am drawing one last time on Deleuze, this time from his understanding of actuality—that which exists in time and space—as conditioned by what is possible, that is, by potentiality. If there is something actual, it is because it has "unfolded" from the potentiality that subtends it. Thus, "We should see the actual not as that from which change and difference take place, but as that which has been effected from potentiality"—with the necessary rider that, in the above sequence, absurdism has been elevated to the status of that potentiality.[59] One way to put all this would be to say that absurdism has here become the punchline to an abject worldview, the sudden swivel in a shift of registers that reveals abjection's ultimate contingency, its transformability. Another would be to say that such moments impossibly actualize the redemptive promise of absurdist thought to make it a principle of the world's altering. The impossible tenet of an absurdist faith, *Louie* finally suggests, is simply this: that the innovating powers of the absurd be realized not in the realm of thought alone; that they not be limited—as even Deleuze argued they must—to the realm of "pure, ideational events," but instead become manifest as real states of affairs.[60] For only this would be the end of abjection.

* * *

C. K. should be so lucky. For the truth was that the rumored misconduct he had long described as "unreal" *had* happened, and in a way that outflanked the possibility of absurdist deferral. Scandal, after all, might be thought of as an exemplary case for the dialectic of potentiality and actuality discussed by Deleuze, only in a way that smashed the machinery of escape imagined in C. K.'s comedy. Scandal dead ends such evasion when it involves sex, because it divulges the abject compulsions of the sex drive as the potentiality of which the artist's body of work comes irreparably to be viewed as the actuality. It turns the artwork into a symptom of what it is trying to avoid. There would be no transfiguration of real states of affairs by absurdist desire, no escape via speedboat for C. K. The front door was opened after all, for all to see inside.

Notes

Color versions of images in this chapter may be found at http://scalar.usc
.edu/works/abjection-incorporated-insert/index.

1 Emily Nussbaum, "One-Man Show," *New York Magazine*, May 15, 2011, http://
nymag.com/arts/tv/upfronts/2011/louis-ck-2011-5.

2 The next sentences quickly correct the misdirection: "With his laptop open,
he mimes the requisite jerky motions below his waist, rolling his head from
side to side. The camera rolls with him, making Louis's image bob like a cork
on the wave."

3 "Which Beloved Comedian Likes to Force Female Comics to Watch Him Jerk
Off?" *Gawker*, March 19, 2012, http://gawker.com/5894527/which-beloved
-comedian-likes-to-force-female-comics-to-watch-him-jerk-off?.

4 "Louis C. K. Responds to Accusations: 'These Stories Are True,'" *New York
Times*, November 10, 2017, https://www.nytimes.com/2017/11/10/arts
/television/louis-ck-statement.html.

5 Kathryn VanArendonk, "Why Some Artists Are Never Separated from Their
Work (and Why Louis C. K. Was)," *Vulture*, November 14, 2017, http://www
.vulture.com/2017/11/louis-c-k-and-separating-artists-from-their-work.html
(emphasis added).

6 Sonia Saraiya, "I Admired Louis C. K.: What a Mistake," *Variety*, November 11,
2017, http://variety.com/2017/tv/news/louis-ck-scandal-sexual-harassment
-mistake-louie-1202612558. Saraiya's assessment of C. K.'s "self-awareness" is from
"'Louie' Returns as Hapless and Sublime as Ever," *Salon*, April 8, 2015, https://
www.salon.com/2015/04/08/louie_returns_as_hapless_and_sublime_as_ever.

7 Jesse David Fox, "Truth in Comedy after Louis C. K.," *Vulture*, November 10,
2017, http://www.vulture.com/2017/11/louis-ck-influenced-generation-of
-comedy-what-now.html.

8 Emily Todd VanDerWerff, "Why *Louie* Is the Next Stage in the Evolution of
the TV Sitcom," *AV Club*, September 27, 2012, http://www.avclub.com/articles
/why-louie-is-the-next-stage-in-the-evolution-of-th,85474; Dan Calvisi,
"Writing Comedy—Interview with Louis C. K.," Act Four Screenplays,
July 16, 2010, http://actfourscreenplays.com/screenwriting-blog/writing
-comedy-interview-with-louis-c-k.

9 Katy Waldman, "Wasted Reckonings," *Slate*, November 14, 2017, http://www
.slate.com/articles/arts/culturebox/2017/11/what_do_we_want_from_public
_apologies_by_accused_sexual_harassers_like_louis.html.

10 Willa Paskin, "*Louie* Was Propaganda for Louis C. K.'s Decency: How Does
It Look Now?" *Slate*, November 10, 2017, http://www.slate.com/blogs
/browbeat/2017/11/10/watching_louie_in_light_of_allegations_against
_louis_c_k.html.

11 Julia Kristeva, *Powers of Horror: An Essay on Abjection*, trans. Leon S. Roudiez
(New York: Columbia University Press, 1982), 12.

12 Steve Heisler, "Louis C. K.: Lucky Cut-Up Earns Creative Freedom," *Variety*, December 3, 2010, http://www.variety.com/article/VR1118028109.

13 Andrew Wallenstein, "Emmys: Louis C. K. in Seventh Heaven," *Variety*, July 19, 2012, http://www.variety.com/article/VR1118056811.

14 Nussbaum, "One-Man Show"; Carina Chocano, "The Best Sitcom of the Past 30 Years, Round One: *Seinfeld* vs. *Louie*," *Vulture*, March 27, 2013, http://www.vulture.com/2013/03/seinfeld-vs-louie-sitcom-smackdown.html.

15 The term "life experience" is Marc Maron's, from "Louis C. K., part 2," episode 112, October 7, 2010, wtf, produced by Marc Maron, podcast, http://www.wtfpod.com/podcast/episodes/episode_112_-_louis_ck_part_2.

16 Jonah Weiner, "The Man Who Loves to Hate Himself," *Rolling Stone*, December 22, 2011, 44–48, http://jonahweiner.com/RS_Louie_CK_Jonah _Weiner.html; Jason Zinoman, "Louis C. K.'s Blue Collar in First Class," *New York Times*, December 19, 2011, http://www.nytimes.com/2011/12/20 /arts/louis-c-ks-working-class-roots-and-success.html?_r=1&; Ian Goldstein, "Burn It Down and Start Again: 4 Comics Who Threw out Their Material and Reinvented Themselves," *Splitsider* on *Vulture*, July 2, 2014, https://www .vulture.com/2014/07/burn-it-down-and-start-again-4-comics-who-threw -out-their-material-and-reinvented-themselves.html.

17 Weiner, "The Man Who Loves to Hate Himself."

18 Richard Zoglin's study of 1970s stand-up in fact relies on this myth as a basic historiographic framework for the entire modern stand-up tradition: "Stand-up comedy from the borscht belt to the '70s could be described as a long march from joke telling to truth telling." Zoglin, *Comedy at the Edge: How Stand-Up in the 1970s Changed America* (New York: Bloomsbury, 2008), 63.

19 Zinoman, "Louis C. K.'s Blue Collar in First Class"; Neil Genzlinger, "Loving Ice Cream and an Older Woman," *New York Times*, January 29, 2014, https:// www.nytimes.com/2014/01/30/movies/louis-c-k-releases-his-tomorrow-night -from-1998.html.

20 Stephen M. Deusner, "Interviews: Louis C. K.," *Pitchfork*, June 20, 2011, https://pitchfork.com/features/interview/7926-louis-ck; Ramsey Ess, "Louis C. K. Discusses 'Louie,' Censorship, and Treating Others Nicely," *Split-sider* on *Vulture*, December 7, 2012, https://www.vulture.com/2012/12/louis-ck -discusses-louie-censorship-and-treating-others-nicely.html.

21 John Limon, *Stand-Up Comedy in Theory, or, Abjection in America* (Durham, NC: Duke University Press, 2000), 4, 6.

22 The routines, respectively, are from *Shameless: An hbo Comedy Special*, di-rected by Steven J. Santos (New York: hbo Video, 2007), dvd; and *Louis C. K.: Hilarious*, directed by Louis C. K., aired September 18, 2010, on Comedy Central.

23 Calvisi, "Writing Comedy."

24 Louis C. K. from "Louis C. K., part 1," episode 111, October 4, 2010, wtf, produced by Marc Maron, podcast, http://www.wtfpod.com/podcast/episodes /episode_111_-_louis_ck_part_1.

25 "Introduction," *Short Films of Louis C. K.*, directed by Louis C. K. (New York: Circus King Films, 2001), DVD.

26 Gilles Deleuze, *The Logic of Sense*, trans. Mark Lester (1969; New York: Columbia University Press, 1990), 135.

27 See Sigmund Freud, *Jokes and Their Relation to the Unconscious*, trans. James Strachey (New York: Norton, 1963), 175–78.

28 *Louis C. K.: Hilarious.*

29 Deleuze, *Logic of Sense*, 136.

30 Deleuze, *Logic of Sense*, 136.

31 The routine in question is from his earliest HBO appearance, August 19, 2005, on *One Night Stand*, directed by Steven J. Santos. C. K. subsequently transformed this routine into the basis for the first scene of the pilot for *Lucky Louie*, directed by Gary Halvorson, which aired June 11, 2006, on HBO.

32 And is the use of language in "Jabberwocky" really so different from that of C. K.'s script for *Pootie Tang* (e.g., "Sine your pitty on the runny kine")?

33 Deleuze, *The Logic of Sense*, 11.

34 Kristeva, *Powers of Horror*, 22.

35 Kristeva, *Powers of Horror*, 23.

36 Kristeva, *Powers of Horror*, 41; Limon, *Stand-Up Comedy in Theory*, 73.

37 Gilles Deleuze, "Bartleby; or, The Formula," in *Essays Critical and Clinical*, trans. Daniel W. Smith and Michael A. Greco (London: Verso, 1999), 68–90.

38 Zinoman, "Louis C. K.'s Blue Collar in First Class."

39 *Louis C. K.: Live at the Beacon Theater*, online release, directed by Louis C. K. (New York: Pig Newton, 2011), https://buy.louisck.net/purchase /live-at-the-beacon-theater.

40 Georges Bataille, *Essais de sociologie, Oeuvres complètes* (Paris: Gallimard, 1970), quoted in Kristeva, *Powers of Horror*, 56.

41 Kristeva, *Powers of Horror*, 3.

42 Kristeva, *Powers of Horror*, 1.

43 Kristeva, *Powers of Horror*, 43–44.

44 "Louis C. K.: Louie on FX," August 22, 2012, *The Treatment*, hosted by Elvis Mitchell, produced by Harriet Ells and Jenny Radelet, podcast, http://www .kcrw.com/culture/shows/the-treatment/louis-c-k-louie-on-fx.

45 *Louis C. K.: Hilarious.*

46 Lewis Carroll, *Alice's Adventures in Wonderland* (London: Macmillan, 1865), at Project Gutenberg, https://www.gutenberg.org/files/11/11-h/11-h.htm.

47 *Louie*, season 3, episode 2, "Telling Jokes/Set Up," directed by Louis C. K., aired July 5, 2012, on FX.

48 Freud, *Jokes*, 293.

49 Allison Benedikt, "Louie recap, 'Looking for Liz/Lilly Changes': Is Louie Afraid of Women?" *Slate*, August 24, 2012, https://slate.com/culture/2012/08/ week-9-louie-recap-looking-for-liz-lilly-changes-is-louie-afraid-of-women .html.

50 Kristeva, *Powers of Horror*, 4.

51 *Louie*, season 3, episode 25, "Daddy's Girlfriend, Pt. 2," directed by Louis C. K., aired July 26, 2012, on FX.

52 Jacques-Alain Miller, "On Perversion," in *Reading Seminars I and II: Lacan's Return to Freud*, ed. Richard Feldstein, Bruce Fink, and Maire Jaanus (Albany: SUNY Press, 1996), 313.

53 "Louis C. K. Responds to Accusations."

54 David Marchese, "In Conversation: Louis C. K.," *Vulture*, June 2016, http://www.vulture.com/2016/06/louis-ck-horace-and-pete-c-v-r.html; David Itzkoff, "Marc Maron Reckons with Louis C. K.'s Misconduct," *New York Times*, November 13, 2017, https://www.nytimes.com/2017/11/13/arts/television/marc-maron-louis-ck.html; Cara Buckley, "Asking Questions Louis C. K. Doesn't Want to Answer," *New York Times*, September 11, 2017, https://www.nytimes.com/2017/09/11/movies/louis-ck-rumors-wont-answer.html.

55 Mike Hale, "'Louie' Is Back: His Issues Are, Too," *New York Times*, April 6, 2015, https://www.nytimes.com/2015/04/07/arts/television/louis-cks-louie-returns-for-season-5.html.

56 Several examples of this are afforded in the first season's eighth episode, "Dog Pound" (aired August 10, 2010, on FX), in scenes in which Louie struggles with a marijuana hangover—as when, for example, he enters a coffee shop and cannot make sense of anything he hears. C. K. conveys Louie's confusion here not by making use of the conventional codes of subjective disorientation (murky sound, etc.) but by having the actors speak actual gibberish, thereby placing the perception *on the side of the object.*

57 *Louie*, season 3, episode 8, "Dad," directed by Louis C. K., aired August 16, 2012, on FX. The understanding that informs C. K.'s script here—that abuse without physical or sexual contact is still abuse—was obviously disregarded by the comedian in his private life.

58 This is in contrast with the earlier season three episode "Something Is Wrong" (episode 1, aired June 28, 2012, on FX), in which C. K. buys a motorbike and soon crashes it.

59 Claire Colebrook, "Actuality," in *The Deleuze Dictionary*, ed. Adrian Parr (New York: Columbia University Press, 2005), 9–11.

60 Deleuze, *The Logic of Sense*, 35.

contributors

MEREDITH A. BAK is an assistant professor in the Department of Childhood Studies at Rutgers University–Camden. Her research interests include children's toys, media, and visual and material cultures from the nineteenth century to the present. Her work has appeared in *Early Popular Visual Culture*, *Film History*, the *Moving Image*, and *Velvet Light Trap*. Her current book project considers the role of precinematic visual media from optical toys to early pop-up books in shaping children's media culture. A second project in development considers the history and theory of animate toys from talking dolls to augmented-reality apps.

EUGENIE BRINKEMA is associate professor of contemporary literature and media at the Massachusetts Institute of Technology. Her research in film and media studies focuses on violence, affect, sexuality, aesthetics, and ethics in texts ranging from the horror film to gonzo pornography. Articles have appeared in the journals *Angelaki*, *Camera Obscura*, *Criticism*, *differences*, *Discourse*, the *Journal of Speculative Philosophy*, *qui parle*, and *World Picture*. Her first book, *The Forms of the Affects*, was published with Duke University Press in 2014.

JAMES LEO CAHILL is director of the Cinema Studies Institute, associate professor of cinema studies and French at the University of Toronto, and general editor of *Discourse: Journal for Theoretical Studies in Media and Culture*. He is author of *Zoological Surrealism: The Nonhuman Cinema of Jean Painlevé* (2019) as well as numerous articles and chapters on animals and media, French cinema, and critical theory.

MICHELLE CHO is assistant professor of East Asian popular culture at the University of Toronto. She's published on Asian cinemas in *Cinema Journal*, the *Korean Popular Culture Reader*, and *Simultaneous Worlds: Global Science Fiction Cinemas*. Her research on Korean wave television, video, and pop music appears in *Asian Video Cultures*, *Hallyu 2.0: The Korean Wave in the Age of Social Media*, and the *International Journal of Communication*. Her first monograph analyzes millennial South Korean genre cinemas, and her current project theorizes *vicarious media* in the convergence of platforms, affect, and the globalization fantasies characteristic of K-pop and its fandoms.

MAGGIE HENNEFELD is an assistant professor of cultural studies and comparative literature at the University of Minnesota, Twin Cities. She is author of the award-winning *Specters of Slapstick and Silent Film Comediennes* (2018). Her articles have appeared in volumes and journals including *Camera Obscura*, *Discourse*, *Film History*, *Feminist Media Histories*, *Film Quarterly*, and *differences*. She is coeditor of *Unwatchable* (2019), as well as *Cultural Critique*, a themed issue of *Feminist Media Histories* on "Gender and Comedy" (Spring 2017) and the In Focus section on "Comedy and Humor Studies" in the *Journal of Cinema and Media Studies* (Spring 2019).

ROB KING is a professor of film and media studies at Columbia University's School of the Arts. He is the author of *Hokum! The Early Sound Slapstick Short and Depression-Era Mass Culture* (2017) and the award-winning *The Fun Factory: The Keystone Film Company and the Emergence of Mass Culture* (2009). He has also coedited the volumes *Beyond the Screen: Institutions, Networks, and Publics of Early Cinema* (2012), *Slapstick Comedy* (2011), and *Early Cinema and the "National"* (2008).

THOMAS LAMARRE teaches in Asian and Middle Eastern studies and art, art history, and visual studies at Duke University. He is author of numerous publications on the history of media, thought, and material culture, with projects ranging from the communication networks of ninth-century Japan (*Uncovering Heian Japan: An Archaeology of Sensation and Inscription*, 2000), to silent cinema and the global imaginary (*Shadows on the Screen: Tanizaki Jun'ichirô on Cinema and Oriental Aesthetics*, 2005), animation technologies (*The Anime Ma-*

chine: A Media Theory of Animation, 2009), and television and new media (*The Anime Ecology: A Genealogy of Television, Animation, and Game Media*, 2018).

SYLVÈRE LOTRINGER is a literary critic, cultural theorist, and editor. He is the Jean Baudrillard Chair at the European Graduate School, where he teaches philosophy and is professor emeritus of French literature and philosophy at Columbia University. He is the founder and editor of *Semiotext(e)* and has authored several books with Paul Virilio (including *Pure War* [1983], *Crepuscular Dawn* [2002], and *The Accident of Art* [2005]), as well as three with Jean Baudrillard (*Forget Foucault* [1986], *Oublier Artaud* [2005], and *The Conspiracy of Art* [2005]).

RIJUTA MEHTA is an assistant professor of English at the University of Toronto. Her research focuses on postcolonial literature, visual culture, and critical theory. Her work is published in *South Asian Film and Media, Interventions: International Journal of Postcolonial Studies*, and is forthcoming in the *Journal of Middle Eastern Women's Studies*.

MARK MULRONEY (www.markmulroney.com) refused to supply us with a serious bio. Instead, he sent us this: "He is the son of an accountant and a worrier. He grew up in Southern California, where he would often steal baseball cards from Ralph's Supermarket until he got caught and had to start stealing from Sav-On Drugs. He went to Catholic School and never played organized football. He started to draw in college and liked it. He has never been convicted of a felony and has never caught a fish that weighed more than two pounds."

NICHOLAS SAMMOND is director of the Centre for the Study of the United States and a professor of cinema studies at the University of Toronto. He is the author of *Birth of an Industry: Blackface Minstrelsy and the Rise of American Animation* (2015), *Babes in Tomorrowland: Walt Disney and the Making of the American Child, 1930–1960* (2005), and the editor of and contributor to *Steel Chair to the Head: The Pleasure and Pain of Professional Wrestling* (2005). Both *Birth of an Industry* and *Babes in Tomorrowland* received the Katherine Singer Kovacs Award from the Society for Cinema and Media Studies.

YIMAN WANG is associate professor of film and digital media at the University of California, Santa Cruz. She is the author of *Remaking Chinese Cinema: Through the Prism of Shanghai, Hong Kong, and Hollywood* (2013). She is currently writing a book on Anna May Wong, the best-known early twentieth-century Chinese American screen-stage performer. Her articles have appeared in journals including *Feminist Media Histories, Quarterly Review of Film and Video, Film Quarterly, Camera Obscura, Journal of Film and Video, Literature/Film Quarterly, Positions: East Asia Cultures Critique,* and *Journal of Chinese Cinemas,* and in volumes including *Silent Cinema and the Politics of Space* (2014), *American and Chinese-Language Cinemas: Examining Cultural Flows* (2014), *New Silent Cinema* (2015), and *Vamping the Stage: Female Voices of Asian Modernities* (2017).

REBECCA WANZO is associate professor of women, gender, and sexuality studies at Washington University in St. Louis. She is the author of *The Suffering Will Not Be Televised: African American Women and Sentimental Political Storytelling* (2009). Her essays have been published in journals such as *American Literature, Camera Obscura, differences: A Journal of Feminist Cultural Studies,* the *Journal of Popular Culture, Women and Performance,* and numerous edited collections. Her research interests include popular culture, African American literature, critical race theory, and feminist media studies. She is currently completing *The Content of Our Caricature,* under contract with New York University Press, which traces the history of African American cartoonists' engagement with racist caricature as a means of commenting on citizenship genres in the United States.

index

CPSIA information can be obtained
at www.ICGtesting.com
Printed in the USA
FSHW011935180520
70353FS

9 781478 003021